Y0-EDQ-688

Studies in Military and Strategic History

General Editor: **Michael Dockrill**, Professor of Diplomatic History, King's College, London

Published titles include:

Nigel John Ashton
EISENHOWER, MACMILLAN AND THE PROBLEM OF NASSER
Anglo-American Relations and Arab Nationalism, 1955–59

Peter Bell
CHAMBERLAIN, GERMANY AND JAPAN, 1933–34

G. H. Bennett
BRITISH FOREIGN POLICY DURING THE CURZON PERIOD, 1919–24

David Clayton
IMPERIALISM REVISITED
Political and Economic Relations between Britain and China, 1950–54

Paul Cornish
BRITISH MILITARY PLANNING FOR THE DEFENCE OF GERMANY, 1945–50

Michael Dockrill
BRITISH ESTABLISHMENT PERSPECTIVES ON FRANCE, 1936–40

John P. S. Gearson
HAROLD MACMILLAN AND THE BERLIN WALL CRISIS, 1958–62

Stewart Lone
JAPAN'S FIRST MODERN WAR
Army and Society in the Conflict with China, 1894–95

T. R. Moreman
THE ARMY IN INDIA AND THE DEVELOPMENT OF FRONTIER WARFARE, 1849–1947

Kendrick Oliver
KENNEDY, MACMILLAN AND THE NUCLEAR TEST-BAN DEBATE, 1961–63

G. D. Sheffield
LEADERSHIP IN THE TRENCHES
Officer–Man Relations, Morale and Discipline in the British Army in the Era of the First World War

Adrian Smith
MICK MANNOCK, FIGHTER PILOT
Myth, Life and Politics

Martin Thomas
THE FRENCH NORTH AFRICAN CRISIS
Colonial Breakdown and Anglo-French Relations, 1945–62

Simon Trew
BRITAIN, MIHAILOVIC AND THE CHETNIKS, 1941–42

Roger Woodhouse
BRITISH FOREIGN POLICY TOWARDS FRANCE, 1945–51

Studies in Military and Strategic History
Series Standing Order ISBN 0–333–71046–0
(*outside North America only*)

You can receive future titles in this series as they are published by placing a standing order. Please contact your bookseller or, in case of difficulty, write to us at the address below with your name and address, the title of the series and the ISBN quoted above.

Customer Services Department, Macmillan Distribution Ltd, Houndmills, Basingstoke, Hampshire RG21 6XS, England

The French North African Crisis

Colonial Breakdown and Anglo-French Relations, 1945–62

Martin Thomas
Reader in International History
University of the West of England
Bristol

in association with
KING'S COLLEGE, LONDON

First published in Great Britain 2000 by
MACMILLAN PRESS LTD
Houndmills, Basingstoke, Hampshire RG21 6XS and London
Companies and representatives throughout the world

A catalogue record for this book is available from the British Library.

ISBN 0–333–71560–8

First published in the United States of America 2000 by
ST. MARTIN'S PRESS, LLC,
Scholarly and Reference Division,
175 Fifth Avenue, New York, N.Y. 10010

ISBN 0–333–71560–8

Library of Congress Cataloging-in-Publication Data
Thomas, Martin.
The French North African crisis : colonial breakdown and Anglo-French relations, 1945–62 / Martin Thomas.
p. cm. — (Studies in military and strategic history)
Includes bibliographical references and index.
ISBN 0–333–71560–8
1. France—Foreign relations—Great Britain. 2. Great Britain—Foreign relations—France. 3. France—Foreign relations—1945–1958. 4. France––Foreign relations—1958–1969. 5. Great Britain—Foreign relations—1945– 6. Algeria—History—Revolution, 1954–1962—Influence. I. Title. II. Studies in military and strategic history (New York, N.Y.)

DC59.8.G7 T46 2000
965'.0461—dc21

00–033268

This book is printed on paper suitable for recycling and made from fully managed and sustained forest sources.

10 9 8 7 6 5 4 3 2 1
09 08 07 06 05 04 03 02 01 00

Printed and bound in Great Britain by
Antony Rowe Ltd, Chippenham, Wiltshire

Contents

Preface and Acknowledgements

In 1997 the French postal service issued a commemorative 3 franc stamp. In the foreground a French trooper crouches on a rock outcrop superimposed on a map of Morocco, Algeria and Tunisia, above which is written 'In homage to French servicemen in French North Africa, 1952–1962'. This marked a rare gesture to the veterans of France's worst colonial conflict, almost 3 million in total, whose activities in the protectorates of Morocco and Tunisia and, above all, within the colony of Algeria, still cause deep unease in France. The uncomfortable juxtaposition of French colonial enforcer and North African freedom fighter, and the obvious parallels between the French struggle for liberation against Nazi Germany and Algeria's quest for national independence, make the Algerian conflict a memory almost as challenging to modern-day France as the years of the Vichy state. The less traumatic withdrawals from Morocco and Tunisia in 1956 were both eclipsed and, in their final stages, shaped by the rebellion in neighbouring Algeria. France's protracted crisis of decolonisation in North Africa had a profound effect on the country's international position. Britain figures among those nations most engaged by the course of events in Morocco, Algeria and Tunisia. The reasons behind this have yet to be subjected to detailed scrutiny although the problems of the North African Maghreb had a major bearing on the course of Anglo-French relations after 1945. Hence this book – a study of France's North African crisis within the fabric of the western alliance and within France's partnership with Britain in particular.

Research on subjects so recent and with such powerful contemporary resonance requires the support and indulgence of archive staffs for whom much of the documentary evidence in question has only recently been catalogued or released. I am especially grateful to the personnel of the Service Historique de l'Armée and the Service Historique de l'Armée de l'Air at the Château de Vincennes as well as the staff of the French Foreign and Colonial Ministry archives at the Quai d'Orsay and the Archives Nationales Centre d'Outre-Mer in Aix-en-Provence. In all cases, I received invaluable help with inventories and requests for access to particular files. Reference to the Georges Bidault papers at the Archives Nationales is by kind permission of Mme Bidault.

I am also indebted to the staff of the Public Record Office in London. Crown Copyright material from this source is reproduced by permission of the Director of the Public Record Office. My thanks go to the Trustees of the Churchill College archive in Cambridge for permission to consult the collections in their care. The Bodleian Library archive staff in Room 132 were always welcoming. I am particularly grateful to the Trustees of the Harold Macmillan archive for permission to consult Harold Macmillan's diaries, and to the Master and Fellows of Balliol College, Oxford, for permitting access to the Walter Monckton papers. Reference to material from the Conservative Party archives at the Bodleian is by permission of the Chairman of the Conservative Party. The archivists and staff of the US National Archives and Record Administration at College Park, Maryland, were equally helpful and generous with their time. I have received vital funding support from the British Academy, the Scouloudi Foundation at the Institute of Contemporary History and the Humanities Research Committee of the University of the West of England.

Many friends and colleagues have provided crucial advice and encouragement, among them Robert Aldrich, Matthew Connelly, Kent Fedorowich, Chris Goscha, Jeffrey Grey, Peter Jackson, Bob Moore, Alistair Parker and Glyn Stone. Along the way, Martin Alexander, Martin Evans, Robert Holland and the British International History Group kindly gave me the opportunity to present papers on Algeria at the School of Oriental and African Studies, the University of Salford, the University of Lancaster and the Institute of Commonwealth Studies. I am especially grateful to Irwin Wall for his valuable comments on the manuscript and for allowing me to consult the manuscript version of his important new book, *France, the United States and the Algerian War.* I owe Michael Dockrill a great deal for his generous support of the project. Karen Brazier and Ruth Willats have been generous and scrupulous editors. Chris Hearmon did sterling work on the maps. As always, my greatest thanks go to my wife Suzy – I dedicate the book to her.

Abbreviations

AFL	American Federation of Labor
ALN	Armée de Libération Nationale (military arm of the FLN)
BAOR	British Army of the Rhine
CCE	Comité de Coordination et d'Exécution (inner-cabinet of FLN leadership)
CGT	Confédération Générale du Travail (French trade union confederation)
CIO	Congress of Industrial Organisations
CNRA	Conseil National de la Révolution Algérienne (FLN executive council)
CRS	Compagnies Républicaines de Sécurité
CRUA	Comité Révolutionnaire d'Unité et d'Action (successor to OS and forerunner to FLN executive)
DGER	Direction Générale des Etudes et Recherches (French foreign intelligence service, 1944–46)
DST	Direction de la Surveillance du Territoire (French internal security service)
EDC	European Defence Community
FLN	Front de Libération Nationale (Algerian nationalist front, founded 1954)
MNA	Mouvement National Algérien (Algerian [Messalist] party founded after the schism within the MTLD)
MRP	Mouvement Républicain Populaire (Christian Democrat Party, founded 1944)
MTLD	Mouvement pour la Triomphe des Libertés Démocratiques (Messalist successor to PPA, founded in October 1946 after the banning of the PPA)
NEACC	Near East Arms Co-ordinating Committee (established 1952)
OAS	Organisation de l'Armée Secrète
OS	Organisation Spéciale (militant Algerian nationalist organisation, founded 1947)
PCA	Parti Communiste Algérien
PCF	Parti Communiste Français
PPA	Parti Populaire Algérien (Algerian [Messalist] nationalist party, founded 1937)

RGR	Rassemblement des Gauches Républicaines (alliance of Radicals and UDSR, founded 1946)
RPF	Rassemblement du Peuple Français (Gaullist movement, founded 1947)
SACEUR	[NATO] Supreme Allied Commander, Europe
SAS	Sections Administratives Spécialisées (French military administrative corps)
SDECE	Service de Documentation Extérieure et de Contre-Espionnage (French foreign intelligence service, succeeded the DGER in 1946)
SFIO	Section Française de l'Internationale Ouvrière
UDCA	Union de Défense des Commerçants et des Artisans (Poujadist organisation)
UDMA	Union Démocratique de Manifeste Algérien (Algerian Party led by Ferhat Abbas, founded 1945)
UDSR	Union Démocratique et Socialiste de la Résistance (Centre-left Party established in 1945 from five French resistance movements)
UGTT	Union Générale des Travailleurs Tunisiens (Tunisian trade union federation)
UNR	Union pour la Nouvelle République (Fifth Republic Gaullist Party)
USRAF	Union pour le Salut et le Renouveau de l'Algérie Française

Archives

AN	Archives Nationales
ANCOM	Archives Nationales Centre des Archives d'Outre-Mer
MAE	Ministère des Affaires Etrangères (Quai d'Orsay)
NARA	National Archives and Records Administration (USA)
PRO	Public Record Office
SHAA	Service Historique de l'Armée de l'Air
SHAT	Service Historique de l'Armée de Terre

Heads of French Government, 1944–62

Premier	Ministry formed	Ministry resigned
Charles de Gaulle	10 September 1944	13 November 1945
	General Election, 21 October 1945	
Charles de Gaulle	21 November 1945	20 January 1946
Félix Gouin	26 January 1946	12 June 1946
	General Election, 2 June 1946	
Georges Bidault	24 June 1946	28 November 1946
	General Election, 10 November 1946	
Léon Blum	16 December 1946	16 January 1947
Paul Ramadier	22 January 1947	(first Ministry reconstructed in May)
Paul Ramadier	22 October 1947	19 November 1947
Robert Schuman	24 November 1947	19 July 1948
André Marie	26 July 1948	28 August 1948
Robert Schuman	5 September 1948	7 September 1948
Henri Queuille	11 September 1948	6 October 1949
Georges Bidault	28 October 1949	24 June 1950
Henri Queuille	2 July 1950	4 July 1950
René Pleven	12 July 1950	28 February 1951
Henri Queuille	10 March 1951	10 July 1951
	General Election, 17 June 1951	
René Pleven	11 August 1951	7 January 1952
Edgar Faure	20 January 1952	29 February 1952
Antoine Pinay	8 March 1952	23 December 1952
René Mayer	8 January 1953	21 May 1953
Joseph Laniel	28 June 1953	12 June 1954
Pierre Mendès France	19 June 1954	5 February 1955
Edgar Faure	23 February 1955	24 January 1956

	General Election, 2 January 1956	
Guy Mollet	1 February 1956	21 May 1957
Maurice Bourgès-Maunoury	13 June 1957	30 September 1957
Félix Gaillard	6 November 1957	15 April 1958
Pierre Pflimlin	14 May 1958	28 May 1958
Charles de Gaulle	1 June 1958	8 January 1959
	General Election, 23 November 1958	
	Presidential Election, 21 December 1958 (De Gaulle elected President)	
Michel Debré	8 January 1959	14 April 1962

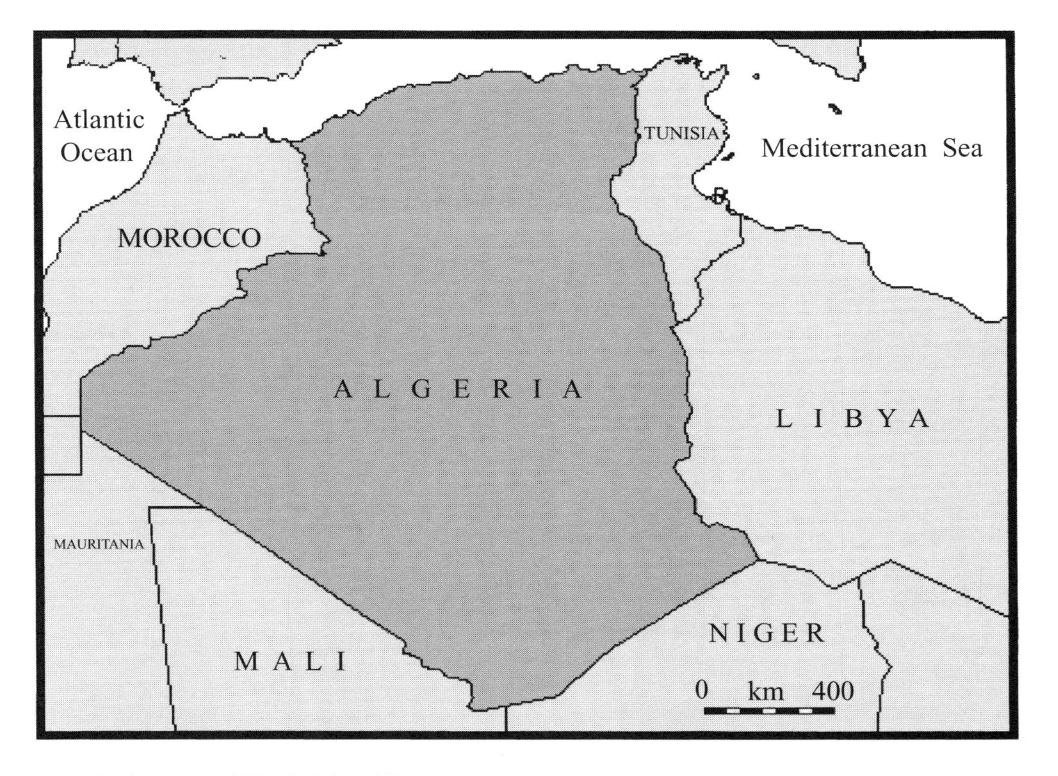

Map 1 Algeria and North–West Africa

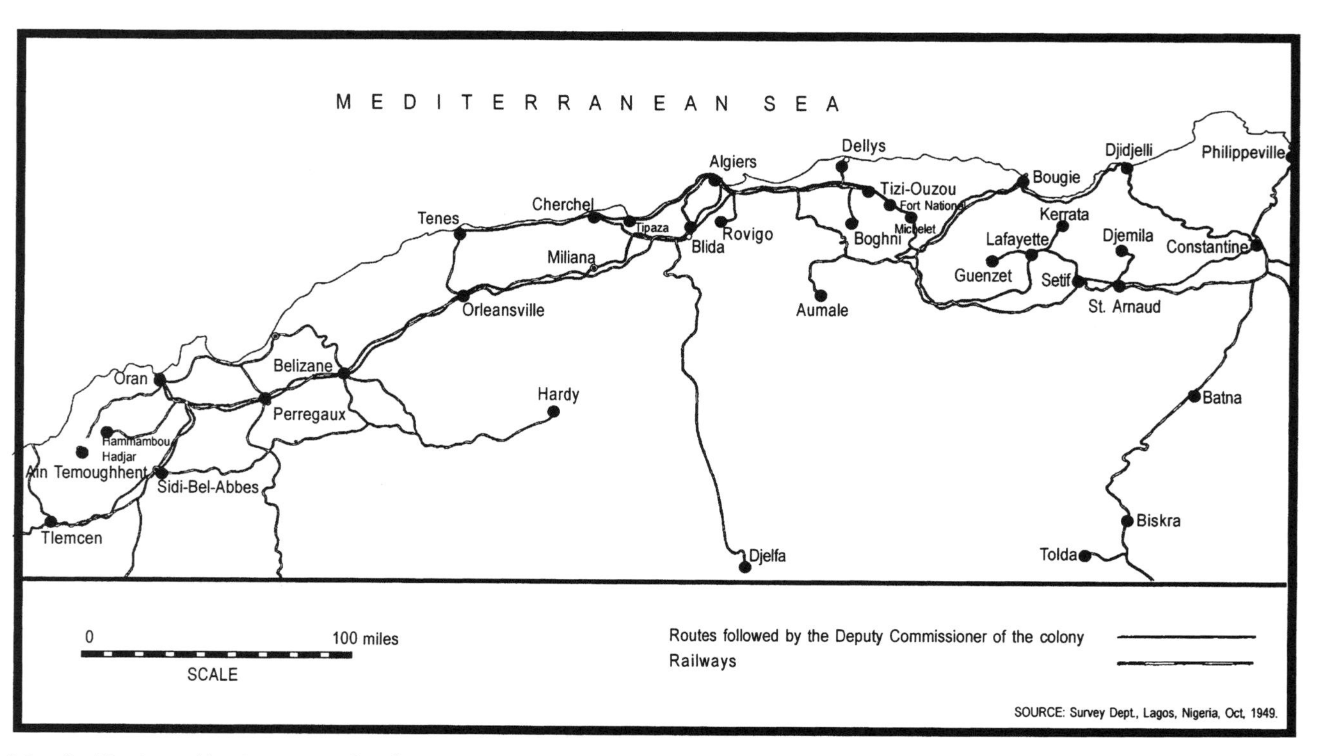

Map 2 Northern Algeria, route taken by Major J. G. C. Allen, 1949

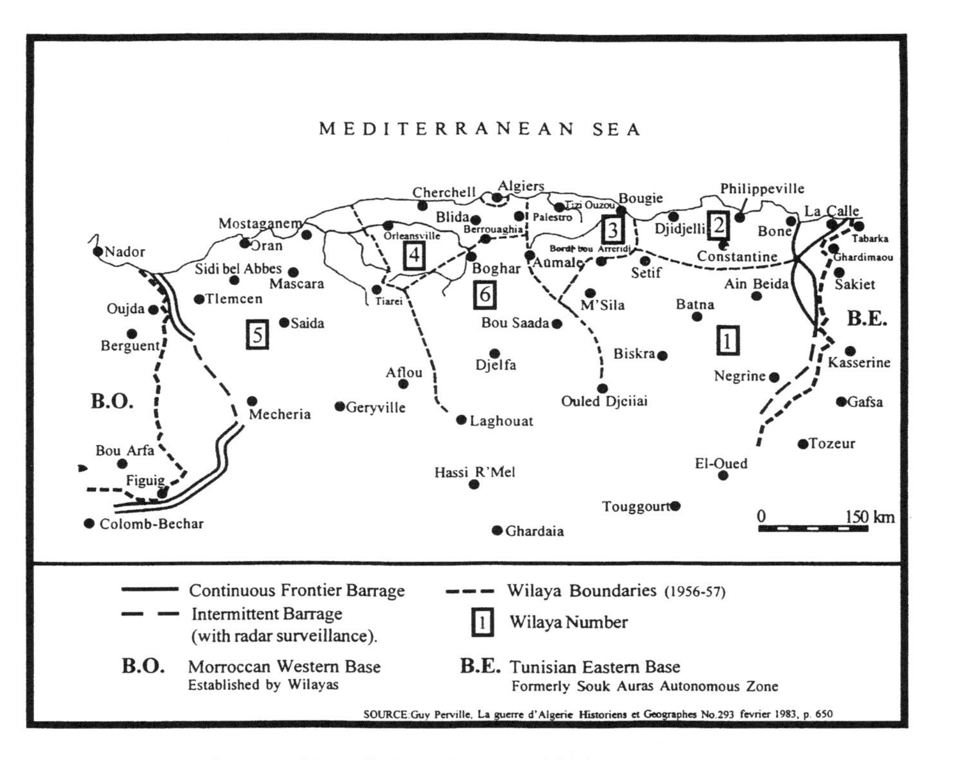

Map 3 A.L.N. *Wilayas* and French Army Barrages, 1956

Introduction

During a post-dinner stroll through the gardens of his official residence at the Hôtel Matignon in Paris on 29 June 1958, General Charles de Gaulle, newly installed as premier of what would soon become the French Fifth Republic, told British prime minister Harold Macmillan of the problems he faced in Algeria:

> Morocco was a State; Tunisia was a State; but Algeria had never been a State. It was nothing but a heap of dust. It had never had any reality and when the French arrived there 120 years ago they had found nothing to build on. There were the tribes and disconnected and separate groups. The effect of the colonisation had been to destroy the tribal organisation without putting anything in its place. They therefore were now faced with a country that was the hardest of all to deal with because it had no real life.[1]

By this point, the Algerian nationalist war of independence against French colonial rule was in its fourth year. The conflict began, officially at least, on 1 November 1954, All Saints' Day, with a series of over 70 orchestrated attacks, explosions and other acts of sabotage largely concentrated in the Aurès mountains and the Grande Kabylie region, and claimed by the *Front de Libération Nationale*, then a little known nationalist movement launched only three weeks earlier. By the time de Gaulle returned to power in 1958, the Algerian conflict had eclipsed the earlier struggles for decolonisation in Morocco and Tunisia. It had become a hugely divisive issue in France, destabilising the Fourth Republic, catalysing schisms within some political parties whilst promoting the emergence of others and, perhaps most importantly, unravelling the constitutional ties binding the military authorities to the civil power. Within Algeria and the Maghreb more broadly, French efforts to contain the rebellion and the FLN's savage determination to succeed produced a widening and cruel war which would ultimately claim hundreds of thousands of, mainly civilian, lives. Internationally, North Africa had become France's Achilles' heel, alarming its allies, draining its financial and military strength, undermining its moral authority and isolating it at the UN and elsewhere. Worse was yet to come. The war still had four years left to run, its end in 1962 proving far more violent and cataclysmic than its more obscure beginning.

Albeit chronically exaggerated, de Gaulle's emphasis on the problem of defining Algerian statehood and, *ipso facto*, the country's future relationship with France, cut to the heart of the Algerian problem. In French school text-books, a conventional justification for the French conquest and colonisation of Algeria from 1830 onwards was that the new arrivals brought order, investment and the rule of western law where previously there was Ottoman exploitation, inter-tribal feuding, endemic disease and virtual anarchy. Children's books are now well recognised as an excellent vehicle for imperial propaganda. But the misrepresentation of Algeria's capacity for self-rule extended far beyond the classroom.[2] Albert Camus, the Nobel prize-winning author born of settler parents and raised in the working class Algiers district of Belcourt, occasionally criticised French military and Algerian terrorist violence and became an increasingly isolated supporter of peaceful Franco-Algerian co-existence. Yet while Camus pleaded for equality of treatment for settlers and Muslims, he dismissed the notion of Algeria as a pre-existent nation with a legitimate claim to outright independence. Opposed to the 'virtual' Arab state conjured up by Algerian nationalists, Camus remained wedded to the still more unrealistic ideal of an overarching French Algerian heritage in which settlers, Berbers and Arabs shared a common attachment to the Algerian soil regardless of their political, ethnic, religious and economic divisions.[3] Camus thus articulated an idea entrenched among the *colon* community – that of a specifically Mediterranean culture which, in Algeria at least, had developed beyond the merely colonial aspect of European settlement. For many settlers, the French identity grafted on to the surface of Algerian colonial politics disguised the absence of any deeper social transformation in the relationship between rulers and ruled.[4]

Anachronistic as this sentiment may appear, it was common currency amongst politicians, *colons* and French people directly touched by life in Algeria, amongst whom Camus, who had joined the Algerian Communist Party as a young man in 1935, seemed decidedly progressive in his genuine commitment to reform. Writing in *Le Monde* in February 1956, the Social Republican Senator and de Gaulle's future Prime

Minister, Michel Debré, captured the outlook of the many French voters across the political spectrum for whom any recognition of Algeria's right to an independent existence was a treasonous affront. For Debré, France's ties to North Africa were vital and indissoluble, an opinion he expressed with the phrase 'Plus d'A[frique] F[rançais du] N[ord], plus d'Afrique française, plus de France.'[5] Nor were French settlers and defenders of *Algérie française* alone in their dismissal of Algerian statehood. Former premier, Paul Reynaud, for example, told a New York audience at a *Herald Tribune* forum in October 1955 that the concept of colonialism was inapplicable to Algeria because the settler community had forged the national identity of the country and salvaged it from economic chaos.[6] Among the many liberal intellectuals, journalists, politicians, conscripts, clerics and work-a-day French people outraged by revelations of torture and inhumane military operations in Algeria from 1957, few automatically concluded that France should leave the colony. Until de Gaulle's decisive break with the official commitment to a French Algeria in 1959, a cross-section of French liberal opinion preferred further reform to outright decolonisation.[7] And, in spite of British and US reservations about French policies in postwar North Africa, one notable triumph of French colonial propaganda was to persuade western observers that the Algerian polity was, for better or worse, a French creation. A State Department briefing paper prepared in anticipation of a UN consideration of the Algerian problem in July 1955 acknowledged France's unique relationship with the colony: 'When France began to occupy the area now constituting Algeria in 1830, it took over in a political vacuum. Algeria was in no sense a political entity – not even a province of Turkey.'[8]

In fact, the porousness of Algeria's pre-colonial frontiers and the complex variations in local political organisation between east and west, and between the northern coastal belt and the pre-Saharan interior, were more the product of pastoral and economic migration, religious pilgrimage and the abiding power of local Muslim notables than of Ottoman neglect. As Julia Clancy-Smith reminds us, 'an ecology of political action existed prior to 1830 and would determine the terms of the colonial encounter for decades after the French conquest.'[9] However, although the French colonial authorities increasingly emulated earlier Turkish practices of periodic tax collection, selective fortification of strategic centres and the cultivation of local notables and religious leaders, the myth persisted of order salvaged from chaos. In general, the French military much preferred Roman imperial precedents to recent Ottoman example during the early phases of conquest and colonisation. Senior officers drew on their classical education for descriptions of ancient warfare against Arab tribes, whilst French military units exploited Roman roads and architectural remains to facilitate campaigning and the construction of fortifications. The very abundance of Roman construction in Algeria and Tunisia encouraged the mutually reinforcing opinions that the North African Maghreb could indeed be colonised and that the indigenous population had contributed little to the 'civilisation' of their own lands since the Romans departed.[10] Again, this fuelled the misconception that only Europeans could build a viable country out of Algeria. What one French historian has recently termed the 'founding myths' of French colonialism in Algeria imposed a dichotomy between the progressive, civilising force of French soldiers, agriculturalists, doctors and engineers and the backwardness of Arab tribal groups. Crudely put, pacification was portrayed as a disinterested, modernizing struggle against the obscurantism of an indigenous population beset with endemic illness and consumed by suspicion.[11]

The large Berber population in the Algerian interior, notably in the mountains of Kabylie and the Aurès, compounded French colonial policies, which assumed both an intrinsic opposition and a clear hierarchy between races. As colonial pacifiers, the French arrivals thus created a modern Algerian society and, in the process, released the Berbers from creeping Arab domination. In this 'Kabyle myth', the Muslim Arabs were the original invaders of Algeria, imposing alien Oriental values on a pre-existing Mediterranean culture which was only superficially Islamicised. In Morocco, too, the French authorities demarcated boundaries – both physical and cultural – between the Berber tribes and the Arab population. Legislation passed in 1930 transferred judicial power in Berber tribal areas from the Arab caïds to local *djemaa* councils and made Berber regions subject to the Napoleonic legal code. The intention was to tie Berber society more closely to France by breaking the Muslim hold upon customary law in Berber regions.[12] The historical inaccuracies of these colonialist stereotypes did not lessen their impact in Third Republic France.

The technology of French imperialism further cemented France's self-image as moderniser and nation-builder. In this characterisation, France's military pioneers developed the materials required to master the North African climate, while French governments showed a breadth of administrative vision unmatched in the Ottoman era. During the 1830s French military doctors introduced quinine treatments to combat the virulent malaria which decimated garrisons in coastal Algeria. French engineers built overland telegraphs and laid a supplementary trans-Mediterranean cable between Port Vendre and Algiers in 1861. The breech-loading rifle and mobile artillery ensured French superiority in encounter battles with indigenous rebels. And from the early 1870s, ministers and entrepreneurs toyed with a trans-Saharan railway project to bring greater economic and strategic cohesion to France's growing African empire.[13]

This reflected a wider shift in the importance of empire to governments of the early Third Republic. The conquest and early colonisation of Algeria attracted only fitful interest in France prior to 1870. French merchants, notably in Lyons and the port cities of the Mediterranean, were eager to exploit the perceived wealth of the Algerian cities to the south. But the early years of France's colonial presence were dominated by the military, a fact exemplified by the army's assumption of direct control over colonial administration in 1834 and the parallel consolidation of a specialist *Armée d'Afrique* to uphold French control.[14] The years 1830–70 forged the bond between the French professional army and North Africa. Early colonial administration was military in character and the army controlled the filtration of news about French advances and achievements within Algeria back to France.[15] Furthermore, the early use of French Algerian forces to help suppress metropolitan dissent in 1834 and 1848 illustrated the gulf which separated the professional troops of the French empire from the urban population at home. It was hardly a feat of imagination to see similarities between the savage military repression of the Communards and the concurrent suppression of renewed uprisings across Algeria from January 1871. Although nineteenth century in origin, the tendencies to see military administrative control as a colonial norm and to identify French colonial forces with an anti-democratic authoritarianism reached their *apogée* in the Indo-China and Algeria wars after 1945.[16] In the mid-nineteenth century then, popular French attachment to the Algerian prize was slow to develop. But, under the Third Republic, the gathering influence of Eugène Etienne's *Parti Colonial* lobbyists plus increased party political and general staff interest in France's overseas possessions from the 1880s onwards gave Algeria, and later the Tunisia and Morocco protectorates, pride of place among the territories of the French empire by 1914.[17]

For years after the initial French conquest of Algiers successive British governments rejected France's stigmatisation of pre-colonial Algeria, and throughout the 1830s and 1840s Britain remained actively hostile to the French presence in North Africa. Only after France's suppression of Amir Abd al-Qadir's long-running rebellion did the British formally acknowledge French dominion in Algeria in 1850.[18] Even then, the British tolerated a steady stream of illicit arms and gunpowder trafficking from Gibraltar and Malta to Algerian rebels, perhaps quietly satisfied that rebellion in Algeria and its Saharan interior was proving more costly to France than the imposition of British rule in India. This arms smuggling continued well beyond the formal French declaration in 1857 that Algeria was fully pacified.[19]

We can hardly be surprised at France's wild distortion of fact to justify its early imperialism in North Africa, and it is worth recalling that in the early 1860s Napoleon III made genuine efforts both to prevent wholesale French expropriation of Muslim land and to assimilate Algerian landowners into the French system of land tenure and legal practice. Napoleon III's reforms failed, not least because they were attempted in the aftermath of a series of bruising revolts from Abd al-Qadir's protracted resistance of the 1830s and 1840s in western Algeria to the mahdist uprisings across southeastern Algeria in subsequent years. France expended an enormous military effort on the pacification of the country after its Algerian conquistador, General Thomas-Robert Bugeaud, first adopted a policy of total occupation as Governor-General in 1841. By the time Abd al-Qadir capitulated in December 1847, there were some 108,000 French troops in Algeria, the largest European force deployed in Africa prior to the second Boer War. More importantly, in putting down the rebellion, Bugeaud's forces pursued a scorched earth policy sufficiently vicious to cement the popular links between Islamic observance, defence of Muslim land and property, and armed resistance.[20] Regardless of the obvious gulf between a privileged religious leader like Abd al-Qadir and the secular leadership of the *Front de Libération Nationale* (FLN) a century later, the threat to Muslims' religious, economic and cultural interests that fed the proto-nationalism of the 1840s remained equally relevant in the 1950s.

After Bugeaud's military success, Algeria was subsequently regarded as the primary location for French colonial settlement rather than as a country in its own right, whose Arab and Berber population would be made French.[21] European settlers secured preferential access to land, skilled employment, capital facilities and administrative posts, all of which negated assimilationist ideals in practice. This tendency towards a segregation of economic opportunity and a cultural division of labour, all to settler benefit, was particularly evident in those coastal cities where European colonisation was most pronounced in the late nineteenth and early twentieth centuries.[22] In short, Algeria was always first and foremost a colony to be exploited for the benefit of France. This view was accepted by the Republican colonialists of the 1880s and 1890s, who were susceptible to the influence of the imperial interest groups loosely moulded into the *Parti Colonial*.[23] By the turn of the century, Muslim agriculturalists had learnt from bitter experience that where the mark of French administration was strongest – in the so-called *communes de plein exercise* run on the model of metropolitan local government – taxation and land allocation was likely to be most heavily weighted against them. In 1884 Algeria was tied to France through a one-sided customs union. From that point forward, over 80 per cent of Algerian export produce was shipped directly to France. After 1918 Algeria's economy grew more dependent on sustained French public investment – itself a substitute for private venture capital – to maintain local economic growth.[24] Until 1919, when exclusively Arab taxes (the *impôts Arabes*) were reorganised, the Muslim community contributed an average of 60 per cent to Algeria's annual budget although less than 5 per cent of French social spending in the colony was specifically aimed at improving Arab living standards.[25]

A highly organised system of colonial exploitation in Algeria was thus taking shape whilst France acquired its Tunisia protectorate under the 1881 Treaty of Bardo, and had become an incontrovertible fact long before the French acquired full protectorate rights in Morocco under the 1912 Treaty of Fez. This brings us back to the central problem of French-ruled Algeria as a nation. It helps account for the apparent anomaly of a colonial territory sandwiched between two ethnically and culturally similar states whose nationhood was theoretically recognised and respected by France. As Douglas Johnson pointed out not long after the end of the Algerian war, many French people remained convinced that the concept of Algeria as a nation-state was simply a nonsense without basis in previous history.[26] Commenting on Professor Johnson's work in the light of French historical writing on North Africa, Michael Brett further developed this point. In 1952 Charles-André Julien, then France's pre-eminent scholar of the Maghreb, published a pioneering study of North African nationalism. His conclusion that nationalist protest represented the popular will of the region's Muslim population and was the natural consequence of past French misrule was far ahead of its time. In acknowledging a genuine nationalism in the French North African territories, Julien questioned France's historic role as nation-builder. If there were indeed proto-national Muslim communities supportive of self-determination in Morocco, Tunisia and even Algeria, what right had France to remain in North Africa?[27]

Moreover, official justification for the police repression of nationalist parties in all three North African territories in the early 1950s characterised Maghreb politicians as unrepresentative and unhistorical in their repudiation of France's achievements as law-giver and guardian of inter-communal order. Typically, Algiers' Governor-General Marcel-Edmond Naegelen defended a crackdown in April–May 1950 against the *Organisation Spéciale* (OS), a covert paramilitary group formerly linked to the nationalist *Mouvement pour la Triomphe des Libertés Démocratiques* (MTLD), with the Hobbesian logic that France alone prevented a reversion to anarchy. As Naegelen put it, 'It has been said that I have caused a reign of terror in Algeria; in truth, we have broken the terror which certain persons intended to impose on the Muslim population, as it was before our arrival in this country.' In a bizarre critique of alleged Anglo-American interference, three months later, the French military commander in North Africa, General Jean Callies even claimed that the spread of Islamic observance, Koranic education and Arabic language usage across Algeria over the preceding century was primarily the work of enlightened French administration.[28]

In fact, the influence of Islamic teaching and its foremost purveyors, the Association of Reformist Ulama, played a crucial role in the development of nationalist sentiment. Founded in 1931 and led after the Second World War first by Muhammad al-Bashir al-Ibrahimi and then by Larbi Tebessi, the Association was pivotal to the growth in support for rebellion against France, especially among young Algerians educated in Ulama schools or clubs. Here was an excellent example of unfettered colonialism misfiring. In applying France's law of 1905 separating church and state to Algeria on the basis that the colony was French, the colonial administration surrendered direct control over local religious practice. Despite the colonial authorities' efforts to corral practising Muslims into state-approved Muslim Cultural Associations, the growth in support of the Ulama, who operated outside state control, undermined French cultural and political hegemony. Not surprisingly, the central question of who ultimately disposed of a town mosque – the French political authorities or the Islamic ritual authorities – had become an explosive political issue by the early 1950s.[29] Sensitive to Ulama influence, FLN propaganda, and the Front's official mouthpiece *El Moudjahid,* claimed a direct inheritance from the Ulama's efforts since the 1930s to inculcate a self-consciously Arab and Muslim Algerian national identity. It was commonplace within FLN publications to assert that there was indeed an Algerian 'nation' before the French arrived in 1830. The FLN claimed a legitimate heritage as modern representative of an oppressed Muslim people whose recognition as a 'nation' demanded a 'decolonisation of history' to match the French withdrawal that the FLN sought to achieve.[30]

The violence of the argument in 1950s France and Algeria over the concept of Algeria as a nation helps one understand the Algerian war as a unique phenomenon. Unlike the more straightforward 'emergencies' in the Morocco and Tunisia protectorates in the early 1950s, the violence in Algeria between 1954 and 1962 engaged the French nation to a far greater extent because, whereas France's protectorate administrations were already in the process of transformation, colonial rule in Algeria was set to continue indefinitely. Political debate in Morocco and Tunisia soon hinged on the schedule and the precise terms for French withdrawal. In Algeria, discussion of a French evacuation remained entirely taboo for much of the war's duration. Not simply a war between opposing armies, a Cold War struggle or a limited colonial insurgency, the Algerian conflict of 1954–62 still defies exact description. In certain respects at particular times, the war in Algeria was all of the above; but its terrible novelty lay in the unbalanced clash between massive French conventional forces and a revolutionary nationalist movement, the FLN, whose military arm, the *Armée de Libération Nationale* (ALN), became adept at techniques of guerrilla warfare, urban terrorism and popular control. The mixture of professional soldiers, colonial troops and, later, French reservists and conscripts, who served in French North Africa during the 1950s covered a broad age range. Many were left traumatised by the experience and yet were for many years denied the formal recognition accorded to veterans of other French conflicts. In hindsight, much like the Vietnam War, the Algerian rebellion is perhaps becoming less well remembered for particular events than for its cumulative impact upon those who survived it.[31]

North Africans, particularly Algerians, formed the largest non-European immigrant group within France. The militant nationalism of Messali Hadj's *Parti Populaire Algérien* (relaunched as the MTLD in 1946) first found expression amongst the Algerian immigrant community in the outer suburbs of Paris. The fact that interwar Algerian nationalists based in France used the organisational example of the French Communist Party (PCF) and the vocabulary of working-class radicalism to articulate their ideas also fuelled counter-arguments that Algerian nationalism was neither representative nor 'national' at all. Throughout the Algerian conflict, the French police fought a parallel, sometimes brutal, war against FLN fundraisers and supporters within this immigrant community. North African immigration to France had taken off during the First World War when batches of workers were ferried to Marseilles in semi-military formations to work in designated occupations under close French supervision. Although initially outstripped by the influx of Spanish workers, both during the Great War and in the interwar years, Moroccans, Tunisians and, above all, Algerians, congregated in industrial cities, notably Paris, Lille and Marseilles.[32] This high level of immigration, and the visibility of North African labour within the industrial sector and the urban life of France, brought an additional aspect to the Algerian conflict. The crises of decolonisation in French North Africa were made tangible to metropolitan France by a highly politicised North African community whose regulation demanded increasing police resources. The Vietnamese community never attracted similar public attention during the Indo-China war, even though several leading Indo-Chinese revolutionaries, including Hô Chi Minh, spent vital formative years in interwar France. Perhaps inevitably, as the Algerian war became more unpopular within France, those still eager to defend French involvement came principally from within the armed forces and a settler community directly touched by the conflict itself.

The fragmentation of the French Right in the aftermath of the Second World War, and the growing divisions over imperial issues among Gaullist and Christian Democrat politicians in the mid-1950s, compounded the political confusion wrought by the war in Algeria. Between 1954 and 1958 the factionalisation of the Gaullist movement, the Christian Democrat MRP and the Radical Party destabilised a succession of ministries in the second legislature of the Fourth Republic. By the time de Gaulle returned to office in June 1958, the Gaullist movement was irrevocably split by the Algerian problem. Many of the most violent opponents of withdrawal organised around Jacques Soustelle's *Union pour le Salut et le Renouveau de l'Algérie Française* (USRAF) were former de Gaulle supporters unwilling to end the Algerian colonial connection.[33] One is therefore left with a doubly confusing image: of a bloody colonial crisis which touched millions of French lives, but over which only a narrow spectrum of mainly right-wing military and settler opinion was prepared to defend France's place as a colonial power.[34] This sense of confusion and unease is hardly surprising. The Algerian conflict was the dirtiest of colonial wars. It did not end in a dramatic and final defeat akin to the fall of the Dien Bien Phu garrison in May 1954. Yet its outcome was no less humiliating.

Crucially for governments in Paris, the introduction of conscription for service in Algeria in the spring of 1956 stimulated far greater public interest in the situation in Algeria than was ever the case during the professional soldiers' war in Indo-China between 1946 and 1954. The fighting in Algeria fractured a succession of Fourth Republic coalitions and undermined France's contribution to the defence of Western Europe. The rebelliousness of French Algerian settlers and a core of France's elite colonial troops ushered in de Gaulle's Fifth Republic in 1958. Massive counter-insurgency operations failed to stem rebel activity and at the same time diminished France's international standing as the cradle of modern democracy. Ultimately, having lost their privileged status, a large part of the French settler community, and those Algerian Muslims who had supported colonial rule to the bitter end, fled the country. The sloganised threat of the FLN – 'the suitcase or the coffin' – acquired a terrible authenticity for thousands of Muslim auxiliaries, their families and the dispossessed *colons*. In every respect, the Algerian conflict was a national disaster for France.

The scale and intensity of this colonial war surpassed anything in Britain's recent imperial past. Much as there are limits to the useful comparisons to be made between the 'emergency' in British Malaya and the French conflict in Indo-China which, by 1950, had come to resemble a Cold War contest of opposing armies, so the Algerian war shared little in common with Britain's more episodic postwar Middle Eastern crises in the Palestine Mandate (1945–48), Mosaddeq's Iran (1951) and the former client-states of Libya and Iraq (1958).[35] To French Algerian settlers, the Algerian struggle was more akin to a civil war. It became a cardinal objective of settler and soldier 'ultras' in the latter stages of the conflict to convince the French nation of this. To the FLN, their rebellion was, at once, a quest for Arab liberation, a socialist new order and a distinctive national identity. To many French voters, before 1958 the Algerian war was essentially perceived as an intractable 'problem' which refused to go away. Fourth Republic leaders proved unable either to win or to contain the rebellion or, alternatively, to negotiate a phased French withdrawal. It has been argued that this reflected a broad 'colonial consensus' based on a widespread conviction that Indo-China and North Africa were too integral to French power to be relinquished. Only gradually did this turn to frustration as successive governments failed to stem colonial conflicts in both regions. Even so, the importance of empire was still generally accepted; even the Communist Party shifted to a clearer anti-colonialist position only after Stalin's death in 1953.[36] In short, until de Gaulle returned to office and forced the country to acknowledge the futility of the Algerian conflict, France had buried its head in the Saharan sand, hoping that the army would triumph, but reluctant to accept the requisite *effort du sang* needed to ensure victory.

British governmental perceptions and reactions to France's painful decolonisation from French North Africa form the core of this book. Here, the historical neglect of the Algerian war remains marked. This is readily understandable. Officially, from 1945 to 1962 British governments consistently maintained that France should be left to deal with its colonial problems alone. British policy was to remain publicly disinterested, not least in the UN General Assembly. But, at the deeper level of British policy formulation towards France, the Mediterranean region, North-West Africa and the Middle East, French decolonisation of the Maghreb territories was of critical importance. The Algerian conflict was always read by those Whitehall departments most concerned as part of a sequence, unique in its violence, but certainly not an isolated event. Where French politicians laid emphasis on the unique constitutional position of Algeria as the colony most closely integrated with metropolitan France, British policy-makers viewed the Algerian war as the last in a series of forced retreats from French North Africa and, more widely, from Arab territories as a whole. By setting Algeria within the framework of events in neighbouring Morocco and Tunisia and in the Middle East, British politicians and officials saw little reason why France should buck the trend towards withdrawal from empire.

This point bears emphasis, for it suggests that Britain neither understood nor accepted the French characterisation of Algeria as more than a precious colonial possession. This French view was based on four primary considerations. First, Algeria was administered through the Ministry of the Interior via a government-general in Algiers which controlled the vast Algerian 'departments' of Oran, Algiers and Constantine. This signified a commitment, albeit more apparent than real, to the integration of Algeria within the constitutional system, the politics and the economy of metropolitan France. Unlike the early years of conquest, only in the Saharan southern territories (*Territoires du sud*) was the country under military administration when the rebellion began. Secondly, Algeria had a symbolic importance as the cornerstone of the modern French empire. Ever since Charles X's government first approved the expedition to Algiers in 1830, successive French rulers sought to fashion a colonial prize worthy of front-rank among French possessions. After conquest, this was a task based on European settlement – a third vital consideration. Fundamental to France's ability to tap the wealth of Algeria, the largest settler community anywhere in the empire helped recast the towns and cities of coastal Algeria and its hinterland in a latinate image.

After 1945 the heterogeneous collection of French, Spanish, Maltese and Italian *colons* formed an embattled, largely urban community, vigorously loyal to France.[37] Their self-conscious gallicism tended to increase as Muslim nationalism and decolonisation gathered momentum across the Arab world. Partly in reaction to this, after the launch of the manifesto of the Algerian people in February 1943, the bourgeois, French-educated, 'Europeanised Algerians' who had sought political and cultural equality with the *colon* population moved inexorably towards a more nationalist position. After 1945, those, like Ferhat Abbas, the key author of the manifesto and leader of the *Union Démocratique de Manifeste Algérien* (UDMA) founded in 1946, gradually despaired of limited reform. While Abbas and his supporters had originally campaigned for an equitable coexistence with the settler population, ultimately they saw little alternative to confrontation with the resident Europeans.[38] Entrenched *colon* privilege was perhaps the ultimate reason for the ferocity of the war. This raises the final element in the equation – the special role of French North Africa within the planning and ethos of the French military. After the loss of French Indo-China, the North African territories provided a vital *raison d'être* for an army increasingly attuned to colonial warfare whose politicisation both before the Algerian conflict and during it constituted the most dangerous threat to French political stability.

For the British politicians and officials who monitored events in French North Africa after 1945, political crises and military confrontation were a more or less constant theme. This coloured British policy formulation towards France, NATO and the Middle East and generated numerous comparisons with Britain's experience of decolonisation. In Britain's postwar foreign and imperial policies the shadowy presence of French North Africa merits closer examination.

1
Divergent Imperialism? Britain and the Restoration of French Power in North Africa, 1945–49

> The evolution of French North Africa had been discernible ever since 1935–6 and we had done nothing. Our empire's loyalty at the time of our defeat in 1940 had temporarily obscured its fragility. But as early as 1945 the revolt in the province of Constantine and the grave developments in Syria and Indo-China ought to have claimed our attention and led to important political decisions. Instead, owing to political paralysis in Paris and the conservative influence of the overseas French, rigidity was the order of the day... (General André Beaufre)[1]

Written by a general later to serve as French task force commander during the Suez expedition in 1956, André Beaufre's harsh judgment on French colonial policy in 1945 reveals several elements common in assessments of France's postwar North African crisis: decisive opportunities for reform were missed; consideration of imperial withdrawal was impossible owing to the imperative of French recovery after defeat in 1940; there was a failure of political will in Paris; and, ultimately, the *colon* settlers were principally to blame for the impending disaster. This chapter revisits these themes by examining the degree to which British policy-makers, diplomats and specialist officials regarded French North Africa as a looming problem for France, Anglo-French relations and the western alliance in the immediate postwar years.

Early Causes of Friction

The end of the Second World War in Europe saw imperial control in the three French North African territories weakened by the interlocking problems of chronic economic hardship, entrenched settler power and the lasting damage to French prestige inflicted by defeat in 1940. This last problem was compounded by the subsequent arrival of Anglo-American forces in the Maghreb and the Levant mandates of Syria and Lebanon. From November 1942 the presence of allied occupation troops disrupted French control over the dissemination of information to the local population and led to heightened international interest in the postwar future of the Maghreb. Across the region the major nationalist parties were better organised and more broadly based than in the pre-war years. And the experience of global war made colonial emergencies a greater source of international concern.[2] A major theatre of operations, North-West Africa had become familiar to the English-speaking world as never before.

With the crucial exception of Messali Hadj's Parti Populaire Algérien (PPA), the Maghreb nationalist parties, notably the Moroccan Istiqlal and the Tunisian Néo-Destour, cultivated British and, especially, American backing for their reformist programmes. In nationalist calculations, if the US government indicated its support for their proposals, Britain might follow.[3] During the Second World War, both Sultan Sidi Mohammed ben Youssef of Morocco and Moncef Bey of Tunisia increasingly identified with the urban professionals and Arab intellectuals who led the Istiqlal and Néo-Destour. Both rulers also sought allied support for their national cause. To the Gaullist administration across North Africa in 1944–45 it took little imagination to conjure up a conspiracy between 'les Anglo-Saxons', local nationalists and the native dynasties of Morocco and Tunisia intended to drive France from the Maghreb. On the ground, the bitter competition between Jacques Soustelle's expanding intelligence service, the *Direction Générale des Etudes et Recherches*, and Paul Paillole's more seasoned counter-espionage network in Morocco and Algeria sometimes distorted the local intelligence picture. This resulted in further wild accusations against British, US and Axis operatives in wartime North Africa, all of which fuelled French suspicions of Anglo-American policy.[4] The lingering presence of US and British troops in bases, port installations and public buildings across French North Africa for several months after the end of hostilities in 1945 inflamed opinion among settler communities. Angered by the distortive impact on the local economy of relatively high-spending British and American service personnel, the French authorities pressed the Foreign Office and State Department to accelerate the repatriation of their forces. Recurrent quarrels over the withdrawal of allied units poisoned the local atmosphere in several Maghreb port cities against Britain and the US throughout the years 1945–48.[5]

By 1945 both the Istiqlal and Néo-Destour claimed full 'internal independence', a demand which conceded France a privileged relationship with any future Moroccan and Tunisian states, but which necessarily involved full internal autonomy prior to the abolition of protectorate status. In pursuit of this, during 1945, the Néo-Destour leader, Habib Bourguiba, even supported a formal alliance to underpin economic and security co-operation between an independent Tunisia and France.[6] President of the Néo-Destour since 1937, Bourguiba was never instinctively hostile to France. Like Hô Chi Minh, his nationalism was forged in 1920s Paris where he completed his legal training at the Ecole des Sciences Politiques and met his French wife, Mathilde Lorrain.

With neither links to London and Washington nor much contact with the newly established Arab League secretariat in Cairo, Algerian nationalists were less well placed to channel popular protest into a campaign for international recognition. This helps explain the more desperate and volatile nationalist protests against the resumption of French colonial control in Algeria in May 1945. VE day marked a new phase of bloody conflict in the history of French North Africa. Within a matter of weeks, the savagery of the Sétif uprising in eastern Algeria was exceeded by the ferocity of the French repression which followed it. The Ministry of Interior's preliminary report on the anti-settler outbreaks in Sétif, Kherrata, Guèlma and several outlying settlements catalogued a series of killings rendered more horrifying by the systematic mutilation of victims and sexual violence against women. A distinctive aspect to these outbursts was the 'military' precision which characterised ostensibly spontaneous unrest. As a prelude to individual attacks, electricity supplies to villages and *colon* farms were cut and automatic weapons made available with remarkable speed. Unarmed demonstrators in Guèlma, who sang the banned Algerian national anthem *Anachid* and pleaded for the release of Messali Hadj on the morning of 8 May, had become a deadly mob by the evening. The fear that the Pandora's box of Muslim unrest might reopen underpinned the vigorous French repression unleashed over the subsequent fortnight.[7] The French military authorities responded to the appalling massacres of numerous *colon* families in and around Sétif with a series of sweep operations backed by the use of aircraft and naval bombardments of Muslim villages along the Constantine coast. This amounted to retributive butchery, occasionally pursued with the active participation of settler vigilantes bent on revenge. André Achiary, a French intelligence officer and sub-prefect of Guèlma at the epicentre of the violence, was even briefly imprisoned for his role in orchestrating the repression.[8] Although quickly suppressed, the Sétif 'outbreak' could not be dismissed as an isolated event confined to a notoriously lawless region. In the words of historian Jean-Charles Jauffret, this was 'the first act of the Algerian war'.[9]

The tragedy for Algeria was that, with no external challenge to French rule comparable to Britain's support for Syrian and Lebanese independence, and with no hostile forces for returning French soldiers to evict as in French Indo-China, international interest in North-West Africa in the summer of 1945 was relatively muted. Led by Egypt, Arab states appealed for US diplomatic intervention in Paris against the clampdown in Algeria. But the Truman administration was anxious to avoid a public row with France and confined itself to a backdoor protest.[10] The Sétif uprising generated lengthy discussion within the Foreign Office African and Western departments, particularly after the Algiers consul obtained figures from France confirming the deaths of at least 6,000 Algerian Muslims in the ten days to 17 May. Yet the events were never discussed in full Cabinet. Quite the reverse. Having read conflicting estimates of the death toll in Algeria, the outgoing Foreign Secretary, Anthony Eden, simply appended, 'What is this all about?'[11] Across Whitehall, in the first months after the war, France's colonial problems were a minor diversion next to the monumental task of reconstruction and the projection of British international power. Discussing the Labour government's approach to colonial policy, D. K. Fieldhouse has distinguished between those imperial problems of immediate international significance which were put to Cabinet, and other, more detailed issues of long-term British colonial rule which were dealt with at departmental level 'below the horizon' of Clement Attlee's chief ministers.[12] If we apply this model here, the Algerian crisis in 1945 clearly fell into the latter category. Still, the crisis of authority in the French Maghreb was real enough.

The Foundations of British Policy

From North Africa in early 1945 British consuls, military personnel and visiting politicians and dignatories predicted major nationalist unrest across the Maghreb once the war in Europe ended. These pessimistic reports variously stressed French reluctance to contemplate autonomy for the North African territories, the radicalisation of nationalist parties after years of repression and the predominance of settler communities whose politics were governed by narrow self-interest.[13] From 24 January, Tunisia's Resident General, Charles Mast, had made repeated requests to Paris for urgent troop reinforcements. Aware that political instability was aggravated by a severe wheat shortage across French North Africa, Mast advised the Foreign Minister, Georges Bidault, that insurrections were already in preparation.[14] Following informal conversations with members of Governor Yves Chataigneau's Algiers administration, British consular officials warned in April 1945 that all three French governments in North Africa planned to extend their local powers in peacetime. This was seen as a pre-emptive strike against nationalist parties, who the French expected would foment popular protest in an effort to keep North Africa in the international eye after the conclusion of the inaugural conference of the United Nations in San Francisco. Symptomatic of this general tension, by May 1945 the already severe press restrictions in French Morocco were extended, leaving only one venal Arab newspaper, *Al Saada*, in circulation. Meanwhile, the French residency in Tunis sought the assistance of the British occupation authorities in neighbouring Libya in an unsuccessful bid to prevent Bourguiba from travelling to Cairo, from where it was feared he would enlist US support for the Néo-Destour programme.[15]

As expected, once Bourguiba arrived in Egypt on 26 April, he devoted most attention to the US consular authorities and to the executive of the Arab League, a seven-nation grouping launched at the Alexandria conference in September–October 1944. Though directed by Egypt, the League was widely considered to be a tool of British imperial policy in the Middle East. This remained axiomatic to both the Quai d'Orsay and French military intelligence despite rising Arab League criticism of British Middle Eastern policy in 1946.[16] When drawing up the Arab League pact, the organisation's secretary-general, Abdul Rahman Azzam, personally supported the inclusion of non-independent Maghreb states. But Azzam did not distinguish between French- and British-controlled territories in his endorsement of independence movements across the Middle East and the Maghreb. Whatever the national priorities of its members, the Arab unity movement was necessarily anti-imperial. If anything, Azzam's pro-Egyptian imprint on Arab League activities was more problematic for Britain than his largely rhetorical support for nationalist causes in French North Africa. As such, French accusations of a hidden British hand at work in Arab League activity after 1945 were misguided; a hangover from France's acrimonious withdrawal from Syria and Lebanon in 1946.[17]

It was none the less obvious that Bourguiba and the Néo-Destour leadership regarded Britain as a potential ally against France, a view strengthened by the Anglo-French confrontation in the Levant States.[18] Fraught discussions between the Quai d'Orsay and the Foreign Office over the handling of Bourguiba were eclipsed by the shock of Sétif. The uprising confirmed the reservations expressed within the Foreign Office and the Colonial Office over preceding months. On 3 June 1945, Ronald Speaight, a senior Foreign Office French expert, summarised their findings: 'I am sure much bloodshed might have been avoided if the French military had not been so eager to engage in wholesale slaughter. As Syria has shown even more forcibly, they do not know how to deal with native unrest.' This was a view shaped by the damning reports from Terence Shone, British minister in the Levant and a stinging critic of French repression. To make matters worse, during summer 1945 the French administration in Morocco was swollen by an influx of bureaucrats displaced from Syria and Lebanon and seething with resentment at Britain's role in their humiliation.[19]

Whatever their underlying doubts, in public Churchill's outgoing administration, its Labour successor, the chiefs of staff and the Foreign Office endorsed French rule in the Maghreb. Assured possession of the North African territories was judged vital to French domestic recovery in the short term, principally because a violent imperial crisis might destabilise the working coalition between Free French Gaullists and the metropolitan resistance which underpinned the French provisional government. In a much publicised interview in *The Times* printed on 10 September 1945, de Gaulle reminded British readers that France, too, had a distinct imperial mission pivotal to its international status.[20] Speedy reconstruction in France was also vital to British economic and strategic interests in Western Europe. French ministers insisted that North Africa would play a key role in this. Although Jean Monnet's modernisation plans were not extended to the Maghreb territories until 1948, his Commissariat au Plan identified increases in North African agricultural and industrial output as vital stimuli to French imperial recovery. This process began in late 1945 with an investment scheme designed to mechanise agricultural production in Morocco and Tunisia. By increasing productivity and so improving the purchasing power of the indigenous peasantry, a general improvement in living standards was anticipated.[21]

In hindsight, such grandiose schemes of economic regeneration seem unrealistic. War-shattered France could ill-afford the immense sums required to reimpose imperial control. With a few notable exceptions, neither French nor British investors seemed eager to plough money into capital projects in colonial territory.[22] But in 1945 the British had no wish to dispute France's stake in North West Africa. This diffidence was stimulated by three further British concerns. First, with no prospect of Anglo-French reconciliation in the Levant, additional imperial controversy was unwelcome.[23] Secondly, British strategic paramountcy in the Mediterranean and Middle East demanded a friendly presence in North-West Africa. British naval deployments and wider strategic planning required an expanding French role in the defence of both the western Mediterranean and north–south land access to the African continent; and thirdly, aside from the bitter, though containable, Levant dispute, it was essential to keep Anglo-French relations on an even keel.[24] France had yet to agree a new constitution and the most dynamic forces in French party politics – a loose Gaullist coalition and a much expanded Communist Party – posed enough difficulties to Anglo-French relations without adding colonial complications to the equation. The British inclination to avoid controversial quarrels over French North Africa, which would remain a feature of policy through to 1962, established itself at the end of the war in 1945.

Among Britain's concerns to avoid another Levant-type dispute, to cement Anglo-French co-operation and to safeguard regional security in the Mediterranean and Middle East, it was the last of these that predominated during the late 1940s. In September 1945, the Labour Cabinet approved the findings of a conference of Britain's Middle Eastern representatives and regional military experts which concluded that Britain's Middle East supremacy should be maintained. British suzerainty across the region would henceforth depend on increasing economic and political support for client Arab regimes rather than military influence alone. This was underlined by the role assigned to the development division within the newly established British Middle East Office. To Foreign Secretary Ernest Bevin, if Britain's Middle Eastern influence was to endure without perennial recourse to repression, attempts to broaden local support for a British connection were essential.[25] In a memorandum to the Cabinet in January 1946, Bevin linked negotiations with Egypt over the long-term presence of British forces in the Suez Canal zone with a new security partnership with Arab partner states.[26] In spite of worsening acrimony over Palestine and Britain's abrupt military withdrawal from Greece and Turkey in February 1947, during the Anglo-American Pentagon talks in the autumn, the US government made British paramountcy in the Middle East a 'cornerstone' of its global strategy. This chimed nicely with that strand of Foreign Office thinking, typified by Bevin and Permanent Under-Secretary, Sir Orme Sargent, which envisaged a form of Monroe Doctrine of non-interference in Britain's Mediterranean and Middle East interests.[27]

Until the devaluation crisis in autumn 1949, the Foreign Secretary was wedded to the concept of a British-led Euro-African 'third force' which made control of key Middle East bases and colonial co-operation with France across Africa pivotal supports to Britain's global power.[28] Specialist co-operation between the British and French Colonial Offices regarding economic policies, social welfare and, to a lesser extent, constitutional development in neighbouring West African territories grew rapidly between 1945 and 1948, and was informed by a shared wish to contain communist infiltration, violent nationalist protest and American political interference.[29] But these exchanges were never extended to Africa north of the Sahara. More important, as John Kent has shown, both Bevin and the service chiefs were muddled in their strategic arguments about the vital importance of Middle East bases in any Cold War contest with the Soviet Union. Suggestions that British bombers could retaliate most effectively against any Soviet aggression from Middle Eastern air bases concealed the technical difficulties involved in such long-distance operations and overlooked intelligence indicating that the Soviet threat to the region was remote. Foreign Office and chiefs of staff insistence that the Middle East was dangerously exposed to Soviet incursion thus revealed more about the determination of strategic policy-makers to preserve British prestige and regional influence in the face of Attlee's long-standing scepticism about the value of Britain's Arab ties.[30] By March 1947 it was established that the British army should protect these key bases despite their questionable utility in the short term. Bevin's preoccupations were shared by the Cabinet Palestine Committee, which also stressed the need to maintain Britain's prestige across the Arab world.[31] British support for an immediate French withdrawal from the Levant states is wholly explicable in this light. While French accusations of a British plot to supplant France in both territories were baseless, from December 1945 British negotiators played to an Arab gallery in the talks over a final Anglo-French withdrawal from Damascus and Beirut.[32]

British worries about the fragility of the French provisional government and its successors gradually diminished, even though de Gaulle's abrupt decision to quit office in January 1946 renewed fears about French stability and the likelihood of a decisive communist breakthrough either at the polls or in the streets. Henceforth, the Colonial Office provided British overseas governors with key Foreign Office memoranda detailing the machinations of French domestic politics. Such reports rarely included information about French North Africa.[33] The US State Department took a keener interest than the Foreign Office in the growing links between the French Communist Party and North African nationalist leaders prior to French elections in October 1946.

The US ambassador to France, Jefferson Caffery, drove this process forward. On 26 July he spelt out the threat as he saw it to Secretary of State James Byrnes:

> In many ways, it would appear that Communism wears a cloak of nationalism and local autonomy in North Africa and perhaps more especially in Algeria. Thus, while it can be said that the Communists as such have not succeeded in developing (or perhaps have not attempted to develop) an extensive following under their own banner in Algeria, one must not forget the potential allies they have in the followers of Ferhat Abbas and of Messali Hadj.[34]

Alarmed by the PCF's entertaining the idea of an electoral pact with Algerian nationalists in particular, the State Department office of Near Eastern and African affairs instituted a long-term system of fortnightly reports on communist activity across French North Africa.[35] Britain's diplomats in France and the Maghreb by contrast were more phlegmatic about alleged communist influence. Less worried about ideological affiliations among nationalist groups, in their policy advice on the Maghreb, Foreign Office French specialists stressed the glaring iniquities in French North African administration, such as the allocation of over 80 per cent of Morocco's tax revenue to metropolitan France, unfair land distribution in Algeria and undue French interference in Tunisia's beylical administration.[36] The economic edge to nationalist protest in Morocco and Tunisia also sharpened in January 1946 following the alignment of the protectorate currencies with a newly devalued metropolitan franc. The Quai d'Orsay argued that, since the Maghreb territories received $220 million in metropolitan assistance to finance essential imports, the benefits of close economic union with France outweighed the disadvantages.[37] This cut little ice with nationalist politicians, aware that the settler community swallowed a disproportionate share of both metropolitan aid and inward investment funding. But these issues were scarcely raised at inter-governmental level. French practices in North Africa were always secondary to European concerns. Discussion of overseas misrule was anyway liable to degenerate into a trading of insults over French and British colonial misdeeds.

During 1947 the announcement of the Truman doctrine in March and the launch of the European Recovery Programme of Marshall Aid in June underscored greater US political and material investment in the new French Fourth Republic. By the end of that year communist support in France and North Africa had diminished. Although Franco-British-US disagreements persisted over policy towards Germany, French alignment with the major Western Powers was not in doubt.[38] In March 1947 Britain and France concluded a mutual assistance pact against future German attack. The Treaty of Dunkirk and the Brussels and North Atlantic Treaties which followed it in March 1948 and April 1949 were primarily European in focus. But the developing Cold War did not respect continental boundaries. Inevitably, French imperial rule in North Africa and British strategic predominance in the Middle East became intertwined as each rested on a primordial need to maintain control of the Mediterranean. After the breakdown of the Council of Foreign Ministers at the London Conference in December 1947, Bevin stressed this common threat in a Cabinet paper tabled on 5 January 1948:

> If the Soviets secured control of France and French North Africa, of Italy, and of Greece, and particularly if they could undermine our position in the Middle East, they would effectively dominate the Mediterranean and could (if they wished) deprive us of access to extensive markets and raw materials, especially oil, without which our economic recovery would be difficult or impossible and the strategic position both of ourselves and of the United States gravely jeopardised.[39]

The redistribution of Italy's former African colonies – Libya above all – also underscored the bonds between western imperial control and regional security requirements in the early Cold War. Situated between Egypt and French Tunisia, Libya was strategically vital to Britain and France. To the British service chiefs, the Cabinet defence committee and the Foreign Office, strategic base rights in Libya acquired additional importance as British imperial control disintegrated in Palestine and Anglo-Egyptian negotiations became mired in disputes over permissible British force levels.[40] After the Soviet Union dropped its claim to a trusteeship over Tripolitania in 1946, the remaining options were to place Libya's component territories of Tripolitania, Cyrenaica and the Fezzan under UN supervision, to return the colony to Italian control as part of a final peace treaty with Rome, to divide the territories between trustee powers, or to grant immediate independence to a new Libyan state. Here, the respective imperial interests of Britain and France intervened. British interest in military facilities within Cyrenaica was nourished by difficulties in securing a revised Anglo-Egyptian treaty to meet British base requirements in the eastern Mediterranean. On 1 August 1946, the French ambassador, René Massigli, pleaded for greater caution in Whitehall policy towards Libya owing to the destabilising effect within Tunisia of rumoured British support for Libyan nationalism.[41] This remained a constant French preoccupation.

When the issue was discussed in December 1946, Léon Blum's government was adamant that Libya should not be granted immediate independence for fear of the repercussions within French North Africa. Although sensitive to French reactions, Britain's strategic requirements, its international reputation and its status within the Arab world precluded the obvious alternative of restoring Italian colonial control. Furthermore, the British had taken the leading role in the allied occupation of Italy's colonial territories after the end of the war.[42] In the absence of agreement within the Council of Foreign Ministers over the future status of Libya, from February 1948 the Attlee government pressed for unilateral control over the country on the understanding that Libya would be granted a high degree of autonomy prior to full self-government.[43] Whereas British planning was predicated on the establishment of a friendly and dependent Libyan regime, in the French-garrisoned Fezzan in southern Libya, plans were well advanced for the assimilation of the region into French Africa. In return for its assent to Britain's preferred solution of a UK trusteeship in Libya, Henri Queuille's government demanded firmer British support for French rule in the Maghreb. Britain's Mediterranean and Middle East security requirements thus produced a clearer political endorsement of French policies in North Africa.[44] This made no difference to British policy in practice. Attlee's government was always torn between its primary concern to see French political stability and economic recovery enhanced and its general sympathy for the pro-western nationalists of French North Africa. Convinced that the frustration of reform would generate long-term conflict in the Maghreb liable to spill over into the wider Arab world, the British government none the less estimated that to press France towards concessions would only poison Anglo-French relations and thus serve no useful purpose.[45] With mounting discomfort, British politicians and officials either scratched the Maghreb from the agenda of cross-Channel talks or confined discussion to specialists outside the mainstream of policy-making.

Sources of British Unease

By 1945 it was commonplace for maghrebi nationalists to emphasise their links with the wider Arab world. Whatever its cultural basis in fact, this tactic helped secure Arab backing, including sanctuary for exiled leaders in Middle Eastern capitals. In addition, the stress on a common Muslim and Arab identity cemented popular support for otherwise secular nationalist parties. Identification with the Arab world also challenged France's claim that its North African territories were distinct from the Middle East, and that Algeria was a society built to French design. Nationalist tracts often played on this theme. Witness a 1944 'Free North Africa' communiqué issued in Algiers:

> 'Algeria is French ground', 'It is a prolongation of France', 'It is a parcel of French soil thrown by chance over the Mediterranean onto the African continent'; such are the slogans that one finds in the writings and the speeches of French officials, politicians, publicists, economists and historians when they speak of our country. Over the past century, French imperialism has made considerable efforts to keep the Algerian Arab separated from North Africa and from wider Arab culture . . . but it is Islamic and pan-Arab solidarity above all that unites Algeria to Islam and to the entire Arab world.[46]

Hence the immense importance attached to the consolidation of the Arab League in 1945. Apart from backing North African nationalism directly, the League enabled maghrebi nationalists to solicit wider international support against France. Although member states did not take up the Moroccan or Tunisian national cause unanimously, both the Istiqlal and Néo-Destour always regarded the League as the primary conduit through which to put their claims for independence before a UN audience. The two main Algerian nationalist parties lagged behind, although the UDMA was ultimately more successful than the PPA-MTLD in winning support from the Arab League secretariat in Cairo.[47] This caused alarm in Paris. As events in Palestine unfolded in 1945–48, President Vincent Auriol recalled that successive French governments attached increasing weight to evidence of Arab League influence across the Middle East.[48] The identification of secular nationalism with a pan-Arab ideal suggested that neither the Moroccan sultanate nor the beylical administration in Tunis could serve as an effective channel for a more limited reformism. Instead, the North African dynasties might be bypassed or trodden underfoot by a radical nationalist stampede.

Habib Bourguiba was the most successful of the nationalist leaders across French North Africa in cementing ties with the Arab League. But, during 1945, there was little suspicion of a deliberate British scheme either to advance the Néo-Destour programme or to support the restorationist claims of the exiled monarch, Moncef Bey, against his

French-backed successor, Sidi Lamine Bey. On 12 February, Charles Mast told Bidault that British consular officials in Tunisia were a model of propriety.[49] In the following year this goodwill evaporated. The French authorities regularly intercepted mail sent to and from leading North African nationalists. Cumulatively, this pointed to a network of contacts with the British. Two examples convey the tenor of this material. On 30 October 1945 Bourguiba allegedly recorded that Arab League secretary-general Azzam had told him that Britain wished to see the French North African territories placed under international trusteeship.[50] On 17 June 1946 the Tunis residency produced a further report, probably based on information gathered by operatives of the French foreign intelligence service, the *Direction Générale des Etudes et Recherches* (DGER). (During 1946 this organisation was being remoulded into the *Service de Documentation Extérieure et de Contre-Espionnage* (SDECE).) This claimed that secret agents of 'a certain great power' worked with Néo-Destour as part of a wider strategy to manipulate the Arab League and deflect Arab criticism from British policy in Palestine. If such a strategy existed, it was failing. As Mast conceded, during 1946 Britain's worsening predicament in Palestine diverted Arab and UN attention from Maghreb problems.[51]

Anglophobic intelligence reports prepared for Mast's administration proliferated following a residency decision in December 1945 to use intelligence operatives to collect evidence of British contacts with Tunisian nationalists in Tunis and Cairo. As a result, from March 1946, the residency pressed the Quai d'Orsay's Afrique-Levant section to confront the British government with the evidence gathered. There were three main aspects to this. First, it was alleged that the British government exploited the Arab League as an intermediary to notify the Néo-Destour of Britain's tacit support. Second, British consular officials were accused of working to reunite the leaderships of the Destour and Néo-Destour parties, which had been divided since the early 1930s. Finally, and most sensationally, it was even claimed that British agents had offered to arm nationalist groups throughout French North Africa provided that they agreed to mount a general rebellion at Britain's behest.[52]

On 22–23 August 1946 allegations of British misbehaviour in North Africa were further advertised during an acrimonious parliamentary debate over a draft constitution for Algeria presented by Ferhat Abbas's UDMA. Buoyed by his party's strong showing in the recent elections for the second college of the French Constituent Assembly (boycotted by the PPA), Abbas proposed immediate Algerian self-rule. His plans were generally mocked, only the PCF lending any support to the UDMA's position. To the Socialist deputy Christian Pineau's quip, 'You are ten years too early M. Abbas', Abbas retorted that, on the contrary, Pineau was a decade behind the times.[53] But it was the anglophobic aspect of the debate that caught Ambassador Alfred Duff Cooper's attention. In his maiden speech as newly elected deputy for the Moselle, de Gaulle's former rival, General Henri Giraud, focused on international interference in North Africa, hinting that Britain encouraged local sedition during 1945.[54]

From London, Massigli noted that none of the 'evidence' of British conspiracies in Tunisia could be authenticated; the French intelligence service's wild theories were a gambit to justify increases in its budget. To act on the allegations made would be to accept that British diplomats contravened Bevin's promise to Bidault in January 1946 to support France in North Africa. Bidault agreed with Massigli and tried to close the matter in a meeting at the Foreign Office on 9 September. As expected, Sir Orme Sargent categorically denied any British wrongdoing.[55] But three weeks later, on 28 September, the Tunis residency, which had continued its customary surveillance of the British consulate, claimed that Salah Ben Youssef and Sala Ferhat, two prominent leaders of the divided Destour factions, visited the consul's home at La Marsa to discuss Britain's terms for supporting inscription of Tunisia's case for international trusteeship status at the UN. Sala Ferhat allegedly rejected British demands to end Destour support for Moncef Bey, so preventing any agreement.[56] Whatever the truth of the accusations, little came of the alleged contacts.

The confirmation of extensive French monitoring of British diplomatic activity in the Maghreb and the Middle East more generally, plus the readiness of senior French officials to swallow the idea of British malevolence towards French imperial rule, confirmed that distrust of Britain was endemic within the administrative elite across North Africa. Even Governor Chataigneau in Algiers insisted that the British consulate in Tangiers and British commercial representatives in Algeria were part of a Maghreb intelligence network whose activities were incompatible with cordial Anglo-French relations.[57] In December 1946, during preparations for premier Blum's first postwar ministerial visit to London, Mast even claimed that British support for Néo-Destour was a lever to persuade Blum to serve as mediator in Palestine.[58]

On the final day of Blum's visit to London on 16 January 1947, the Foreign Office learnt that the French government was recalling Mast from Tunis. This helps explain British enthusiasm for Blum's decision to revive an administrative innovation of the pre-war Popular Front by re-establishing a secretariat for Muslim affairs within the Quai d'Orsay headed by a junior minister, Georges Gorse. British officials hoped to work with the restored secretariat – effectively a special office for North African affairs – to break down French paranoia over Anglo-American malevolence towards French imperial policy. Since the Quai's Afrique-Levant section occasionally succumbed to this, an alternative department with which to communicate over North Africa was particularly welcome.[59] In late January 1947 the British heads of mission from the North African territories suggested that, as an adjunct to the imminent negotiations for the Dunkirk Treaty, the secretariat for Muslim affairs should be encouraged to co-operate with Britain's Middle East bureau, sharing technical advice on how best to improve Arab living standards.[60]

With the Dunkirk negotiations looming, as an additional precaution, Bevin reiterated on 27 February that, whatever their personal sympathy for moderate nationalist aspirations, British officials should not oppose French colonial rule. Consular contacts with North African nationalists were to be kept to the bare minimum required to keep abreast of local politics. This was an unequivocal statement of the primacy of French regional security over the claims of Arab nationalism in North West Africa.[61] In mid-April the British urged the State Department to follow suit, suggesting that UN consideration of French North Africa be discouraged since, regardless of British dislike of French colonial administration, 'no other means of assuring stability in the region were at present discernible'.[62] As Maghreb politics grew more confrontational, such aloofness justified on grounds of strategic interest made less sense. The firm French hand applied to North Africa was the principal cause of the instability that Bevin was so anxious to avoid.

While French suspicions of British intelligence activity in North Africa could be dismissed, the Foreign Office could not ignore the mounting evidence of a breakdown in the dialogue between France and Tunisian and Moroccan nationalists in 1946–47. In January 1946, Gabriel Puaux, the experienced Resident General in Morocco, warned Bidault that French protectorate administration had to move with the times. There were few fresh ideas to match this sentiment. France remained committed to a reform plan launched in November 1944. This scheme included a clearer separation of executive and judicial power, a reform of Morocco's penal code and greater access for native Moroccans to senior administrative posts. But the central element in Puaux's reforms was to invest in the modernisation of Moroccan agriculture in order to increase rural living standards and so consolidate popular loyalty to France.[63] A dreadful harvest in 1946 and a widespread typhus epidemic indicated that these reforms were not working. In fact, French government spending in the North African territories was inevitably dependent on the revitalisation of the home economy. Substantial capital funding only made a marked impact upon the Maghreb economies following the expansion of public investment from 1949 onwards.[64] Alone of the North African territories, Morocco was theoretically open to international free trade. But, as Robert Schuman had warned in 1945, since the protectorate administration put the interests of the settlers and the tribal caïds first, free trade access to the Moroccan market only served the interests of a narrow elite.[65] The US consul in Rabat, Maurice Pasquet, also argued consistently that whilst French settler and military interests barred communist penetration of Morocco, they also blocked the reform process.[66] This was bound to provoke American diplomatic protest since the US government retained its capitulatory trading rights in Morocco and was taking a closer interest in the country's economic potential and strategic importance.[67]

The governing tripartite coalitions of Socialist, MRP and Communist ministers attempted to breathe new life into Morocco's reform process in 1946 by appointing a forward-thinking Resident, Eirik Labonne. Rumoured to have links with Britain's Secret Intelligence Service, during the course of the year, Labonne spurned *colon* interests in pursuit of accelerated constitutional and economic reform.[68] Meanwhile, as President of the French Union, Vincent Auriol sought to arbitrate between the Paris government and the protectorate administrations. While Auriol was anxious to restore Franco-Tunisian co-operation on the basis of the original protectorate treaties, his only administrative support was his adviser on Maghreb affairs, Cherif Mécheri. Since imperial policy was rarely debated extensively either within the French Cabinet or among senior Socialist ministers, the Foreign Minister and the Resident Generals in post in Rabat and Tunis had leeway to implement policy changes with relative impunity provided that they carried the local administrations with them.[69] This tendency became more pronounced after the MRP's underlying colonialism was boosted by the admission of like-minded Radical, UDSR and conservative Independents to the governing coalition in January 1947. All of these parties were prepared to make their resistance to colonial democratisation an issue of confidence. This intransigence set the MRP and the UDSR apart from their Socialist colleagues, and gave them considerable leverage over colonial policy, making Auriol's arbitral task near impossible.[70] In Morocco, Labonne's initial progress was impeded by his misguided appointment of General Jean Lecomte to head the Department of the Interior which replaced

Morocco's Department of Political Affairs in June 1946. Lecomte combined with veteran administrator Philippe Boniface, the former director of political affairs in Rabat who had been made regional commissioner in Casablanca, to block administrative liberalisation. Without a supportive administration behind him, Labonne had little hope of overcoming settler and Istiqlal opposition to limited reform. He was recalled from Rabat on 14 May 1947.[71]

The completion of the constitutional proposals for the French Union in late 1946 further blocked the reform process in all three North African territories. As protectorates, and therefore nominally sovereign countries, Morocco and Tunisia were to become 'Associated States' of the French Union, rather than full members, whose subject peoples were to be accorded French imperial citizenship. In contrast to the special status of the North African protectorates, Algeria, which as a colony might logically have become a full Union member, was the subject of a special statute. This was intended to acknowledge Algeria's unique position as the colony most closely assimilated to France. In fact, consideration of the Algerian statute divided successive tripartite governments. It undermined the credibility of SFIO support for assimilationism and it set the MRP against its erstwhile Socialist and Communist coalition partners. Within Algeria, Muslim disappointment at the final terms of the Algerian statute, clearly articulated by Messali Hadj, destroyed popular support for the French Left and fed the growth of autonomist and nationalist Algerian political parties.[72] Taken together, the terms of the October 1946 French Union and the August 1947 statute for Algeria crystallised a constitutional relationship between France and the three North African territories which set Algeria apart from its neighbours, leaving Algerians without hope of reforms akin to those planned for Morocco and Tunisia. Twice debated by the Constituent Assembly in October 1945 and April 1946 before coming to a final vote of the National Assembly on 27 August 1947, the statute underwrote settler control over the Algerian electoral, administrative and fiscal process by perpetuating separate voting rights for French citizens and Algerian Muslims.[73]

The military reorganisation of French colonial forces necessitated by the French Union project illustrated the complexity of the project itself. Appointing a general staff for the French Union to co-ordinate colonial commands was relatively straightforward in so far as individual colonies within the Union were still disbarred from raising their own armed forces. But the outbreak of the Indo-China war hastened plans for the creation of Vietnamese, Cambodian and Laotian armies to assist the

French war effort. As Associated States the protectorate administrations in Morocco and Tunisia could justifiably argue that they, too, should be allowed to raise their own national defence forces. This prospect caused unease within the French defence establishment. In a worst-case scenario, French-trained Moroccan and Tunisian troops might turn their French-supplied weapons upon their French protectors. The solution adopted was to emphasise the unique circumstances of Indo-China, thus precluding military autonomy for the North African territories.[74]

As Duff Cooper noted, French North Africa was tangible proof of the irreconcilable tendencies in French colonial policy between greater federalism as applied to the protectorates, and an abiding belief in assimilationism in established colonies like Algeria. His prediction was remarkably accurate:

> The process of turning Arabs into Frenchmen is a difficult one to reverse; and if the centrifugal forces should ever prove strong enough to disrupt the present relationship, the almost complete integration which has been achieved would probably make impossible the orderly transformation of Algeria into a self-governing member of the French Union.[75]

Although neither Moroccan nor Tunisian nationalists were entirely satisfied with the new obligations of an 'Associated State', in late 1947 the greater militancy of Algerian nationalist opposition was more noticeable since the statute endorsed an indefinite continuation of French colonial rule. Passage of the statute also marked the triumph of a group of right-wing parliamentarians representing *colon* interests over those moderate Algerian deputies united under the umbrella of Ferhat Abbas's reformist programme. Abbas and other 'Europeanised Algerians' like him who had received a French education, had served in the French armed forces or local bureaucracy, and who wrote and spoke in French throughout their professional lives, were thus alienated from a colonial power with whom they were culturally inclined to co-operate. The UDMA, previously the best bet as a 'constructive nationalist' party with whom to negotiate, was instead driven towards integral nationalism. This was both in reaction to French administrative abuse and in order to prevent a haemorrhage of support to the more radical MTLD, the Messalist Party founded in October 1946 as a successor to the outlawed PPA.[76]

Marcel-Edmond Naegelen's appointment as governor-general in Algiers as successor to Yves Chataigneau on 11 February 1948 confirmed this shift to the right in French colonial policy. The centrist 'third force' governments that held sway in France during 1948–51 were dominated by MRP and Radical Party figures determined to slow down the reforms contemplated in the tripartism period. Drawing on information from the chiefs of staff joint intelligence committee (JIC), in February 1949 British Colonial Secretary Arthur Creech Jones notified Britain's colonial governors that, if it altered at all, French imperial policy was likely to become more reactionary. MRP fears of a loss of support to the Gaullist *Rassemblement du Peuple Français* (RPF) only confirmed this assessment.[77] From the inception of the RPF in April 1947 until de Gaulle's return to office in 1958, the movement's rank and file proved more hostile to colonial reform than the General himself. Most RPF supporters endorsed secretary-general Jacques Soustelle's vigorous defence of French imperial privilege.[78]

Although a Socialist Deputy with a proud resistance record, Naegelen quickly reinforced settler predominance in Algerian politics. Recalling his formative political experiences in Alsace, Naegelen attacked Algerian nationalism with the same vigour with which he had previously opposed Rhenish separatism. From 1945, and especially after Naegelen's arrival, the Algiers governorship became a more overtly politicised posting. Those appointed tended to be political figures rather than career colonial officials. As the US consul, George Tait, noted ruefully in March 1950, direct settler pressure upon the governor – exerted by French Algerian Deputies, the Algerian Assembly, the immensely powerful Algiers press or by direct street protest – took root during Naegelen's term of office.[79] The new governor undermined the free operation of the dual college electoral system instituted under the 1947 statute. Instead of permitting the election of an Algerian Assembly with limited financial powers whose 120 members were legitimately chosen by French Algerian citizens and Algeria's Muslim voters, Naegelen engaged in wholesale gerrymandering in the April 1948 elections to ensure that the Muslim electoral college would contain suitably compliant appointees. He defended corrupt practice on the grounds that Muslim voters 'expected' guidance from the local authorities. Were it not forthcoming, respect for the French administration would evaporate.[80] In all, 464,000 French Algerian citizens, including 58,000 Muslims, were eligible to vote for the first electoral college. Algeria's remaining 1,400,000 Muslim voters were to elect the second college. Thanks to Naegelen's electoral engineering the statute for Algeria merely created 'rotten boroughs' dedicated to French colonialism.[81] Just as revealing as the election results were the actions of René Mayer. Radical Deputy for Constantine and Finance Minister in Robert Schuman's 1948 administration, Mayer helped orchestrate the campaign for Chataigneau's dismissal and then intervened to ensure Ferhat Abbas's defeat as electoral candidate in the Sétif district.[82]

The rigged elections in Algeria during April 1948 confirmed a return to the old practices of government in Algiers. In the crucial poll for the settler-dominated first electoral college, the overwhelming victory of Gaullist and right-wing candidates enabled the government-general to rule without concession to nationalist demands. Overall, Socialist and Communist candidates to the first electoral college secured only five of the 60 seats, while the Gaullist-dominated coalition, the *Union Algérienne et Rassemblement du Peuple Français,* took 40.[83] Meanwhile, the 'success' of pro-French Muslim candidates for the less influential second electoral college was much celebrated by Naegelen's administration. Even so, the triumph of radical Messalists in Constantine over their more moderate rivals loyal to Abbas's UDMA revealed increasing Muslim militancy in eastern Algeria.[84] This was evident elsewhere too. Across the country, 19 Messalist MTLD candidates and six of their UDMA equivalents were arrested for sedition immediately after campaigning ended. In the week following the April ballot, 400 prominent nationalist and Algerian communist supporters were detained. At Aumale, 80 miles south of Algiers, the *Garde Mobile* killed several demonstrators protesting at the manner and outcome of the elections.[85] More serious in the long term, those Algerian Muslims who agreed to serve within this tainted colonial system inevitably lost touch with the population they were supposed to represent. This fed the radicalism of the emerging generation of Muslim activists who would lead the Algerian rebellion. They saw little prospect of significant reform within the existing structure of tight French political control and compliant '*Beni-oui-oui*' Muslim representatives closely linked by family ties, economic interests or political background to the colonial establishment in Algeria's principal cities.[86]

The same trend towards arbitrary French rule was apparent across Algeria's western border. Confronted with the disintegration of Puaux's and Labonne's reform plans, and with accumulating evidence that the Sultan sympathised with Istiqlal objectives, France applied a firmer hand to Morocco during 1947. This dismayed British diplomats and North Africa watchers within the Foreign and Colonial Offices, who saw in the Istiqlal – a party committed to secular modernisation and prepared to sign a post-independence treaty of alliance with France – the kind of pro-western movement that Britain hankered for in Egypt.[87] Following bloody rioting in Casablanca on 7 April and an incendiary speech by the Sultan in Tangiers calling the legitimacy of French rule into question, on

27 May a new Resident General arrived to reassert French authority.[88] This was the Algerian-born Alphonse Juin, the only serving Marshal in the French army, and a man with unrivalled military experience in the Maghreb. In anticipation of high office in North Africa, Juin had already refused Paul Ramadier's offer of Admiral Thierry d'Argenlieu's former post as French High Commissioner in Indo-China.[89] Juin's appointment at the behest of Bidault and his MRP colleague, deputy premier Pierre-Henri Teitgen, was facilitated by the dismissal of the PCF ministers from Ramadier's Cabinet. It was confirmation of the rightward lurch in French colonial policy, which would soon become more apparent with the promulgation of the statute for Algeria and the subsequent consolidation of third force government in 1948. The more strident MRP approach to colonial matters and the incoherence of SFIO imperial policy had grave long-term consequences. Anxious to stamp their mark on Moroccan affairs, Juin and his fellow *colon*, Regional Commissioner Boniface, made it their first task to bring the Sultan's administration back into line.[90]

Since Juin was convinced that the Sultan sought Anglo-American support for the Moroccan national cause, North Africa was bound to remain a thorny issue in Anglo-French relations.[91] His repression drove the Istiqlal underground, increasing the risk of a more violent outburst of nationalist activity. Worried at this radicalisation of Moroccan nationalism, and pressed by the Sultan and Istiqlal leaders through the UN to oppose Juin's disruption of the original protectorate treaties, by 1948 it was once again difficult for the British government to endorse French rule.[92] The outbreak of widespread Arab–Jewish clashes across Morocco's cities as British withdrawal from Palestine drew closer in the early summer heightened British embarrassment. This was not an apposite moment to take the moral high ground. Such was the escalation of disorder across numerous territories of the British empire during the course of 1948 that Attlee's government also adopted Draconian security measures from the Gold Coast to Malaya.[93] Moreover, Foreign Office representatives could hardly criticise the inadequacy of French economic support for the Maghreb territories when the Middle East Office was struggling to advance any of the development projects so much favoured by Bevin owing to stringent Treasury cuts and the equivocal Whitehall backing for the new organisation.[94]

For the French, the security position in Tunisia was no better than that in Morocco. On 23 August 1946, during a session of the Destour National Congress in Tunis, the French authorities arrested 46 senior party figures and their leading supporters within the Tunisian trade union movement.

The Destour executive promptly begged the British government to intercede on its behalf.[95] The outbreak of the Indo-China war in December 1946 added to anxiety in the Quai d'Orsay about reform in French North Africa. The gradual reinforcement of the French expeditionary force, achieved largely by drawing off forces from other colonial commands, made the military authorities in French North Africa more sensitive to any local political dissent.[96] A month before the arrests of Destour leaders, in July 1946 the ministerial North Africa committee approved a series of reforms for Tunisia proposed by Charles Mast. During the late 1940s and early 1950s the committee served as an advisory body to successive French governments, bringing together the Resident Generals with the Quai d'Orsay and Ministry of National Defence ministers and officials. The North Africa committee's readiness to alter the fabric of French rule in Tunis by increasing Tunisian ministerial representation, extending the franchise and reforming the structure of local government across the protectorate was quickly tested once the conflict in Indo-China began.[97] The breakdown in discussions with Destour, Mast's recall in January 1947 and the decision to pursue talks with the incumbent Sidi Lamine Bey rather than his more popular rival, the deposed monarch, Moncef Bey, confirmed that the French government intended to impose reform as it saw fit.[98]

As with Naegelen's appointment to Algeria, the appointment of Jean Mons as Resident General in Tunis was determined by the emergence of a powerful Gaullist challenge to the dominance of centre-left tripartism in France. With a strong resistance record and proven administrative skills as a former *directeur de cabinet* to Blum, Mons suited the reformist inclinations of the Socialist Party. But, like his fellow resister Naegelen, once in office in North Africa Mons blocked accelerated reform. This was quickly confirmed by the arrest of the entire Tunisian section of the protectorate Grand Council in December 1947. Invested with limited powers to scrutinise and sanction the Residency's annual budget for Tunisia, the Grand Council had become a battleground in which Tunisian representatives sought to trade their approval of the budget against the implementation of long-promised administrative reforms. The resulting arrests and resort to rule by decree exposed the bankruptcy of the joint French–Tunisian co-operation supposedly enshrined in protectorate administration. Although Mons increased Tunisian ministerial representation within Mohammed Kaak's protectorate government, French backroom control was assured by civil advisers posted throughout the central administration.[99]

By 1948 the patterns of repressive control in Morocco and Tunisia, and of corrupt electoral practice in Algeria, were clearly set. Constrained by its self-denying ordinance to avoid questioning French actions, British policy towards French North Africa was ineffective. At the fourth session of the UN General Assembly in 1949 the British delegation faced a powerful anti-colonial bloc of states reluctant to distinguish between British and French dependent territories. Arab delegations were determined to make an issue of the Maghreb, and Anglo-French solidarity within the UN trusteeship council in particular was beginning to crack. The political cost of tacit support for French North African rule was increasing.[100]

The fundamental ambiguity in British policy towards French North Africa was nicely illustrated by internal Colonial Office discussions between 1949 and 1951 over two exploratory visits to Algeria and Morocco conducted by Major J. G. C. Allen, a deputy colonial commissioner in Nigeria (See Map 2). Allen submitted Alice-in-Wonderland reports on French administration in both countries: racial tension had disappeared, elections were conducted scrupulously and social equality was everywhere apparent. The hapless commissioner was clearly shepherded from one model project to another by his French hosts and lapped up their political hostility towards local self-government. After the Colonial Office sought advice from Ronald Robinson of Nuffield College, Oxford, on the accuracy of Allen's report on Algeria, it was meticulously demolished by Robinson's colleague, Sybil E. Crowe, Oxford's leading Maghreb expert at the time. But, as official reports, Allen's views on Algeria and Morocco were widely circulated to British colonial administrations, whereas Crowe's unofficial corrective was kept under wraps. This spoke volumes for the contradictions in British policy.[101]

*

The spectacular emergence of the Gaullist RPF in 1947, and the growing sensitivity of the MRP leadership towards de Gaulle's accusations of softness on imperial security, quickly offset the minimal success hitherto achieved in dissipating French suspicion of a hidden British agenda towards overseas France. Meanwhile, the humiliation of Palestine and the chequered path of Anglo-Egyptian negotiations undermined Bevin's claim that Britain held Arab interests in high esteem. Whitehall's passive response to French behaviour in North Africa lent further weight to Arab criticism of British policy. But the US administration was also struggling to balance its intrinsic hostility towards French policies in North Africa with the overarching requirements of European reconstruction and western security co-operation. Both countries faced mounting difficulties as disorder increased in Morocco and Tunisia in the early 1950s.

2
Towards Independence for Morocco and Tunisia: British and American Concerns, 1950–56

By 1950 France had made little progress towards enduring and stable postwar relationships with its North African protectorates. In October 1949 the Socialist Deputy, Pierre-Olivier Lapie, a delegate to the most recent UN General Assembly session, informed Foreign Minister Robert Schuman of the growing international criticism of French colonialism. Schuman had no solution; he was exasperated by unaccountable colonial pro-consuls whose readiness to impose order by force prevented meaningful dialogue with nationalist leaders.[1] Pressure from Pakistan and several Arab governments for UN consideration of self-government for Morocco and Tunisia continued to mount and, to the annoyance of the Rabat and Tunis residencies, the Istiqlal and Néo-Destour communicated directly with the British and US governments and their UN delegations in New York.[2]

UN recognition of Libyan independence added to the tension in Tunisia and facilitated the traffic of arms via Libyan territory to Tunisian guerrillas. But the Attlee government dismissed French complaints in order to conserve British influence in Tripoli.[3] In a keynote speech to Néo-Destour's youth movement at Gabès on 19 March 1950, Bourguiba praised British readiness to withdraw from South Asia and Egypt, contrasting this with French repression in North Africa. He told his young audience to prepare for a guerrilla war to liberate Tunisia.[4] When he visited Paris in the following month, Bourguiba was more conciliatory. Though shunned by the French government, in a press conference at the Salle Wagram he outlined a seven-point programme built around universal suffrage, the election of a representative Tunisian parliament with powers to draft a new constitution and select its own executive, and the strict limitation of French advisory rights and security interests within Tunisia.[5]

In May 1950, Schuman's nomination of Louis Périllier – a super-prefect from his home department of the Moselle – as Resident General in Tunis, seemed to herald more generous concessions, albeit based on the proposals elaborated by Périllier's predecessor, Jean Mons. Speaking at Thionville on 10 June, Schuman affirmed that Périllier's dual objective was to develop Tunisia's natural resources whilst leading the country towards independence. In August a more overtly nationalist Tunisian government took office headed by Mohammed Chenik and containing three Néo-Destour ministers, Salah Ben Youssef among them. The advisory posts reserved for French officials within six key Tunisian ministries were immediately abolished, ending the requirement for Tunisian ministers to submit their departmental acts and policy papers to a French scrutineer.[6] Sir Oliver Harvey, Britain's ambassador in Paris, remained sceptical, predicting that daily contact with residency officials and Tunis colons would bring out Périllier's underlying conservatism. So it proved. After a brief return home to Metz in October, Périllier imposed a 'go-slow' on administrative reform in Tunis.[7] The appointment of Chenik's administration had raised contradictory expectations. The residency acknowledged the need for a more representative Tunisian Cabinet, but still expected docile compliance with the limited reforms proposed to central and municipal government. Meanwhile, conscious of broad public support and subject to increasing Néo-Destour influence, Chenik's ministers became more intransigent during the course of 1951.[8]

On 8 February 1951 Chenik approved decree legislation instituting strict parity between Tunisian and French ministers within the Cabinet and trimming the power of the French-nominated secretary-general to the government. But this détente soon collapsed over the issue of municipal elections. In April the government refused to present its budget to the Tunisian Grand Council arguing that a truly representative Parliament should be elected instead. Weeks later, Néo-Destour began a rolling campaign calling for parliamentary democracy, in effect a demand for full independence.[9] As for Morocco, it was painfully obvious that Resident General Juin still opposed major concessions. Returning from the Indo-China war to resume his post in Rabat in late 1950, Juin reassured the settler crowd that greeted him at the airport with the ominous statement: 'I have come back and I am staying.'[10] As in Tunis, the Rabat authorities hoped to pursue dialogue over Moroccan autonomy with compliant local representatives sitting on a joint Franco-Moroccan reform commission.

When push came to shove, in early 1950 Britain still stood shoulder to shoulder with France within the UN in opposing pressure for colonial disengagement. In talks with US Secretary of State Dean Acheson on 9–10 May, Bevin emphasised that colonies remained an essential 'foundation of European economic existence'. Schuman said much the same to Acheson later that week, although he concentrated on the position in Indo-China to the virtual exclusion of North Africa.[11] But the Labour government underestimated the intra-party division and political insubordination which would mar French policy in North Africa in the early 1950s. Where Schuman was prepared to consider full autonomy for the two North African protectorates, Bidault still led a substantial MRP bloc opposed to the reduction of French prerogative in the Maghreb. The resurgence in support for right-wing parties in the June 1951 legislative elections weakened any surviving reformist impulse within the leaderships of the MRP and the Radical-RGR coalition. The results left the RPF as the largest single group in the Chamber with 106 seats. Faced with powerful RPF and Communist parliamentary opposition, centrist third force administration was fatally weakened.[12] Moreover, among the settler communities of French North Africa, the RPF was most influential in Tunisia. Whereas memories of extensive Vichyite collaboration among the *colons* of Algeria diminished Gaullist sympathy for Algeria's settlers, the RPF leadership championed settler rights in Tunis.[13]

Preoccupied with European questions during 1951, Schuman handed the supervision of North African reform to Maurice Schumann, Secretary of State at the Quai d'Orsay. Alarmed by the loss of MRP support to the Gaullists, Schumann gave a more conservative stamp to the Foreign Ministry's North African policy after the RPF's decisive electoral breakthrough in June. On 15 December René Pleven's government reiterated France's right to co-sovereignty as Tunisia's protecting power, disregarding the Bey's vocal support for a new parliamentary regime. This provoked a Tunisian general strike and an upsurge in violent protest, both of which underscored Néo-Destour's claim to speak for the mass of the urban population.[14] In one of its final acts in office, in January 1952 Pleven's Cabinet ruled out concessions by appointing Jean de Hauteclocque as replacement to Périllier in Tunis. In the same week, Schumann's advisers warned of the need for extensive French security operations in Morocco if anti-French agitation continued or western strategic interests came under threat.[15]

This change in the French political climate put British indulgence towards French policy in North Africa under strain. In his public pronouncements Bourguiba consistently used the analogy of the British Commonwealth both to explain his preferred model for Franco-Tunisian co-operation and to justify his rejection of the French Union. The BBC's Arabic broadcasts drew attention to this, angering the Quai d'Orsay's North African section as a result.[16] Matters came to a head when Bourguiba visited Britain in August 1951, conducting press interviews, meeting Labour MPs and participating in a BBC radio debate. The inevitable French government complaint was that Bourguiba had been 'treated in London like the real leader-in-waiting of an independent Tunisia'.[17] While Tunisia caused the first new frosts in Anglo-French diplomatic exchanges over North Africa, Moroccan nationalists were quicker to exploit these tensions at the UN. From late 1951 Istiqlal-backed propaganda in the US highlighted the inconsistencies between Britain's backing for France as a fellow imperial power and the Churchill government's eagerness to court American support.[18]

Ramifications of the Indo-China War

Meanwhile, in Indo-China, the experiment with a unified Vietnamese regime under Bao Daï was fast unravelling amidst worsening losses of seasoned colonial troops and freshly trained French officer cadres.[19] At the start of 1950, 162,400 of France's 651,330 serving military personnel were stationed in Indo-China. The maintenance of expeditionary force strength deprived the French army of the equivalent of six metropolitan infantry divisions. The disastrous French defeat at Cao Bang in October 1950 heightened demands from the Indo-China command for urgent reinforcements. Meeting in Tunis a month later, the three North African governors appealed to the general staff not to weaken their security forces by sending Maghreb troops to South-East Asia.[20] In early 1951, however, General Jean de Lattre de Tassigny, newly appointed as commander-in-chief and high commissioner in Indo-China, redoubled the call for more soldiers and equipment. Determined to take the war to the Viet Minh, de Lattre's eponymously-named year of command involved a constant search for additional manpower and resources. Schuman ruled out the further depletion of French military capacity in Europe. Much to the annoyance of Juin in particular, the bulk of the reinforcements dispatched to the war during 1951 – the *année de Lattre* – came from units stationed in French North Africa. The Maghreb commands had become the French empire's 'strategic reserve' just as a powerful military presence in North Africa assumed added political importance.[21] The reassignment of units to the Far East also complicated the work of the North African permanent secretariat for national defence in ensuring strategic co-ordination across the Maghreb territories. By early 1952, the committee of national defence in Paris considered the French North African commands dangerously under strength.[22]

Mao's victory in China in October 1949 and the outbreak of the Korean War in June 1950 led to massive increases in US assistance to the French war effort against the Viet Minh. France began a major rearmament programme which heightened the inflationary pressure generated by increased raw material prices soon after the Korean conflict began. In an 850 billion franc military budget for 1951, 240 billion was earmarked for Indo-China, it being anticipated that the US would pick up much of the tab.[23] De Lattre lobbied the US administration directly for increased supplies during a high-profile visit to America between 14 and 26 September 1951. Something of a media 'hit', de Lattre further persuaded General Eisenhower and more sceptical State Department specialists, including Dean Rusk and Livingston Merchant, that the conflicts in Korea and Indo-China were two sides of the same Cold War coin.[24] The Americans were by this point convinced by Britain's commissioner for South East Asia, Malcolm MacDonald, and his regional military commander, General Sir John Harding, that the defence of Tonkin and Burma was fundamental to the protection of British Malaya, a strategic outlook clarified at the tripartite Anglo-US-French Singapore conference in May 1951. Hence, de Lattre's mission was always likely to succeed. But the US Defense Department was slow to provide the promised additional consignments of military hardware. Citing intelligence that Communist China was providing training and equipment for at least six new Viet Minh divisions, de Lattre reeled off lists of incomplete US military deliveries.[25] According to the Indo-China command, by the end of 1951 combined expeditionary force and Vietnamese army forces in Tonkin and Annam were seriously outnumbered by highly mobile Viet Minh units.[26] In June 1952 Jean Letourneau, long-serving Minister for the Associated States of Indo-China, and General Paul Allard, expeditionary force commander, followed up de Lattre's earlier success, pressing Washington to underwrite further expansion of the Vietnamese national army.

Increased aid was no guarantee of strategic harmony. The US joint chiefs of staff found much at fault with planned French offensives in 1953. Their British partners shared these concerns, alarmed that Generals Allard and Raoul Salan had invested so much trust in a strategy of perimeter defence based on the ill-fated forts strung across the interior of Tonkin. Yet an increasing flow of US supply funding remained assured, especially once the war spilled over into Laos in 1953 threatening neighbouring Thailand more directly.[27] British material support for the

Indo-China conflict was, in contrast to American aid, minimal. Stretched by their own overseas obligations, the service departments responded coolly to French attempts to purchase modern hardware – helicopters in particular.[28] As it was, during 1952–53, greater American material support did not alleviate the short-term pressure on French military manpower in South-East Asia. Following NATO Council discussions on Indo-China in December 1952, from March of the following year Prime Minister René Mayer and Foreign Minister Bidault redoubled French calls for additional US assistance in funding an indigenous Vietnamese army in order to permit France to retain a strategic reserve within Europe.[29] By this point most of the 80,000 metropolitan troops within the Far Eastern expeditionary force were serving beyond their legal service term. According to figures provided by ambassador Massigli on 19 May, 25 per cent of all French army officers and 40 per cent of all NCOs were on active duty in Indo-China. The conflict had absorbed £1,280 million in French budgetary funding since 1945, of which £459 million was allocated in 1952 alone.[30]

Massigli released these figures following the angry reaction within Mayer's Cabinet to Churchill's call for France to introduce two-year military service backed by the introduction of French conscripts to the Indo-China war. Churchill's outspoken remarks stemmed from his irritation over the blockage of the European Defence Community (EDC) project in the French Assembly. Intended to create a more closely integrated Western European military force built around a Franco-German axis, the EDC aroused widespread opposition in France. In Churchill's view, if France wished to remain both an imperial power and the major contributor to a Western European military alliance, extended conscription was inevitable. Armed with information from Sir Hubert Graves, the British minister in Saigon, the British service chiefs also criticised the French war effort. Graves condemned the Indo-China command for inadequate leadership and poor 'offensive spirit'. But he did not consider insufficient manpower a major problem. General Harding agreed, lambasting the French general staff for 'failing to make their minds up' about their requirements.[31] Whether sending conscripts to Indo-China made sense or not, in the absence of decisive action, Churchill's sympathy for France's imperial defence needs waned further.[32]

British insensitivity to France's very real manpower dilemma implied a misunderstanding of the pressures faced by French commanders in the Maghreb. Indo-China's drain on French resources was felt acutely in French North Africa largely because of the simultaneous pressure on French manpower within NATO's European defences. From 1952 until the end of the Indo-China war in May 1954, political controversy over the EDC dogged plans for the reinforcement of the Indo-China command. It was politically suicidal to transfer forces from continental Europe to the Far East whilst the military standing of France and a potentially rearmed West German state remained unresolved. But the US government, the key arms provider in Indo-China, backed the EDC project.[33] The Maghreb garrisons were expected to plug the manpower gaps in Indo-China wherever possible. As in 1951, Juin remained the most vociferous critic of this reduction in North African forces. In November 1952 he warned that the 21st Division, the backbone of the regular army in Algeria and a strategic reserve for NATO units in Europe, was so under-equipped that it could scarcely undertake 'large-scale local police action'.[34] More important to the later conflict in Algeria, de Lattre's inspirational year of command in Indo-China caused a sea-change in attitudes among the professional troops of the expeditionary force. Persuaded by de Lattre that victory was achievable, after the General's death on 11 January 1952, these colonial regiments were more inclined to blame their impending defeat upon the shortsightedness of the government in Paris, the incomprehension of the French public and the mean-spiritedness of US arms deliveries.[35]

These were prejudices largely immune to counter-argument, and they permeated the commands of French North Africa in the early 1950s as the interchange of forces between Africa and South East Asia gathered momentum. As the war reached its climax in the spring of 1954, the British joint intelligence committee (JIC) advised the chiefs of staff that the high quality of French forces in Indo-China was offset by the dismal standards of their Vietnamese national army protégés. Defeatism was by then prevalent in France, where the will to fight on had 'almost disappeared'. The French professional forces that would be redeployed from the Far East to North Africa between 1954 and 1956 returned from a conflict in which their Viet Minh opponents held the military initiative throughout the last year of the war. This had compelled the French command to disperse the reinforcements laboriously built up into a mobile striking force as the Viet Minh launched co-ordinated assaults in five separate areas, the most important being northwestern Tonkin. To many of the French officers involved, this was as much a failure of French political support as it was a Viet Minh military victory.[36]

As French financial and military dependency on the US reached its apogée in the early 1950s, so French anti-Americanism reached new heights. The European Recovery Program, US support for the war effort in Indo-China and Washington's enthusiasm for West German rearmament all served to emphasise the real decline in French international power. But the extent of US material support, and its backing for General Henri Navarre's unsuccessful plan to defeat the Viet Minh in Tonkin, meant that Dien Bien Phu marked the failure of American as well as French policy.

Churchill's government had anticipated this. On 18 March 1954 the Foreign Secretary, Anthony Eden, warned his Cabinet colleagues that Eisenhower's administration had invested too much in Indo-China to be sanguine about a Viet Minh victory. If the terms of French withdrawal did not suit Washington, an 'agonising re-appraisal' of Franco-American relations was bound to result.[37] Unlike his joint chiefs, Eisenhower remained sceptical about direct US intervention against the Viet Minh, sensitive to adverse public and congressional reaction to direct engagement in the closing stages of the war. None the less, French Chief of General Staff General Paul Ely's intensive lobbying in Washington and the National Security Council's protracted discussions of Indo-China in the weeks prior to the Geneva conference suggested that US policy hung in the balance.[38] Matters came to a head on 24 April when Secretary of State Dulles proposed a joint 'declaration of intention' affirming the American, French and British resolve to keep South East Asia free of communism. If approved, this would serve as the basis for congressional sanction of operations against the Viet Minh and their Chinese backers. Since Joseph Laniel's government seemed willing to go along with the plan rather than face impending defeat, British hostility to the scheme was decisive. According to the US ambassador in Paris, Douglas Dillon, the relationship between Dulles and Eden never recovered.[39] To Dulles's further annoyance, Eden's pivotal role at the July 1954 Geneva conference alongside Chinese Foreign Minister Chou En-lai extricated France from Indo-China with a temporary partition settlement. This belied the extent of France's defeat by concealing the fact that the Viet Minh had controlled at least five-sixths of Vietnamese territory.[40]

A Nationalist Threat?

The expansion of US rearmament in 1950 also stimulated interest in North Africa's strategic resources. The heightened importance of North Africa within US strategic thinking brought the issue of communist penetration in the Maghreb to the fore. On 26 September 1950, provision of additional raw material supplies and discussion of the communist threat dominated Franco-American talks on co-operation in Africa. Although Washington was attentive to any link between nationalism and communism in French North Africa, successive French governments in the early 1950s failed to convince the Americans that significant ties existed.[41] Faced with the PCF's inability to seize power in France, from late 1946 the Algerian Communist Party (PCA) promoted a communist-nationalist front against French rule. But the divisions between nationalist groups, the hostility of the Ulamas to communism and awareness that the still marginal PCA would gain most from an association with its more popular nationalist counterparts impeded collaboration. By mid-1951 both Ferhat Abbas and Messali Hadj opposed UDMA or MTLD contact with communist leaders.[42]

Across the border, by 1950 the Istiqlal leadership openly questioned Morocco's co-operation with NATO and sought to barter continued US military base rights against Truman's endorsement of Moroccan independence. On 11 September the Istiqlal executive committee accused the 'western democracies' of placing NATO strategic interests above the political requirements of the Moroccan people, further alleging that this betrayal of Morocco's contribution to allied victory in 1945 freed Istiqlal of any obligation to the western alliance.[43] But neither the party's charismatic figurehead, Allal el Fassi, nor the pragmatic Istiqlal secretary-general, Ahmed Balafrej, were remotely pro-Soviet. A quadripartite pact between the principal Moroccan nationalist parties signed on 9 April 1951 rejected any co-operation with local communists and affirmed that the Istiqlal was the legitimate voice of the Moroccan people.[44]

Notwithstanding their efforts to convince Washington and London that communist sedition in North Africa represented a major threat, the Maghreb administrations directed their security apparatus to containment of organised nationalism. The Rabat residency always feared that Sultan Mohammed Ben Youssef's public endorsement of the Istiqlal would galvanise Arab opinion throughout the protectorate. Hence Juin's insistence in late January 1951 that the Sultan should denounce the Istiqlal or face deposition. The Sultan refused to comply. Unable to persuade either Foreign Minister Schuman or Socialist Minister of National Defence Jules Moch to support the Sultan's overthrow, Juin's residency turned on the nationalist leadership.[45] Stringent censorship of the pro-nationalist press and restrictions on trade unions with strong links to the Istiqlal contrasted with a more even-handed approach to Morocco's communists. Across all three territories, censors and police chiefs were generally more sensitive to Arab language material than to communist propaganda in French.[46]

French suspicion of possible Anglo-American interference grew in direct proportion to the virulence of nationalist protest. Certain that nationalist leaders in Morocco and Tunisia fomented civil disorder in order to cultivate international interest, Arab support and UN sympathy, the North African authorities considered the Anglo-Saxon powers pivotal to worsening unrest. In French estimations, the Istiqlal and Néo-Destour were playing to a western and Arab gallery, rather than seeking the backing of the communist bloc. It was thus incumbent upon the US and Britain as, respectively, the leading UN power and the dominant force in the Middle East not to encourage such nationalist tactics.[47] Conversely, during 1951–52 the Arab League and pro-western Arab leaders repeatedly urged the British and American governments to intercede in North Africa. In May 1952 Acheson warned Schuman in Paris that Anglo-American endorsement of French North African rule depended upon prior consultation over France's reform plans.[48] After the Conservatives' election victory in October 1951, Churchill's administration backed the US line: France could only expect close support from its western allies if they were apprised of its North African policies. In practice, these demands meant little as it became clearer in 1952 that negotiations in Tunisia had collapsed, the French Assembly having failed to agree upon minimum reforms.[49]

The Tunisian Crisis, 1952

On 9 January 1952, General Garbay, French land forces commander in Tunisia, predicted a dire year ahead for the protectorate:

> Tunisian nationalist propaganda is being fed by fresh causes of agitation. These stem from the failure of recent nationalist demands and Egypt's attitude towards England. The independence granted to neighbouring Libya has also encouraged the agitators. Order has certainly not been challenged so far, but the population has been profoundly infiltrated by Néo Destour and, on a simple pretext, an incident could degenerate into riot and then rebellion.[50]

Garbay's pessimism was based on the popular acclamation which greeted Bourguiba's return to Tunis on 2 January. The Tunisian leader urged his supporters to take to the streets. A fortnight later, a demonstration organised by the Association of Tunisian Muslim Women, in which Bourguiba's nieces played a leading role, sparked more general urban protests in the week ahead.[51] This marked the climax to the gradual breakdown of negotiations between Paris and Tunis. As seen above, having ruled out immediate self-government, in mid-December 1951, with Prime Minister Pleven's approval, Schuman instead proposed a continuation of French control in the guise of Franco-Tunisian 'co-sovereignty'. Sent to implement this policy, the new Resident General, Jean de Hauteclocque, was confronted by a public service strike. He called in *Gardes Républicaines* units from Algeria to help contain the unrest and safeguard French naval installations from attack.[52]

On 14 January the Néo-Destour ministers in Mohammed Chenik's Cabinet lodged a renewed appeal for UN intervention. The Pakistani government, headed by Zafrullah Khan, agreed to sponsor Tunisian complaints against French repression, invoking Article 32 of the UN Charter whereby non-member states could raise grievances in the Security Council.[53] This complicated the British response. Britain could easily support France in the Security Council on the legal technicality that only the protectorate authorities themselves could inscribe Tunisian questions on the UN agenda. But the endorsement of the Tunisian case by Pakistan, a friendly client-state, made the Foreign Office squirm. Should the British urge Islamabad to alter its position? Or should London impress the need for concessions on the French in return for a Tunisian climb-down over a UN debate?[54] Neither option looked promising. The Iraqi government was prepared to take Pakistan's place as sponsor for Tunisia if required. And France was between governments in the second and third weeks of January. In the absence of a confirmed Cabinet, on 18 January an ad hoc ministerial committee directed by Maurice Schumann ordered the re-arrest of Bourguiba, his close associate Mongi Slim and three Tunisian communist leaders. In the disorders which followed, ten Tunisian protestors were killed.[55]

The Radical Party leader, Edgar Faure, whose brief administration held office for six weeks in early 1952, could not break the impasse. Stung by virulent Socialist criticism of the repressive measures enacted, Faure devoted his investiture speech to the Tunisian problem and virtually repudiated Schuman's December 'co-sovereignty' plan. Still, the fundamental tenets of French policy remained: France was to retain its politico-military presence and negotiations were confined to internal autonomy, not full independence. Bourguiba's arrest was counterproductive. Popular support for Néo-Destour increased and Bourguiba simply directed party affairs from detention at Tabarka on the western coast.[56] Antoine Pinay's centre-right government, which succeeded Faure's short-lived administration on 8 March 1952, was determined to act decisively. In doing so, Pinay's Cabinet made the security position in Tunisia worse. On 25 March Schuman, who had been Foreign Minister continuously since July 1948, acquiesced in the arrest of senior ministers within Chenik's Cabinet. This brought Tunisia to UN attention once more.

The arbitrary dismissal of Chenik's Cabinet revealed French contempt for the concept of partnership with a protectorate administration, making it impossible for the UK and US administrations to endorse French policy. The reaction was sharper in the US. In response to news of the general strike in Tunis, on 3 February the executive council of the American Federation of Labor (AFL) called for immediate 'home rule' for Tunisia.[57] By this stage, there were powerful links between the AFL, the Congress of Industrial Organizations (CIO) and the foremost Tunisian union federation, the *Union Générale des Travailleurs Tunisiens* (UGTT). With CIA backing, the AFL executive council supported the anti-communism and moderate nationalism of Ferhat Hached's UGTT. Able to distance itself from these inter-union contacts in public, the State Department encouraged AFL–CIO interest in French Africa, recognising the benefits of cultivating support for the West among colonial workers. Under the impetus of its leading foreign affairs specialist, Jay Lovestone, and his close associate, Louise Page Morris, with CIA encouragement the AFL cultivated ties with Bourguiba, Hached and, subsequently, the Tunisian, Moroccan and Algerian envoys to the UN.[58] On 8 April the New York-based Committee for the Freedom of North Africa, an umbrella organisation which lobbied on behalf of Maghreb nationalist parties, including the Istiqlal, the MTLD and the Néo-Destour, pleaded for a change in US regional policy. These events culminated in unprecedented national press coverage of the North African situation during March and April, with most editorial comment hostile to French behaviour. On 25 April the French ambassador to Washington, Henri Bonnet, warned Schuman that the underlying community of Franco-American strategic interest in North-West Africa was thoroughly undermined by US disdain for French rule in the protectorates.[59] Acheson later confirmed that the Pinay government failed to 'give us the minimum means of supporting them'.[60] The US delegation duly abstained in the vote inscribing the Tunisian situation on the UN General Assembly agenda. Since the State Department had already upheld the General Assembly's right to discuss the Moroccan situation, its only concession to France was to reserve the US position in the resultant debates.[61]

In spite of its reluctance to antagonise Pakistan and Iraq, in April 1952 the British delegation blocked consideration of the Tunisian crisis by the Security Council. Pressed to explain this decision by Fenner Brockway, the leading anti-colonialist voice within the Independent Labour Party, Eden maintained that internationalisation of the Tunisian problem would merely generate greater extremism on both sides.[62] Arbitrary French rule in Tunis and Rabat made this position harder to justify. The arrest of Chenik's ministers had made Néo-Destour pressure for inscription of the Tunisian problem at the UN a rallying point for newly independent Afro-Asian member states.[63] Still, the Foreign Office recognised that Pinay was a hostage to the diffuse right-wing parties which propelled him into office, including a breakaway group of 27 dissident Gaullist deputies. As US ambassador Dillon pointed out from Paris after the fall of René Mayer's successor ministry in June 1953, since the Gaullists were split both on a left–right axis and over the issue of participation in Fourth Republic governments, any Cabinet reliant upon Gaullist backing was inherently unstable.[64]

During Truman's final months in office in late 1952, Bonnet's staff in Washington noted a deeper State Department pessimism about French policy within Morocco and Tunisia nourished by fear of eventual communist infiltration to North Africa. Eisenhower's Republican victory in November 1952 did not mark a significant change in this regard. Yet both Pinay's administration and Mayer's reshuffled Cabinet which succeeded it in January 1953, anticipated firmer American support. Before Schuman made way for Bidault's return to the Quai d'Orsay, on 2 January he received Bonnet's assessment of the probable US attitude towards French North Africa. The ambassador predicted that Republican eagerness to reduce economic support to France would necessarily prompt greater US interest in North Africa's capacity to aid French economic growth. More importantly, Bonnet was convinced that Eisenhower's administration grasped the strategic importance of western paramountcy in North Africa. To capitalise on this, France faced three tasks. First was to allay State Department suspicion that France was the major obstacle to the development of cordial relations between Arab states and the West. Second was to demonstrate sufficient commitment to reform to disarm Moroccan and Tunisian nationalist critics within the US. Third was to promote long-term economic development in North Africa under French direction.[65] Unable to deliver on any of these proposals, Mayer found Secretary of State Dulles reluctant to underwrite French policy in the protectorates during meetings in Paris and Washington in February and March.[66] Meanwhile, the Istiqlal and Néo-Destour redoubled their propaganda drive in the United States, aware that western unity over French North Africa was cracking.[67]

From Tunis de Hauteclocque argued that the monarchical precepts of Tunisia's beylical administration and the *dirigisme* of the Néo-Destour programme were antithetical to western-style democracy. Were France to leave, Tunisia would descend into a dictatorship in which European settlers would soon lose everything. De Hauteclocque considered it his key task to restore a protectorate system based on a loyal beylical government. His staff also tried to 'disorganise' Néo-Destour by freezing it out of the electoral process. These strategems highlighted the deteriorating co-operation between the Tunis residency and the Quai d'Orsay. Ironically, de Hauteclocque stood at the apex of a protectorate administration which was less accountable than the beylical government it supervised. On 4 March 1953 Maurice Schumann alerted Bidault to this. The Foreign Ministry's protectorates subdivision complained that de Hauteclocque treated policy instructions as merely provisional advice.[68] But Paris had not provided a lead. Still reeling from the disastrous arrest of the Chenik government in late March, on 20–21 June 1952 the National Assembly had spent two days in bitter debate over Tunisia without agreement on any plan of action.[69]

Anglo-American Responses to the Moroccan Situation, 1951–54

British observers considered de Hauteclocque, and first Alphonse Juin and then General Augustin Guillaume in Rabat, irretrievably compromised as residents general.[70] All three at various points coerced the principal nationalist groups whilst at the same time coaxing the monarchical authorities towards acceptance of limited internal autonomy. This was never likely to succeed. The concessions offered were tainted by association with crackdowns against populist nationalism. In October 1951, Gaston Soulie, the leading figure within Guillaume's Civil Cabinet in Rabat and a chief adviser on North African matters to the French UN delegation, admitted that the Resident General's relentless attack on the nationalist leadership was failing. In forcing educated, non-aligned Moroccans to make a stark choice for or against French policy, General Guillaume, Juin's successor as Resident General, alienated the critical constituency which might otherwise have favoured a compromise settlement.[71] France could not pursue reform and repression simultaneously. Since repressive measures were untenable over the long term, the only alternative was genuine self-government.

Compared with Tunisia, the French security position in Morocco was less exposed throughout 1952. But the underlying causes of tension were much the same. French readiness to negotiate on the basis of Moroccan internal autonomy was frustrated in practice by the abiding strength of the Istiqlal which, like its Néo-Destour cousin, demanded a firm French commitment to Morocco's independence. As in Tunisia, faltering negotiations were punctuated by popular disorder, French repression and nationalist appeals for UN intervention. Istiqlal leaders including Allal el Fassi, Ben Aboud and Ahmed Balafrej, plus members of Hassan Ouezzani's rival Democratic Independence Party (*Parti Démocrate de l'Indépendance* – PDI), regularly lobbied US, British and other UN representatives in New York. In addition, from September 1952 onwards the 13-strong Arab–Asian bloc of UN states pressed for consideration of Moroccan, as well as Tunisian, complaints against France.

To British and American discomfort, in early October 1952 Sultan Mohammed Ben Youssef released details of his exchanges with the French over the preceding two years. These made plain that successive Paris governments had stalled over the central questions of Moroccan self-government and parliamentary democracy. The administrative reforms put forward were largely confined to local initiatives and economic modernisation designed to undermine nationalist support. This provoked further anti-French protests at the UN. At a press conference on 8 October the Sultan called for the establishment of a provisional government in Rabat with plenipotentiary powers to negotiate a definitive Franco-Moroccan settlement.[72] Cornered by the Sultan's intervention and angered by nationalist success, Guillaume capitalised on rioting in Casablanca in December 1952 to order a police clampdown against the Istiqlal and the Moroccan Communist Party, both of which were outlawed. In early January 1953 he returned from Paris with a package of the very administrative reforms that the Sultan had pilloried three months earlier.[73] Talks over municipal government and rural *djemaa* councils failed to ignite popular interest and ultimately ran into the sand.

As negotiations over municipal reform ground on into the summer of 1953, the Sultan's temporal authority caused fresh controversy. In August the simmering dispute between Sultan and residency over local government reform and the disputed introduction of Franco-Moroccan councils to 'advise' the Sultanate administration became more heated. Although presented as a democratisation of the monarchical system of government, conferring an executive role on a combined Franco-Moroccan Council of Ministers at the expense of the Sultan's personal authority violated the Treaty of Fez. The Sultan's power to legislate by royal decree (*dahir*) was compromised by permitting a French-controlled Council of Ministers to override his decisions. Yet this transformation of central government was the centrepiece of reforms which excluded universal suffrage and offered no guarantees of political rights. The State Department's office of western European affairs concluded that, without freedom of speech, press, assembly or association, talk of an emerging Moroccan democracy was farcical.[74]

Since the Sultan refused to give ground, the residency set about undermining his position. Throughout the year, two of the Sultan's preeminent local rivals, the Pacha of Marrakech, El Glaoui Hadj Thami, and Sherif el Kettani, exploited Ben Youssef's increased political exposure to spearhead a campaign for his dethronement. They drew on petitions of prominent Berber tribal chiefs and *caïds*, which Juin's administration had encouraged since at least 1951, to call for the Sultan's uncle, 65-year-old Sidi Mohammed Ben Moulay Arafa, to be made 'Imam of the Faithful'.[75] Significantly, in the political violence which erupted between supporters of the Sultan and those of the Glaoui and Ben Arafa, European settlers remained the primary target. According to conservative official estimates, in the worst incidents at Oujda, the regional capital of eastern Morocco, on the evening of 16 August, rioters killed 26 people, including 14 settlers. After the police fired on the crowd, killing 'about 40', a further 29 settlers were butchered by the demonstrators.[76] Although violence against the settler population was primarily an urban phenomenon, the underlying French hope of cultivating Berber support outside the principal Arab-dominated cities of Morocco was doomed to fail. While the residency exploited clan factionalism and Arab–Berber tensions in order to undermine the Sultan's position, no stable regime could be built on a 'Franco-Berber master–servant relationship'.[77]

Anxious lest this Moroccan dynastic factionalism descended into widespread inter-communal violence, on instruction from Paris (though without the full assent of the Council of Ministers), Guillaume pressed the Sultan into abdication on 20 August. French troop reinforcements ensured that the more compliant Ben Arafa took office without a breakdown in civil order. Within a month the new Sultan signed up to the core political reforms which his predecessor had resisted. Although a planned restructuring of the Moroccan judicial system remained outstanding, the French secured the main pillars of their reform plan. A clearer separation of executive, legislative and judicial power curbed the Sultan's political authority while the gradual democratisation of local government encouraged the growth of a loyalist administrative class.[78]

Having wrecked his political career through association with OAS terrorism, when Bidault wrote his memoirs in 1965 he made no secret of his decision as Foreign Minister 12 years earlier to depose Mohammed Ben Youssef. He received strong support from Interior Minister Léon Martinaud-Déplat, administrative president of the Radical Party and controller of its influential North African federations. Already directing a political campaign against the PCF at home, for him Guillaume's fervent anti-communist, pro-colonial policies made sense. According to Bidault, confrontation was inevitable once the Sultan implicitly rejected French authority during his famous Tangiers speech in April 1947. Bidault further insisted that his action saved the Sultan from the wrath of the Moroccan people and was more justifiable than Edgar Faure's subsequent revocation of the deposition in November 1955.[79] This was a monumental self-delusion. Although Bidault drew parallels between conditions in Indo-China and Morocco, the deposition of Mohammed Ben Youssef made no sense as a pre-emptive strike against encroaching communist influence. The Moroccan Communist Party was driven underground following Guillaume's December 1952 ban, and its efforts to build a united front with nationalist groups got nowhere. Bidault and his fellow MRP leaders were accomplices to the reactionary imperialism of entrenched settler interests and leading military figures with a hand in North African policy, such as Juin and Guillaume.[80] This was as fatal to MRP unity as it was to the success of North African policy in 1953. Ultimately, the prosecution of major constitutional reform in the Maghreb in 1954–55 was only made possible by the MRP's departure from government.[81]

By this point the progress of Moroccan nationalism was irreversible. Growing international sympathy for Moroccan and Tunisian independence were important factors in this. On the one hand, the Sultan's deposition solidified Egyptian support for Moroccan nationalism. Mohamed Fathi Al Dib, General Gamal Abdel Nasser's nominee as liaison to the Maghreb nationalist movements, increased Egyptian propaganda attacks on French colonialism, principally through Radio Cairo's *Voix des Arabes* broadcasts. On 4 April 1954 he also convened the first of several co-ordinatory conferences between Istiqlal, Néo-Destour and Algerian nationalist representatives under the aegis of the Arab League.[82] On the other hand, after the Sultan's deposition, the State Department office of Near Eastern affairs warned that American passivity in the face of intensified French repression might provoke terrorist attacks against US air bases and NATO installations in North Africa.[83] The Foreign Office, too, was critical of Ben Youssef's deposition. The fact that implementation of limited reforms was used to justify France's arbitrary actions merely confirmed that the French right could not unite around a more ambitious scheme for genuine Moroccan self-government.[84] Even so, Churchill's Cabinet stopped short of condemning French behaviour outright.

Foundations of British Policy

Increasingly, Britain stood apart as the major power most reluctant to press France directly over its North African policies. What, then, was the point of British policy, and was British influence of much importance? Like France, Britain was strategically overstretched when the Korean war erupted in June 1950. Although the Malayan Emergency did not drain resources in a manner akin to the Indo-China war, Australia and New Zealand's definitive alignment with the US in the September 1951 ANZUS pact confirmed the irreversibility of Britain's military decline in South-East Asia. Australia's primary concern for its 'Near North' further undermined British hopes that Australian and South African forces would continue to play a leading role in Middle Eastern defence. By 1950 the US air force was also reluctant to accept British plans to use Middle Eastern bases as a front line for a strategic counter-offensive against any Soviet attack. As Attlee had persistently warned, beyond the Cyprus colony, the tenability of Britain's Middle Eastern base facilities was bound to become more problematic as Arab nationalism gained impetus.[85] Much as France faced mounting disorder in North Africa, so by 1952 the British garrison in Egypt was hard-pressed to contain urban rioting, strikes and guerrilla activity. Plans for a restructured Middle Eastern Command to underpin British regional power in the years ahead were at variance with the general upsurge in Arab nationalism, the incipient breakdown of British control in Egypt and the limited number of British troops and aircraft available for Middle Eastern reinforcement.[86]

Here, the parallel with France's military dilemma in Morocco and Tunisia was particularly strong. Committed by treaty to a renegotiation of relations with the local governments in Egypt and the French North African protectorates, in each case the British and French governments were reluctant to make concessions until their strategic and economic interests were assured. Churchill and Eden were keenly aware of the security implications for British interests in the Middle East and East Africa if their plans for negotiated withdrawal from Egypt were disrupted. The added complication of a Sudanese settlement further increased Tory sensitivity to any unforeseen disorder across North Africa. Ministry of Defence plans to withdraw Egyptian garrison forces to Cyprus, and to prepare facilities on the island for up to four divisions of reinforcements in the event of renewed crisis in the Middle East, were scarcely more viable than French schemes to conserve their military privileges in Morocco.[87] The critical point to note here is that both

Churchill and Eden viewed colonial problems through the perspective of global strategy. Neither was much interested in colonial development plans or the minutiae of Colonial Office schemes of constitutional reform. The Cabinet was still dominated by ardent imperialists who overestimated the capacity of the colonial powers to hang on to strategic assets in the face of nationalist opposition.[88] By extension, there was some sympathy for French efforts to safeguard their Maghreb interests. For Churchill's ministers, French North Africa was a rumbling irritation to western unity, secondary to more global foreign policy concerns.

In May 1950 France joined Britain and the US in signing the Tripartite Declaration to uphold the territorial status quo in the Middle East. A similar commitment to French North Africa was never contemplated. In January 1951 Foreign Office refusal to provide Schuman with details of the Commonwealth Heads of Government Conference just concluded in London suggested an abiding British distrust of French policy in the Middle East and a growing sensitivity to Asian Commonwealth states hostile to French colonialism.[89] At British insistence, the French were excluded from Anglo-US strategic talks over common Middle Eastern and Mediterranean problems held in Malta between January and March 1951. Fear of French security leaks offered a convenient excuse to avoid Arab criticism of any Anglo-French regional co-operation. In an attempt to soften the blow, British NATO representatives in Paris proposed additional talks with their French and American colleagues over Far Eastern defence, an issue not yet as divisive as the Middle East and North Africa. The Americans concurred, ultimately brushing aside French protests about their exclusion from the Malta meetings. The Department of Defense shared British security concerns about any detailed discussion of global strategy with French delegates. And the State Department's Policy Planning Staff estimated that French standing in the Middle East was at its lowest ebb since the May 1945 bombardment of Damascus.[90]

Although the British sanctioned low-level discussions between Foreign Office and Quai d'Orsay specialists over common Middle Eastern problems in May 1953, these produced few results beyond a reaffirmation of the Tripartite Declaration.[91] As Eden pointed out to the Cabinet in January 1954, while British direction of Egyptian foreign and military policy might suit French strategic interests in the Maghreb, the reverse did not apply. Whether Britain's Middle Eastern power continued to rest on control of Suez and co-operation with client regimes in Iraq, Jordan and Libya, or whether the British invested more heavily in collaboration with the more powerful regimes in Israel and Turkey, close identification with French policy in the Maghreb would complicate British relations with its chosen Middle Eastern partners.[92] From Cairo, ambassador Sir Ralph Stevenson warned that the Neguib regime's fears of a coup d'état compelled it to advertise its xenophobic, anti-western credentials. This only increased Eden's unwillingness to back France openly at a time when he was also trying to curb Churchill's enthusiasm for a showdown in the Anglo-Egyptian treaty negotiations.[93] Any appearance of an Anglo-French front was sure to make things worse.

The apparent cohesion of the Arab League was an added complication. An Arab League security pact signed in April 1950 came into force in August 1952. Over subsequent months member states signed a series of agreements to integrate their trade and communications systems more closely. With Libya's accession to the League in March 1953 and the presence of Palestinian observers in Cairo, all Britain's historic Arab partners or subjects were now associated with the Arab League project.[94] Quai d'Orsay Arabists still misjudged the significance of these British connections, overestimating Britain's capacity to moderate Arab League criticism of France. Their Foreign Office counterparts reckoned that French intransigence in the Maghreb encouraged the anti-westernism which bound the League together.[95]

During 1953 Churchill's administration grew more impatient at France's refusal to risk a bold initiative in the North African protectorates. Both René Mayer's administration and its successor under Joseph Laniel flogged 'co-sovereignty' for Morocco and Tunisia although the idea was obviously a dead horse. Close to *colon* politicians and deputy for Constantine since 1946, Mayer's centre-left credentials as a co-founder of the *Rassemblement des Gauches Républicaines* did not dent his die-hard support for the French presence in North Africa. He typified the excessive influence a leader with a major stake in Maghreb affairs could exert on cabinets that lacked countervailing cross-party support for ambitious colonial reform. On 23 January 1953 an inter-ministerial committee convened by Mayer to prepare for Anglo-French governmental talks in London on 12–13 February concluded that the protection afforded to Britain's South-East Asian position by the French war effort in Indo-China and Britain's steadfast refusal to permit discussion of French North Africa at the UN revealed common Anglo-French colonial interests.[96] This was a mirage. In practice, the stalled EDC treaty and the worsening security position in Indo-China dominated Anglo-French relations in early 1953.

In June, the inclusion of Gaullist RPF ministers within Joseph Laniel's Cabinet again weighted the governing coalition against far-reaching

North African reforms. The faltering progress of negotiations in Tunis and Rabat between 1950 and 1954 was thus the mirror-image of the protracted and unsuccessful campaign to secure parliamentary approval for the EDC project. In both cases, the majority of the political community found fault with the proposals tabled but were either unwilling or unable to devise viable alternatives with any chance of broad support in the National Assembly.[97] At the tripartite Bermuda conference in December 1953, Foreign Minister Bidault sought renewed assurances regarding Anglo-American force levels in Europe and the consolidation of ties between NATO and the developing European Community, knowing that the still unratified EDC treaty remained an obstacle to the consolidation of Franco-British-US relations.[98] After the inconclusive four-power conference in Berlin in February 1954, Bidault secured additional concessions from Britain over the EDC. But opposition to the EDC treaty in the National Assembly remained insuperable. Fifty-nine of the 105 Socialist Deputies opposed it, Gaullist and Communist criticism persisted, and an influential triumvirate – Edgar Faure, Marshal Juin and former President Vincent Auriol – all spoke out against the project during the spring of 1954.[99]

As for North Africa, a discernible 'I told you so' attitude crept into Foreign Office reportage as nationalist terrorism intensified in Tunisia and Morocco during 1953. Néo-Destour's boycott of Tunisian local elections in May and the assassination of heir-apparent, Prince Azzuddine Bey, on 1 July suggested that even the replacement of de Hauteclocque by the more liberal Pierre Voizard in early September could not break the political log-jam in Paris. The leading trio of colonial progressives in Laniel's new administration – Faure, Pierre-Henri Teitgen and François Mitterrand – all opposed Voizard's appointment, aware that the new Resident would not give ground on the central question of greater authority for the Tunisian executive.[100] In exchanges during December 1953 neither the Quai d'Orsay's North Africa specialist, Jean Basdevant, nor former Tunis Resident, Jean Mons, could persuade British officials that the prospects for settlement had improved. The best that could be expected was that the negative achievements of the previous year – such as the containment of terrorism and the frustration of nationalist pressure at the UN – could be repeated.[101]

Towards Independence for Morocco and Tunisia, 1954–56

It required a major change of political direction before France could bow to the inevitable and withdraw from its North African protectorates. On the eve of his departure from the Paris embassy, in late February 1954 Oliver Harvey remained pessimistic, noting 'a nineteenth century atmosphere of paternal government' and a determination that self-government should actually involve continued dependency upon France.[102] What de Gaulle would be to Algeria after 1958, so Pierre Mendès France was to Tunisia and Morocco during his brief term of office between June 1954 and January 1955. The cult of Mendès France as a leader of principle and the last hope of the Fourth Republic is most persuasive when one makes a simple reckoning of his colonial policies.[103] By pursuing self-government talks for the North African protectorates and negotiating the withdrawal from Indo-China, Mendès broke the stalemate in the Assembly. In the crucial parliamentary debate on 10 August, Mendès capably defended his government's commitment to accelerated reform in Morocco and Tunisia.[104] At a stroke he shattered the tacit consensus observed by right-of-centre parties during 1952–53 to avoid consideration of a pull-out from either North Africa or Indo-China. This was the key to US and British enthusiasm for a Mendès ministry. Hostile to narrow partisanship, Mendès seemed capable of revitalising the centre-left at communist expense by forcing the French political community to weigh the relative advantages of imperial engagement next to a clearer commitment to political and strategic co-operation with the western powers.

On all counts, caution is essential. As Britain's new ambassador to Paris, Gladwyn Jebb, noted, there was something of the sacrificial lamb about Mendès France. At the risk of mixing metaphors, to his political opponents Mendès was the ideal scapegoat; he would do the necessary dirty work of extricating France from Indo-China and finally killing EDC and would bear the brunt of any public backlash. Then he could be easily removed.[105] By the time Mendès took office, the Indo-China war was lost. His achievement was to negotiate and sell the Geneva settlement to the French electorate. As for the EDC, neither Churchill nor Eden was much impressed by Mendès's decisive action. The abrupt French abandonment of the project in late August caught the British government and its US ally off-guard, uncertain of how best to respond. The Conservative Party was itself divided over the merits of the EDC. Both the right-wing 'Suez Group' and the pro-European 'Strasbourgers' disliked the plan, albeit for different reasons.[106]

The premier's surprise visit to Tunis on 31 July to announce his government's recognition of Tunisian autonomy and its readiness to transfer power to a sovereign government was certainly a decisive stroke. The 'Carthage Declaration' pulled the rug from under the parliamentary opponents of Tunisian independence; its apparent finality undermined the efforts of *France-Tunisie* lobbyists to rally support for continued French rule. Still adjusting to its vote over the EDC, the National Assembly's two-day debate on the government's North Africa policy on 26–27 August was decidedly apathetic. With minimal debate, the Chamber supported Mendès by a vote of 419 to 112, with 77 abstentions.[107] But the Carthage Declaration was made possible by preliminary talks with Néo-Destour representatives in Geneva in which French negotiators demanded cast-iron guarantees of French base rights, commercial privileges and a *droit de regard* over Tunisian foreign policy. Since the government was not, in fact, committed to immediate independence for Tunisia, the persistence of terrorist *fellagha* violence and later problems in securing parliamentary ratification of the Franco-Tunisian conventions on internal self-government might be laid at its door.[108]

Mendès's capacity to surprise client governments was also apparent in the initial stages of the Algerian rebellion in late 1954. His was the administration that committed France to suppress the FLN uprising. On 2 November Mendès ordered a three-fold military reinforcement of Algeria, a reflex reaction made in substantial ignorance of the immediate causes of the outbreak and as a counterweight to the rush towards decolonisation in earlier months.[109] The premier and his Minister of Interior, François Mitterrand, tried to revitalise the administrative reforms built into the 1947 statute, but Mendès's Algerian policy was that of a convinced economic determinist. For him, social and economic imbalance in Algeria and the poverty of Muslim agriculturalists were better explanations for popular dissent than the absence of political rights.[110]

Early French security measures in Algeria hardly affected Arab indulgence towards the Mendès government. Although Radio Cairo continued its criticism of French repression, Syrian ambassador, Dr Farid Zeineddine, spokesman for the eight Arab governments represented in Washington, acknowledged France's effort to secure Tunisian and Moroccan settlements.[111] Fearful lest events in Algeria should force Mendès to back-peddle over protectorate reform, Dulles pressed Arab League governments not to raise North African issues at the UN in the short term, warning that the US government would vote against inscription.[112] For some months, the parliamentary fragility of Mendès France's administration silenced Arab and Anglo-American criticism of French policies in the Maghreb. Persuaded that Guillaume's successor as Resident General in Rabat, Francis Lacoste, was committed to reform, the escalating urban terrorism and arson attacks against settler farms which formed a backdrop to Franco-Moroccan negotiations in late 1954 generated little response in Washington and London.[113] This Anglo-American goodwill could not, however, be taken for granted. Dulles expected quicker results in North Africa now that the more pressing French problems over the Geneva settlement, German rearmament and the future of the Saar had been resolved. On 18 October the US National Security Council affirmed its support for the Carthage Declaration but warned that France should grant Tunisian self-government quickly in order to avoid renewed UN criticism.[114]

As so often before, the Quai d'Orsay reacted with suspicion to muted State Department and Foreign Office enquiries about *fellagha* activity in Tunisia and the worsening violence in Morocco. Even moderate expressions of concern were perceived as implicit Anglo-Saxon support for nationalist interests.[115] During talks in Washington in December 1954, Mendès threatened to drag the whole issue of Arab propaganda in French North Africa before the NATO Council. This was most unwelcome to Britain so soon after the signing of a new Anglo-Egyptian treaty in October.[116] Sensitivity to US 'interference' generated a broad hostility to US policy which was quite unprecedented in its cross-party appeal. Jean-Paul Sartre's initial suspicion of a hidden US hand in Maghreb politics made him almost possessive about Algeria, despite the fact that he would later emerge as perhaps the most famous intellectual opponent of the Algerian war, notably in the influential journal *Les Temps Modernes*.[117] Until 1954, the Eisenhower administration was criticised in France for working to a double standard – supporting French colonial control in Indo-China whilst cultivating the nationalist opposition in North Africa in anticipation of French failure.

In February 1955 the Mendès France government was voted out over North Africa by Conservative *modéré* deputies and anti-Mendèsist Radicals who then formed the backbone of Edgar Faure's Radical-led administration. This left Faure with little room for manoeuvre. In Rabat, Francis Lacoste pushed ahead with wage reforms, the reorganisation of judicial powers, decentralisation of administration and the relaxation of French controls over the Rabat government. But, as he admitted, this counted for little amongst nationalist opinion next to the restoration of Mohammed Ben Youssef. Although urban terrorism had declined from a peak of 300 incidents during August 1954 (the first anniversary of the Sultan's deposition), in Casablanca and Rabat – always the principal centres of unrest – *'la question dynastique'* still dominated public protest.[118] The longer France blocked Ben Youssef's restoration, the more he became the focus of popular nationalism. Ben Arafa was irrevocably tarnished, as were his main local backers, the regional *pachas* and *grand caïds*, whose corrupt self-interest in preventing any reassertion of Arab power in Rabat was increasingly exposed.[119] The fall of Mendès France also marked the decisive defeat of administrative reforms for Algeria put forward by his embattled Interior Minister, Mitterrand. And the campaign against Mitterrand exposed the parliamentary influence and formidable power-base of reactionary French settlers in Algiers in whose interests René Mayer had led the charge against Mendès within the Chamber in February.[120] Only over Tunisia was the new government able to register quick progress. On 21 April Faure and Tunisian premier, Tahar Ben Ammar, signed a Franco-Tunisian convention conceding internal autonomy, transferring judicial power to the Tunisian state and confirming Tunisia's customs union with France.[121]

Faure tried to rekindle the reform process in Morocco by appointing a progressive Gaullist, Gilbert Grandval, as Resident General on 20 June. Whoever took over in Rabat was sure to face a gargantuan task. Grandval, the former head of the French diplomatic mission in the Saar, was only offered the post after both Naegelen and Paris prefect of police, André Dubois, refused it. In the weeks preceding his replacement, Lacoste warned that Moroccan negotiators were bound to demand concessions at least equivalent to those granted in Tunis. And the assassination on 11 June of the prominent industrialist, Jacques Lemaigre-Dubreuil, heralded an upsurge in counter-terrorist violence amongst the French settler community. Lemaigre-Dubreuil was proprietor of the *France-Presse* media group whose Rabat newspaper *Maroc-Presse* supported extensive liberalisation. He was gunned down in Casablanca by supporters of *Présence française*, a Moroccan forerunner to the OAS in Algeria.[122] Faced with an increasingly tense atmosphere in Morocco's major cities, the measures that Grandval was sent to implement were too ambitious for Faure's more right-wing Cabinet colleagues to accept. Like his predecessor, Grandval warned that the issue of restoration dominated all others. Yet the requirement to proceed in accord with the traditionalist *pachas*, the Glaoui of Marrakech above all, blocked any compromise. A choice would have to be made between conciliating the main nationalist parties – the Istiqlal and the PDI – by restoring the Sultan, or banking on the conservative tribal chiefs who stood behind Ben Arafa. In reality, only the former could ensure long-term stability in Morocco, albeit at the price of tribal dissent within the Rif interior.[123]

On 5 June US Ambassador Dillon warned Dulles that North Africa was 'both France's number one problem and number one sore spot in Franco-American relations'. Alarmed by the deteriorating French security position, on 2 July US Under-Secretary of State for European affairs, Livingston Merchant, suggested that Dulles should warn French ministers at forthcoming talks in Geneva that urgent remedial reforms were required. He recommended joint Anglo-American pressure for greater concessions. But the fragile basis of government support in the Chamber imposed a sequential, go-slow policy towards North African reforms.[124] Faure's Cabinet, with the hardliners Maurice Bourgès-Maunoury and General Pierre Koenig at the key Ministries of Interior and National Defence, was anyway disinclined to soft-pedal on local security measures, particularly as the clamour for increased military involvement in Algeria, directed from Algiers by Governor Jacques Soustelle, increased. In Morocco, Grandval's replacement by the more conservative General Pierre Boyer de Latour threatened a renewed stalemate. The new resident arrived in Rabat following a spate of urban terrorism, protests in 19 major cities and the massacre of 50 Europeans in settlements at Oued-Zem and Ait-Amar on the second anniversary of the Sultan's deposition on 20 August. In the previous year, as Resident General in Tunisia, Boyer de Latour implemented the Carthage Declaration, concluding a ceasefire accord with the Tunisian *fellaghas* in November 1954. But in Rabat he was out of his depth in the face of the Glaoui's reluctance to give ground and settler opposition to reform.[125]

The key breakthrough was made in France and not Morocco during a week of government discussions from 22 August at Aix-les-Bains with representatives of all shades of Moroccan opinion from the Istiqlal to the key *pachas*. This cleared the way for the removal of Ben Arafa and the creation of a Regency Council to govern pending the return of Ben Youssef.[126] Leading figures in the Chamber who had sat in Laniel's 1953 Cabinet, including Bidault, Pleven and Henri Jacquinot, were almost bound to oppose the Sultan's restoration having helped secure his deposition.[127] Edgar Faure had also sat in Laniel's administration. But, like Mitterrand, he had protested at Ben Youssef's removal. Perhaps recalling this, two years later he acted decisively against his die-hard Gaullist colleagues in Cabinet to reverse the 1953 deposition. The Gaullists themselves had driven Faure into a corner. On 5 October the National Committee of the Gaullist movement (renamed the Social Republicans after the final demise of their previous incarnation – the RPF – in November 1954), called for a 'government of public safety' to cope with the Moroccan crisis. This first major attempt to precipitate de Gaulle's return to office was a flop. Faure demanded the resignation of intransigent Gaullist ministers, including Raymond Triboulet and General Koenig, and was left with a Cabinet reconciled to Moroccan self-government. Following preparatory talks with Georges Catroux between 2 and 9 September, the former Sultan, then still in exile in Madagascar, returned to Rabat as King Mohammed V on 16 November. In the interim, Catroux's discussions prepared the ground for the implementation of the plans discussed at Aix-les-Bains – the removal of Ben Arafa, the creation of a Regency Council in which Ben Youssef's close ally, Si Bekkaï, played the leading role, and the Sultan's triumphal return to Morocco via France.[128] At the close of a three-day debate, on 8 October the National Assembly voted 462 to 132 in favour of Moroccan self-government.[129] This marked a remarkable *volte-face* for French Conservatives, who less than a year before had been vicious opponents of reform. Whilst opposition to colonial concessions was an obvious route to conservative unity in 1954, the escalation of violence in Morocco and Algeria from August 1955 onwards demanded a more realistic evaluation of the costs of colonial rule which split the right once more.[130]

Having been the focal point of North African protest against French rule in 1950–52, by 1955 Tunisia was less violent than its Maghreb neighbours. On 23 November 1954 curfew restrictions were lifted and the Tunis residency announced an armistice for all *fellagha* who surrendered their arms. Some 2,700 rebels responded to this offer. Agreement over Tunisian control of finance, public services and education was reached by February 1955. But three months of often tetchy negotiations followed before Faure's Cabinet conceded full internal autonomy to Tunisia on 3 June. Approved in the Chamber of Deputies by a vote of 540 to 43, this arrangement was confirmed by an exchange of conventions between Paris and Tunis on 31 August.[131] Although this accord rested on the Tunis government's acceptance of an underlying community of interest with France, Néo-Destour was instinctively opposed to continued French base rights and formal guarantees to the settler population.[132]

These matters lay at the heart of renewed confrontation with Paris in early 1956. By this point Bourguiba had ran rings around his main rival, the Néo-Destour secretary-general, Salah Ben Youssef, strengthening his hand in negotiation with France in the process. Bourguiba and Tunisian deputy-premier Bahi Ladgham duly convinced the chief French negotiator, high commissioner Roger Seydoux, that the Youssefists were a major threat to future Franco-Tunisian partnership. Hence, the Tunisian negotiators pressed for complete control over foreign policy, policing and a national army.[133] As the negotiations in Rabat and Tunis neared conclusion, so the full implications of 'inter-dependence' with France had to be faced. Understandably, the Moroccans and Tunisians sought unequivocal French acceptance of their national independence before agreeing to maintain economic, strategic and political ties with France. But, as Alain Savary, the Foreign Ministry Secretary of State responsible for Moroccan and Tunisian affairs, stressed, the idea of independence first and talks on interdependence later was unacceptable. The Quai d'Orsay's economic and financial affairs directorate agreed. Future French economic support was conditional on Morocco and Tunisia remaining within the franc zone and sustaining their customs unions with France.[134]

In practice, all parties to the negotiations recognised the trade-off inherent in the independence settlements between French economic aid, the temporary maintenance of French base rights and military privileges, and an informal French *droit de regard* over Moroccan and Tunisian foreign policy. Alain Savary, the principal French negotiator, was himself a *pied-noir.* Born in Algiers in 1918, he had an outstanding record in the resistance and was a leading Maghreb expert within the SFIO. A frequent contributor to the Socialist mouthpiece *Le Populaire*, he was a prominent critic of Juin's North African policies and of military insubordination in general. His attitude to the negotiations was generally constructive. Perhaps responding to this, during the final round of Franco-Tunisian independence talks in Paris between 29 February and 12 March, Bahi Ladgham even suggested that ties with France might be reinforced once a fully functioning Tunisian regime was established.[135] But quite how France could uphold these rights should the Moroccan and Tunisian governments decide to repudiate or ignore them was never fully resolved.

Franco-Moroccan discussions resumed in Paris three weeks after the 2 March joint declaration abrogating the Treaty of Fez and recognising Moroccan independence. In this second round of negotiations, the mechanics of French financial support, Moroccan defence policy and diplomatic representation had still to be worked out – theoretically according to the precepts of interdependence. On 20 March Foreign Ministers Christian Pineau and Tahar Ben Ammar formally abrogated the 1881 Treaty of Bardo. Theoretically, Tunisia could raise its own armed forces and conduct an independent security policy.[136] But, again following the Moroccan model, talks on Franco-Tunisian interdependence in defence policy and foreign affairs began in Paris on 4 April. The conflict of interest between unfettered Moroccan and Tunisian responsibility for internal security and a limited French role in the external protection of both states was always apparent. On the one hand, French negotiators exploited examples of interdependence, such as the retention of French commanders and advisers within the Royal Moroccan Army, as evidence that Morocco wanted nothing to do with pan-Arabism. On the other, Bourguiba was adamant that the 20 March protocol gave the Tunisian government unrestricted control over foreign and defence policy. In 1956, Guy Mollet's government could fairly point out that, as yet, Tunisia had neither the means nor the international recognition to chart an entirely separate course in international affairs. It remained axiomatic in Paris that the governments in Rabat and Tunis should not be allowed to solicit British or US material aid as a substitute for French economic and military provision.[137]

These differences of interpretation became more acrimonious as FLN operations conducted from Morocco and Tunisia intensified in the months ahead. This brought into question the effectiveness of Moroccan and Tunisian internal security as well as the right of French forces to pursue ALN bands within the now independent states. It also provoked angry exchanges regarding France's May 1956 promise to provide equipment to the Moroccan and Tunisian armies, the fulfilment of which was conditional upon the implementation of effective frontier surveillance.[138] Eventually, the principles of interdependence to which all sides had paid lip-service in early 1956 settled upon the final independence accords like a thin film of dust – near invisible, untidy and always liable to be swept away by a vigorous bout of spring-cleaning in Rabat and Tunis.

Anxious to keep in step with France, Eden's government delayed British recognition of Moroccan and Tunisian independence until the French Assembly ratified the March 1956 protocols. This was more than mere politeness. To varying degrees, western governments withheld recognition to support French efforts to secure the most favourable terms for the interdependence accords still to be agreed in Rabat and Tunis. The British backed French demands for base rights, economic privileges and guarantees for the settler populations in Morocco and Tunisia, conscious that France might be asked to reciprocate in future cases of British decolonisation.[139] This set the British government apart from its American partner.

State Department fears that French obstructionism would only drive Moroccan and Tunisian leaders into the arms of Nasser or the Soviet block fuelled French suspicion that the US government sacrificed 'western unity' in pursuit of its North West African interests. With two Moroccan airfields in use by the US air force and a further two on stand-by, the Department of Defense had invested over $350 million on air force facilities alone. The Moroccan air bases, in addition to naval facilities at Port Lyautey and a communications station at Sidi Yaya, were important complements to NATO forces in the Mediterranean. But American eagerness to preserve them was nothing new.[140] In truth, French irritation stemmed from America's greater success in retaining its strategic facilities. This soon turned to mutual recrimination. On 20 May an exchange of letters between France and Morocco made no mention of the US base rights agreed in November 1950. But on 7 July the Rabat government indicated its intention to negotiate direct with Washington, leaving France out in the cold.[141]

Bourguiba's government was always unenthusiastic about an alliance treaty with France that would keep French forces on Tunisian soil for years to come. As a result, British ambassadorial representation in Tunis was delayed until Roger Seydoux was appointed France's first ambassador to Tunisia on 21 June.[142] Again, these diplomatic end-games were more than a simple matter of protocol. British, Italian, German and, above all, US recognition of Tunisia's independence consolidated Bourguiba's political standing at the expense of his more radical opponent, Salah Ben Youssef. Self-styled leader of a 'Tunisian Army of Liberation', Salah Ben Youssef seemed committed to violent struggle against the essentially pro-western policies favoured by Bourguiba.[143] In an effort to steal his opponent's thunder, from late March Bourguiba railed against any continuation of a French military presence in Tunisia. Behind the scenes, his chief negotiator, Abdelhamid Chelbi, secretary-general in the newly created Ministry of National Defence, was less intransigent. Meanwhile, settlers left the country in increasing numbers. By the time Franco-Tunisian talks over future interdependence began on 26 June the two sides had adopted irreconcilable positions. Bourguiba's government demanded the complete evacuation of French forces, while Pineau and Savary insisted that French forces remain indefinitely to discharge French obligations to Mediterranean defence, to safeguard the European population and to cover Algeria's eastern flank. Inevitably, the discussions broke down on 13 July. They were not formally resumed until the following February. Savary's successor, Maurice Faure, reopened direct negotiations in Tunis, only to run into deadlock once more over the duration of the French military presence.[144]

During the interdependence talks, the Tunisian government claimed that full independence, even if not yet ratified by the French Parliament, necessarily invalidated any military agreements made before it was conferred. In similar vein, Ahmed Balafrej, now installed as Morocco's first Moroccan Foreign Minister, insisted that, under the independence accords, France's remaining troops in Morocco were to serve only as advisers, trainers and guardians of French base installations. They held no jurisdiction over Moroccan internal security, the protection of settlers or the policing of frontiers. With an eye to mounting Anglo-Egyptian tension, this was not a principle the Foreign Office wished to see conceded. Furthermore, the defensive works and military installations built in the two protectorates in earlier years posited the operational unification of the three Maghreb commands in time of war. Even after independence, French forces expected to co-ordinate the defence of North-West Africa, with the Algeria garrison serving as a central strategic reserve.[145] Although impressed by the Tunisian refusal either to jump onto the Arab League bandwagon or to come out in support of Nasser, Eden's government backed the French case throughout.[146]

In Morocco the quest for international recognition and the issue of Franco-Moroccan interdependence were less fraught. Although the Rabat government was equally suspicious of any preconditions to French financial, developmental and military assistance, it was more confident than its Tunisian partner of the country's ability to negotiate support without in the process undermining hard-won independence. Neither the Sultan nor the Moroccan Cabinet were as reticent as the Tunisians in admitting their readiness to co-operate with the western powers. The Moroccan government was more eager to secure membership of the UN than to join the Arab League. The Istiqlalist regime foresaw a unique role as the pivot between the West and the Islamic world. This became more pronounced from August 1956 when the Istiqlal challenged the power of its main political rival, the PDI, which had secured eight ministerial posts within M'Barek Bekkaï's coalition Cabinet.[147]

*

Throughout these initial post-independence exchanges, the Algerian situation presented the main obstacle to close relations with France, and with the West more generally. Far more than Suez, the Algerian war dominated French relations with the Maghreb capitals in the months and years after the 1956 independence agreements. On 22 June an incursion by Foreign Legion troops in pursuit of Algerian guerrillas who had cut telegraph communications to the Legion base at Colomb Béchar near the Saharan Algeria–Morocco frontier provoked a cycle of protests and counter-protests. These became a familiar feature of Franco-Moroccan relations. The subsequent French bombardment of the Moroccan village that served as hiding place for these Algerian fighters suggested that French inability to localise the Algerian war would gradually erode Moroccan goodwill.[148] In discussions with Pineau and the

British ambassador in Rabat a month before Nasser's nationalisation of the Suez Canal Company on 26 July, Foreign minister Balafrej dismissed the Egyptian situation in order to focus upon Algeria. Happy to reassure his listeners of Moroccan coolness towards Nasser and the Arab League, Balafrej was none the less outspoken in his condemnation of French military policy in Algeria. The massive reinforcement of French forces then underway was bound to drive the FLN into the arms of Egypt, thus undermining any prospects that either Morocco or Tunisia could successfully mediate a settlement of the Algerian conflict. Understandably, when ambassador Jebb suggested that Anglo-French unity over the Suez crisis might be cemented by direct British military aid to the war effort in Algeria, neither Selwyn Lloyd nor Eden were prepared to pursue the matter.[149] Just as Algeria rather than Suez dominated Moroccan and Tunisian relations with France in 1956, so it dominated French policy towards Nasser. The British government glimpsed this but never fully understood it. To appreciate this more fully we need to consider the colonial environment in which the Algerian rebellion developed.

3
The Algerian War as a Colonial Problem: British Responses, 1954–58

The Eden and Macmillan governments always looked on the Algerian rebellion as a colonial problem. The war's impact on France's international power and its repercussions within French domestic politics were shaped by the manner in which France struggled to avoid decolonisation from Algeria. This chapter focuses on the final years of the Fourth Republic when withdrawal from Algeria was officially ruled out. It analyses the four aspects of the conflict which stimulated most discussion in British government circles. These were the viability of Franco-Algerian integration, the changing nature of colonial government in Algiers, the military policies pursued in the field, and the prospects for dialogue with Algerian nationalists.

The Politics and Economics of Integration

In the six years prior to the outbreak of rebellion in November 1954, the imbalance in Franco-Algerian trade worsened dramatically. Whilst imports from France increased by some 135 per cent over the years 1948–54, Algeria's exports to France expanded by only 32.5 per cent. Algeria was flooded by imports of French textiles and manufactured goods. Although Algerian foodstuff exports to France commanded higher prices by the mid-1950s, the country did not attract complementary private investment sufficient to underpin significant growth in its industrial sector. Instead, Algeria was increasingly reliant on French state investment to help extend the country's industrial base and so provide work for the expanding urban population and the country's youth. In November 1953 Joseph Laniel's government approved a second four-year economic modernisation plan for Algeria costing 277,501,000 francs. This was to fund investment in industrial equipment and development of the nation's economic infrastructure.[1] The initiative failed. Total industrial employment in Algeria increased by only 145,000 over the period 1948–56, a figure dwarfed by the overall increase in population facilitated by a sharp postwar drop in infant mortality. Over the five years from 1955 to 1960, Algeria's registered population grew from 8,811,100 to 9,875,000. In the same period the number of Muslims living in the country's cities mushroomed from 1,624,000 to 2,072,000. Urbanisation and increased Muslim unemployment went hand in hand. One indicator of this was the sharp rise in Algeria's commercial deficit between 1950 and 1956. Government investment mitigated the economic effects of a deteriorating deficit position but did little to promote longer-term economic growth.[2] Jacques Marseille summarises Algeria's economic position by 1954 thus: 'Increasing budgetary disequilibrium, a commercial deficit of worrying proportions, stagnant cereal production in the face of a rapidly growing population, the great majority of whom possessed only the bare essentials: such was the paradox of Algeria's economic and social development....'[3] The myth of economic complementarity between France and Algeria proved hard to dispel. A series of 1956 *Paris-Match* articles written by the journalist Raymond Cartier prompted more general media discussion of the costs and benefits of empire. But the dispassionate evaluation of the Algerian connection implicit in 'Cartiérisme' drew broad criticism.[4]

Given the strength of *colon* influence upon successive Algiers Governments General, the challenge of reform in Algeria was always less to devise a plan of political and economic change than to persuade the settler community to accept it. This helps explain British scepticism towards French assimilationist doctrine in general and Algerian reform plans modelled on greater integration with France in particular. In 1955 Prime Minister Edgar Faure suggested that Algerian workers in France – reckoned at some 275,000 by this point – sent home wage packets which helped provide for 1.5 million people. Five years later, de Gaulle told Indian premier Jawaharlal Nehru that these figures had increased to some 400,000 Algerians in France supporting 2.5 million people back home. Whatever the accuracy of these statements, their obvious implication was that the Muslim population of Algeria could not sustain itself. French withdrawal meant economic misery. But since French rule had utterly disrupted the indigenous system of land tenure, once Algeria's population explosion took off after 1945, it was inevitable that the indigenous population would face worsening poverty unless France either invested more heavily in agricultural modernisation or altered the basic fabric of landholding. To do so would, in turn, alter the basis of Arab–settler relationships across the colony. In the absence of such fundamental reform, Algerian Muslims were bound to flock to the coastal cities in search of work. A rootless and increasingly radicalised young labour force scratching an existence on the margins of a French-controlled economy provided a hard core of nationalist support which the French could not sway without relinquishing their own political control and reordering Algeria's economic system.[5] This picture of an unenfranchised, underemployed and increasingly militant young Algerian population dominated the proceedings of a British inter-departmental study group on French North Africa, first convened at the Foreign Office in January 1956 to provide policy advice about the Maghreb. Advised by Algiers Consul D. J. Mill-Irving, the African department specialists within this group accepted that settler opposition was the essential barrier to progress.[6]

In spite of increasing urbanisation, most Algerian Muslims relied on the agricultural sector. If the preferential French distribution of Marshall Aid funds to projects run by, or on behalf of, the *colon* population was any indication, then new funding for agricultural modernisation might spark alarm among Muslim cultivators afraid that they would be largely overlooked. Rural development programmes in British territories such as Kenya and Cyprus had triggered just such a reaction.[7] In June 1955 Paul Reynaud, chairman of the parliamentary finance commission, warned Minister of the Interior Maurice Bourgès-Maunoury that a clear programme of French strategic investment in Algeria was critical both to maintain and justify colonial control. During a tour of Algeria three months earlier Reynaud antagonised settler leaders by suggesting substantial tax increases to make good France's reform plans.[8] De Gaulle, too, was by 1955 appealing for a more far-sighted programme of constitutional reform and economic investment in Algeria. But, after floating his ideas at a June 1955 press conference, the general retreated to his Colombey residence and the manuscripts of his *Mémoires*, refusing to intervene decisively over Algeria until 1958.[9]

During Churchill's final term as Prime Minister, debates over the merits of colonial development raised many of the same questions of economic cost versus potential political benefit that the French confronted over Algeria. Whatever the Colonial Office enthusiasm for such projects, Churchill signalled his personal disinterest by abolishing the ministerial committee on colonial development. Beyond the Cabinet, inter-departmental argument persisted over the distribution of funding between development projects, imperial policing and defence. While recognising that colonial reform was inescapable, few of Churchill's

Cabinet colleagues were enthusiastic about it.[10] It remained a first principle of negotiated reform in Africa that the metropolitan power should not concede ground under pressure of a breakdown in law and order. Surely then, there were grounds for a sympathetic British response to France's dilemma in Algeria?

In June 1955 the African department assessed French prospects. Apart from military pacification, long-term plans to keep Algeria French hinged on economic investment, broader educational opportunity and infrastructural development. Commendable in themselves, these efforts to raise Algerian living standards remained open to criticism because of the legal fiction that Algeria was part of France. If that were the case, then French investment would need to be hugely multiplied to reduce the actual economic imbalance between metropolitan and Algerian departments. Similarly, Algerian citizenship rights and political representation in Paris would at some stage have to be massively increased – logically to the point where up to 120 Algerian Deputies would sit in the National Assembly. This would mark the biggest shift in French electoral demographics since the introduction of female suffrage in 1944. And most of the new deputies involved could be expected to side with the PCF in voting for secession.[11] The Algiers consulate painted a dismal picture in early July:

> Now that the implications of assimilation and integration are gradually being brought home to the French in Algeria, their instinctive repugnance to such measures is revealing. Perhaps, if left to themselves, local French politicians could imagine no better state than the one which now prevails at the antipodes. Unfortunately for this view, Algeria has neither the resources nor the wealth of the Union of South Africa and, what is more, is dependent on France for financial aid on an ever increasing scale.[12]

Simply put, integrationist arguments that Algeria was more than a colony and official insistence that Algeria required years of French material assistance both ran into the brick wall of France's actual incapacity to transform a developing state with a distinctive Muslim identity into a mythical 'French Algeria'. By insisting that under the 1947 statute 'Algeria was France', successive governments faced an insoluble dilemma. To make the concept a reality would require a full equalisation of political rights and a massive injection of capital to narrow the economic chasm between metropole and colony. Neither was remotely likely. Nor was there convincing evidence that most Algerian Muslims wanted to become French anyway.[13] Foreign Secretary Macmillan agreed with his advisers; it was nonsense to call Algeria 'French' on the basis that it had a metropolitan departmental structure and a large settler population. Its Arab culture ran far deeper and its Muslim population constituted the great majority. On 10 June 1955 he told Jebb that the only long-term solution in Algeria was the phased introduction of self-government backed by a long-term programme of infrastructural investment.[14]

By the start of 1956 the African department was convinced that the incoming French government faced a stark choice between the hugely expensive root-and-branch integration favoured by Governor Jacques Soustelle or prompt recognition of Algerian autonomy on the model of the neighbouring protectorates. From Algiers, consul Mill-Irving stressed that the underlying premise of either policy was that an educated Algerian Muslim 'governing class' could still be persuaded to work with France. This was most unlikely. Furthermore, since integration implied Franco-Muslim partnership within a single Algerian Chamber, it was never endorsed by the *colon* leaders of *Algérie française*.[15] Before premier Guy Mollet's fateful visit to Algiers on 6 February, his nominee as resident minister, Georges Catroux, tried to reassure his settler critics in interviews with *Le Monde* and *France Soir* that reform would build on the uniquely Gallic-Muslim 'personality' of Algeria. Catroux thus promised to respect the settler contribution to Algeria and the innate pro-westernism which separated Maghreb Muslims from their Arab cousins.[16] This characterisation had little basis in fact. There was no local political tradition of joint Franco-Algerian administration to compare with that in the protectorates. And settler commerce had stifled the emergence of a substantial Algerian Muslim bourgeoisie. Nor were the UDMA, the Messalist *Mouvement National Algérien* (MNA) or the FLN avowedly committed to a uniquely maghrebian politics which might be welded to a pro-western foreign and defence policy. French efforts to keep the Sultan, the Istiqlal, Bourguiba and the Néo-Destour in the western camp could not be emulated in Algeria where the dominant nationalist group had seemingly emerged from obscurity in a matter of months.[17] During 1956 these hard realities became starkly apparent.

In June 1956 Algeria's departmental structure was reorganised. Twelve newly established departments were superimposed upon the restyled 'regions' of Oran, Algiers and Constantine. This followed the creation of unified civil and military commands in the Aurès and Kabylie, the first centres of rebel activity. Here, specialist 'native affairs officers' (*officiers des affaires indigènes*), many with previous experience in administering Moroccan tribal areas, set about restoring the fabric of local administration, working with community leaders to introduce additional public services.[18] This restructuring of departments and communes was intended to increase Muslim representation in departmental politics by introducing single college elections to municipal councils. But implementation of this new electoral procedure was confined to those areas already pacified, and it was generally undermined by the FLN boycott of elections.[19] On 6 December 1956 the Algiers government reported that 1,460 Algerian Muslims had been recruited into the central bureaucracy. In 200 out of a target of 500 communes local administration had been overhauled. Interrupted by the Suez crisis, when these communal reforms resumed, the dissolution of additional regional and town councils caused immediate settler protest. This culminated in a spate of *colon* killings in Algiers following the assassination on 28 December of Amédée Froger, president of the Algerian federation of Mayors. The intensity of this violence confirmed that the introduction of a single college voting system at national level – ending the discrimination between the existing European and Algerian Muslim colleges – would be a far more difficult proposition bound to provoke still more extreme settler reaction.[20]

In this sense, kick-starting the reform process at local level made sense. But here, other complications intervened. Widespread crop burning and the FLN's brutal enforcement of Muslim boycotts of 'European' goods and French export products, including wine and tobacco, disrupted the economy as this ban spread westwards from Constantine in early 1955. On 4 June 10,000 reservists were called up in an effort to protect the 1955 harvest. In spite of a vigorous offensive led by Foreign Legion units, by January 1956 attempted pacification in the Aurès and Kabylie commands was also undermined by the escalation of rebel activity in the eastern coastal region based upon Bône, Constantine and Philippeville.[21] On the other side of the military divide, a key reason for the army's readiness to prosecute a long war was that the Algiers military command accepted that integration could only succeed if implemented from the bottom up in areas that had been cleared of rebels.[22] This was a more sophisticated equation between order and reform than rhetorical government commitments to implement constitutional change once a ceasefire was in place. But from 1956 onwards it widened the gap between a French political community increasingly persuaded that integration was unachievable and a professional army that remained determined to spearhead the social transformation of Algeria. To the permanent military secretariat in Algiers, implementation of the administrative reforms built into the enabling law (*loi cadre*) eventually passed in 1958 presented a new opportunity to make integration work rather than the beginning of genuine Algerian autonomy. In other words, as more Algerians were inducted into the colonial administration or took jobs as railwaymen or postal workers within an expanding Algerian public sector, so the ideal of Franco-Muslim integration could be revitalised. The army's task was to make Algeria safe for integration if not for real democracy.[23]

The Problems of Algiers Government

An important point to note here is the broad French consensus that political unrest in Algeria arose from adverse economic circumstances. This principle informed the postwar training programme at the advanced study centre for French administrators in Muslim territories. Improved rural living standards would guarantee political stability by preventing greater urbanisation and proletarianisation of Algeria's Muslim population.[24] This outlook found echoes within Bevin's Foreign Office during the late 1940s, particularly in British Middle East Office support for economic development among Arab client-states. But whereas this economic determinism fell out of favour in Whitehall during Churchill's final term, it remained integral to French schemes for Algeria as cross-party and *colon* opposition to more fundamental political concessions left a gaping hole in reform planning. The preservation of the discriminatory twin college electoral system within the 1947 statute for Algeria, Governor Naegelen's staunch defence of settler interests between 1948 and 1951, and the inability of the non-Communist left in France to reject assimilationist thinking outright: all condemned Algeria to political stalemate during the late 1940s. The Socialists, in particular, underestimated settler power within Algerian and metropolitan politics and overestimated Muslim tolerance of French rule so long as infrastructural development continued.[25]

This tendency to emphasise the material benefits of economic reform to the exclusion of more fundamental constitutional change was soon reinforced. In early 1955 François Mitterrand, Minister of the Interior in Mendès France's Cabinet, proposed an equalisation of educational and political opportunities for French and Algerian citizens across the colony. Misjudging the potential scale of the Algerian rebellion, Mitterrand and Mendès estimated that prompt administrative reforms combined with vigorous repression of terrorist violence could restore the situation.[26] Mitterrand therefore advocated extended powers for local councils (*Conseils généraux*) in the administration of departmental affairs. On

6 January *Le Monde* leaked details of his plans. This provoked bilious right-wing parliamentary attacks, orchestrated by the Radical senator Henri Borgeaud, upon Mitterrand and his main ally within Algeria, the liberal mayor of Algiers, Jacques Chevallier. This criticism was amplified in the French press and in *colon*-owned newspapers in Algeria. Argument over implementation of the reform plan also paralysed the Algiers Assembly and divided settler opinion. For the first time Algeria's problems were politically exploited as a means to bring down a sitting government. To make matters worse, Mitterrand was also immersed in the 'affaire des fuites' scandal, having been falsely accused of leaking defence secrets to the PCF, the Soviets and the Viet Minh.[27] Most important, in an unsuccessful bid to hold his coalition together whilst removing a potential thorn in his side from Paris, Mendès appointed Jacques Soustelle as Governor-General in Algeria only days before his government fell. An act of appeasement intended to conciliate opponents of reform in Paris and Algiers, this set the tone for subsequent government capitulations to settler pressure. It is none the less worth noting initial *colon* suspicion of Soustelle based upon his closeness to de Gaulle and his status as an appointee of Mendès France. Once in office in Algiers, Soustelle quickly dispelled these reservations.[28]

From Algiers, US Consul Lewis Clark warned the State Department bureau of western European affairs of the *colons'* ability to block all but limited economic reform, singling out the *grand colon* elite in Algeria's major cities:

> These few families, the colons, practically control the country. Through election to political office, through the press which they own, and through lobbies they maintain in Paris they greatly influence, if they do not in fact determine, French government policy in respect of Algeria. The ignorance of the average Metropole Frenchman on the subject of Algeria is abysmal and he is very likely to accept the judgment of his co-citizen who lives there. Accordingly, the selfish, short-sighted task of the colon is made easier.[29]

Clark was right. The appointment of Soustelle was a foretaste of Mollet's surrender to *colon* protesters a year later when the selection of Georges Catroux as replacement to Soustelle was overturned by sectarian protest. As the *New York Times'* banner headline put it on 7 February 1956, settler power in Algeria had become a 'Dictatorship of the Populace'.[30] Mollet almost admitted as much in a conversation with Jebb a fortnight after the Algiers *jour des tomates*. While the premier liked to claim that his trip to Algiers proved that most protesters were of solid working-class and artisan stock, he confided that the *grands colons* and their allies within the Algiers administration formed a powerful reactionary alliance. Ironically, Mollet expected Catroux's replacement, Robert Lacoste, Socialist deputy for the Dordogne, to purge the Algiers government of these unnamed officials. Lacoste's impressive resistance record, a fund of negotiating experience working with the CGT in the late 1940s, and his willingness to give up the Finance Ministry to go to Algiers, suggested that he would be a determined political operator. But, as Jebb warned, the vested interests that Lacoste faced in Algiers would sooner challenge the government than depart quietly.[31]

Cowed by the settler mob on 6 February 1956, Mollet's appointment of Lacoste destroyed all prospect for the immediate introduction of bold political reform. The circumstances of Lacoste's appointment left him at the mercy of the diehard *colons* in the Algiers Assembly, the local press and Amédée Froger's Algerian federation of mayors. The war veterans, *petits commerçants* and young supporters of Pierre Lagaillarde's Student Action Committee that formed the protester hard-core saw their stake in Algerian society threatened as never before. They were not about to back down.[32] Lacoste could hardly implement wider reforms in the face of bitter *colon* opposition when his very selection represented the government's capitulation to these settlers' interests. Infuriated at being replaced, Soustelle drove home this point by pandering to the settler crowds that turned out to mark his departure from Algiers.

Controversy over the appointment of a governor-general – or, in the case of Catroux and Lacoste, a resident minister – was both a reflection of the power that an effective governor might wield and proof of the fact that, as a political appointee without assured backing in the French Assembly, individual governors and residents usually built up a constituency of political support by courting settler opinion. Appointed by the Council of Ministers and responsible for the implementation of government policy in Algeria, in practice a governor's authority rested upon the broad delegation of metropolitan powers to his administration in Algiers. In a period of internal unrest, the governor's civil powers were augmented by the role of his military cabinet as principal liaison to the three French corps commanders across the country. From 1954 the governor-general/resident-minister was the civilian face of both economic reform and the war effort. And as his deputy, the secretary-general of the civil government, supervised the day-to-day working of the central administration, the governor had time to cultivate a political following among the *colons* that dominated the proceedings of the Algerian

Assembly and the street politics of the northern cities. Short of the French government deciding to remove the governor altogether, there was little constitutional constraint on the exercise of his personal authority since the organisation established for the purpose by the statute for Algeria was wholly inadequate. The Algerian council of government, with six appointees chosen by the governor himself and by the Algerian Assembly, was assured of a European majority. Its competence to challenge government decisions was strictly limited. The combination of an intransigent governor enjoying widespread settler support and a sympathetic Minister of the Interior hostile to nationalist pressure was a difficult axis to break.[33]

Initially, Soustelle liaised with the Paris-based inter-departmental coordinatory committee for French North Africa over policy formulation. But by January 1956 he clearly expected to pursue his integrationist ideas in the teeth of Ministry of the Interior scepticism. He justified his defiance by warning that the abandonment of integration would confront the government with the alternative of conceding Algerian independence. Born into a Protestant family in Montpellier, Soustelle's belief in integration derived in part from his academic training as an ethnologist. His pre-war research into Aztec culture took him to Mexico where the Indian population appeared to have been assimilated into modern Mexican society, though at terrible human cost. Evidently this convinced Soustelle that the process had to be thorough.[34]

Although the post of governor was discarded in February 1956 in favour of a resident minister more directly responsible to the Council of Ministers, the delegation of power from Paris to Algiers remained considerable during Lacoste's term as resident until April 1958. Ultimately, Lacoste proved no easier to control than Soustelle, although he was less confrontational with metropolitan governments. Within four months of taking up his appointment, Lacoste was censured by the SFIO congress, which endorsed Mollet's Algerian policy but criticised the resident minister's failure to implement it.[35] Again, settler pressure was decisive. Throughout the rebellion, the Foreign Office African department, the Paris Embassy and the Algiers consulate monitored the *grand colon* politicians, landowners and businessmen who controlled both the French-language press and Algeria's wine, tobacco, milling and shipping industries. Settler politicians, such as Algiers senator Borgeaud, the most powerful proprietor within the Algerian wine industry, and the deputies Georges Blachette and Marcel Paternot also enjoyed a disproportionate influence within the National Assembly. They could readily expose party divisions over Algeria by demanding an unequivocal defence of the *colon* population. After this settler oligarchy was dubbed 'The Masters of Algeria' by the journal *L'Express* in January 1955, Algiers consul, C. O. Wakefield-Harrey, warned that *colon* leaders concealed their opposition to any structural political change by objecting to the method and timing of planned reform. Since 1947, every attempt to implement the Algerian statute had been frustrated, and Mitterrand, the first Interior Minister to challenge the settlers directly, was vilified for doing so. The principal Algiers newspapers were so reactionary that Wakefield-Harrey estimated that only the Communist press was reporting objectively on Algiers politics.[36]

Mitterrand's painful experience exerted a lasting influence over his successors at the Ministry of the Interior. The selection of an Interior Minister with a track-record of opposition to far-reaching reform became a key ingredient in cabinet selection between 1955 and 1958. Edgar Faure's appointment of Maurice Bourgès-Maunoury in February 1955 and Guy Mollet's choice of Jean Gilbert-Jules twelve months later exemplified this shift. Bourgès-Maunoury and Gilbert-Jules were less readily identifiable with the formulation of reforms than with the extension of emergency powers, huge increases in troop numbers and the arrest of five key FLN leaders in October 1956. As Hugh Roberts has indicated, the imputation of economic motives to Algerian political demands became 'a staple ingredient' of French official thinking.[37] Successive French governments hid behind a misguided economic determinism to avoid the unpalatable truth that there could be no successful negotiations without discussion of Algerian independence.

The Search for *'Interlocuteurs Valables'*

Seen from London, France faced two central problems in finding representative Algerian leaders – *interlocuteurs valables* – with whom to negotiate a compromise settlement. First, the combination of direct colonial rule and repression of nationalist politicians had prevented the growth of a mass-based Algerian political party capable of persuading the majority of the civil population to accept the phased introduction of self-government. Secondly, no French government could convince the settler population of the requirement for unconditional talks with the FLN. These were problems for which the Algiers authorities bore primary responsibility. Police harassment and periodic arrests of MTLD and UDMA politicians persisted throughout Naegelen's three-year governorship, but peaked during campaigning for the April 1948 and February 1951 Algerian elections. But when Naegelen tendered his resignation on

16 March 1951, he insisted that he had implemented the Algerian statute as far as was possible. To no avail, the three Algerian Socialist federations and numerous mayors and councillors, still loyal to their man, urged Naegelen to stay.[38] In the months following his departure, the Algiers administration rejected political dialogue, bolstered by its disruption of the established nationalist parties and the break-up of the *Organisation Spéciale* (the paramilitary forerunner to the FLN) in 1950. On 27 July 1951 the MTLD, the UDMA, the Algerian Communist Party (*Parti Communiste Algérien* – PCA) and the organisation of religious Ulamas formed the Algerian Front for Defence and Respect of Freedom. This coalition quickly fell apart owing to the ill-concealed rivalry between the two main nationalist parties and their mutual disdain for communist orthodoxy. But the underlying evidence of widening opposition to French repression elicited little reaction in Algiers or Paris.[39]

From November 1954 the previous decade of alternating French manipulation and repression of Algeria's major political leaders facilitated the rapid ascendancy of the FLN. French exploitation of the schism within the leadership of Messali Hadj's MTLD, the party's refusal to contest elections to the Algerian Assembly while Messali himself remained in detention, and the re-emergence of the MTLD's bitter feud with the PCA during late 1953, weakened Messalist influence in the months before the Algerian rebellion began.[40] After the breach between Messali loyalists and the MTLD's central committee under Hocine Lahouel emerged into the open at the Party's Algiers congress in April 1953, it extended further when the rival factions held competing congresses in Brussels and Algiers a year later. The Foreign Office estimated that the PCA's decision to align with the anti-Messalist MTLD central committee and the latter's production of a new party newspaper, *La Nation Algérienne*, killed off any prospect for talks between the French authorities and the party which, hitherto, represented the broadest swathe of nationalist opinion. Messali Hadj's decision to establish a new party, the *Mouvement National Algérien* (MNA), backed by the majority of former MTLD supporters among the immigrant community in France, also marked a rejection of dialogue. Remarkably, in May 1956 Mollet told the British Labour Party leader, Hugh Gaitskell, that he thought the MNA might agree to serve as interlocuteur between the government and the FLN. In fact, police repression and the violent contest for support between MNA and FLN organisers in France only hardened nationalist resolve. With almost 4,000 Algerians in France either killed or injured in the MNA-FLN feuding during 1957 alone, MNA mediation between the French authorities and the FLN was hardly likely.[41]

In early 1955 Governor-General Roger Léonard bent to settler pressure and arrested the MTLD supporters on Algiers city council for sedition. Ironically, this prompted his own dismissal alongside a government purge of senior police officers in Algiers.[42] With the MTLD fatally weakened, members of the PCA executive targeted for arrest and Ferhat Abbas's UDMA still unable to generate a mass following beyond the educated urban Algerians at its core, the onward march of the FLN was further assisted by the French rejection of talks during the first year of the war. Instead, the French security services tracked the movements of senior FLN figures, most notably Ahmed Ben Bella, convinced that a pan-Maghrebian uprising was being planned.[43] The one remaining Muslim voice close to the central administration – the second college of the Algerian Assembly – had no credibility as a representative institution. The cantonal elections held across Algeria on 17 and 24 April 1955 were the first in a string of local and Algerian Assembly ballots which revealed the FLN's capacity to impose its will on much of the Muslim electorate. Despite the best efforts of the authorities to ensure that eligible voters turned out, the April 1955 elections attracted barely 50 per cent participation. This figure declined further in subsequent ballots.[44] By late 1956 no credible Algerian politicians were prepared to negotiate with France for anything less than national independence. This fuelled the Mollet Cabinet's determination to prosecute the war to a final conclusion. In June Mollet stated that, unless the rebels agreed to a ceasefire, the administration would 'create' its own interlocuteurs.[45] This was a nonsense, based on the specious hope that, once the army reimposed general order, a hitherto silent Muslim majority would record an overwhelming debt of gratitude in national elections.

On 13 September 1956 *France-Soir* published accurate details of government plans to extend local autonomy and abolish the dual college voting system. This scheme was further refined by Lacoste's directorate of political affairs which worked closely with Marcel Champeix, a Socialist senator appointed as Secretary of State with special responsibility for Algeria within the Ministry of the Interior. Algeria was to be administratively reorganised. Each department would elect a single college assembly responsible for local taxation and regional government. A single college assembly would also be established at national level, although France was to retain control over defence, foreign affairs and external trade. In spite of gerrymandering to ensure settler predominance within key urban constituencies, Muslim majorities were anticipated in most local government elections in addition to the selection of deputies and senators to sit in Paris. But the limited powers of elected bodies in Algeria and the overarching authority of the resident minister in Algiers were little altered. Furthermore, these measures were to be implemented without prior discussion with any nationalist representatives.[46] This was reform as a substitute for negotiation rather than as a product of it. Again, the fundamental dilemma was that no respected Algerian political figure would endorse French policy. This became still more apparent in 1957. In February, a spate of arrests of Muslim professionals in Algiers and the discovery of a cache of bombs in the house of Abderrahmane Bouteleb, President of the Association of Caïds and a former member of the Algerian Assembly, led British consul Roderick Sarell to conclude that the FLN could now claim substantial support among Algeria's educated Muslim elite.[47]

Apart from the main nationalist parties, the Muslim Association of Reformist Ulama, by turns tolerated and persecuted since its foundation in 1931, was also systematically repressed between 1955 and 1957. This followed two years of bitter jurisdictional argument over control of key mosques, particularly in Constantine, and French accusations that Ulama religious funds were channelled to the FLN. Although one cannot put a precise figure on it, many of the young Algerians educated in the Koranic schools and the influential Ben Badis Institute run by the Ulama in the 1940s and 1950s fused their Islamic learning with the radical nationalism of the MTLD and the FLN.[48] This emerging generation of Algerian nationalists connected the integral nationalism of radical Messalists on the one hand, and the Ulama leader Muhammad al-Bashir al-Ibrahimi's condemnation of assimilationist efforts to undermine Muslim religious identity on the other.[49] With hindsight, it seems clear that the Algiers administration blundered in its rejection of peaceful Ulama pressure for the separation of Islamic establishments and schools from civil administrative control in 1950–51. At this point, the mayor of Algiers, Jacques Chevallier, and the influential proprietor of the *Echo d'Alger*, Alain de Serigny, both accepted that a clearer demarcation of central administrative control and local Ulama jurisdiction might diminish the force of religious protest.[50] Had this concession been granted earlier, the radicalisation of the Ulama leadership might conceivably have been tempered prior to the rebellion.

As it was, al-Bashir al-Ibrahimi stepped up Ulama opposition to French colonialism from 1951 onwards. In March 1952 he visited Pakistan and Saudi Arabia to publicise the impact of French administrative control on Islamic observance. In meetings with fellow clerics he stressed the difficulties Algerian pilgrims faced in performing the *hajj* to Mecca. Moving on to address the Arab League in Cairo, he discussed external support for religious teaching in Algeria and secured additional places for Algerian students to study in Egyptian universities. Beyond these Islamic concerns, al-Bashir al-Ibrahimi emphasised the importance of a common approach to Maghreb problems among the Arab and Asian Muslim delegations to the UN. On 17 February 1955 he joined a fellow Ulama leader, Foudil el Ouartalani, at a key inaugural meeting of the FLN organised by Nasser's aide, Mohamed Fathi Al Dib, in Cairo. Although no Muslim cleric equalled the political impact of Archbishop Makarios in Cyprus, in January 1956 the Association of Reformist Ulama issued a manifesto demanding French recognition of Algeria's separate national identity and its right to full self-government.[51]

Beyond the nationalist parties and Algeria's religious leadership, British and American observers recognised that both sides in the conflict increasingly sought the allegiance of Algerian women. Although the women who fought and secretly raised funds for the FLN acquired hero status in the hagiography of the movement, the leadership remained torn between an appeal to educated Algerian women as a force for secular modernisation and the need to court orthodox Muslim opinion. But by 1958 Lakhdar Ben Tobbal, commander of the northern Constantine *wilaya,* was the only prominent FLN figure who openly advocated a Muslim state. The fact remained that the PCA stood alone in selecting women to major national positions, a reflection of its affiliation to the Soviet-sponsored International Federation of Democratic Women.[52] On the other side of the war's divide, Mitterrand encountered strong local opposition to his inclusion of women's suffrage within his 1955 reform plans. In any event, successful proposals for the emancipation of Muslim women had to originate from within the community to which they were to be applied.[53] This was confirmed by experience in Tunisia and especially Morocco, where women played leading roles in single-issue political protests, most notably in favour of the restoration of Sultan Mohammed V.[54]

Apart from offering the vote, a key element in French policy in rural Algeria was to improve living standards and public health among young Algerian women. From 1958 the army's specialist colonial administrative corps, the *Sections Administratives Spécialisées* (SAS), spearheaded the effort to mobilise local support among Muslim women. Women's Clubs became a common feature of villages under army/SAS protection. These offered a public information service backed by the provision of free health care and vaccination programmes, often administered by female doctors.[55] Yet, while Muslim women were no more politically or culturally homogeneous than their male counterparts, colonial administrators and proffered reforms too often treated them as such. Typical in this regard was the mounting French political and press hostility to the wearing of traditional veils or head-scarves by Algerian women. The engagement of Muslim women in the war either as rebel combatants, as a targeted constituency of the French rural reform drive or, most often, as victims of violence could make wearing the veil appear either an act of defiance or subversion. Conversely, the image of a face hidden by the veil was frequently exploited in French propaganda as a symbol of Islamic oppression of women. Yet, controversy over the veil only confirmed that in war the tendency was to render complicated issues of gender in reductive terms. In fact, the wide spectrum of Algerian women's writing on the war makes plain that conversion to the French cause had no clear gender basis.[56]

The Military Dimension

As the likelihood of Algerian negotiations receded, British respect for French military objectives diminished. This estimate drew on British experience. Whereas in Malaya the Briggs Plan gradually isolated the Communist insurgents whilst cultivating a workable political alliance with Malay parties and the non-Communist Malayan Chinese Association, in Kenya, a larger and more influential settler population and the radicalisation of the nationalist leadership during the Mau Mau emergency blocked a political solution.[57] In this respect, Algeria resembled Kenya, but on a far greater scale. The Algiers authorities could not isolate the FLN from their international backers. A vigorous prosecution of the war only consolidated FLN primacy over its nationalist rivals. From December 1957 Britain's major anti-colonialist organisation, the Movement for Colonial Freedom, chose to maintain contact with the FLN alone. Boasting a range of Labour Party and trade union affiliates, the Movement for Colonial Freedom had previously been as sympathetic to the less doctrinaire MNA as to its FLN rival. Ultimately, however, the FLN was endorsed as the more authentic nationalist voice.[58]

Within France, liberal criticism of army practices and the lack of political progress stumbled on the issue of viable alternatives. Whatever the ideological gulf between them, before 1958 the few advocates of outright Algerian independence and those demanding a war without limits against the FLN at least accepted the logic of Algeria's situation. Noting the realism which linked anti-war radicals and proponents of a revolutionary war strategy, Philip Dine captures the liberal's dilemma: 'the war in Algeria could not be made more humane, since the conflict's political and military logic defied all attempts to impose moral limits upon it.'[59] As the conflict intensified, it became more important to justify its human and material costs by clarifying precisely what would occur once order was restored. Successive governments failed to do so because they could not divine any middle ground between the settler and nationalist positions. Again, those on the political fringes from Communists to Poujadists who advocated French withdrawal or a simple return to the *status quo ante* were at least clear about their final objectives.

Meanwhile, with the escalation of conflict, the slim chance of Muslim acceptance of a French-imposed settlement disappeared. In this sense, the army was the victim of its bloody success: the means it employed to reimpose control alienated the constituency of Algerian Muslim opinion that it had hoped to conciliate. The FLN was quick to recognise the dynamic at work here. By terrorising civilians it undermined French military claims that life under the French tricolour was qualitatively better than an uncertain future in an independent Algerian state. Although grassroots support for the FLN progressively increased, the movement never entirely abandoned this use of what Martha Crenshaw Hutchinson termed 'compliance terror'. French government figures for the years 1954–56 suggested that the FLN had assassinated six times as many Muslims as Europeans. In May 1957 the slaughter of the male population of a small village near Melouza south of Algiers accused of support for the MNA caused revulsion in France and overseas. But its political message was sickenly clear.[60] A night of vicious reprisals for a village's alleged collaboration with the civil-military authorities could unravel months of patient French effort by *quadrillage* patrols, military doctors, teachers and technicians in building up local support for the French presence. Notwithstanding the success of French mobile forces (especially the *Commandos de chasse* established by commander-in-chief General Maurice Challe in 1959) in clearing areas of ALN *katibas* (units), the supposed eradication of the rebel threat in one zone often proved temporary. As Challe later put it, in such a war it was pointless to play Napoleon seeking out an Austerlitz; real victory was measured in the political allegiance of the civilian population. Algeria then was first and foremost a political war.[61] Military success in one area often stimulated the re-emergence of additional threats elsewhere as the ALN commanders of the six administrative regions, the *wilaya*, established across Algeria endeavoured to sustain the tenor of the rebellion (see map 3).[62]

In the first months of the rebellion the Algiers command also suffered from the fragmentation of its deuxième bureau military intelligence capability over the preceding decade. The removal of state of siege restrictions in Algeria on 12 December 1945 signified that the country was no longer considered an active zone of operations. Military intelligence-gathering and the readiness of field commanders to act on intelligence information gradually declined. Reports by deuxième bureau staff of the Algiers-based *10e région militaire* were still forwarded to the Ministry of National Defence. But the civilian intelligence-gathering agencies – the *sûreté nationale*, the *Direction de la Surveillance du Territoire* and the secret intelligence SDECE post in Algeria – played a more prominent role. These organisations reported directly to the Ministry of the Interior and the Prime Minister's Office, but were less attuned to the mood among the Algerian population than local military commands, particularly in outlying areas. This explains why General Henri Jacquin, chief of the deuxième bureau in Algiers in 1954, judged the early intelligence battle against the FLN a failure.[63]

After the public tumult over Mitterrand's frustrated reforms in early 1955, the Ministry of the Interior focused instead on the implementation of state of emergency restrictions in the regions most affected by rebel attacks. Commanded by Mustapha Ben Boulaïd, the guerrillas in the Aurès-Nementchas *wilaya* made the greatest inroads against French colonial control in the first quarter of 1955.[64] On 22 March Bourgès-Maunoury tabled enabling legislation introducing special military powers in the Tizi-Ouzou region of Kabylie and a swathe of Constantinois territory from the foothills of the Aurès mountains around the town of Batna, through the Tebessa region to the Tunisian frontier. Soustelle's administration suggested the delimitation of this initial round of emergency legislation which came into force on 6 April 1955. Although martial law was supposedly restricted to areas of known rebel strength, according to US consulate figures, these measures covered an area with a population of over 1.2 million Muslims and 15,000 Europeans.[65] Just as important, the application of the state of emergency provisions within Constantine required closer liaison between civilian prefects and divisional commanders and, beneath them, sub-prefects and the army colonels commanding individual sectors.[66] Slowly but surely these civil–military relationships acquired a sharper political edge. As the prefectural administration and its local army command worked hand-in-glove against the rebellion, so the distinction between the political objectives of the former and the military tasks of the latter became blurred. This extension of martial law was the Faure government's only significant contribution to the Algerian conflict. Gripped by the Moroccan dynastic crisis in the summer and autumn of 1955, Faure's administration did not formulate a coherent scheme of reform.[67] 1955 was thus a year of transition from limited rebellion to outright war in Algeria while French policy-making in North Africa was still dominated by the problems of Tunisia and Morocco. The commitment to restore law and order was a convenient means to conceal the lacunae in French policy.

This tendency became still more apparent in early 1956. Lacoste's regular directives to all officers serving in Algeria implored the troops to redouble their efforts to crush the FLN.[68] From March onwards, military operations against ALN bands were intensified with the introduction of the *quadrillage* system dividing the country into zones progressively swept and then garrisoned, generally by conscript forces. Started in the Bône plain, this system underpinned the offensives conducted across rural Algeria for the rest of the year. In response, the hard-pressed FLN turned towards more widespread acts of terrorism and economic sabotage to sustain the rebellion. Aside from its tragic human consequences, this shift in emphasis had three immediate consequences for the direction of Algiers government policy. First, the extension of urban terrorism hardened settler opposition to reform still further. At its most extreme, this produced unqualified official sanction of settler violence and reprisal. Maurice Papon, the now notorious former Vichy official who was then serving as an Inspector-General in the Constantinois, told a press audience on 5 September 1957 that the local *colon* population should be prepared to fight the FLN directly since the region faced 'total war'.[69] Second, from the start of 1957, the professional army's ruthless offensive against the FLN cells in Algiers and other urban centres cemented the bond between key sections of the military command, leading professional regiments and the *petits colons* that suffered most from urban bombings. This common sympathy soon took on the character of a political alliance with seismic consequences in 1958.

Finally, the less well-publicised ALN war against the economy of French Algeria rocked the very foundations of economic modernisation. As French reinforcements began to pour across the Mediterranean in March 1956, the management of the Ouenza iron mines, the largest single industrial enterprise in Algeria, warned that acts of sabotage had brought the company to its knees. Algeria's mineral production, the main pillar of the country's industrial sector before the exploitation of Saharan oil began in earnest, was based on three principal mining works: the iron ore and phosphate mines at Ouenza (near Tebessa in eastern Constantine) and the phosphate mining enterprise south of the coastal town of Bougie. These and other newly developed production facilities around Philippeville were all reliant on railroad links to transport their output. Sabotage of these industrial railway lines, as well as disruption of the arterial Casablanca–Tunis line, became endemic in 1956. So, too, attacks on road traffic and telephone and telegraph communications increased markedly over the year, a problem which accelerated the army's construction of long-distance radio transmitters as an alternative to telegraph transmissions.[70] Such was the increased danger of commercial travel that the US consulate estimated a 50 per cent drop in Algerian petrol consumption in the first quarter of 1956. French and Algerian commercial managers were now prime assassination targets alongside *colon* agriculturalists.[71] Economic reforms to the exclusion of fundamental political change made still less sense when the economy of Algeria was so thoroughly disrupted. Mollet's avowed commitment to economic reform, including plans for the expropriation of large estates in readiness for a land redistribution scheme, was out of tune with the worsening economic dislocation and extensive rural violence across the country.[72]

From 1956 to 1959 the theories of revolutionary warfare and the requirement to exceed the enemy's politico-military capacity to control the civilian population dominated the pages of French military journals, official and unofficial. The *Revue Militaire d'Information*, the *Revue de Défense Nationale* and the less widely read *Message* published numerous articles suggesting that revolutionary war held the key to Muslim loyalty and defeat of the FLN. In his unfailingly upbeat 'general directives' to French officers in Algeria, Lacoste, too, emphasised that psychological warfare was a vital military priority.[73] In real terms, by 1957 the army was the only face of French administration across much of Algeria. General Quenard, commander in the Saharan southern territories, even suggested that the army might as well run the transport system since it directed most other public services within the Algerian interior.[74] This extension of military control offered unprecedented opportunities to adapt counter-insurgency to the tenets of revolutionary war. Inherently political owing to the military methods involved, revolutionary war acquired a sharper ideological edge as its die-hard protagonists opposed the scaling down of operations and the reorientation of French defence policy towards nuclear deterrence under de Gaulle.[75]

Historical interest in the French army's revolutionary and psychological warfare practices began soon after the war ended and has been sustained ever since. So, too, the vital importance of the politico-administrative work of the *Sections Administratives Spécialisées* has recently been recognised.[76] In its pursuit of psychological warfare and in the commitment to improve rural living conditions, the French army in Algeria went further than its British counterpart. This was partly a reflection of the differing French and British jurisdictional controls over psychological warfare operations. Through a psychological action committee organised by Lacoste's cabinet staff in July 1956, the Algiers residency supported psychological warfare planning. Far from restraining military action, the civil authorities encouraged its extension.[77] Where the military imposed its stamp on psychological warfare within French imperial territory, in British African and Far Eastern territories, propaganda, broadcasting and political warfare were jointly controlled by the Foreign Office, the Colonial Office and the colonial governments concerned. Civilian specialists thus determined the contents of psychological warfare material, while colonial governors generally controlled such activity at local level.[78] A still more important explanation for the greater scope of French imperial psychological warfare was the interplay between two colonial conflicts following closely on one another.

In September 1954 the Ecole de Guerre in Paris instituted a psychological warfare course, based on techniques learnt from experience in Indo-China. Since the essential objective of warfare was to impose one's will on the adversary, military practice had to adapt to colonial conflict where success or failure depended on the insurgents' ability to control the local population.[79] Recalling Viet Minh success in the war for Vietnamese hearts and minds, the Algiers command was also quick to organise a distinct psychological warfare unit to combat the FLN's propaganda and its terrorisation of the Muslim population. A *bureau régional d'action psychologique* was established in March 1955. Commonly termed the *bureau psychologique*, this unit was subsumed within the cinquième bureau of the Algiers combined forces command in January 1957. Colonel Goussault, the director of the cinquième bureau appointed by General Salan, shared his commander's intimate knowledge of Viet Minh techniques. Captured at Cao Bang in 1950, he spent four years as a Viet Minh prisoner before applying the lessons he learnt as a POW to psychological warfare in Algeria. Convinced that communism was the underlying threat in North Africa, he was persuaded that Franco-Algerian integration was the only counter-measure. For his part, Salan was determined to convince France's NATO allies that the FLN's rural insurgency drew upon Viet Minh methods. From Algiers on 4 January 1957 he conveyed his historically jumbled views to Admiral Arthur W. Radford, chairman of the US joint chiefs of staff:

> Personally I can tell you that what we are seeing here is the installation of a political regime identical with that of the Viet Minh. The

> analogy is disturbing. It is essentially a Communist type system which tends to infiltrate quickly and contaminate a population which is built around the family and which reveres its traditions and its village. The acts of terrorism which are committed bear the mark of the Reds and are similar to those committed during the period of the Communist regime in Spain.[80]

Clearly, the Indo-China experience informed psychological warfare in Algeria, nourishing the self-confidence of its cinquième bureau protagonists. Henry Descombin, a member of the Oran command's psychological warfare staff between 1958 and 1960, recalled the feeling among his colleagues: 'Because, rightly or wrongly, the cinquième bureau believed it understood modern revolutionary war and how to devise appropriate responses to it – in this case, cancelling out the rebellion and substituting it with pacification – it thus saw itself as the brain of the French army in Algeria.'[81] Certain of its effectiveness, the cinquième bureau continued its psychological warfare activities until it was re-organised on de Gaulle's instructions in March 1959. Thereafter, the army's effort to sway Algerian opinion fell to the more gently named *Section problèmes humaines*.

Ultimately, the 'lessons' of Indo-China were misapplied in Algeria. The unprecedented interest among senior French colonial officers recently returned from the Far East in Viet Minh and Chinese Communist methods of warfare was understandable. So too was their enthusiasm for British resettlement and re-education practices against the Min Yuen insurgency in Malaya. General L-M. Chassin, former air force commander in Indo-China, even wrote the first French-language biography of Mao Tse-tung. But the FLN was never rooted in communist ideology, nor could its external backers, Egypt prominent among them, match China's massive investment in the Viet Minh. Further, the enormous costs involved in the resettlement of rural Algerians far exceeded the relocation programme enacted in Malaya under the Briggs Plan. In November 1957 Lacoste's civil cabinet estimated that expenditure on the permanent resettlement in purpose-built villages of those Algerians evicted from centres of ALN activity might reach 2.5 billion francs in Oran alone. This was based on a figure of 15,000 families relocated across the Oranais. In Constantine, where relocation took place on a far greater scale, the regional authorities anticipated that up to 320,000 people would be relocated by the end of 1958. In some districts, such as the hinterland of Philippeville and Collo, up to half the rural population was to be moved. From frontier districts close to the expanding eastern barrage, the Algiers army staff planned to resettle a further 60,000 Algerians.[82]

In practice, the so-called *centres de regroupement* established from 1955 onwards were primarily a by-product of military operations rather than the vanguard of a systematic programme of social engineering. As more rural Algerians were shunted into these camps their material conditions deteriorated. Inevitably, between 1955 and 1959 the *centres de regroupement* heightened Muslim opposition to military policy.[83] Despite this, the army remained confident that forced relocation of rural populations from rebellion heartlands would deny the rebels logistical support, insulate civilians from the FLN's revolutionary warfare and confirm the benefits of French protection. Villagers anxious to stay put also had a powerful incentive to form self-defence units in order to avoid compulsory resettlement. In March 1958 Colonel Peynaud, head of the Algiers permanent military secretariat, justified the regrouping of the rural population by noting the success achieved at the margins of the Blida plain south of Algiers:

> The mountain populations of the Blida Atlas who, until recently, were at the mercy of outlaws and were constrained to offer them aid and shelter, are today regrouped at the foot of these mountains and are efficiently protected by the security forces. Meanwhile, rebel troops deprived of support which, though enforced by coercion, was no less effective, are constrained to change their deployments, to disperse their [military] effort and to organise their supplies in more difficult circumstances.[84]

In December 1958 Sarell again warned that Indo-China veterans like Goussault and Colonel Charles Lacheroy, the leading protagonist of revolutionary warfare within Algeria, saw analogies between France's major colonial conflicts where few really existed. It made little sense, for example, to employ Viet Minh interrogation methods with civilian internees in an effort to redeem them from FLN influence – a practice exposed in *Le Monde* in January 1958.[85] Elsewhere, the South-East Asian influence was most apparent in the Algiers command's revolutionary warfare practices. Lacheroy established his reputation as a strategic theorist with a series of papers written in 1954 describing Viet Minh manipulation of the Vietnamese population despite nominal French military control of territory. On 19 August 1955 General Guillaume, then chief of general staff, warned his senior colleagues that French misunderstanding of these techniques had been a major contributory factor to defeat in

Indo-China. He concluded that the appreciation and application of revolutionary warfare was now integral to any Cold War conflict, including Algeria. This thinking underpinned the creation of the Jeanne d'Arc specialist officer training school in May 1957. Under the command of Colonel Marcel Bigeard this became the focal point for the protagonists of a total war against the FLN among the professional officer corps in Algeria until de Gaulle dismissed senior staff members at the school, including Bigeard, during 1958–59.

For all its interest in psychological and revolutionary warfare, especially between 1955 and 1959, the Algiers command remained unclear about the distinction between the two. While revolutionary warfare was inseparable from Marxist and Maoist ideology and hinged on guerrilla warfare as a prelude to popular control, psychological warfare was more generic and was sometimes understood as little more than the dissemination of propaganda amongst the Algerian population.[86] By 1959 the two strategies were sometimes treated jointly as facets of 'subversive war' which, as General Jacques Massu conceded in a command directive on 24 February 1959, began from a recognition that neither side could achieve outright military victory. To Massu, the real battle was between the French pacification measures intended to win over the Muslim population and the FLN terror designed to undermine this.[87] This tendency to conflate the ruthlessness of revolutionary war with the military effort to influence Muslim opinion had far-reaching consequences. As we have seen, it encouraged undue comparison between the Viet Minh and the FLN. The ideological coherence and sophisticated strategies of the former were too readily ascribed to the latter, hardening the determination of senior commanders to fight a war with few restrictions. Admittedly, FLN insurgency, its fratricidal war against the MNA and its bloody purges revealed a ruthless singularity of purpose. And the FLN, like its OS forebear, attached greater importance to control over the civilian population than to conquest of territory. But this was imposed by the imbalance between opposing forces. Moreover, French commanders attached excessive importance to psychological warfare, convinced that the Muslim settlements of the Algerian interior were a key battlefield. Yet press and radio propaganda, leaflets and loudspeaker vans were no substitute for tangible socio-economic support and sustained local security. In its pursuit of an intensified war for hearts and minds, by 1957 the cinquième bureau was promoting operations never properly sanctioned in Paris. Thereafter, the commitment to the 'long haul', so important to the supporters of psychological warfare, helped drive a wedge between local army commanders and their political masters back home.[88]

In mid-July 1958 the British War Office sent Lieutenant-Colonel A. J. Wilson, a Camberley staff college specialist in subversive warfare techniques, to observe French operations in Algeria. Wilson, who had already visited the country during 1957, noted a marked improvement in the military situation. But his conversations with leading French officers confirmed the dangerous politicisation of those most committed to outright victory in Algeria. General Marguet, recently promoted to chief of staff within the Algiers command, commented that before 13 May the army's main enemies were 1) Bourguiba; 2) prefects appointed by the Ministry of the Interior; 3) civilian officials within the governor general's office; 4) the *grands colons*; and 5) the FLN. This was not what British military planners wanted to hear.[89]

The SAS were always more successful in winning over Muslim opinion than their colleagues in psychological warfare. FLN targeting of SAS officers underlined the point.[90] Similar to the civil affairs sections within British colonial forces, in East Africa in particular, the SAS were none the less unique in the impact and scope of their work. Based on the four pillars of public health provision, educational support, agricultural aid and rudimentary engineering and housing projects, the work of the SAS provided concrete benefits. Well trained and resourceful, many SAS personnel also favoured land redistribution to improve rural living standards. Harking back to the *bureaux indigènes* and native affairs officers of early French colonialism in North Africa, SAS personnel still had a vital role to play in the last years of empire. Their impact was greatest within those regions most difficult to pacify militarily, such as the Blida plain, the Aurès and Ouarsenis mountains. Within individual *communes de plein exercise* SAS officers often served as patrons for the Muslim population conveying their concerns to the local mayor. This mediation gave rural Algerians an unprecedented stake in local administration, even though it involved no formal 'reform' at all. Practical, unsensational and inexpensive, this model of military administration was much admired by British military and diplomatic specialists.[91]

In the Berber centres in Kabylie, too, the SAS were considered essential. The Berber population had long been considered better educated and more politically conscious than the Arab peasantry. Yet the Berbers of Kabylie remained chronically poor. The relatively high population density in Grand Kabylie added to problems of unemployment and land hunger, increasing Berber family dependency on relatives working in metropolitan France where FLN influence was growing stronger. The army faced an enormous task if it was to sway this population. The French command in Grand Kabylie had established 40 village self-defence (*auto-défense*) units in Kabyle villages by 1957. But it then blockaded all eastern routes into the region in an attempt to induce uncooperative village communities to re-establish contact with the local French administration, even if only to complain at the economic hardship induced by the blockade itself. By March, General Lacome, infantry commander in Kabylie, admitted that he needed an additional 30,000 troops to suppress local Berber dissent.[92] To make matters worse, the FLN conducted terrifying purges against French-educated Berbers within Kabylie which further compromised the success of SAS policies after 1957. Here, it seems the SAS was foredoomed to failure.

From 1957 the SAS attracted considerable interest amongst British officials. Whereas the Foreign Office was chiefly interested in SAS capacity to affect national opinion in Algeria, the Colonial Office and the War Office explored the technical details of SAS work and its local impact.[93] British estimates of the numerical imbalance between French forces and ALN units suggested that, even with a superiority of 14:1, the army could not crush the rebellion. This added to interest in alternative solutions. From Algiers, Sarell concluded that the 600 or so SAS officers deployed across Algeria by the end of 1957 were as important as the rolling programme of local government reform based on the establishment of elected communal authorities with devolved administrative powers. In either case, Muslim contact with the SAS or involvement in communal politics signified a repudiation of the FLN ban on any such co-operation.[94]

In contrast to the high-quality training of SAS personnal, the first wave of reservists and conscripts sent to Algeria in 1956 typically received only a few weeks of preliminary training before embarkation. Induction concentrated on the firing range, the exercise yard and, sometimes, basic classroom explanations of counter-insurgency.[95] The speed with which men were put into uniform and packed off to Algeria alarmed the Armed Forces Minister Max Lejeune. On 13 April he instructed the army's inspector general to conduct frequent visits to military bases to assess whether new recruits were adequately prepared for what awaited them in North Africa. As matters stood, it appeared that on several occasions troops were shipped out without completing the basic training prescribed by the general staff.

Few conscripts were directly involved in the army's offensive against urban terrorism during 1957. The human rights violations that occurred during the battle for Algiers aroused strong reactions in Whitehall, on the floor of the House of Commons and in the British press. But British military and consular observers were struck by two other aspects of these operations. First, comparisons were drawn between French actions and similar, if more low-key, British military policing in Kenya and Cyprus. 'Operation Anvil' conducted in Nairobi during April 1954 and army interrogation of captured EOKA terrorists had obvious parallels with the clampdown in Algeria's cities. A second point of note was the arrogation of civil–military power by General Massu, commander of the elite 10^{e} parachute division, in order to pursue his clean-up of the *casbah*. British officials in Algiers roundly condemned the practice of turning soldiers into policemen, judge and jury without the safeguards of due legal process. Sarell criticised the acceleration of capital trials in Algiers as an act of unprincipled military expediency.[96]

The consul's judgement was particularly astute, thanks in part to his frank discussions with key officers serving under Massu. On 9 August 1957 he sent Selwyn Lloyd details of the army's use of torture as explained by Captain Robert Frequelin, a military intelligence officer of Colonel Bigeard's colonial parachute regiment, the most famous of the elite units reassigned from the *bled* to Algiers. Massu's counter-terrorism was modelled on ruthless operations conducted by this regiment in the Nementcha mountains during the first two months of the rebellion. Frequelen reiterated the soldiers' contempt for the urban terrorist compared to the rural guerrilla whom they had come to respect. He conceded that this, and the need to extract information without delay, could lead to violence, such as the death in custody of FLN commander, M'Hidi Ben Larbi. Again the dangers of conflating civil, judicial and military power emerged from Sarell's report:

> Captain Frequelin said that their operation differed fundamentally from that of the police. When a crime was committed the police objective was to catch the criminal and bring him to justice. The objective of the parachutists was also to catch the criminal, but having caught him they had no interest in bringing him to justice and their whole operation was designed to climb up the chain towards the leaders by extracting from him information: – who had equipped him with his weapon or his bomb, and who had given him his instructions. They had had eight interrogation centres in Algiers each with some five officers conducting interrogations, and outside a party would be standing by ready to go off at a moment's notice to exploit information as and when it was obtained. As remarked above, Captain Frequelin made no attempt to deny that forceful measures of

> interrogation had been used...but he added that in many cases very little force was necessary to obtain the information required. In their interrogation they were only interested in working back to the higher levels...[97]

Sarell concluded that the professional army in Algeria was fast becoming a law unto itself, a fact underlined by Massu's comments in an interview with America's CBS network on 6 August. The General warned 'that for the moment the French Army had a government in Paris which they could support, but that he could not predict whether this would be the case with any succeeding government'.[98]

Beyond the infamous battles against urban terrorism, the British military attachés and Service Ministry personnel invited to visit front-line units during the course of the war invariably submitted positive reports about the quality of French personnel and tactics. But two questions about longer-term French military strategy were persistently raised: could the Muslim population really be won over in the face of FLN terror, and would the army ever prevent the ALN from replenishing its ranks by military means alone? On both counts, the broad conclusion in London was 'no'. Until 1959, even with conscript forces garrisoning huge sectors of territory, professional units generally pursued ALN bands after receiving intelligence regarding their activities rather than conducting sweep operations over entire sectors. This was sometimes unfavourably contrasted with the success of British tracker patrols in Kenya or the jungle clearance operations in Malaya. Even protracted operations, the installation of a garrison or the provision of small arms to co-operative Muslim auxiliaries or self-defence groups could not always prevent the reappearance of the guerrillas. As long as this remained the case, the local population was bound to serve two masters – loyal to the French authorities by day but ready to meet ALN exactions or abide by FLN embargoes by night. Many Algerians were being taxed by the French authorities and the FLN. A village which agreed to raise an *auto-défense* unit equipped with French small arms in order to keep out ALN fighters made itself a target. Its livestock, its crops, its water supply and its most exposed family members were all under threat. In this circumstance, it was far wiser to hedge one's bets whatever the quality of the SAS, the impressiveness of French soldiering or the promises of economic development.[99]

To meet the escalation of the conflict in 1957, the British military attaché's office in Paris seconded an assistant attaché, Lieutenant-Colonel Acworth, to the Algiers consulate. Acworth's first report in

August 1957 was unequivocal. The army command could point to high morale and tactical successes in all directions. But the war remained a strategic stalemate. This was likely to endure for years to come.[100] The appearance of an army increasingly at odds with the Muslim population it claimed to protect emerged more strongly in British observation reports from 1958 onwards. The reverses in French attempts to convert dissident rebel leaders into allies were key to this. As a result of the FLN–MNA conflict, factionalism within the *wilaya* commands and local Arab–Berber tensions, by early 1958 three major rebel bands, each several hundred strong, had changed sides. The former Messalist commanders Mohammed Bellounis and Si Chérif each controlled large sectors of territory in co-operation with French forces. But Bellounis proved unreliable and was killed by French forces on 16 July. This was two months after Belhadj Djilali, perhaps the most important of the MNA dissident leaders, was murdered by his own men in the mountainous Ouarsenis region, his decapitated body left symbolically with a tricolour thrust into the neck.[101] Despite the failed co-option of rebel bands, the army still employed thousands of Algerian Muslims either as regular soldiers, *harki* auxiliaries or in rural self-protection squads organised into *groupes mobiles de sécurité* or *auto-défense* teams. British recognition of the scale of this local contribution was offset by awareness that the loyal Muslim ex-servicemen and officials that formed the backbone of these paramilitary formations faced mounting personal danger.[102] This became clearer in the final years of the rebellion before many suffered dreadful retribution in 1962.

During the summer of 1958 the military attachés in Paris and Algiers also reported much strengthened ALN units operating from Tunisia, rejecting the official French figures of under 5,000 and suggesting that up to 20,000 fighters were involved. The ALN supply network just across the Tunisian frontier, collectively termed its eastern base (*base de l'est*), was by then the principal focus of French operations. A newly constructed and heavily defended Algeria–Tunisia frontier barrier, the Morice line, plus a similar though less extensive frontier barrage along the western border with Morocco, impeded arms supplies and the movement of ALN companies back and forth.[103] This strategy of layered frontier fortification and pursuit operations mounted as soon as incursions were detected was made possible by the Minister of National Defence, André Morice's transfer of border protection tasks to full military control in the autumn of 1957. Although the Algiers residency retained ultimate responsibility for customs controls, border checks and frontier surveillance, the establishment of military no-go areas along the frontiers gave the Constantine and Oran army commands control over any individuals or groups found within these zones. This allowed unfettered pursuit of any rebels caught entering Algeria illegally and signalled a marked increase in the relocation of village populations from eastern Constantine.[104] ALN losses increased dramatically as the rebels tried to maintain the flow of men and materials to the interior *wilaya* commands. Practically and symbolically, from 1958 onwards victory in the 'battle of the frontiers' became a key indicator of the French capacity to defeat the rebellion outright. In October 1958 the Algiers command made the closure of the frontiers a higher priority than the destruction of the ALN's administrative organisation within Algeria itself.[105]

*

After 1954 Conservative Cabinets in Britain, Whitehall Africanists, defence analysts and intelligence specialists, British observers, both civilian and military, in France and Algeria, and British journalists and media commentators were generally agreed on one point: French efforts to turn the tide of rebellion in Algeria were unlikely to succeed. French integrationist thinking was intrinsically alien to British conceptions of empire, increasingly at variance with the trend towards decolonisation from Africa and never unequivocally adopted as official French governmental policy in Algeria anyway. Mounting evidence of insubordination and local authoritarianism within the civil–military apparatus of colonial government in Algiers was deeply worrying to the British government; its implications for French policy in Algeria and the stability of governance in France more generally causing growing concern after 1956. And the absence of any prospect of meaningful dialogue with the leaders of the rebellion as French efforts to contain the war focused upon Algeria's land frontiers in 1957–58 indicated that no short-term end to the conflict was in sight. This intensification of the frontier war had profound international consequences. It damaged French relations with the Moroccan government and completely undermined those with Bourguiba's Tunisia. In the process, Britain and the US became more directly affected by the diplomatic fall-out of the Algerian war. The gradual internationalisation of the conflict is discussed in detail in chapter 5. But before examining the broad international ramifications of colonial disorder in the Maghreb, it seems sensible to consider the links between France's North African crisis and Anglo-French actions in the Suez crisis.

4

1956: the Algerian War Extended and the Suez Intervention

As 1956 began, French policy towards Algeria was in limbo pending the imminent general election and the widely anticipated victory of a centre-left Republican Front coalition of Socialists, *Mendésiste* Radicals, Mitterrand's UDSR and the Gaullist followers of Jacques Chaban-Delmas' Social Republicans.[1] British and American diplomatic observers recognised that Edgar Faure's caretaker administration would avoid major policy statements. According to Ambassador Jebb, the government considered it 'electorally dangerous' to send additional troops to Algeria. During the initial round of campaigning Faure promised voters that 'not another man would be sent'. In response, Governor Soustelle gave an interview to *France-Presse* on 22 December 1955 in which he lambasted Faure's administration for failing to deliver promised reinforcements or viable reforms.[2] Throughout the election campaign, the government was further pilloried for its attempted cover-up of the murder of an Algerian prisoner, shot in cold blood by an Algiers gendarme before the cameras of America's Fox-Movietone news. The newsreel was not shown in France, but it was widely broadcast in North America and was even replayed at the UN General Assembly in a debate over inscription of the Algerian problem. The Ministry of the Interior attempted to prosecute the US network, but, Georges Chassagne, the photographer involved, discredited the accusation that he had urged the policeman to commit the crime once stills of the killing were published in *L'Express* and *Life* magazine.[3]

Algeria was becoming the best stick with which opposition leaders could thrash a sitting administration. Mendès France did so with aplomb, suggesting that Faure's successor should leave the Hôtel Matignon and reside in Algiers to ensure that the government carried through its policy pledges.[4] Meanwhile, the outlook in Algeria deteriorated further. Chief of Army Staff General André Zeller was considering resignation over shortages of military manpower in North Africa.[5] Yet by 1 January 1956 the French army had 324,534 soldiers deployed across French North Africa: 180,451 in Algeria, 104,692 in Morocco and 39,391 in Tunisia.[6] New year bombings in Bône and Tizi-Ouzou confirmed the escalation of FLN terrorism. Following a boycott by Muslim deputies of the second Algerian Assembly organised by Dr Mohammed Bendjelloul in late September 1955, three months later Ferhat Abbas resigned his seat altogether. His UDMA supporters and other Algerian politicians followed suit, withdrawing from the Assembly's second college and regional and town councils in protest at the government's failure to deliver constitutional reform.[7] Faure had long since reached the limit of his capacity to secure cross-party support for imperial change in order to push through the Grandval Plan for Morocco. As several scholars have noted, parliamentary acquiescence in Faure's decisive acceleration of Moroccan and Tunisian reform carried with it an unspoken assumption to redouble the French effort to keep Algeria. Faure's one bold step was to dissolve the National Assembly for the first time in almost eight years after losing a parliamentary vote of confidence on 29 November 1955.[8]

The expectation that a new government would have to face up to Algerian reform, the Fox-Movietone scandal and the crude, sometimes racialist, electioneering of Pierre Poujade's right-wing extremists, kept the Algerian war in the foreground of the election campaign. Built on a *petit bourgeois* constituency of shopkeepers and artisans, the Poujadist movement, organised into the *Union de Défense des Commerçants et des Artisans,* attracted widespread support amongst Algerian *colons* and held its first conference in Algiers in November 1954 – the month the war began. The 51 Poujadist deputies elected in January 1956 took the appellation *Union et Fraternité Française* and immediately figured amongst the most reactionary and vocal supporters of *Algérie française*. Poujade even dispatched two of his deputies to Algiers to mobilise the movement's local organisation in readiness for Guy Mollet's visit to the capital in February.[9] With Paris preoccupied by the elections, and Poujadist street politics proclaiming the settler cause, at the turn of the year Governor Soustelle had a rare opportunity to seize the initiative. A government commission was at work on a report into Algerian administrative reform and was expected to pronounce on Soustelle's well-known preference for an integrationist policy. In what many saw as an act of spiteful revenge against his detractors, Faure planned to pass on its findings to his successor.[10]

As a result, the Foreign Office and the State Department were anxious to establish the most probable French reforms should either Pierre Mendès France or the Socialist leader, Guy Mollet, become premier of a Republican Front Cabinet. If, as expected, these politicians finally abandoned the quest for political and economic integration between France and Algeria, opting instead for some form of federal solution, then conflict with Soustelle, Algeria's influential city mayors and their *colon* backers seemed likely. Jebb had suggested that, under the impetus of Alain Savary in particular, the SFIO was 'feeling its way' towards federal reforms for Algeria and black Africa. But Socialist and Mendésiste reforms were necessarily imprecise since their implementation depended upon the complexion of the Chamber of Deputies. R. C. Blackham, first secretary in the Foreign Office African department caught the mood of his colleagues: 'It is nothing short of disastrous that the vital question of future policy in Algeria should become the shuttlecock in the party political game; and the party with the most progressive ideas on the question (i. e. the Socialists) seem to have least conception of the practical difficulties.'[11] In the month before his removal from office in February 1956, Soustelle amplified his support for integration, increasing the political temperature among the Algiers settler community. In early January a *Mendèsiste* Deputy addressing a political meeting in the capital had to be rescued from a settler mob by the police. Days later the mayoral federations of the departments of Algiers, Constantine and Oran insisted that the new government should rule out any dialogue with Algerian nationalists while the rebellion persisted. The tired rhetoric of 'order before reform', the hopeless quest for 'moderate' interlocuteurs willing to accept limited Algerian autonomy, and parliamentary obstruction of an enabling law to reorganise Algerian local and national elections all continued throughout 1956.[12]

With these multiple disappointments yet to emerge, the turn-out at the polls in France on 2 January was the highest recorded in the Fourth Republic. The outcome heralded a transformation in the scale of the Algerian war. The election results were devastating to two major political groups. The MRP, for so long the arbitral party in French colonial policy, fell back decisively, whilst the Gaullist vote collapsed from over 4 million in the 1951 election to less than 850,000 in 1956. This left the Socialist Party holding the balance of power. Mendès France's Radical Party supporters made the most dramatic electoral gains, but their leader was ill at ease with Socialist direction of the Republican Front. In May Mendès resigned from the Cabinet, unimpressed by the government's financial policy and disconcerted by Mollet's Algerian strategy.[13]

The Mollet Government and Algeria

Recalling Mendès France's famous 1953 dictum that 'governing means choosing', Robert Frank has criticised the Mollet government for its naive attempt to combine ambitious social spending, further European integration and an expanded war effort in Algeria.[14] Certainly, a defining feature of Mollet's administration was the apparent ease with which it contracted new commitments. In the North African context, this is remembered in two respects above all: first, in the hasty reversal of policy over Algeria following Mollet's hostile reception in Algiers and, secondly, in the enthusiastic embrace of collusion with Israel in preparation for the Suez expedition. The first two months of the Mollet government in February–March 1956 marked a watershed in the Algerian war, arguably of greater importance on the ground than de Gaulle's return to power in May 1958 and the resurgence of military insubordination from 1960 onwards. Mollet's government adopted a colonialist agenda after the premier's uncomfortable brush with the *colon* protesters who surged through the CRS cordon around the *Monument aux morts* in central Algiers on 6 February. Ostensibly committed to political reform for Algeria, in fact the new government was determined to crush the FLN by military means. This involved a second departure: to hasten victory the French army in Algeria was to be allowed the use of conscript forces. Within weeks of being elected, partly on the promise of progressive reform and negotiation in Algeria, the Mollet coalition changed its spots entirely.[15] By March, the administration supported the prosecution of all-out war as a prelude to any meaningful talks with Algerian nationalists. Mollet's Algerian policy was dominated by the effort to come to terms with this initial *volte-face*. The French role in the Suez crisis must be seen in this light.[16]

It bears repeated emphasis that the new government enacted policies in Algeria diametrically opposed to the pre-election plans of the governing Socialist Party, the handful of left-leaning Gaullists and their pro-*Mendèsiste* Radical Party allies in the 'Republican Front' coalition. In 1947, the last time the Socialists had directed a coalition, Paul Ramadier's government had tried to pursue a policy of restoring order to Indo-China before negotiating with representative Vietnamese politicians, only to find its good intentions thrown off course by a deteriorating military situation.[17] So there was a certain *déjà vu* as Mollet's government ran into the sand in Algeria. Mollet himself had a pedigree as a liberal colonial reformer and an Anglophile. As a prisoner of war in Germany he wrote a textbook on English grammar. This was published by Hachette soon after Mollet became secretary-general of the Socialist Party in which capacity he criticised the expanding war effort pursued in Indo-China by the Blum and Ramadier governments in late 1946 and 1947. Like many leaders of the non-Communist left, Mollet insisted that French colonial control was theoretically justifiable only in so far as it advanced the living standards and political freedoms of the colonised.[18] In practice, Mollet, like Blum and Ramadier before him, found it harder to enact bold reform in office than to espouse it in opposition. Many SFIO members, notably the Young Socialists led by Michel Rocard, were appalled at the leadership's Algerian policy. And after 1958 the French left exploited its newfound support for Algerian self-rule and regular protests against reactionary OAS violence to draw a veil over Socialist and Communist involvement in the crucial extension of the war in 1956. But some blue-collar supporters of both the SFIO and the PCF showed contempt for Algerian nationalism, sometimes tinged with racial antagonism to North African immigrant workers in France.[19] Rank-and-file suspicion of Algerian nationalism *per se* was reinforced by the sentiment among more seasoned left-wing observers of Algerian politics that Messali Hadj and his *Mouvement National Algérien* alone represented the authentic voice of Algerian nationalism. Yet the PCF leadership stuck to Maurice Thorez's argument, first articulated in 1939, that Algeria was a 'nation in formation' in which the settler population had a legitimate role. To many Communists, in 1956 the FLN was an upstart which spurned the international politics of East and West and the doctrinaire Marxism of class struggle. This view was reinforced by the gathering internecine violence between rival MNA and FLN supporters among the Algerian population in France. This erupted into outright civil war in the autumn. FLN indulgence towards Islamic custom further alienated Socialists in particular, for whom *laïcité* and secular modernisation were cherished values. This added weight to Mollet's determination to prosecute the war more effectively.[20]

Mollet's extension of conscription to cover service in Algeria indicated that the key lesson derived from the Indo-China war was not that generous reform was essential but, on the contrary, that the regular French army should not be abandoned once more by an indifferent political elite in Paris. 1956 thus transformed the French experience of the Algerian conflict from colonial rebellion to major war effort. At its height, fewer than 70,000 metropolitan Frenchmen were fighting in the Indo-China war. Within a year of the announcement of conscription, French force levels in North Africa approached 500,000.[21] The primordial requirement for a negotiated solution in Algeria was subsumed within a new phase of ambitious offensive planning, political re-education and more brutal counter-insurgency. Far from diluting the dirty war practices of the professional shock troops, the arrival of conscripts brought a new opportunity to implement the revolutionary warfare techniques learned by the officers of the Indo-China expeditionary force.[22]

British reaction to the parliamentary vote which conceded Mollet's government 'Special Powers' to prosecute the war was largely determined by the broad cross-party support for the measure in France.[23] Even the PCF voted in favour of the Special Powers on 12 March. This was a remarkable turnaround for the Communists, who had consistently opposed the Indo-China war and argued for speedy withdrawal from Morocco and Tunisia. Léon Feix, the PCF executive member responsible for North African affairs, had welcomed the fall of Mendès France in February 1955, claiming that the administration was insufficiently committed to negotiated reform. The Algerian Communist Party (PCA) had taken the same line before it was again banned by the Algiers authorities along with its associated worker and student 'front' organisations in late April 1956.[24] The PCF's long years of political isolation since the collapse of tripartism in 1947 engendered an unusual indulgence towards Mollet's plans for Algeria. Although the premier did not respond warmly to Communist approaches, PCF support for Mollet was a by-product of the Party's attempt to recreate a Popular Front-style 'United Front' which would bring the PCF into coalition alongside the Socialists. The abrupt reversal of Communist policy towards colonial war also revealed a deeper truth: within French domestic politics the ramifications of the Algerian war could give rise to unusual political alignments.[25] Despite widespread grassroots opposition to the introduction of the Special Powers, before the Suez crisis erupted the PCF leadership defended its support for the measure and disavowed Party members who supported protests by reservists and conscripts reluctant to serve in Algeria. Ironically, the government utilised the Special Powers legislation to curb press freedoms, barring publication of the Communist daily *L'Humanité* on 11 May. At the PCF's annual congress weeks later Maurice Thorez still insisted that the quest for a United Front was paramount.[26]

Whatever the official PCF line, there was sufficient unrest in France among those most directly affected by the government's extension of the Algerian conflict – the 1953 class reservists (*Rappelés*) recalled for service and the conscripts (*Appelés*) assigned to Algeria – to suggest that the Assembly's extension of the war antagonised a swathe of opinion across the French left.[27] From September 1955 onwards, sporadic protests occurred in Paris, Rouen, Limoges, Lyons and other marshalling centres; troops and airmen refusing to board the boat trains to their ports of embarkation. Once the Special Powers legislation was applied from March 1956 these protests widened, attracting considerable civilian support for the *Mouvement des Rappelés et Appelés*.[28]

Fragile Anglo-French Unity

Though colonial affairs still weighed heavily in British and French Cabinet discussions in 1956, outside black Africa – about which regular discussions between Colonial Ministry officials and academic specialists on both sides of the Channel were well established – there was little community of interest between the two governments.[29] Albeit tentatively, this was beginning to change. On the initiative of Selwyn Lloyd, from spring 1956 onwards the Foreign Office, the Quai d'Orsay and the Colonial Offices in both countries liaised more closely over communist penetration in colonial Africa. On 21 April Lloyd alerted the French, Belgian and Portuguese governments to Foreign Office worries about the proliferation of Communist Front organisations, such as the World Federation of Trade Unions, the World Peace Council and the International Union of Students, within black Africa. More seriously, he stressed the increasing number of African specialists within Soviet governmental agencies in Moscow and abroad.[30] Although sub-Saharan Africa was the main focus of British concern, Robert Lacoste's crackdown in April and May against the PCA, its affiliated front organisations and its newspaper concentrated the minds of Foreign Office Africanists on Algeria for several weeks prior to the Suez crisis.[31] The North African bureau of the Quai d'Orsay's Africa–Levant directorate welcomed this. It provided selected governments with extracts of Ministry of the Interior reports and Algiers military intelligence indicating communist infiltration of the FLN. In November 1955, for example, the bureau sent Jean Chauvel documents relating three instances of FLN–PCA collusion in Algiers, Oran and the Aurès, telling him to make best use of this material with his host government.[32] This African dimension was central to British and French efforts to persuade the US administration of the connection between Nasserism and communism in the months ahead.

Regardless of these increasing Anglo-French contacts, before the Suez crisis broke in July, Anthony Eden's ministers rarely debated imperial strategy as a whole, instead tackling individual colonial problems as and when the need arose. Sir Evelyn Shuckburgh, Foreign Office Under-Secretary for Middle East affairs, complained about Eden's refusal to address long-term strategic planning in the Middle East. Shuckburgh saw in Eden's absorption in policy minutiae a short-termism which suggested a deeper lack of clarity and vision.[33] Still Chancellor of the Exchequer and preoccupied by his battle to secure major defence cuts, Harold Macmillan also thought the Cabinet too absorbed in immediate problems. He caught the tone of Cabinet discussions over colonial difficulties in his diary. On 28 June he recorded the day's Cabinet meeting: 'terrible agenda – Cyprus, Malta, Libya, Egypt – all trouble and mostly blackmail.' On 5 July he lamented that a three-hour Cabinet session had 'dart[ed] about from home to abroad', noting that 'every question gets more difficult. Cyprus, Ceylon, Middle East . . . etc.'[34]

Anglo-French collusion with Israel during the Suez crisis obviously made a comprehensive Middle East settlement much harder to achieve. But the key British decision to undermine Nasser antedated the nationalisation of the Suez Canal Company and resulted from the failure of the Anglo-American 'Project *Alpha*' to broker a definitive Egyptian-Israeli settlement. As is well known, matters came to a head on 1 March with King Hussein's dismissal of Lieutenant-General Sir John Glubb as head of Jordan's Arab Legion, a measure that Eden and Lloyd attributed to malign Egyptian influence.[35] Still, the British decisions to confront Nasser, to oust Syria's pro-Egyptian government and to reconstruct Hashemite leadership of the Middle East by supporting Iraq's regional primacy drew upon more long-standing regional strategic planning. By 1956 the British were the principal backers of the one multilateral anti-Soviet alliance within the Middle East – the Baghdad Pact, concluded between February and October 1955. Although US representatives sat on the Pact's military planning committee, with no prospect of a definitive Israeli–Arab territorial agreement, the chances of eventual American adherence to the Pact evaporated. The 'Northern tier' of Baghdad Pact states, based on a British-sponsored alliance of Turkey, Iraq, Pakistan and Iran, was not likely to be further consolidated.[36] To make matters worse, British intervention against Nasser was bound to harden opposition to the Baghdad Pact, and to British Middle Eastern policy more generally, among the leaders of the non-aligned states at the UN, Nehru's India above all.[37]

In its existing form, the effectiveness of the Pact hinged on Britain's capacity to build up Pakistan's military and air power. This was problematic. Field Marshal Claude Auchinleck warned the Minister of Defence, Walter Monckton, of this in March 1956:

> The Baghdad Pact which is designed to secure the Middle East is at present like a bridge which has two abutments but nothing in

> between. The abutments are Turkey and Pakistan, both reasonably strong and firm and willing to help. Between them, so far there is nothing but a gap, caused by the political instability and inherent military weakness of Iran and Iraq ...[38]

If Nasser humiliated Britain the Baghdad Pact would inevitably be damaged, and its chief Arab opponents, Egypt and Syria, correspondingly strengthened. The strategic gap between Turkey in the west and Pakistan in the east would become a chasm.[39] Until March 1956 material support for Israel and abiding hostility to the Baghdad Pact remained the most salient features of French Middle Eastern policy.[40] Much to Eden's irritation, Foreign Office efforts to diminish French opposition to the Pact in its present form achieved nothing.[41] The Quai d'Orsay preferred a Middle East Colombo Plan offering financial backing and development aid as opposed to a full-blown military alliance which hardened Soviet opposition to western policies and added to Nasser's credibility as the authentic voice of Arabism. The existence of the Baghdad Pact also increased the temptations for Moscow and Cairo to dabble in the affairs of French North Africa in order to destabilise western strategic interests wherever possible. Moreover, French officials resented persistent criticism of their North African policies by Nuri al-Sa'id's Iraq, Britain's Baghdad Pact stalwart.[42]

The concomitant French resentment over Egyptian support for the FLN could not provide a basis for co-operation with Britain whilst British diplomats still worked to reconcile the Cairo government to Project *Alpha* and the Baghdad Pact. But the collapse of *Alpha*, rising British hostility to Nasser and the closer ties with the Israeli regime that this encouraged, made Britain more receptive to the French. The coincidence of the French vote over the Special Powers and the decisive reorientation of British Middle Eastern policy against Egypt and Syria was of lasting importance. The National Assembly's decision to widen the war in Algeria gave added import to the effort to cut the external sources of FLN supply just as British policy, too, focused on Cairo as the key to the survival of Britain's regional power. Whether understood primarily as a challenge over control of Suez, over western interests in the Middle East more generally or over France's determination to keep French North Africa from the clutches of pan-Arab Orientalism, Nasser's actions between July and September 1956 drove Britain and France together. On 27 July Eden and the French Foreign Minister, Christian Pineau, both informed Washington that the use of force against Egypt might become necessary. Lloyd and Pineau concerted their efforts to 'frighten'

Dulles's envoy, Under-Secretary Robert Murphy, into reporting that Britain and France could not be restrained.[43]

The British and French foreign intelligence services, MI6 and the *Service de Documentation Extérieure et de Contre-espionnage* (SDECE), consolidated links with the Israeli security forces from whom they obtained precise information regarding Egyptian deployments. The SDECE was not inclined to be cautious. For years it had been gathering intelligence about support for Maghreb nationalists among the non-aligned states at the UN, and using a slush fund to dissuade certain delegates from voting for inscription of North African questions within the General Assembly. Within Algeria, the SDECE counter-intelligence chief, Lieutenant-Colonel Germain, and the former Guèlma sub-prefect André Achiary, directed plans to 'neutralise' key members of the FLN leadership.[44] SDECE operatives and those of the French internal intelligence service, the *Direction de la Surveillance du Territoire* (DST), were immersed in clandestine operations against the Egyptians – including bugging and thefts of documents from Egypt's Paris Embassy and surveillance of a military attaché, Tharwat Okacha – as part of the intelligence war against FLN fundraising inside and outside France. The Minister of National Defence, Maurice Bourgès-Maunoury, Army Minister Max Lejeune and General Paul Ely's chiefs of staff also regarded Israel as a natural ally. On 7 August Bourgès led French military discussions with Shimon Peres, then director-general of Israel's Ministry of Defence, in which the principle of joint military collaboration against Egypt was sealed by the provision of 48 Mystère IV fighters to Israel.[45]

Meanwhile, Macmillan and the Lord President, Lord Salisbury, two of the leading members of the Egypt (Suez) committee, established by the full Cabinet to handle the Canal crisis, were moving in parallel to the Bourgès group. On 3 August Macmillan convened a meeting at 11 Downing Street with Gladwyn Jebb and other Foreign Office officials to agree a statement of Anglo-French military objectives. In this discussion the possibility of eventual French alignment with the Baghdad Pact was raised once France extricated itself from Algeria.[46] Macmillan utilised Jebb's analysis of France's Middle Eastern concerns to press the case for joint operations at the Egypt committee meeting on 7 August. Though he revised his opinion after the events, at the time Jebb favoured joint military intervention in order to conserve western interests.[47] Macmillan, the leading 'hawk' within the civil–military planning of the Suez campaign, acted as the cipher for Chief of Imperial General Staff, General Sir Gerald Templer, and General Sir Hugh Stockwell, principal architect of the revised operational plan put to the Egypt committee on 8

August. Sensitive to the service chiefs' concerns, Macmillan insisted that preliminary agreement with France and Israel over operations against Egypt was a strategic imperative.[48] While the Egypt committee was considering the revised *Musketeer* plan, Admiral Pierre Barjot, who would command the French forces assigned to the operation, and Admiral Nomy, representing Ely's general staff, were nearby in London. The two Admirals were anxious about the slowness of British preparations and pressed for more detailed joint planning. Ironically, neither was immediately informed of the *Musketeer* revisions for fear of leakage in France.[49]

This rocky start to joint operations was compounded by French coolness towards Stockwell and abiding doubts about the appointment of British supreme commanders to which the French force commanders – Rear-Admiral Lancelot, Major-General André Beaufre and Brigadier-General Raymond Brohon – served as deputies. As deputy commander-in-chief, Barjot was determined to push his own ideas regarding the direction of the initial operations. But he liaised effectively with the overall task force commander, General Sir Charles Keightley. This was a testament to the skill of the army commander, Major-General Beaufre, in many respects the brains behind proposals ostensibly proposed by Barjot. The admiral himself was animated by French intelligence indicating further Soviet arms deliveries to Egypt. He estimated that, if left unchecked, Egypt would pose a far more serious military threat by the spring of 1957. His concern chimed perfectly with French anxieties over the heightened tempo of external arms supply to the FLN.[50]

Jebb confided happily to Macmillan that French toughness stemmed from the government's realisation of the implications of military failure, a remark which ignored the divisions over Egyptian policy within Mollet's Cabinet and the Socialist Party as a whole.[51] Labour's former Minister of War, John Strachey, warned on 3 September that the utmost British error would be to permit French forces to use Britain's Cyprus or Malta bases prior to an attack on Egypt, thus immersing Britain in a desperate French bid to undermine legitimate Arab support for Algerian independence.[52] This was precisely what happened, the Egypt committee having agreed on 23 August that ships of the French expeditionary force should set out from Marseilles as if making for Algiers, when in fact destined for Cyprus. (In fact, this concentration of land and naval forces on Cyprus was later ruled out.) That same day the French air staff created the first combined air group made up of two fighter squadrons, a reconnaissance squadron and 40 transport aircraft, to be deployed to two Cyprus airbases.[53] Only Walter Monckton, soon to register his opposition by moving from the Ministry of Defence to the less contentious post of

Paymaster General, questioned the Egypt committee's determination to use force against Nasser.[54] A day after Strachey's warning, as expected, Nasser rejected the proposals of the Canal users conference in London to place the operation of the Suez Canal under the authority of an international board. The subsequent attempt to establish a Suez Canal Users Association as a means to dilute Egyptian control was no more successful, nor did the British or French governments expect it to be.

Eisenhower's administration recognised the North African concerns which underpinned France's belligerence. During the spring, the French service attachés in Washington submitted new purchase requests for American equipment for use in Algeria, including up to 300 light aircraft.[55] Dulles found Pineau agitated by the issue of foreign arms supplies to the FLN during their first exchanges at a SEATO meeting in Karachi on 7 March. This was a tense encounter. Neither man came away with a high opinion of the other. In addition, Lloyd was antagonised by Pineau's hostility to the Baghdad Pact. After Britain's unstinting support for the French presence in North Africa it was a poor reward to find French opposition to the Pact as uncompromising as Nasser's criticism of it.[56] Dulles was at this stage preparing to isolate Nasser by dragging out negotiations over the financing of the Aswan Dam and withholding aid and arms export licences to the Cairo government whilst increasing US material provision to Egypt's pro-western neighbours.[57] A clash with France over its Algerian fixation was unlikely in the short term at least.

On 6 June Lewis Clark warned from Algiers that Lacoste was now calling the shots in Algerian policy, his support for the settler position meeting little opposition within Mollet's fractious Cabinet.[58] State Department suspicions of French policy only increased once the Suez crisis broke. The FLN's spokesman in New York, Hussein Aït Ahmed, played on this, pointing out that selfish concern with Algeria explained French eagerness to march on Cairo. In early August, Lacoste used the tension caused by the Suez crisis to postpone the further democratisation of Algerian local government.[59] Washington received a string of reports confirming that Lacoste's civilian staff and the French military command were convinced that defeat of Nasser held the key to victory in Algeria. Even Jacques Chevallier, the moderate mayor of Algiers who remained the principal source of US political information in Algiers, shared this view.[60] The Interior Ministry's publication of administrative reforms for Algeria in mid-September 1956 suggested that the government was losing faith in Lacoste's ability to direct policy effectively.

So, too, did the ongoing series of secret French diplomatic contacts with members of the FLN's external leadership. These peaked in Rome on

2–5 September when Mollet's close colleague, the SFIO's interim secretary-general, Pierre Commin, resumed discussions with FLN executive members, including Mohammed Yazid and Mohammed Khider. Commin built on earlier clandestine meetings held in Belgrade in late July. In the light of Lacoste's intransigence, this was encouraging. But there was little reason to expect a more conciliatory FLN attitude towards any pre-ceasefire negotiations, particularly as its executive in Cairo was uneasy about the wisdom of talks held exclusively with SFIO representatives. Furthermore, the more moderate voices among the FLN's external leadership were much weakened after the reorganisation of the FLN's executive structure at a secret congress held in Algeria's Soumman Valley in August. In practice, the negotiation process was shaped by the course of the Suez crisis, the Belgrade talks having been undermined by Nasser's announcement of nationalisation on 26 July.[61] Two overwhelming obstacles to political reform remained. First, the widespread disorder across Algeria prevented either a national election campaign or a rolling programme of local elections. Second, promises of electoral reform and Algerian autonomy were rejected out of hand by the FLN. French hopes that Muslim voters would turn out to endorse limited autonomy measures were soon disappointed.[62]

The marginal success of administrative reform and the army's inability to defeat the FLN completely fed the Mollet government's interest in an external solution to the Algerian impasse. As Georgette Elgey and Charles-Robert Ageron have recently reiterated, all the ministers most closely involved in foreign policy formulation, strategic planning and intelligence-gathering shared the Algerian fixation. Military and secret intelligence reportage linking FLN operations to Cairo since November 1954, the introduction of conscripts to Algeria and Pineau's personal frustration at being manipulated by Nasser produced an unblinking resolve to tackle Egypt head-on. The fledgling Moroccan and Tunisian regimes shared an interest in the containment of the Algerian rebellion and both dreaded any consolidation of Nasserite influence within Algeria. But their warnings that Egypt required sensitive handling in order to prevent a dangerous upsurge in anti-French sentiment across the Maghreb evoked no response in Paris.[63] In mid-April Mohammed V and Moroccan government representatives had held preliminary discussions in Madrid and Seville with FLN leaders. But the mediation offers that emanated from Rabat during the spring and summer of 1956 were never endorsed by Mollet's Cabinet. Having just extended the war, the government would not curtail operations at the request of North African intermediaries in whom it placed little trust. By contrast, the Foreign

Office was eager for Moroccan and Tunisian mediation to proceed, not least because the Algerian conflict prevented the normalisation of relations with the governments in Rabat and Tunis. British warnings that the new regimes might be swept away on a tide of radical Arab nationalism were never likely to alter French policy because closer Moroccan or Tunisian involvement in an Algerian settlement was bound to complicate the effort to safeguard French base rights and military privileges in both countries. Without an assured military presence in the former protectorates the French army in Algeria would be more seriously exposed to cross-border attacks. So the withdrawal of forces from Morocco and Tunisia could not form part of a mediation bargain.[64]

The conscription commitment in Algeria made strong action against Egypt inevitable.[65] The implementation of 'Plan Valmy' – the reinforcement of Algeria with reservists and conscripts – was not expected to yield immediate military gains. As we have seen, these additional troops received minimal weapons training or familiarisation with counter-insurgency techniques before leaving France for Algeria. A further scheme, 'Plan Bugeaud', was devised by the army's operations section to prepare the new arrivals for active service in the field. Inevitably, this took time. Hence, in spite of the massive reinforcement of the French army in Algeria during the spring and early summer of 1956, the Algiers command could not immediately pursue an all-out offensive against the FLN. The Suez operations were planned in this interval period.[66] The arrest of four key FLN leaders, including Ahmed Ben Bella, and an FLN information officer, en route by plane from Rabat to Tunis on 22 October, and the seizure of the steamer *Athos* six days earlier, added to the government's conviction that action against Egypt could break the log-jam in Algiers. The French security services insisted that 12 kg of FLN executive documents allegedly found aboard the FLN leaders' plane confirmed Egypt's role in directing the Algerian rebellion.[67] By 25 October the French press in Algiers was full of allegations supposedly based on the captured documents. According to these reports, the FLN relied on Egyptian arms deliveries, the implication being that if this supply line were cut, the ALN would be unable to sustain long-term operations. It was further alleged that the Moroccan government was complicit in an ALN plan to establish an Algerian Republic-in-exile prior to an assault on the western Algerian city of Tlemcen.[68] It emerged later that the *Athos* was carrying weapons from Egypt, principally small arms and machine guns, for use by the FLN. Many of these guns were British Second World War surplus stores previously sold to the Egyptian, and other Middle Eastern, governments.[69]

Whatever the expediency of detaining the FLN leaders, details of the arrests revealed worrying limitations on French government authority in Algiers. Mollet had supposedly granted the FLN leaders safe conduct across Algerian air space in order to let the Moroccan and Tunisian governments pursue their efforts as intermediaries. Air Marshal Frandon, Armée de l'Air commander in Algiers, ordered the French pilot of the FLN plane to divert to Algiers without clear government authority to do so. Max Lejeune, the Secretary of State for the armed forces in Algeria and perhaps the most vocal Socialist advocate of an Egyptian solution to the Algerian crisis, approved the measure. So, too, according to US records, did Bourgès-Maunoury, the Minister of National Defence. But neither Mollet nor the full Cabinet did so until it was presented to them as a *fait accompli*.[70] Mollet's acquiescence in the illegal arrests on the grounds that the FLN executive would be significantly weakened was also misguided. The detention of Ben Bella and his colleagues and their subsequent incarceration in the Paris prison de la Santé actually facilitated the emergence of a more hardline ALN strategy to which Ben Bella and Mohammed Boudiaf had been opposed. The temporary eclipse of the external directorate only consolidated the influence of the FLN's internal leadership within the five-member *Comité de Coordination et d'Exécution* (CCE) established at the Soummam congress. According to Jacques Chevallier, who maintained unofficial contacts with the FLN from Algiers, the military leaders Belkacem Krim, Ramdane Abbane and Omar Ouamrane were now the three pre-eminent individuals within the movement.[71]

Moreover, the seizure of the aircraft was an affront to Moroccan sovereign rights. Although French-registered, the aeroplane belonged to the Moroccan state aircraft company and had been chartered by the Sultan, who insisted that it fell under his royal protection.[72] This Moroccan dimension was vital. In conversation with Alain Savary, the much-respected Secretary of State for Moroccan and Tunisian affairs, on 3 October Foreign Minister Ahmed Balafrej reiterated Morocco's hostility to Soviet influence in Egypt and Nasser's claim to leadership of the Arab world. But while the Algerian rebellion continued, popular support for Nasser across the Maghreb and the risk of military insubordination in the Royal Moroccan Army could only increase.[73] In the aftermath of the arrests crisis, 30 European settlers in Meknès were massacred and Savary, who opposed the arrests, felt compelled to resign. According to his *chef de cabinet*, Chazelle, the scheme to detain the FLN flight was arranged by the DST and the Algiers military authorities in consultation with Lacoste. Chazelle stated that Mollet originally opposed the arrests, was staggered when they occurred, but warmed to the idea when the French public reaction proved so favourable. This stifled the chances of Moroccan and Tunisian involvement in a negotiated Algerian settlement just weeks before the Suez expedition began.[74]

The evidence of Nasser's policy adviser on Algeria, Mohamed Fathi Al Dib, and former Algerian premier Redha Malek's recent history of the secret Franco-Algerian negotiations between 1956 and 1962 suggest that there were several points at which the extent of the FLN–Egypt connection was revealed. According to Fathi Al Dib, Nasser sanctioned the shipment of arms to the Algerian guerrillas immediately the rebellion began, selecting an Egyptian naval officer, Azzat Soliman, to help find suitable vessels and crews. On 8 December 1954 the yacht *Intissar* completed the first shipment of Egyptian small arms to Algeria. Over the next two years this maritime smuggling increased in tempo, especially to the more remote ALN units in the Oranais. By the time the *Athos* was intercepted in October 1956, at least ten successful shipments had been made to ALN units in western Algeria.[75] Meanwhile, according to Keith Kyle, the Egyptian military attaché in Madrid, Colonel Abdul Mun'im al-Nagar, was permitted by Franco to supply ALN units via Spanish Morocco where the attaché also organised guerrilla training.[76]

In his account of Suez, the influential Cairo journalist and Nasser confidant, Mohamed Heikal, suggested that Nasser considered the reassignment of French NATO forces to Algeria an act of western aggression against an Arab people to which he felt bound to respond. Heikal also links French resentment at Egypt's support for the FLN to the consolidation of the Franco-Israeli alliance. But in his account of Pineau's Cairo meeting with Nasser in March 1956 Heikal makes no mention of any agreement over the cessation of arms supplies, stating only that the Egyptian leader met his promise to arrange unofficial talks between French representatives and the FLN's external executive. Redha Malek also stresses that Nasser's role was to relay to the FLN leaders in Cairo unofficial French proposals relayed by Mollet's fellow Socialist, Georges Gorse. Secret talks were then conducted over several weeks in April and early May between Mohammed Khider and the Socialist vice-president of the French Union Assembly, Joseph Begarra. These stumbled over the French demand for a ceasefire before elections to a unified Algerian Assembly and Khider's insistence on a recognition of Algeria's right to independence. As for the later Franco-FLN conversations in Belgrade, these were something of a second best after President Tito prevented the Algerian delegation from addressing his fellow leaders of the non-aligned movement – Nasser and Nehru – at a July meeting on the

Yugoslav island of Brioni. The Egyptian leader's involvement in these negotiations was marginal. Even so, the Brioni declaration expressing support for Algeria's freedom was enough to antagonise the French government, not least as the three leaders concentrated their fire on France and made no criticism of the Baghdad Pact.[77]

Despite Egypt's encouragement of the FLN's Belgrade talks and its provision of the *Athos* shipment in October, Algeria was a secondary concern to Nasser's government. In his memoir of Egyptian diplomacy during the Suez crisis, Foreign Minister Mahmoud Fawzi did not see fit to mention the Algerian problem at all.[78] But, to the Quai d'Orsay, it seemed incontrovertible that Egyptian backing for the FLN had increased markedly over the course of 1955–56. As this support took many forms, when added together it made frightening reading. In addition to propaganda and diplomatic action against France, the presence of FLN leaders in Cairo, mounting financial aid to the rebels, extended training facilities for North African guerrillas and, of course, arms trafficking, all suggested deepening Egyptian involvement in the Algerian war. The inflammatory broadcasts of Radio Cairo's *Voix des Arabes* which had earlier been toned down thanks to the efforts of Ambassador Armand du Chayla, resumed once the Canal crisis began. Having offered renewed arms contracts with Egypt in return for an end to anti-French propaganda, the French were obviously concerned by Radio Cairo's influence on a largely illiterate Algerian Muslim population for whom the radio was a powerful medium. Intelligence reports also indicated that the Egyptian government had given the FLN approximately £100,000 to organise its Cairo executive. Egypt also released some £15,000 a year through the Arab League's Maghreb bureau to fund the FLN's Cairo activities. The FLN further benefited from a 'special help fund' for nationalist causes. As for arms trafficking, this had increased markedly since the first major seizure of Egyptian weapons (destined for the Aurès) south of Gafsa in December 1955. Some of the heavier Soviet weaponry supplied to Egypt from Czechoslovakia, including bazookas and heavy machine guns, was also said to have reached the ALN. According to the Quai d'Orsay, the practice of training Maghreb guerrillas was well established, dating back to March 1953 when Kamal Eddine Hussein, a member of the Egyptian Revolutionary Council and commander of the National Guard, decided to make facilities available. North African students studying in Cairo were offered basic commando training and from August 1954 this was organised by Lieutenant-Colonel Sulieman Azzat's Egyptian Special Services, which liaised directly with the FLN's *Comité commandement extérieur nord africain*. By October 1956 some 200 trainees per month allegedly passed through Egyptian training camps.[79]

Much of this intelligence was relayed to London. The Foreign Office, the War Office and the British intelligence services also endeavoured to quantify overseas arms supplies across North Africa and establish the provenance of the equipment provided. In anticipation of the Anglo-Egyptian treaty in 1954, an *ad hoc* committee of Foreign Office, service department and Joint Intelligence Board representatives began monitoring Egypt's arms imports and its armaments manufacturing capacity. As a result, the Joint Intelligence Committee (JIC) noted in June 1954 that Nasser's regime was stockpiling small arms far in excess of the country's requirements. This included at least 20,000 Swedish sub-machine guns – sufficient to equip Egypt's army and its paramilitary forces 'on a very liberal scale'. While this accumulation of weaponry was largely explained by Cairo's fear of Israeli attack, the JIC noted that small quantities of arms were provided to rebels in French North Africa.[80] The Foreign Office and the JIC also shared the Quai d'Orsay's interest in Radio Cairo, considered the most effective propaganda medium at Nasser's disposal. French annoyance at violent Radio Cairo broadcasts stretching to Morocco and French West Africa was matched by British irritation at transmissions extending to the Persian Gulf in the east and Zanzibar to the south.[81] By late 1956 the Egypt Committee was content to proceed on the general assumption that French accusations against Nasser were broadly justifiable.

Prior to 1956 French ministers and officials rarely made any secret of their conviction that the Cairo government was a major arms provider to the FLN.[82] Within three weeks of the start of the Algerian rebellion, Sir Roger Makins, British ambassador in Washington, warned that French diplomats intended to seek US, British and NATO backing to protest against Egyptian material aid to the insurgents. [83] During acrimonious talks with Mendès France in November 1954, Eisenhower and Dulles, who had agreed to a freeze on US aid to France after the collapse of the EDC, discounted warnings about foreign interference in Algeria. Exasperated by the new French government, Admiral Radford even told his NSC colleagues that if Algeria went the way of Vietnam, the United States should itself provide arms for the Arabs.[84] In consequence, London became the key focus of French lobbying within the western alliance.

The Quai d'Orsay advised the British Embassy that Egyptian arms deliveries to French North Africa had increased significantly following the Constantine massacres in August 1955. Captures of rebel arms suggested that, wherever possible, *wilaya* commanders provided their troops with the M.A.B. sub-machine gun, a weapon previously sold in large quantities to the Egyptian government. Since many of the French conscripts posted to garrison duties were equipped with Second World War era rifles, the increased sophistication of ALN small arms was a matter of real concern.[85] This alleged upturn in Egyptian support occurred at the same time as Nasser's government finalised its own purchase of Soviet arms from the Czechoslovakian government in late September. Although the high-grade equipment obtained from the Eastern bloc had little in common with the weapons infiltrated to the ALN, it underscored the connection in French eyes between Nasser's support for North African nationalism and his links with the Soviet Union. In Cairo on 4 October 1955 Allal el-Fassi proclaimed a unified Moroccan–Algerian 'National Liberation Army' which had begun co-ordinated guerrilla operations in eastern Morocco and the Oranais. Thanks to the efforts of Mohammed Fathi Al Dib, this alliance between Moroccan Liberation Army and ALN units received Egyptian material aid shipped in by the poignantly named vessel *Good Hope*.[86] In response, the Quai d'Orsay pressed the Foreign Office to redouble its efforts to ensure that the Libyan authorities prevented rebel activity or arms trafficking across their territory.[87]

Britain's treaty relationships with Egypt and Libya inevitably dragged it into the disputes over terrorist arms supplies. Churchill's government concluded a twenty-year treaty with Libya in July 1953, promising to finance Libyan development over five years.[88] A comparable Franco-Libyan treaty concluded in July 1955 never bore fruit. It remained unratified owing to French refusal to withdraw from the Fezzan until Libya closed its frontiers effectively to arms supplies. (This is discussed further in Chapter 6.) As Libya's main protector, the British government was irritated by this French intransigence despite the signature of Anglo-French military accords in June and August 1955 providing for co-operation between the garrisons on Libyan soil.[89] But Cairo's support for the Libyan republican opposition, apparently orchestrated by Egyptian military attaché Colonel Ismail Sadek, lent weight to the French hard line.[90]

On 24 February 1956 Jebb urged Lloyd to ask Nasser to end his sponsorship of North African terrorism. The French were bound to request this sooner or later having offered to supply arms to the Egyptian government if it withheld support for the FLN. French willingness to bargain in this way had already caused disquiet in Whitehall. This turned to anger following Pineau's visit to Nasser after the SEATO talks in Karachi in mid-March. Annoyed by French hostility to the Baghdad Pact, Eden also felt betrayed since Mollet had personally assured him that the French government had rejected a previous Egyptian offer to mediate in Algeria. France's North African problems were impeding the presentation of a common front towards Nasser. Pineau's mistaken assumption after his Cairo meeting that Nasser would reduce Egyptian involvement in Algeria was an added complication. Indeed, Pineau muddied the waters still further by insisting to Jebb that he was not taken in by Nasser who shared his reservations about the Baghdad Pact.[91]

Since Mollet's government was already talking directly to Cairo, it pressed Britain to intervene in Tripoli to dissuade its client regime from permitting overland arms trafficking or the establishment of FLN training bases on Libyan soil. Eden preferred to increase British material support to the Libyans than meet such French requests.[92] Tripoli ambassador W. G. Graham warned in August that, until the storm broke over Suez, Algeria had dominated public discussion of foreign affairs. If Britain supported French actions the entire basis of Anglo-Libyan treaty co-operation would collapse.[93] After the Special Powers vote, the Libyan, Syrian and Iraqi governments pleaded for British intervention in Paris to secure a reversal of French policy in Algeria. To appease its domestic critics, the Libyan government supported Syrian pressure for a comprehensive trade boycott against France at the Arab League in mid-April.[94] News of the French decision to supply Mystères to Israel led to further Libyan efforts to bring the Algerian situation to international attention. On 22 May Prime Minister Sayid Mustafa Ben Halim told French ambassador Jacques Dumarçay that his attempts to persuade Nasser to stop sending arms across Libyan territory had been wrecked. Whether or not, as Fathi Al Dib claims, Ben Halim had been complicit in Egyptian arms trafficking since late 1954, Libyan police in Tripolitania were now sure to let supplies through whatever the instructions from central government.[95] In early June the Tripoli Parliament protested to all NATO member states at the use in Algeria of French forces theoretically assigned to NATO command. Three months later it joined the protests at the detention of Ben Bella and his fellow leaders. The Libyan premier personally delivered a message to Ambassador Graham pleading for Britain to press for their release, and his government supported Arab League consideration of an extended boycott backed by the severance of diplomatic relations with France.[96]

Towards Collusion

The British government quickly discovered that the October 1956 arrests were not properly sanctioned. Marginalised after the failure of Pineau's efforts to conciliate Nasser, the Quai d'Orsay played little part in the arrests crisis. Nor did it make a specifically French case for intervention in the weeks before the Egyptian landings began.[97] But the decline in Quai d'Orsay influence on policy in Algeria had long been apparent.[98] Following a meeting of the inter-departmental North Africa committee on 21 December 1955, Faure nominated a liaison committee to discuss the Algerian situation with Soustelle. The three men chosen were Paul Demange, a former prefect of Oran then installed at the Seine-et-Oise prefecture, General Jacquot, a government military adviser, and Abel Thomas, then assistant-director of the Ministry of Interior *cabinet*. Sent to encourage closer co-operation between the Interior Ministry and the Algiers government general and to discuss the deployment of troops returning from Indo-China, this liaison mission treated Algeria according to French constitutional precepts as a purely internal problem requiring no specialist diplomatic expertise.[99]

As Keith Kyle and Maurice Vaïsse have highlighted, Abel Thomas, who followed his former ministerial chief to become director-general at Bourgès-Maunoury's Ministry of National Defence in 1956, suggested in his own account of the Suez expedition that Mollet deferred to the Defence Ministry over and above the Quai d'Orsay from the end of May. Reluctant to risk Bourgès's resignation from Cabinet, Mollet acquiesced in the Defence Ministry's appropriation of Middle East policy-making following a confrontation in the Council of Ministers over a speech lambasting Nasser delivered on behalf of Bourgès by his close adviser, Louis Mangin.[100] It was Mangin, a figure at the margins of government, who, with SDECE chief, Pierre Boursicot, organised the first Franco-Israeli preparatory talks at Chantilly on 23 June.[101] And Bourgès still supervised Max Lejeune's administration of the military operations in Algeria. By contrast, the new Minister of the Interior, the Radical senator Jean Gilbert-Jules, saw his jurisdiction over Algerian policy whittled away once Mollet made the rebellion his top priority in February. Although the Interior Ministry retained a state secretary with responsibility for Algerian affairs, in practice he reported direct to Mollet.[102]

This marked a breakdown in French Cabinet government. The assertion of Service Ministry control over strategic planning and Middle East diplomacy facilitated collusion with Israel. This culminated in conclusion of the Sèvres Protocol without inter-departmental analysis or prior Cabinet agreement on 24 October.[103] The die was cast ten days earlier when deputy chief of staff General Maurice Challe and acting Foreign Minister Albert Gazier met Eden at Chequers. Challe delineated the plan for an Israeli offensive into the Sinai to serve as the pretext for the subsequent Anglo-French expedition to 'separate' the warring parties and occupy the Canal zone.[104] As Jebb remembered, 'something was happening completely outside the diplomatic machine of which I had no inkling. Indeed Bourgès-Maunoury had quite frankly told me this. When Eden and Selwyn Lloyd came over to Paris on 16 October and had a meeting of several hours from which all officials were excluded, this became even more obvious.'[105]

In the absence of a dispassionate evaluation of the strategic and political significance of Egyptian support for the FLN, the inner-group of French decision-makers – Mollet, Bourgès, Louis Mangin, Abel Thomas and, more sporadically, Pineau – superimposed their flawed assumptions about the nature of the Algerian rebellion on their planning for war against Egypt.[106] They characterised the FLN and Nasser's regime as alien to the national traditions of their own countries. In refusing to accept that the FLN represented any Algerian popular will, Mollet and his colleagues inevitably attached undue importance to the movement's external backers. By concentrating on breaking the FLN's link to Cairo, the French ministers focused in turn on Nasser's association with the Soviet Union. But it was their inability to acknowledge the FLN as an indigenous Algerian phenomenon that sparked this chain reaction between the Algerian rebellion, action against Nasser and a perceived Communist threat to the Arab world. Throughout, the key decisions rested with a few select ministers and military planners acting on the basis of an unchallenged consensus about the nature of the conflict in Algeria and how best to win it.

The disruption of French governmental procedure did not lead to a re-evaluation of Britain's support for France in North Africa. This was attributable to three factors – the quickening pace of Anglo-French operational planning typified by the collusion with Prime Minister David Ben-Gurion's Israeli delegation at Sèvres; the fact that the Egypt committee, too, had circumvented the processes of Cabinet government; and, finally, the British inclination to accept French claims of an Egypt–Algeria link at face value. Guided by their imperial requirements, Britain and France were equally cynical towards the UN, and ultimately flouted the UN Charter in defiance of international opinion. Once Dulles learnt the full extent of Anglo-French-Israeli collusion on 29 October, he advised Eisenhower that this marked Britain's rejection of an Anglo-US diplomatic partnership in the Middle East in preference for naked imperial aggression. This came as a real shock. During a key session of the US National Security Council on 1 November, Dulles insisted that friendship with Britain and France should no longer imply indulgence towards their colonial policies across the Arab world.

There was more to British policy than this. As Scott Lucas has stressed, it also served Britain's imperial needs to avoid a possible Israeli strike against Jordan as opposed to Egypt in order to conserve the pro-British Iraqi–Jordanian axis and avert the invocation of the Anglo-Jordanian military alliance.[107] But whatever its own justifications for intervention, Britain was also following a French colonialist agenda dominated by Algeria. Unless America clearly signalled its displeasure, Arab states would turn away from the West.[108] On 10 November Mollet warned a British Embassy official in Paris that he remained committed to solidarity with Israel. His government's Algerian requirements demanded the destruction of Nasser's regime.[109] Albeit briefly, Britain was now a party to this.

In his vilification of Nasser's Arabism, Eden lent undue coherence to Nasser's still imprecise and malleable philosophy. Eden's efforts to persuade Washington to support, or at least acquiesce in, Anglo-French intervention against Egypt focused on the imminent threat to western interests throughout the Arab world should Nasser's defiance over the Suez Canal Company succeed. Eden's much quoted remarks to Eisenhower comparing Nasser with Mussolini and warning of the dangers of wrong-headed 'appeasement' were prefaced by the comment that 'Nasser is active wherever Muslims can be found even as far as Nigeria'.[110] Mollet, too, was transfixed by the spectre of Nasserite Arabism and had conflated it with Cold War thinking. In early March he warned Eden that the containment of Nasser's 'pan-Islamism' was now the foremost task of the western alliance.[111] In the British Prime Minister the French government appeared to have an ally who shared their imperial preoccupations. This was confirmed by Eden's readiness within the Egypt committee to contemplate military operations with a significant risk of escalation whose political ramifications might divide the western alliance and split the Commonwealth. But, if successful, the Suez intervention would re-establish an Anglo-French partnership at the heart of European and Mediterranean affairs.[112] At this stage, the Prime Minister was not alone. His colleagues within this Suez inner Cabinet – Macmillan and Lord Salisbury above all – were equally determined.[113]

Eden's nightmare scenario of Egyptian-sponsored young officers' rebellions in Iraq, Jordan, Syria and Saudi Arabia meshed with the French obsession with the FLN's external sources of arms, financial support and political backing. Justifying the assault on Port Said to a sceptical Eisenhower and Dulles, on 5 November Eden made this connection explicit, linking the salvation of Britain's network of Middle Eastern client regimes with the protection of Libya and the Maghreb from creeping Egyptian control. Eisenhower had already rejected Eden's arguments, warning him two days earlier that military intervention against Egypt would only harden anti-western sentiment across North Africa and the Middle East.[114] In similar vein, the Quai d'Orsay tried to alleviate US condemnation by presenting the Suez intervention as a calculated bid to restore security to the Middle East and North Africa. Pineau was stung into action by France's UN representative, Hervé Alphand, who warned on 31 October that State Department and American press criticism might expose the Franco-Israeli collusion. The Quai d'Orsay instructed its ambassadors to emphasise to their host governments that French intervention was intended to restore regional stability to the Middle East, broadly defined to include the protection of French interests in the Maghreb.[115] But French sensitivity to the importance of American hostility was tempered by reports from Jean Chauvel in London indicating the collapse in Foreign Office resolve as the Suez landings rapidly undermined Britain's position among its Baghdad Pact allies and threatened to drag Syria and Jordan into a spiralling Middle East conflict. Meanwhile, in a meeting with Soviet Foreign Minister Dimitri Chepilov on 6 November, the French ambassador Maurice Dejean insisted that Egyptian complicity in the *Athos* affair had confirmed the futility of dialogue with Nasser. He thus rejected the telling Soviet accusation that France was prosecuting a colonial war against an innocent state.[116]

In the fortnight after the Suez operations began, the British chiefs of staff and the Ministry of Defence strategic exports committee reviewed British arms exports policy towards Middle Eastern states. It was judged essential to maintain export contracts with Iraq, Jordan and Lebanon not only to quell potential criticism over Suez, but to bolster their pro-western regimes.[117] This contrast between France's obsession with arms smuggling into Algeria and British concern to conserve regional influence was itself a good indicator of the fundamentally different British and French expectations of the Suez venture. While France attacked Egypt to help win a colonial war, Britain attacked Egypt in the vain hope that this would consolidate the neocolonial relationships with Arab clients which kept British Middle Eastern power alive. Whereas for Britain, its oil interests, the challenge to its international prestige and the avowed fear of Soviet incursion into the Middle East also drove government policy-making during the Suez crisis, for France, Algeria was always the paramount concern.

As the effort to halt the supply of arms to ALN units became a vital focus of the French war effort in Algeria, controversy over external aid blended with the broader debate over the intensified Middle East arms race in which French equipment deliveries to Israel were usually justified by reference to Soviet and Czechoslovakian supplies to Egypt. Moreover, Nasser's pan-Arabist message rankled French politicians proud of their country's imperial achievement in North Africa. The veteran Radical leader, Edouard Daladier, gave voice to this sentiment in a parliamentary debate in early March, pointing out that French social spending in Algeria was four times greater than that of Egypt, where living standards and infant mortality rates were significantly worse than in the French territories.[118] Hardly a measured appreciation of the respective national resources of France and Egypt, Daladier's remarks none the less tapped that vein of French opinion which justified the Algerian campaign in terms of the economic benefits that France alone could guarantee to its subject populations. Daladier's choice of Egypt as the alternative model for Algeria was just as revealing. Ferhat Abbas's defection to the FLN, which he announced from his new political base in Cairo on 25 April, cemented the links in the public mind between Egypt and FLN terrorism. Abbas, previously France's one remaining hope as an interlocuteur, now backed FLN arms trafficking and the organisation of ALN operations by the Cairo-based executive.[119]

As French politicians of all hues became exasperated by the declining situation in Algeria, the breadth of political support for intervention in Egypt seems readily explicable. Nasser's defiance crystallised what Maurice Vaïsse has termed 'the Munich syndrome' amongst the French political and military leadership. Desperate to achieve a breakthrough in Algeria, Mollet's inner cabinet was emotionally conditioned to see any compromise with Egypt as an impermissible surrender.[120] Mollet confided to Eden at Chequers on 11 March that the lessons of failing to confront pan-Germanism in 1938 weighed on his ministers as they confronted pan-Islamism and pan-Slavism in 1956.[121] Public interest in Algeria had been transformed since the start of the year. On 3 October public subscriptions to a national loan to fund investment in the colony raised a record total of 313 billion francs. Popular unity was more easily sustained since Mollet's government averted a run on its currency reserves akin to the US-induced pressure on sterling by securing authorisation to draw upon the International Monetary Fund prior to the Suez landings.[122]

After Suez, Sir Pierson Dixon, the British government's permanent representative at the UN, bemoaned the loss of Britain's moral force in international affairs.[123] By contrast, Mollet's government presented intervention against Egypt as a moral and strategic imperative to shorten the Algerian war. Among the French service chiefs there was no echo of the disagreement between Templer and First Sea Lord, Admiral Louis Mountbatten, for whom operations against Egypt in defiance of

American and UN opinion appeared an unquantifiable risk. To the historian Avi Shlaim, 'The French military had three priorities at that time: Algeria, Algeria and Algeria.'[124] As part of the Foreign Office post-mortem over Suez, on 21 January 1957 Jebb noted that 'in attempting, with the United Kingdom, to impose her will as regards the Suez Canal by force of arms, France was conscious, for the first time since the war, of being virtually united. This very fact produced a strange exhilaration.' This sensation had been still more apparent among the *colon* community many of whom hoped that the defeat of Nasser, 'the evil genius of the Algerian problem', would somehow induce a rapid collapse of the FLN. Failure only heightened French disenchantment with NATO, Britain and the US.[125]

Ironically, the British and, still more so the American government were never convinced that the Egyptian government's material support to the FLN was essential to the movement's success. From June 1955 US consular reports stressed the importance of Egypt's political support for the FLN but correctly placed it within the broader context of the Arab League which also hoped for an FLN victory.[126] Military aid supplies were less significant than the fact that ALN cadres could be maintained in spite of a mounting attrition rate. As long as young Algerian men and women were driven to violence for political ends, the means would be found to arm them.[127] US diplomatic contacts with the FLN leadership in Cairo in December 1955 also suggested that the movement's relationship with the Egyptian government was based upon real affinity. Ben Bella and Aït Ahmed advised US Embassy officials in Libya and Egypt that the FLN supported Egypt's foreign policy, its quest to arm itself against Israel and its Arabist message.[128]

The Suez Aftermath and Relations with Britain

The abrupt abandonment of military operations soured relations between London and Paris. Jebb recalled the atmosphere with characteristic understatement, 'Though they were much too polite to say so, it was evident that the French ministers, who had left the military lead to us, were much shaken by our inability to resist American pressure to call the whole venture off.'[129] Just as the Eisenhower administration gave ample notice that it would not endorse the Suez expedition, so French readiness to take collusion with Israel to its logical military outcome of armed conflict with Egypt was not in doubt. French naval and air support for Israel's initial attacks on Egypt was so blatant that British military observers feared the immediate exposure of their collusion with the Israeli attack. As the French aircraft took off from Israeli airfields to bombard Egyptian air bases and the cruiser *Georges Leygues* pounded the eastern town of Rafah in support of Israeli ground operations, it became obvious that the French commanders cared little about international reaction.[130] Although Mollet accepted the importance of concealment, the French commanders under Admiral Barjot only deferred to his advice on 3 November by which time the concealment of France's support for Israeli aggression was something of an irrelevance.[131] Yet as General Keightley subsequently observed, 'The one overriding lesson of the Suez operation is that world opinion is now an absolute principle of war and must be treated as such.'[132]

The core of the French forces earmarked for operations against Egypt were two elite divisions (the 10^{e} parachutists and the rapid mechanised 7^{e}), a naval support group including an aircraft carrier, cruisers and the only battleship assigned to the joint allied forces, and a combination of fighter and ground attack aircraft intended to protect and support the assault troops. In spite of the scale of this contribution, the French commanders deputised to their British colleagues in all service arms.[133]

French air force commander, General Raymond Brohin, was unimpressed by the effectiveness of the British bombing strikes against Egyptian targets. Like Barjot, Brohin was agitated by the possibility that the wholesale destruction of Egyptian aircraft would count for little if the Egyptian and Syrian air-forces were resupplied with Soviet MIGs. But the larger air assault necessary to destroy the airfields, support facilities and infrastructure of the Egyptian air-force was hardly viable once US opposition to the Suez operation became manifest. And since the French air effort was co-ordinated from Cyprus, British leadership of the joint air effort made obvious sense.[134] While the French air force commanders viewed the Suez operation from the broad perspective of the regional balance of power in the Middle East, Algeria figured more prominently for their army counterparts. Both the French army divisions arrived from service in Algeria, the parachutists' commander, Jacques Massu, having narrowly missed assassination a month earlier when his jeep was machine-gunned on the outskirts of the capital.[135] His troops staged in Cyprus while the rapid motorised division were shipped direct from Algiers. Subsequently, the colonial and Foreign Legion parachute regiments within the the 10^{e} division played a decisive role in the assaults on Port Said and Port Fuad. On 31 October French aircraft mounted the first major air assault against Egyptian naval vessels off Alexandria whilst French fighters provided cover for British bombardments such as the destruction of the Radio Cairo centre at Abu Zabaal on

1 November. In all, Keightley acknowledged that the French performed the more difficult military tasks.[136]

This brief summary of the composition and actions of the French forces at Suez is worth noting here for three key reasons. First, many of the forces selected for the Suez operations were both drawn from, and moulded by, the Algerian conflict. Furthermore, many of the troops involved immediately returned to play the leading role in the impending dirty war against urban terrorism. Secondly, the military success of the French ground and air forces in particular nurtured the belief within the French professional army in Algeria that defeat was snatched from the jaws of victory in Egypt.[137] Hence, the final and most vital point. In this French assessment, Britain was the spineless villain. French commanders intent upon overthrowing Nasser shared Field Marshal Auchinleck's judgment in late November 1956 that Britain's military objectives in Egypt and the Eastern Mediterranean were hopelessly confused.[138] French political and military leaders were also less concerned with the possible alternatives once Nasser were deposed. From Pineau's first conversation with Lloyd two days after the Canal crisis broke in late July, the French government always supported military intervention. When that intervention was abandoned, French ministers and Ely's general staff reacted angrily to the apparent collapse of British resolve. Ambassador Chauvel failed to explain the key divisions within Conservative ranks until 15 November. Castigated by the US, the Soviet Union and the UN for going to war against Nasser, Eden's government was also pilloried by its French ally for failing to go far enough.[139]

Among military leaders accustomed to international and UN criticism of their actions in North Africa, the response to the failure of the Suez operation was less driven by fear of moral censure and incipient financial breakdown than by annoyance at a missed opportunity to win strategic advantage in Algeria. Barjot warned Keightley that the announcement of a ceasefire on 6 November, just as French ground forces were on the point of decisive victory, caused immense frustration among French troops and commanders.[140] Exasperated by the constraints on France's freedom of action, in his assessment of the Suez expedition submitted to Bourgès-Maunoury and the chiefs of staff on 31 December, Barjot stressed the need for a French rapid reaction force capable of amphibious assaults at short notice. In addition, he suggested contingency planning for unilateral operations conducted outside the confines of NATO.[141] Barjot's conclusions were a portent of de Gaulle's later confrontation with Britain and the US over the utility of NATO command, and confirmed that the military leadership were not chastened by the Suez experience. Frustration over a job left unfinished was carried straight back to Algiers. The gap between France and its Anglo-American NATO partners would widen further as the military pursued victory in Algeria and the development of French nuclear capacity. Within a month of the Suez ceasefire Mollet's Cabinet authorised the credits for the development of prototype nuclear weapons.[142]

As news of the Anglo-French failure spread throughout Algeria, terrorist incidents increased markedly. On 13 November US ambassador Dillon reported that Mollet and Lacoste were 'depressed'. Removal of Nasser would have made it easier to impose a settlement, whereas the prospects for a ceasefire and single college elections were now gloomy.[143] Any concession of genuine autonomy in Algeria was bound to produce demands for outright independence. In spite of this, failure at Suez did force Mollet's Cabinet to reconsider a political solution in Algeria. But now the barriers were greater. After the Soummam congress, the arrest of key members of the Cairo FLN, and Egypt's successful defiance, the internal FLN leadership, now controlled by Abbane Ramdane and fellow ALN *wilaya* commanders, was increasingly militant.[144] So, too, were their French military opponents. The core of professional forces in Algeria soon refocused the war against the FLN from Egypt to the Algiers *casbah* in the decisive struggle against urban terrorism during 1957. And by the time the French expeditionary force retreated from Suez, Plans Valmy and Bugeaud had made a huge difference to army capacity within Algeria: of the 520,264 soldiers deployed across French North Africa by 1 December, 394,361 were in Algeria alone.[145]

*

It was hardly surprising in the light of the Foreign Ministry's limited impact on French policy over Suez that Pineau, secretary-general, Louis Joxe, and the Ministry's director of political affairs, Jean Daridan, sought to distance the Quai d'Orsay from the government's linkage of Algeria and armed intervention in Egypt. At Joxe's request, on 10 November the Foreign Ministry completed a preliminary assessment of the long-term consequences of the Suez operations. This emphasised the consolidation of Egyptian and Soviet influence, the lasting damage to French standing in the Middle East and the rupture among the western powers. In addition, the Quai at last spelt out unequivocally that the attack on Egypt could not facilitate the solution of France's difficulties in North Africa. Nasser's involvement in Algeria was real enough, and further increased after the collapse of the withdrawal of Anglo-French forces. But direct action to restrain him only alienated allies and hardened Arab hostility to French colonial policy in general. It was time to defend the French presence in Algeria through argument and achievement.[146] During a visit to Washington in mid-November, Daridan criticised the arrest of the FLN leaders and even suggested that wider US involvement in an Algerian settlement might be welcomed. In like fashion, Pineau admitted that Algerian policy was in disarray. But a month later in talks with Dulles and Dillon prior to a NATO council session in Paris, Pineau and his senior officials were more upbeat. They responded warmly to Dulles's obvious eagerness to mend fences among the western allies. Pineau promised further agrarian and communal reforms in Algeria and even suggested that international – though not UN – monitors might be invited to supervise the eventual polling in Algeria.[147] On 9 January 1957, in his long-awaited televised address to the nation on the Algerian problem, Mollet reiterated previous government offers of an unconditional ceasefire once the rebels accepted French proposals for the organisation of nation-wide elections held under international scrutiny. The 'informal contacts' with the rebels during 1956 were dismissed as irrelevant, except in so far as they confirmed the extent of Egyptian influence over the FLN. In other words, neither French policy nor the government's preconceptions were much altered. On an altogether different plane, with Foreign Ministry encouragement, Mollet and his successors increasingly looked to Chancellor Adenauer's West Germany rather than to Britain, as France's principal partner in international affairs and nuclear policy.[148] Although Suez had not brought an end to the Algerian war any closer, France recovered from the shock of failure more easily than its British ally. Yet while failure at Suez seemed a more containable political problem in France than Britain, the growing internationalisation of the Algerian war continued to erode French power.

5

France Undermined? French International Power and the Algerian War, 1954–58

No postwar British government thought that French North Africa could survive intact as a quasi-colonial confederation. It remains difficult to disentangle the threads of British policy towards the region in the 1950s because Whitehall policy-makers were generally sceptical, and sometimes unsure, about the worth of these territories to France. More importantly from their perspective, there was always a tension between support for France as an ally and the inevitable anger this caused among client Arab states, Commonwealth members and the non-aligned movement. The consolidation of independent nation-states from Syria to Libya further intensified Arab hostility towards the survival of French imperial control.[1]

Jacques Marseille has argued persuasively that the numerous French industries that relied on imperial markets in the interwar period were in full retreat from colonial trade by the 1950s. The primary products typically exported from French Africa were by then more widely available on the open market, and those territories whose currency was linked to the French franc did not produce goods for export at much saving to France. As a result, neither the French industrial sector nor its agricultural market depended on French North Africa remaining under the tricolour. Furthermore, many of the businesses that still traded heavily with the Maghreb territories were uncompetitive and short of private venture capital. It was hardly surprising in light of the uncertain political future of overseas territories that the shrewd French investor did not reckon North-West Africa an attractive proposition by the time the Algerian war began.[2] In real terms, French North Africa was becoming a drain on the French economy before the costs of policing and war turned the trickle of French funds to the Maghreb into a flood. If the economic rationale for retaining Algeria was at least questionable, why was it so often taken for granted that the territory was a vital component of France's international power?

Ambivalent British Support?

Recalling his expectations as he took up his Paris ambassadorial post in 1954, Gladwyn Jebb stressed the underlying malaise in Anglo-French relations at the time:

> Ever since Robert Schuman's startling and unheralded initiative in 1950 there had been a vague feeling in Whitehall that the French were not 'playing the game'; that they were inclined to take an individual and at the same time rather unpredictable line; and that in any case, owing to constant changes of government, the Fourth Republic was a weak sister who must be kept on the straight and narrow path of Western solidarity by a firm, purposeful and self-confident Britain.[3]

Jebb went on to note that the Foreign Office Permanent Under-Secretary, Sir Ivone Kirkpatrick, lacked a sophisticated grasp of French attitudes.[4] This two-dimensional characterisation of French unreliability was common currency among British officials. Middle Eastern and North African problems compounded these British reservations once Indo-China and the EDC were removed from the equation.

In May 1954, as Foreign Secretary, Eden had vetoed plans for greater Foreign Office involvement in the annual cycle of Anglo-French colonial discussions over matters of common interest in Africa. Although the assistant under-secretaries of the Foreign Office and the Quai d'Orsay met regularly to discuss Middle Eastern problems, Eden did not want Britain more closely identified with French policy in the Maghreb for fear of the adverse Arab reaction.[5] As a fellow imperial power, Britain was particularly susceptible to generic criticism of colonialism at the UN and elsewhere. Whilst favourable comparisons might be drawn between British and French decolonisation from Africa, numerous examples of die-hard British colonialism, settler intransigence and bloody colonial insurgency remained. Moreover, since the North African protectorates were clearly capable of self-government, there was much to be gained from cementing political and commercial relationships with friendly independent regimes in Rabat and Tunis. As for Algeria, the intensification of the conflict, its impact on France's financial and military capacity, its effects upon French national unity and Arab opinion, and the human tragedy involved all suggested by 1958 that France's effort to hang on was not worth the cost.

Although the general trend in British official attitudes towards French North Africa is clearly discernible, its outcome in policy terms is harder to measure. Whatever the governmental reservations about support for France, in practice, from the end of the Second World War until the Evian agreements in 1962, British ministers, diplomats and military commanders generally backed the French presence in North Africa regardless of France's actions in the region. Yet the basic equation that successive British governments put good relations with France above the interests of the North African peoples is simplistic and inadequate. It ignores the depth of the French commitment to North Africa and the correspondingly limited opportunities for foreign governments to influence French policy. It dismisses the western security interests involved. Perhaps most importantly, it fails to convey the fact that attitudes towards empire and decolonisation were in gradual transition, affecting various politicians, bureaucrats, soldiers, journalists and writers in different ways at different times. To assume that there was a common British perception of events in French North Africa because a broad consensus existed regarding colonialism, colonial war or France as an imperial power is to misunderstand the fluidity in British opinion and to overestimate the general concern for peoples living under a different flag.

The one British interest unaltered throughout the years of French crisis in North Africa was that France's international power should not be compromised. Jebb summarised Foreign Office thinking in July 1955:

> The fact that France's status as a Great Power depends directly on the maintenance of the French position in North Africa makes it doubly important for both France and France's allies that French policy in Algeria should not only be progressive but wise. Moreover France will only possess the self-confidence required for a liberal approach to the Algerian problem if she considers herself assured of the unswerving support of her Western allies for the French position in that country.[6]

In this respect, the gulf between those within the governmental apparatus and the opponents of rigid colonialism outside it becomes apparent. In June 1956, for example, Kirkpatrick dismissed Chauvel's protest at the invitation issued to Ferhat Abbas to address a meeting of MPs sponsored by the Movement for Colonial Freedom, noting that he could not answer for an organisation 'often more hostile to HMG than to the

French government'.[7] British policy towards French North Africa was formulated with an eye to the western alliance, European integration and the Cold War in Africa and the Middle East. Non-governmental opposition to French policy tended to view the Maghreb in relative isolation. Whether justifiable or not, policy was rarely determined without overarching European, Middle Eastern or transatlantic considerations in mind.

Outside the UN, active British support was largely confined to efforts to impede arms smuggling to Tunisia and Algeria from other Arab states – Libya above all. The British government also pressed the Egyptian government to tone down the anti-French propaganda of Radio Cairo and urged the Libyan regime to keep a close watch on the swelling population of Tunisian and Algerian refugees within its borders.[8] Public squabbles with France were largely confined to the technicalities of international law in colonial matters and the alleged insufficiency of British intervention to restrain its Libyan client. But this reflected a deeper malaise, itself a hangover from the war years. As Jebb put it: 'Nearly every Frenchman at the back of his mind blames British policies in the Middle East for France's difficulties with her Arab populations.'[9]

Typical in this respect was a protracted argument with the French delegation at the UN over Britain's reluctance to admit Morocco and Tunisia as full members of UN-affiliated organisations before their independence was confirmed by treaty in March 1956. Within the Franco-Tunisian convention concluded in June 1955 preparatory to a final independence settlement, the Faure government endorsed Tunisia's application for membership of several bodies, including UNESCO, the International Wine Office and the Union Postale Universelle. Hardly contentious, the Foreign Office none the less objected that a dangerous precedent would be set if technically non-sovereign states were permitted direct affiliation to the UN. On 12 December 1955 Evelyn Shuckburgh even suggested that the issue might jeopardise Anglo-French colonial co-operation more generally. The Quai's Tunisian affairs office retorted that Britain had supported Sudanese admission to UN-linked organisations without consulting Paris.[10] A minor argument soon became a poisonous dispute.

Conservative governments were again sensitive to charges of hypocrisy regarding the nature of French operations in Algeria and the conduct of certain French units. The Foreign Office and the service departments generally accepted the advice of their men on the spot – the consuls and service attachés in Algeria who enjoyed remarkably free access to operational areas and senior French commanders. Within four weeks of the November 1954 outbreak, the Ministry of National Defence approved a War Office request for the first in a series of inspection tours by the British military attaché in Paris and his assistant in Algiers to compare counter-insurgency techniques. Initially, British officers and officials saw more of General Paul Cherrière's command headquarters than their American counterparts, though neither party was as yet permitted to visit units active in the Algerian interior. The first such visit was conducted by George Bowker, British vice-consul in Bône who, in May 1955, toured the Tebessa region where state of emergency provisions were in full force.[11] Subsequent War Office requests to send additional British military observers to Algeria to study French anti-guerrilla tactics, the use of helicopters and combined operations were more often blocked by the Foreign Office than by the French authorities.[12]

Allegations of French military atrocities against Algerian Muslims drew sustained international media coverage following the Constantine massacres of 20 August 1955. The West German press was particularly critical of French actions, condemning 'scorched earth' methods and a 'blood bath' in which some 1,000 Algerians were allegedly killed during the destruction of nine Arab villages around Oued-Zenati in Constantine. Even the official French death toll admitted to the killing of 1,273 'terrorists' between 20 and 27 August for the loss of 122 civilians and French military personnel, including the 35 settlers at the Al-Halia iron ore works whose gruesome deaths had stimulated the wave of repression.[13] Responding to outrage across the Arab world, the Iraqi and Yemeni governments formally appealed to Britain and the US to help end the killings. The Egyptian government joined the chorus on 26 August, demanding that France's western allies should demand the cessation of operations carried out within NATO's strategic perimeter. The Washington administration duly promised to seek assurances from Paris that no US military hardware previously supplied for use in Indo-China and Europe had been transferred to North Africa (a disingenuous concession as the Americans were on the point of supplying additional helicopters for service in Algeria).[14]

By contrast, British military attaché, Brigadier A. C. F. Jackson's detailed report on French operations made no concessions to the rising tide of international opinion, and London press coverage of the repression in late August was so positive that Soustelle sent a message of thanks to the British authorities.[15] Jackson sympathised with French commanders' complaints that they had been unable to arrest known ALN terrorists until 6 April 1955 when state of emergency regulations were introduced in the so-called *zones d'urgence* where rebel activity was most pronounced. Only after the Constantine massacres was this emergency legislation extended, making the entire country a *zone d'urgence*. With numerous British army units in similar colonial glass houses, Jackson thought it ill-advised to throw stones. He vindicated the small minority of French servicemen whose repulsion at ALN killings drove them to violent reprisal:

> One cannot help feeling that it would be too much to expect continued restraint by the young men in the French army in North Africa. It has been said that British troops would not have behaved in this manner, but it is difficult to find a case since the Indian mutiny, when British troops have been so tested as were these young Frenchmen... Since the August period there have been a few cases of injustice but there is no evidence that the number is large considering the size of the force. In order to get a sense of proportion about such cases, it is perhaps worth mentioning that there have been at least four proved cases of atrocities committed by British troops or police in Kenya and they did not make pretty reading. Algeria is perhaps fifty times as big as the Mau Mau country and there are perhaps ten times as many troops in the former as in the latter.[16]

The tenor of Jackson's report captured the dichotomy at the heart of British official responses to the changing nature of the Algerian war. Unwilling to condone extended operations and more ruthless military actions outright, the British government was none the less sensitive to the French army's dilemma and forgiving towards its local excesses. With colonial emergencies of their own to contend with, British policy-makers and specialist observers were unsure whether to view their French counterparts as fellow-sufferers or as dangerous adventurists heaping further discredit on what remained of imperialist rationale. It is worth noting that Conservative Central Office sent its candidates for the 1955 general election a memorandum justifying the detention without trial of Mau Mau suspects in Kenya and pointing out that when the Labour Party lost office in 1951 over 2,500 suspects were similarly detained in Malaya.[17] On the ground, the Algiers consuls, C. O. Wakefield-Harrey and his successor, D. J. Mill-Irving, were far less certain that French repression was proportionate to the scale of the rebellion faced. Wakefield-Harrey accepted that most French soldiers showed commendable restraint, yet stressed that by Christmas 1954 'murder and counter-murder' were commonplace while French arrests already ran into thousands. Those detained included all past MTLD deputies to the Algerian Assembly and

13 students of the Ulama Koranic school in Mostaganem sentenced to terms of between two and ten years for carrying arms.[18] For his part, Mill-Irving admitted on 10 September 1955 that he had completely revised his initial assessment of the success of military operations; in fact, the gulf between the French and Muslim populations looked unbridgeable and the local situation was fast deteriorating. Most African department officials were convinced that the Algiers consul was right. The Foreign Office responded to the February 1956 settler protest against Mollet by activating plans to evacuate the 700 or so Britons in Algeria to Gibraltar. Transmission of a courtesy message welcoming Mollet into office was withheld lest it be wrongly interpreted as a formal expression of support for his Algerian policy. Jean Chauvel shared African department head, Adam Watson's expectation of more severe inter-ethnic violence, confiding his fear of 'something like Ireland or Palestine' – hasty partition once the civil power lost effective control over the warring factions.[19]

Military and UN Problems

French reinforcements began arriving in strength in Algeria after the Chamber of Deputies instituted the state of emergency regulations in early April 1955. Washington ambassador, Maurice Couve de Murville, noted that US military leaders monitored French troop redeployments closely. The removal of two light divisions from NATO duties in Europe to Tunisia in late 1954 produced consternation among France's major allies. French military pressure on Faure to agree the transfer of a French division from West Germany to Algeria caused similar disquiet.[20] Aware that Mendès France had promised to keep Washington apprised of French military plans in North Africa, Foreign Minister Antoine Pinay was careful to explain to US ambassador C. Douglas Dillon the details of the reinforcement proposals agreed by the Council of Ministers on 16 May 1955. He stressed that several battalions were being transferred to Algeria from the neighbouring protectorates. Only a single motorised division had been sent from metropolitan France. Pinay forestalled criticism about the use in Algeria of US equipment supplied under the Mutual Assistance Programme by emphasising that the counter-insurgency in Algeria met NATO's broad strategic requirements.[21]

On 24 May the French committee of national defence met to consider the dispatch to Algeria of two echelons of reinforcements totalling some 20,000 troops. The committee recognised that Faure's government was obliged to consult the NATO Council and General Alfred Gruenther,

Supreme Allied Commander in Europe (SACEUR), before transferring forces to North Africa. This would be a bumpy ride. Gruenther's SACEUR report for 1954 criticised France for retaining only three combat-ready divisions within his European command. This included the 7th regiment of *tirailleurs marocains*, an obvious candidate for reassignment to Algeria. Anxious not to denude its European divisional strength still further, and wary about diminishing French influence within NATO, the committee of national defence urged that the required reinforcements for Algeria be drawn from other units. Care was to be taken not to provide these soldiers with US equipment, supplied for use within NATO alone.[22] The Anglo-American response was muted; it was, after all, self-evident that the Algiers command required more front-line soldiers. On 28 May the NATO Council gave grudging approval to the proposed transfers of troops from the 15^{e}, 25^{e} and 29^{e} divisions. Gruenther, however, registered his disapproval in two letters to the Minister of National Defence, General Pierre Koenig.[23]

Unease within the NATO Council re-emerged over the summer months as the French general staff discussed further reinforcement of North Africa, particularly after the horrific violence in Morocco and Algeria on 20 August. Again, the NATO commanders sent out a mixed message: redeployment of so many French units threatened SACEUR's planning but protection of French North Africa was acknowledged as fundamental to European defence. As before, Gruenther protested that these North African obligations undermined the southern sector of the Rhine command where France's NATO divisions had been concentrated.[24] From Paris, Dillon warned in August that the parliamentary national defence committee was preoccupied with Algeria, not with NATO obligations in Europe. If necessary, the government would commit its entire conventional forces to hold the line in North Africa.[25]

In spite of the indications of the previous year, the British and US governments were surprised that Mollet's centre-left coalition extended the Algerian war decisively by introducing conscripts to the conflict from March 1956. In the weeks between the 2 January 1956 ballot and Mollet's formation of his Republican Front Cabinet a month later, the State Department made ready to publicise its support for the comprehensive reform plan promised during the election campaign.[26] Thereafter, US attitudes towards Mollet's appointment of Lacoste as Resident Minister and the passage of special powers legislation reflected an overwhelming sense that the French government had plunged head-long into the abyss. To the US government, Mollet's Cabinet were agents of their own destruction in North Africa, as reckless over Egypt as they were short-sighted over Algeria. Unwilling to confront settler intransigence and strike out in pursuit of reform, Mollet's administration opted instead for a massively expensive military venture with dubious prospect of success. In the first phase of the 1956 Plan Valmy reinforcement schedule, three infantry divisions were designated for immediate dispatch to Algeria. Abandoning earlier discretion, these troops were armed with a combination of French and American weaponry, notably the US carbine rifle.[27] Bourgès-Maunoury and General Ely insisted that the broad equivalence of NATO and Warsaw Pact conventional forces in Europe made French troop withdrawals strategically insignificant. Divisions reassigned to Algeria were better employed in protection of French interests and the southern perimeter of the western alliance.[28]

On 21 February Mollet warned Dillon that, if France were ejected from the Maghreb, francophone Africa would fall under communist influence. Alarmed at increasing signs of anti-Americanism in France, the ambassador and Henry Cabot Lodge, US delegate to the UN, urged Eisenhower to reaffirm US backing for French efforts to restore order to Algeria. Jebb's statement of British solidarity with France to the Algerian regional press association on 6 March added urgency to the problem as did Selwyn Lloyd's reiteration of Jebb's remarks during Commons questions a week later. But both took pains to explain that Britain offered moral rather than material support. US Under-Secretary of State Herbert Hoover refused to go this far, leaving Dillon to stress Washington's sympathy for France's Algerian predicament in a speech on 19 March. Behind the façade of ambassadorial and ministerial statements, the specialist bureaucrats on both sides of the Atlantic were more candid. On 8 March African department officials advised US embassy staff that the French position in Algeria was untenable regardless of the policies pursued.[29] In the aftermath of parliamentary and press criticism of Jebb's March speech, the Foreign Office prohibited Mill-Irving in Algiers from making public statements of support for French actions. Since Lacoste's reform plans remained vague and Algeria was supposedly an internal French matter, far better to let sleeping dogs lie. Mollet had only requested British 'understanding' of France's Algerian difficulties when he met Eden on 11 March. Annoyed by Pineau's discussions with Nasser in Cairo, Eden was not in a generous mood.[30]

As this Anglo-American obfuscation became clearer, French anger focused on Washington. During the French Senate debate on Algeria on 31 May Lacoste and the Social Republican senator, Michel Debré, later appointed Prime Minister under de Gaulle in 1959, stoked the fires of anti-American sentiment. Debré accused the US government of being 'consistently hostile' to French and British policies in Africa. As a 'battlefield of world conflict' Algeria was pivotal to the West; its loss would bring down the French Republic and usher in a communist regime. Given Debré's subsequent role in bringing de Gaulle to office in May 1958, his criticism of US actions seems ludicrous. But he spoke for a wide spectrum of political opinion in 1956.[31]

Continued pressure from the Afro-Asian group of UN member states for General Assembly consideration of the Algerian situation added to French sensitivity regarding alleged lapses in American or British support. This was brought into sharper focus by concomitant demands from the Afro-Asian bloc for renewed consideration of the situation in Morocco as well. The Moroccan problem had been put before the General Assembly every year since 1951. Pressure for UN consideration of the Tunisian situation also peaked between 1952 and 1954.[32] From 1952 onwards the French delegation did not block inscription of debates over Morocco calculating that to do so would provoke more damaging arguments within the UN bureau which determined the General Assembly's agenda. But Algeria, as a full colony rather than a protectorate, was a different matter. Here, the French delegation contested any UN right to involvement and expected unequivocal Anglo-American backing. As fellow sufferers of anti-colonial criticism, British support was taken for granted, especially after France endorsed Britain's opposition to inscription of the Greek government's proposal for Cypriot self-determination at the September 1954 General Assembly.[33]

Eleven months later, Couve de Murville saw clouds gathering. In the wake of the Bandung Conference, the State Department was acutely sensitive to charges of collusion with the colonial powers and determined to recover lost credibility amongst the newly independent states of Asia. A reassertion of America's lapsed anti-colonialism was an obvious weapon in the contest for the hearts and minds of the Bandung nations.[34] In the annual round of pre-General Assembly talks on colonial matters between State Department officials and British Foreign Office and Colonial Office representatives on 23–24 August 1955 the US delegation stressed the link between the crisis in the Maghreb and the increased cohesion of the non-aligned powers.[35] To ignore the former risked further alienating the latter. Meanwhile, the UN Secretary-General, Dag Hammarskjöld, remained broadly sympathetic to the French interpretation of the UN Charter as applied to French North Africa. But he had to perform a delicate balancing act between the colonial powers and the Afro-Asian bloc. Hammarskjöld could not be expected to rubber-stamp any French 'Non' to UN consideration of Morocco or Algeria.[36]

During the tenth session of the UN General Assembly on 27 and 30 September 1955 Algeria was discussed in open session as delegates considered whether to ratify the Assembly bureau's recommendation against inscription of the Algerian problem. This occasioned the strongest attacks hitherto from Afro-Asian bloc delegates against French colonial oppression and human rights abuses. In reply, Foreign Minister Pinay and France's ambassador to the UN, Hervé Alphand, insisted that, in strict legal terms, Algeria was France. There was no room for equivocation over France's claim that the rebellion was a purely internal affair. Article II, paragraph 7 – the 'domestic jurisdiction clause' – of the UN Charter disbarred member states from debating the internal policies of individual states. Those nations that supported UN consideration of the Algerian problem effectively implied that the Muslim and settler populations could not live harmoniously in a French Algeria. Since French reforms were all built on the foundation of inter-communal coexistence, it was offensive to suggest that government policy was less than colour-blind.[37] The intricacy of this argument did not have the desired result. Most UN delegations did not accept that Algeria was a country moulded by France, recognising instead that the rebellion had catalysed a specifically Algerian national identity defined in opposition to French rule.[38]

The British endorsed Pinay's approach, though it was left to Belgian Foreign Minister Paul-Henri Spaak to defend the French case most strongly on the Assembly floor.[39] In spite of Pinay's protestations, a motion to inscribe Algeria on the agenda was passed by a single vote. This prompted a French walk-out. Alphand saw the comic theatricality of this, the more so as he immediately set about preparations for France's return. But it did isolate France within the UN.[40] Faure even proposed a bill authorising a complete withdrawal – a heat-of-the-moment reaction unlikely to proceed as France was about to assume the presidency of the Security Council. In René Girault's phrase, the 1955 vote established the UN's role as the 'moral tribunal' of the international community. For the first time, France was not only accused, but narrowly convicted.[41] To Foreign Office relief, Quai d'Orsay irritation at this defeat again focused on Washington rather than London, although the Americans too had voted against inscription. This prompted fraught exchanges between Pinay and Dulles in early October over the wisdom of French tactics in the General Assembly.[42] Macmillan helped heal these wounds during talks with Pinay and Dulles in Geneva in early November, when the three foreign ministers agreed to liaise more closely over how best to keep Algeria off the UN agenda in future.[43]

In New York, Hussein Aït Ahmed, now serving as FLN envoy to the UN, consolidated support amongst the Afro-Asian bloc. On 6 April 1956, representatives of the non-aligned movement convened at his request to discuss the alarming escalation of the war.[44] But in June 1956 the Security Council proved unreceptive, rejecting an Afro-Asian group request to debate the threat to international peace posed by the Algerian conflict. As expected, France's fellow colonial powers, Britain and Belgium, each with an eye to Cyprus and the Congo, stood four-square with France.[45] This was hardly cause for celebration. The Security Council's permanent members were never likely to agree amongst themselves over French North Africa. The new Soviet Foreign Minister, Dimitri Chepilov, appointed on 2 June, was an expert on Arab affairs, an Arabic speaker and a keen Algeria-watcher. Khrushchev made no bones about Soviet support for inscription, bluntly telling Moscow ambassador Maurice Dejean on 6 July that France should grant Algeria its independence. This followed the publication of the first leading editorial in *Pravda* explicitly attacking colonialism in Algeria and calling for France's withdrawal.[46] At the PCF Congress in Le Havre a fortnight later, Party leader Maurice Thorez followed the Soviet lead. He rejected the resolution passed at the SFIO Congress in Lille advocating 'a war on two fronts' against the FLN and against the colonialist '*ultras*' who blocked reform. Instead, Thorez called unequivocally for an independent Algeria less than six months after supporting the Special Powers.[47]

The British and US delegations estimated that a strictly limited discussion of Algeria within the eleventh UN General Assembly session in November 1956 might assuage Afro-Asian demands for the Security Council to intervene more strongly with France. The Foreign Office saw little profit in attempting to persuade Commonwealth members – India above all – that Algeria lay outside UN competence. British tactics to prevent UN consideration of Cyprus were increasingly based upon Turkish opposition to *enosis* rather than invocation of the domestic jurisdiction argument favoured by the French.[48] Since 1952 Quai d'Orsay strategy regarding UN consideration of Morocco and Tunisia had been to allow inscription, safe in the knowledge that the Assembly and the Security Council would not vote for a full debate on the floor of the UN. By 1956 this was no longer the case since the General Assembly now contained an additional 16 member states, most of whom were avowedly anti-colonialist. If the French delegation now tried to block inscription of the Algerian problem, there was bound to be an international row before the matter even reached the UN agenda. The FLN would win the publicity war whether or not France successfully opposed inscription. As a result, the Quai d'Orsay's conference secretariat admitted the logic of British arguments. Since it was probably fruitless to oppose inscription, better to follow the British lead over Cyprus. Just as the British had ceased their effort to block debate and instead went on the offensive within the General Assembly against Greek support for Cypriot terrorism, so France could use the seizure of the *Athos* to lambast Egypt's involvement in Algeria.[49]

The international clamour for unrestricted censure of France following the arrest of the four FLN leaders on 22 October made this change of tactic irrelevant.[50] Following the arrests crisis, 25 African and Asian governments condemned the French action at the UN, and Algeria was inscribed on the General Assembly agenda on 14 November. Funds for donation to the Algerian rebels were launched across the Middle East, and the FLN executive took the unusual step of sending a commercial telegram direct to Eisenhower to plead for US help in securing the release of Ben Bella and his colleagues.[51] This elicited no reply, although accusations in the French Algerian press that the captured FLN leaders possessed documents proving the involvement of three US oil companies in funding the rebellion hardly endeared the State Department to French actions in Algeria.[52] The accused directors of Caltex, Standard Oil of California and the Texas Oil Company, denied the allegations made against them, particularly the charge made by the mayor of Oran that Ben Bella had sold exclusive rights to recently discovered Saharan oil to a US consortium.[53] This did not appease Pineau. In January 1957 he complained to Dulles that the Americans misrepresented French policy in Algeria and misunderstood the linkage between national elections and the commitment to negotiations with representative Algerian leaders.[54] This was not how the State Department viewed matters. Most agreed with Lewis Clark's New Year assessment from Algiers: the French were 'in a dream world':

> Lacoste and Mollet insist that if it were not for fear of FLN reprisals [the] vast majority [of the] Muslim population [of] Algeria would be delighted to participate in [the] proposed reform program. That may have been true a year ago but now there is too much evidence that [the] breach between [the] two communities has become so great that it would be hard to find [a] Moslem of substance who is not contributing financially to [the] FLN and who does not hope for its success.[55]

British and American frustration over the diplomatic fall-out from the October arrests was sharpened by the belief that France had also thrown away the chances of Moroccan or Tunisian mediation of an Algerian ceasefire. Although Rabat and Tunis later renewed their offers to broker an Algerian settlement, the Sultan's conspicuous failure to prevent attacks on settlers in Meknès immediately after the Algiers arrests caused understandable pessimism among British and American embassy staffs in Paris.[56]

Throughout 1957 the British and US governments remained torn between encouragement of Moroccan and Tunisian mediation, continued support for France at the UN and direct diplomatic intervention in Paris to hasten French recognition of Algeria's right to independence. None of these alternatives promised much reward. Moroccan and Tunisian plans for Algeria's future were markedly different, the Moroccans still hoping to link a settlement to the creation of a Maghreb federation.[57] British and American diplomats could not agree whether France would accept North African mediation at all. Most accepted that negotiations could only succeed if the French government recognised the FLN and discussed full independence. Mollet's successor, Bourgès-Maunoury, who briefly took office on 13 June, was anyway hostile to outside interference.[58]

Over the next 12 months the Americans took a clear lead. The State Department was convinced that any solution based on the forthcoming *loi cadre* was no solution at all. This was vital. By mid-1957 the US government considered French policy in Algeria fatally flawed. Independence, not autonomy, was the only viable solution. So the plans for constitutional revision and limited Algerian self-government enshrined in an eventual *loi cadre* were bound to be an irrelevance, whatever their precise detail. But the French political leadership was politically and psychologically incapable of admitting this publicly. It was pointless to think otherwise. Increased diplomatic pressure in Paris or at the UN would only drive French heads further into the sand. Accurate and alarming reports of mounting army dissent within Algeria from the US consulate in Algiers further added to American caution. 'Anglo-Saxon' pressure for independence talks risked alienating the Algiers command to whom Lacoste had delegated considerable civil power since the extension of pacification measures at the start of the year. Another condemnation of France at the UN was expected to harden French opposition to reform.[59]

This gloomy prognosis left open one route for indirect US pressure on France. This was economic diplomacy which, according to historian

Matthew Connelly, Washington used to exert a decisive influence on French policy in Algeria after Suez. Eisenhower was determined that France should not undermine the western position in North Africa. In Connelly's view, over subsequent months, the US administration withheld loan funding and military aid until Paris committed itself to troop withdrawals and early negotiation with the FLN. Although Dulles later denied it, this was substantially what the senior Arab ambassadors in Washington had pressed the US government to do. The linkage between US grant funding and a French commitment to return troops from Algeria to NATO duties in Europe was certainly considered by the National Security Council in October 1957. But Irwin Wall has stressed that Dulles disliked the idea, as did Eisenhower.[60] Prior to this, in February 1957 a chastened Pineau promised an acceleration of reform in order to prevent the UN General Assembly from proceeding with a full debate over Algeria. Although this alleviated the pressure on the French delegation in New York, it was clear that Mollet's government could expect little help from Britain or the US within the Security Council if it failed to live up to Pineau's promise to the General Assembly.[61]

Two months later Pineau notified French heads of mission overseas that the government was to set up a 'Commission for the protection of individual rights and liberties'. Whatever the excesses of FLN butchery, France would not resort to similar repressive measures. But the establishment of this Commission was driven by rising UN protest, orchestrated within the Afro-Asian bloc, against the very practices that Pineau insisted were not taking place.[62] As the revelations of army torture spread during the course of 1957, most UN member states considered the equation between the restoration of order and the implementation of reform broken once and for all. On 24 May a delegation of 11 Arab ambassadors in Washington appealed to Dulles for immediate US intervention to end the violence in Algeria.[63] France appeared to have crossed the line into the prosecution of unrestricted colonial war. This sentiment was shared by countless French citizens for whom the news of torture, detention without trial and forced relocation of civilian populations into refugee camps was a painful reminder of their own wartime experiences. To those whose party allegiances were shaped by the experience of occupation and resistance, the Algerian conflict touched their political core. The parallels drawn between the Algerian conflict and French experiences in the Second World War became a powerful political weapon. In Henri Rousso's words, 'Analogy became a way of laying claim to a political heritage.'[64]

This process gathered momentum in 1957, and it drew Foreign Office attention. In late May, for example, four federations of former French deportees successfully lobbied an 'International Commission against the Regime of Concentration Camps' to press Mollet's government to set up an independent enquiry into detention centres in Algeria. The enquiry findings, published in *Le Monde* on 27 July, highlighted widespread arbitrary arrests of young Algerians by the army, the gendarmerie and the DST. Before detainees were properly screened by camp authorities, several instances of beatings and even torture were cited in the one-month period legally permitted for the detention of terrorist suspects. Overall, however, the enquiry rejected claims of systematic torture or disregard for due legal process, and stressed that the concentration camp analogy was invalid. But *Le Monde*'s publication a day earlier of details of the arrest and torture by French parachutists of five staff of the International Voluntary Service for Peace diminished the impact of the enquiry's more favourable report.[65]

An additional commission of enquiry was instituted by government decree on 7 May to investigate allegations of army malpractice. Chaired by former procurator general, Pierre Beteille, this was a more substantial body, its 12 members including leading lawyers and academics, a former military governor of Paris and the much-respected former colonial governor, Robert Delavignette. Here, too, the commission findings that allegations of army brutality were much exaggerated were undermined, first by Delavignette's resignation in September, and second by the circumstances in which the commission conclusions were published three months later. On 13 December *Le Monde* published a leaked copy of the commission report and a secret file from Lacoste's office on military atrocities.[66] Confronted with this *fait accompli*, premier Félix Gaillard's belated decision to publish the Beteille report only added to the impression that the Paris authorities were not the real masters in Algiers. This was quickly proven. Within a week the Chamber of Deputies debated Algeria. Under a barrage of right-wing questions, Lacoste committed the government to stringent preconditions for a ceasefire, including the compulsory surrender of FLN weapons. This destroyed Gaillard's preferred solution of a ceasefire implemented by stages, with each step intended to build up mutual trust.[67]

The Foreign Office did not accept official French figures regarding Algerians held in detention camps, refugees or victims of torture and army brutality.[68] Filtered up to the Foreign Secretary, the Joint Intelligence Committee and to Macmillan's Cabinet, this information added to government unease about support for France in Algeria. It did not, however, produce a tangible shift in policy. For the first time since the rebellion began, the government risked falling out of step with British public opinion, which became more conversant with events in Algeria during 1957. This was largely the result of two factors. First, with the support of the Movement for Colonial Freedom and Labour MPs including Anthony Wedgewood Benn and Barbara Castle, an FLN information office directed by Mohamed Kellou opened in London to publicise the Algerian situation. Second, and perhaps more important, the press reported extensively on the battle of Algiers, in particular the alleged use of torture by French security forces, notably Massu's 10^e^ division parachutists, against Yacef Saadi's urban terrorist network. This fed, in turn, on information drawn from the mass of French press coverage, notably in *L'Express, Esprit, Les Temps Modernes* and *France-Observateur,* as well as the developing anti-war protest movement and its publicisation of atrocities.[69] News of the dirty war in Algeria had particular resonance for those British readers alarmed by reports of British military actions in Cyprus and Kenya which, by 1958, were attracting the attention of the Council of Europe's Human Rights Commission. Press accounts of army malpractice in Algeria culminated in the serialisation of Henri Alleg's *La Question* in the *Manchester Guardian* in March 1958 in which Alleg, the former Communist editor of the Algiers daily *Alger Républicain,* detailed his experiences of torture under interrogation by parachutists under Massu's command. Within days Macmillan's parliamentary private secretary was deluged with letters of protest from constituents.[70]

For the British government the most vital consequence of the intensification of the Algerian conflict during 1957 was the further internationalisation of the war. The annual round of UN debates, the global furore over army brutality, and the shortfalls in the French military contribution to NATO's European shield forces: all indicated that Algeria was a central issue in France's relations with its western partners. While Macmillan moved to repair the 'special relationship' after the Suez disaster at the Bermuda and Washington conferences in 1957, Algeria became a worsening complication in France's relations with the US and Britain. The war was making the Chamber of Deputies ungovernable, the basic equation in Mollet's survival having been the prosecution of an essentially right-wing policy in North Africa in exchange for parliamentary acquiescence in limited social reform within France. During the autumn, the protracted quarrel over the *loi cadre* and the unedifying spectacle of six weeks without a French government following Bourgès-Maunoury's resignation on 30 September highlighted the crisis of the Fourth Republic regime.[71] This was nothing new. In May Pineau told Macmillan that effective governance in the Fourth Republic was impossible. The Foreign Minister joked that 'the best system for France might be to have no Government at all, but only a well organised opposition which w[oul]d command the unswerving allegiance of all parties.'[72]

Troubled relations with the former protectorates made matters worse. Always hostile to French withdrawal, Georges Bidault insisted that Mendès France failed to secure adequate security guarantees from the Moroccan and Tunisian governments before conceding independence in 1956. This problem returned to haunt the French army in Algeria during 1957.[73] In the autumn Bourguiba's government used the spectre of an arms supply deal with the Soviet Union to secure US and British promises of military contracts with the Tunisian government. France was conspicuously frozen out. Small arms were by this point being trafficked across the Tunisia–Algeria frontier in sufficient number to reprovision the FLN military effort in its eastern *wilaya* commands.[74] Over the winter of 1957–58, Tunisia was the nexus between Anglo-US efforts to prevent the newly independent North African regimes from succumbing to Soviet or Egyptian influence and the French military drive to close Algeria's land frontiers, so cutting the flow of weapons to the FLN. The result was a clash between western strategic plans and the more aggressive French war effort.

1958: the Algerian Frontier and Franco-Tunisian Relations

By the spring of 1958 British disillusionment with French policy and Stronger American pressure on France were subsumed within the crisis in Franco-Tunisian relations that erupted after the French air force attack on the Tunisian border settlement of Sakiet Sidi Youssef on 8 February. In an attempt to knock out an ALN support base, French aircraft with US-supplied bombs killed at least 70 Tunisian villagers, many of them children. Alleging that an abandoned mine equipped with anti-aircraft weaponry housed an ALN base several hundred strong, the Constantine army corps command, the army and air force commanders in Algeria, Generals Salan and Edmond Jouhaud, and Jacques Chaban-Delmas' Ministry of Defence defended the intense French aerial bombardment of Sakiet. Led by B26 bombers, this was a major air raid, triggered by the shooting down of a French reconnaissance plane and an earlier successful ALN ambush upon a French unit just across the Algerian frontier on 11 January in which 14 soldiers were killed, their bodies mutilated, and four prisoners taken. To Dulles this was proof that French policy in North Africa was morally and politically bankrupt and inadequately controlled from Paris.

The *loi cadre* had not won Muslim support and, for all their present resolve, the French might yet give up the struggle to communist benefit, as in Indo-China. Information from Lacoste's Algiers advisers, in particular his *chef de cabinet*, Pierre Chaussade, suggested that, while Gaillard's Cabinet approved limited cross-border ripostes against FLN units based inside Tunisia, ministers envisaged army raids rather than an aerial bombardment never properly approved through the chain of command from the Bône Corps headquarters. Yet, while the Sakiet raid was not considered in advance by the French Cabinet as a whole, standing army instructions to pursue Algerian rebels across the Algerian frontier were well known, and Chaban-Delmas above all seems to have been fully cognizant of the planned bombardment.[75]

As Irwin Wall has shown, after Sakiet Eisenhower's administration set about political intervention to hasten an end to the war, even at the cost of destabilising Félix Gaillard's government and the Fourth Republic regime. Although it was not Dulles' intention specifically to weaken Gaillard's administration, Wall makes plain that Sakiet wrought a decisive shift in State Department policy. Convinced that policy formulation in Paris was structurally deficient, that the civil–military bureaucracy in Algiers was running out of control and that Tunisian grievances were, ultimately, justified, Washington was prepared to consider unprecedented direct intervention both to contain the crisis in Franco-Tunisian relations and, more importantly, to seek an end to the Algerian war – the root cause of the instability across the Maghreb.[76]

In a key memorandum on 20 February Dulles's special assistant, Julius Holmes, pressed for this policy shift, arguing that Sakiet proved that the Algerian conflict was the prime threat to regional stability throughout the Mediterranean theatre. In so far as Washington recognised that the Fourth Republic could not withstand the loss of Algeria, US pressure for its abandonment challenged the regime itself.[77] This was a logical next step to systematic economic pressure intended to force an Algerian settlement upon France. According to Connelly, two weeks before the Sakiet attack, in return for the release of $650 million in US loan funding, Jean Monnet faced American insistence upon the withdrawal of 150,000 French troops from Algeria as a prelude to ceasefire talks with the FLN leadership.[78] There was now an economic and political dimension to long-standing French bitterness over the Suez crisis and the eagerness with which Morocco and Tunisia courted US favour. This helps explain why the return of de Gaulle also amounted to a rejection of US leadership in the western alliance.[79]

Although the crisis in Algiers catapulted de Gaulle back into office, his early dealings over North Africa with 'les Anglo-Saxons' turned upon a settlement of the Sakiet dispute. Ever since independence in March 1956, Bourguiba's government complained to Paris, Washington and London about periodic French military incursions into western Tunisia in pursuit of ALN formations based across the frontier. Although less severely affected, the Moroccans did much the same regarding French actions along their eastern border. For Tunisia, the problem was compounded by some 200,000 Algerian refugees living on or near the Algero-Tunisian frontier either side of which the Algiers military command had established a demilitarised zone in order to allow more efficient policing of their frontier barrage.[80] In a sense, this was entirely familiar. Before the Algerian rebellion began, the Algiers deuxième bureau reported incidents of arms trafficking and Algerian terrorist cells operating from across both land borders. General Callies conducted large-scale manoeuvres in the Oranais in March 1954 designed to curb any rebel infiltration from Morocco in particular.[81] Evidence of Middle East and eastern bloc support for the FLN always provoked powerful reaction among politicians and soldiers in Paris and Algiers with recent memories of Chinese aid to the Viet Minh.[82] For them, right of pursuit was fundamental to the developing strategy of fortified barriers along Algeria's desert borders.

Of these, the Morice Line along the Tunisian frontier was the more impressive. Named after the Minister of National Defence who approved its construction in late 1957, the Morice Line ran for over 300 km, eclipsing its western equivalent on the Moroccan border. Massive army investment in this barrage indicated that victory in the so-called 'battle of the frontiers' was pivotal to the strategy of the Algiers command. The barrage's electrified barbed-wire fences, garrisoned block-houses, spotlights, minefields and radar surveillance system promised results.[83] Whether blocking, retarding or merely revealing ALN frontier incursions, the fortified barriers enabled the army to maximise its numerical superiority by concentrating forces against previously detected insurgents.[84]

Jean Basdevant, director of the Quai d'Orsay office of Moroccan and Tunisian affairs, dismissed Tunisian allegations against troops of the Constantine Corps command as political point-scoring rather than legitimate protests against violations of national sovereignty. Bourguiba's Cabinet could thus show solidarity with the FLN and exploit French incursions in its campaign to evict French forces from their remaining military bases in Tunisia.[85] The Moroccan government was less confrontational about incidents along its eastern frontier. Yet tension persisted. The precise delineation of the Morocco–Algeria border was agreed only during the final stages of Franco-Moroccan independence negotiations in late February 1956.[86] There was also genuine confusion between the Algiers command and the Royal Moroccan Army over key sections of the frontier, particularly within the Saharan regions formerly administered by French native affairs officers. After receiving complaints from the governor of Oudja province in eastern Morocco, Maurice Faure, secretary for Moroccan and Tunisian affairs, warned Robert Lacoste in May 1957 that the Rabat authorities could not ignore the strafing of Moroccan frontier settlements and nomad encampments.[87] Frontier policing was impeding the development of working relations with the independent Maghreb states. The army's reliance on fortified barrages just as these governments sought to establish their international status was explosive.

France could hardly demand rigorous Tunisian border policing without conceding the country's right to organise its own armed forces in order to do so. As Tunisian ministers later complained, if the might and technical wizardry of the French army could not prevent ALN infiltration across land frontiers, how could France expect Tunisia's poorly equipped security forces to do any better?[88] But a functioning Tunisian army would doubtless want control over all the country's defence installations, including those still manned by French personnel, it might be supplied by the Soviets or Egyptians, and it was bound to be sympathetic to the FLN. No surprise then that negotiations for the Franco-Tunisian common defence agreement, an adjunct to the 1956 treaty settlement, made little progress. Instead, violent disagreement over French base rights steadily intensified.[89] This was further complicated by the reluctance of the French air staff to reorganise the air force command in French North Africa by taking Moroccan and Tunisian independence into account. The *V^e^ région aérienne* covering the three Maghreb states was not reduced in scope to cover only Algeria and the Saharan territories until 16 February 1959, by which time the prospects for air force co-operation with the Tunisians were poor.[90]

Compared to the low-intensity cross-border violence of 1956, in the following year the more systematic French incursions poisoned Franco-Tunisian relations.[91] Skirmishes with ALN rebels in Tunisia and the resultant Franco-Tunisian diplomatic clashes escalated in September 1957 following a French mortar attack on the Tunisian frontier post at Haïdra. In their protests Bourguiba and deputy premier Bahi Ladgham maintained that France was now conducting full-scale military operations inside Tunisia. The Tunis government threatened to respond with force to any further incursions and appealed for UN observers to monitor the frontier. Facing mounting obstacles on their established entry routes, ALN units began infiltrating Algeria via the southern Saharan territories. This widened the geographical scope of the conflict and threatened French oil installations more directly. The frontier war was escalating fast. Further complaints about French pursuit operations and violations of Tunisian air space followed in the months leading up to the Sakiet bombardment in early February.[92] After Sakiet Tunisian security forces blockaded French bases inside Tunisia adding a new dimension to the friction.[93]

But it was British and American agreement to supply arms to Tunisia in October 1957 that made the worsening Franco-Tunisian tension a central feature of France's relations with the western powers over the next 12 months.[94] In February 1957 Maurice Faure accepted the French military recommendation that all aid to the Tunisian armed forces should be withheld in an effort to curb Bourguiba's support for the FLN. With a common defence agreement looking unlikely, on 20 May the Mollet Cabinet suspended French financial aid to Tunis. By then, the ALN cadres based in Tunisia outnumbered Tunisia's national army.[95] The British reaction was conditioned by Bourguiba's frank discussions with Anthony Nutting in March in which he admitted that he turned a blind eye to arms smuggling into Algeria as part of his 'precautionary plan' to supplant Nasserite influence over the FLN.[96] The State Department also considered Bourguiba a known, pro-western commodity and did not want Salah Ben Youssef's radical Destour faction strengthened. Without western material support, Bourguiba might adopt a neutralist policy. His *de facto* support for the Algerian rebels was obviously irreversible. By the end of May Selwyn Lloyd agreed, having been persuaded by Adam Watson that French economic pressure risked alienating Tunisian ministers for whom public support of the FLN and a warm welcome for its exiled leaders in Tunis were a matter of political survival.[97]

In these circumstances, Eisenhower's administration had little difficulty in carrying the British towards an arms supply deal. The French were less malleable. On 30 September Mitterrand criticised France's NATO partners for failing to recognise that the Mediterranean was now a more important strategic frontier than the Rhine. Weeks later riot police were called out to guard the US embassy in Paris against protesters incensed by the arms agreement.[98] On 15 November Gaillard told the National Assembly that the supply deal was an 'unfriendly act'. In an effort to repair the damage, in late November Macmillan paid a courtesy call on the new premier in Paris. This smoothed some ruffled feathers but did little to end the underlying dispute over Tunisia.[99]

In fact, Macmillan had lost patience with French strategic arguments over North Africa.[100] His description of 'the French scene' to Dulles on 25 November was acid:

> The French appear to be obsessed with their own problems, domestic and North African. But they make a distinction between the two and do not recognise the connexion between inflation and Algeria. They are not interested in world affairs except to the extent that they might be thought to impinge on their own immediate difficulties. At the same time they are sensitive about their standing in the world. They consider that the Americans want to push them about and resent it. They are jealous of us and annoyed with us for appearing to side with the Americans against them. NATO they regard as a means of extracting blackmail.[101]

The interlocking problems of Tunisia and Algeria remained the major cause of argument between France, Britain and the US throughout Gaillard's term in office. The two signpost events in these months – the Tunisian arms deal in October 1957 and the Sakiet crisis in February 1958 – added to French disillusionment with NATO. French irritation turned to fury once the Anglo-American 'good offices mission' set to work. Led by US Under-Secretary of State Robert Murphy and Foreign Office Under-Secretary Harold Beeley, the good offices mission sought to defuse the Franco-Tunisian crisis over the Sakiet bombardment outside the forum of the UN.[102] In practice, good offices mediation between Paris and Tunis hinged on US diplomatic pressure on Gaillard's government to make further concessions over base rights, border security and compensation to Bourguiba's administration. Macmillan and Jebb feared that the mission would threaten Britain's standing in France increasing the likelihood of an impasse over British trade with the European Community.[103]

Disagreement over the strategic importance of the Algerian war within western defence planning was a root cause of these tensions. Although Algeria drew off far larger numbers of French troops than any British colonial emergency, in the wake of the 1957 Sandys defence review the British government made greater cuts to its standing military forces. As a result, by 1958 Britain shared France's difficulty in maintaining its commitment to NATO strength on the continent. Although the French army avoided such major reductions in its front-line units, during 1957 Minister of National Defence André Morice sought to reduce the service term for troops assigned to Algeria from 27 to 24 months. A popular measure in France, this none the less exacerbated NATO troop shortages.[104] The 1958 NATO annual review stipulated the forces required of the alliance's major powers over the subsequent five years. The North Atlantic Council set force levels for the British Army Of the Rhine (BAOR) which the chiefs of staff criticised as beyond the BAOR's manpower and weapons capacity.[105] Far from increasing its commitment, the Ministry of Defence was in the throes of reducing BAOR standing strength to 56,000 by the end of 1958 in anticipation of further reductions during 1959. By that point an Anglo-West German settlement of local defence costs would make possible a further cutback to a BAOR strength of some 45,000 troops. This was in line with the Sandys review which envisaged the implementation of these reductions by 1960–61. If anything, the Cyprus emergency was expected to impose a heavier drain on British troop strength in the short term, such that the service chiefs predicted in June 1958 that the BAOR might need to be cut further to some 35,000 in total.[106] Clearly, there was greater common ground between the British and French positions than might first be assumed when studying the massive deployment of forces in Algeria during the 1956–60 period. But the fact that the western partners faced similar difficulties in maintaining their conventional force commitments to NATO in Europe tended to generate friction between them rather than any parallel approach to a problem shared.

In Foreign Office reports during October 1957 Sir Frank Roberts, head of the UK delegation to NATO in Paris, and Admiral Denny, Britain's representative on the NATO standing group, measured Algeria's military importance to the western alliance. Both men pointed out the fallacy of NATO's strategic assumptions, based as they were upon maintaining Mediterranean sea communications and the Algiers and Oran naval bases after an initial nuclear exchange. The naval and air force facilities in Algeria and the logistic support that French forces in the country could provide to NATO's southern European command would be irrelevant if not obliterated after the first wave of Soviet nuclear attack. The strategic value of Algeria's bases and resources did not justify the reassignment of vast numbers of French troops better employed in European defence. It was politically unwise to count upon the durability of French rule or to expect that an independent Algeria would necessarily become a Soviet or Egyptian lackey. As Roberts stressed, NATO clearly faced a dilemma over Algeria:

> On the one hand, the continuance of the *présence française* would safeguard NATO bases, ensure western strategic predominance and

> give the Russians no chance of establishing a foothold. But it might at the same time delay indefinitely the reconstruction of the French forces where they should be, i.e. in Central Europe. On the other hand, a French political and military withdrawal would remove Algeria from the NATO area, eliminate the NATO bases and perhaps reduce Algeria and even the whole of the Maghreb to chaos which, while not necessarily leading to Soviet predominance in the area, might well result in a situation more dangerous than the present crisis from the NATO point of view, more particularly if the loss of Algeria were to create in France a profound disillusionment with the Alliance. In these circumstances probably the only policy which can usefully be pursued by NATO countries, individually or collectively, is to continue discreetly to encourage the French to come to terms with Arab nationalism while they can still count upon the help of such relatively moderate Arab leaders as the present rulers of Morocco and Tunisia.[107]

Roberts sent this report as the *loi cadre* came before the National Assembly in October 1957. Although the law was finally passed four months later, the bitter parliamentary debate over constitutional reform suggested that Algeria's future as a core element in NATO's western Mediterranean defence remained uncertain. Nor was it any clearer whether, as Gaillard's government insisted, troop reductions could be made in Algeria to permit French reinforcement of West Germany or whether, as Salan's Algiers command maintained, more soldiers were needed to turn the war against the FLN. French contingency plans to return its three 'missing' NATO divisions from Algeria to Europe in the event of a continental emergency were wholly unrealistic. If troop cuts could really be made in Algeria, the political pressure to reduce the military service term once more from 24 to 18 months might well prove irresistible.[108]

In mid-February 1958 the British chiefs of staff also reviewed the strategic importance of Algeria to NATO. This followed African department warnings that, should France be evicted, it might become necessary to link the Maghreb states to the western alliance through a North African version of SEATO. This might ensure that the NATO powers could maintain air bases and port facilities in Algeria at least. The uneasy relationship between NATO and the Baghdad Pact did not, however, augur well for any Maghreb grouping linked to the western alliance. NATO's Scandinavian members in particular had always resisted any extension of their commitments to cover the quasi-imperial interests of

Britain or France in the Middle East or North Africa.[109] This was brought into sharper focus by Gaillard's proposal for a Mediterranean Pact on 7 March. This held out the prospect of Moroccan, Tunisian and Algerian association with NATO in a regional defence agreement linking the states on the Mediterranean's northern and southern shores. If successful, this would underscore the common western interest in the preservation of French military power in North Africa. Gaillard thus hoped to kill two birds with one stone. The Pact would mark an admission by fellow NATO states that the French military effort in Algeria was worthwhile, and yet it would contain the internationalisation of the Algerian conflict by establishing from the outset that the Maghreb was strategically vital to the western alliance. This would make it impossible for the Anglo-American good offices team to reach a verdict over the Sakiet dispute which ignored France's paramount strategic interests in North Africa.[110]

Gaillard's plan was still-born. The NATO Council did not back it, the SFIO and the Labour Party objected to the suggested inclusion of Franco's Spain, and the proposal was soon overtaken by the course of the good offices mission and the mounting Algerian problems that engulfed Gaillard's administration two months later.[111] It bears emphasis, however, that uncertainty over the French and Maghreb role within NATO was a major British concern months before the May 1958 crisis. The later friction between Britain, the US and de Gaulle's Republic over NATO and Algeria was of a different order, but it was not without precedent.

British and American material support strengthened Bourguiba's hand in his dealings with France over the winter of 1957–58.[112] The diplomatic settlement of the Sakiet dispute, brokered by Murphy and Beeley, weakened the French claim to exclusive military privileges and a *droit de regard* over Tunisian foreign policy still further. In its written defence of the Sakiet bombardment to the UN, Maurice Faure's Moroccan and Tunisian affairs secretariat stressed that, while Cairo remained host to the FLN's external executive under the guidance of Colonel Omar Ouamrane, a former leader of ALN operations in Kabylie and the Algérois, Tunis was now the major centre for the co-ordination of FLN military planning and armaments supply. Faure's advisers further alleged that in July 1957 Bourguiba authorised the FLN to establish a full military staff in Tunis to plan operations in eastern Algeria in conjunction with three subordinate frontier command centres at Souk-el-Arba, Tajerouine and Redeyef which liaised directly with the *wilaya* commanders inside Algeria. Since 80 per cent of rebel arms seized during 1957 derived from external sources, of which 90 per cent were trafficked in via Tunisia, intelligence of an FLN logistical base at Sakiet was held to justify the French attack.[113]

These arguments did not impress Eisenhower, Dulles or Murphy, for whom a ceasefire and a negotiated French withdrawal from Algeria seemed essential if France was not to turn the entire Maghreb away from the west. However, whatever the material evidence of rebel organisation across the Algero-Tunisian frontier, the legality of France's claim to a legitimate right of military pursuit into Tunisian sovereign territory was decidedly questionable. Murphy also questioned the strategic utility of French bases within Tunisia which were not properly integrated into NATO, and he accepted Bourguiba's argument that to give in to French demands would destabilise his regime to Nasser's benefit. Ultimately, the Americans were spoiling for a fight with Gaillard's hapless administration and were quite prepared to topple it.[114]

The Foreign Office worked hard to temper US criticism and find a face-saving formula for the French over Sakiet. Whereas the Americans seemed to have accepted the consequences of inducing further political crisis in France, Macmillan's government was more cautious. The success of British efforts to reconcile its preference for a loose European free trade area with the gradual emergence of a functioning European Economic Community, whose institutional structure was taking shape during 1958, demanded a more subtle approach to Anglo-French relations. With free trade access for British exports to the six founder members of the EEC under threat, there seemed to be considerable advantage in moderating Washington's more hard-line approach within the Good Offices mission. This was hardly successful. In a letter to Gaillard soon leaked to the French press, on 11 April Eisenhower warned of a withdrawal of American support for France at the UN if France did not reach an accommodation with Bourguiba on the basis of the good offices proposals originally rejected by the French Cabinet in mid-March. Although the wording of the President's letter was far milder than originally planned, its very delivery in the first place helped tip Gaillard's already shaky administration over the edge. Following a Chamber of Deputies vote opposing the Gaillard Cabinet's proposal to accept the Good Offices recommendations, on 16 April it fell. The British, and far more so the Americans, thus played an integral part in the unfolding Fourth Republic crisis, albeit driven to do so by the glaring inadequacy of French plans in Algeria.[115]

Superficially, British governmental inability to play much of an honest broker rule in the North African frictions between France and the United States in the spring of 1958 suggests that Britain's efforts to limit the internationalisation of the Algerian war were ineffectual. In practice, after 1954 what little room for diplomatic manoeuvre the Conservative governments may initially have enjoyed gradually ebbed away. By 1957, caught between sensitivity to Britain's faltering prestige in the Arab world, the imperative need to rebuild Anglo-American co-operation after Suez and the potential threat of French leadership of a more or less exclusive European Community, British ministers and officials were disinclined to adopt a more proactive policy towards the Algerian conflict. Cold War interests certainly played their part in British and US policy over Algeria between 1954–58. But after Suez this did not work to French advantage. Before considering the May crisis, the Fifth Republic and Algeria in the final chapter, this Cold War dimension to the Algerian conflict needs to be examined in greater detail.

6
The Algerian Conflict – a Cold War Front Line?

Was France fighting the Cold War on behalf of the western alliance in North West Africa? If so, then the Algerian conflict would have to be recognised as far more than a colonial struggle over national independence. Algeria was included within the southern perimeter of NATO's strategic theatre during the original North Atlantic treaty talks in 1949. Articles 5 and 6 of the treaty brought Algeria within the collective defence provisions of the alliance, effectively acknowledging it as an integral part of a European state.[1] French operations thus took place within territory which NATO signatories were theoretically obliged to defend. But since this was constitutionally French soil, successive Paris governments insisted that their NATO partners had no claim to help direct the conflict. Yet, as we have seen, once the war escalated and the FLN's ideological sympathies became clearer, so French ministers pressed for dispensation from France's alliance obligations and justified requests for material aid in Algeria on the grounds that French forces were working on NATO's behalf.

This attempt to have it both ways – at once excluding international involvement in the conflict whilst pleading for concessions from NATO allies because of the weight of the Algerian burden – caused mounting indignation in Britain and the US. In December 1954 a US briefing paper for the first NATO ministerial meeting since the rebellion began put the matter simply: France could not expect a blank cheque for extended operations, nor could the Algerian problem be both domestic and international at the same time. To press the issue of NATO support for French actions would only divide the alliance. The Scandinavian countries did not want to get involved. Britain, Turkey and Greece refused to alienate the Egyptian regime unnecessarily by supporting French repression. And the US would not bank-roll French security operations over which

Washington exerted no control and about which it was increasingly dubious.[2]

This paper was prepared during Mendès France's visit to Washington, where the French premier reportedly found Eisenhower 'panic-stricken' (*très frappé*) over the possibility of Communist involvement in North African unrest. It seems more likely that Mendès was himself responding to reports from the Quai d'Orsay's department of Moroccan and Tunisian affairs indicating increased Soviet interest in the Maghreb.[3] Neither Britain nor the US were much impressed by French use of the Communist bogey to elicit allied support for policy in North Africa. As Irwin Wall puts it, 'Algeria was a case of clear American acceptance of a revolution that Washington was convinced had the capacity of becoming democratic and non-communist'.[4] The methods and objectives of the increasingly dirty colonial war prosecuted in Algeria threatened serious division among NATO members. In their own strategic and intelligence assessments of the Middle East position after 1954, neither the British service chiefs nor their Joint Intelligence Committee (JIC) included the Maghreb states amongst those considered at grave risk of Soviet incursion or communist subversion.[5] This scepticism was fuelled by British and American irritation at persistent French claims that the Istiqlal and the Néo-Destour were either directly linked to the Soviet bloc or, more implausibly still, were serving Soviet interests simply by challenging French rule and draining off French security forces to the Maghreb. As suggested in Chapter 2, these arguments were put most forcibly during Marshal Juin's term as Resident in Morocco. But Juin's use of the Cold War rhetoric of the zero-sum game seemed ridiculous given the manifest pro-westernism of the Moroccan and Tunisian nationalist leaderships.[6]

Within the French command in Algeria, however, the equation of pan-Arabism and Soviet imperialism and the fixation with NATO's southern flank endured throughout the war.[7] Sino-Soviet co-operation, the spread of Nasserite influence and the threat of African communism were all adduced to link the Algerian conflict to a global struggle between western civilisation, Oriental Arabism and a generic Communist threat. From Mao to Mau-Mau, Khrushchev to Kenyatta, the diverse opponents of European colonialism were lumped together as opponents of western values.[8] In 1957 Chief of General Staff Ely still maintained that, with little prospect of conventional war in Europe and the mutual destruction of a nuclear exchange self-evident to East and West, colonial conflicts had to be viewed as proxy wars offering fresh opportunities for communist expansionism. French forces in Algeria were thus defending western interests, NATO's southern perimeter and the African continent against Soviet penetration.[9]

Irritated by French efforts to play the Cold War card to best advantage in Algeria, the British and American governments tended to dismiss sometimes well-justified French arguments regarding the FLN's ideological hostility to the West. Even so, Suez notwithstanding, Conservative governments and Eisenhower's administration generally sought to avoid political clashes with France over North Africa. Though Washington gradually warmed to Maghreb nationalism, France's role as a cornerstone of Eisenhower's European policy remained a more important consideration. Problems arose when the nationalist parties across French North Africa refused to acquiesce in western regional hegemony once independence from France was won. Unfortunately, this only added to the confusion in Paris over America's long-term objectives within North Africa and the Middle East, itself born of the fact that US officials had difficulty mapping the connections between Arab nationalists and the Soviet Union.[10]

The British, too, became caught up in inter-allied disagreement over the nature of the Maghreb conflict. This was brought into sharper relief during the course of 1955, a year in which Jebb's reports from Paris were dominated by two issues – the prospects for détente with the Soviet Union and the deepening French crisis in North Africa.[11] On 28 January a Foreign Office delegation led by Evelyn Shuckburgh discussed the Middle Eastern situation with members of the State Department office of Near Eastern affairs. There was confusion over French objectives in the region. France had no close Arab clients, its colonial policies were generally detested and its growing material support for Israel destabilised the local balance of power. But so long as the British and Americans refused to treat France on an equal footing in discussions over the Middle East, French co-operation was unlikely. Neither party saw much to admire in French policy in North Africa. Yet criticism of France's actions would not achieve much. Politicians genuinely committed to reform would be pilloried as lackeys of the Anglo-Saxon powers, making it more difficult to construct a viable parliamentary majority in favour of negotiated withdrawal from Morocco or Tunisia.[12] This impasse in Anglo-American approaches towards French North Africa was matched by the stalemate in French policies towards Morocco and Algeria. Edgar Faure's government – and the Radical Party more generally – was split between die-hard supporters of Sultan Moulay Arafa and those who accepted that reinstatement of Sultan Ben Youssef was essential. This stymied policy formulation. Moroccan guerrilla attacks escalated over the summer just as the Algerian rebellion, too, was dramatically extended by the Constantine massacres and the retribution which followed in late August.

With the promulgation of the South East Asian Treaty Organisation (SEATO) in September 1954, France, Britain and the US reiterated their commitment to regional alliance networks explicitly designed to resist the spread of communism.[13] Immediately prior to the Algerian rebellion, the western allies thus bound themselves afresh to the war against communism in colonial, or formerly colonial, territory. The Maghreb was no South East Asia. Nevertheless, parallels between the political organisation, the techniques of popular control and the armed insurgency of the Viet Minh and the FLN became easier to find once the conflict intensified after August 1955. By this point, British military intelligence planners sometimes classified Arab 'national liberation movements' as proto-communist since they were expected to seek Soviet material aid and political advice. Communist front organisations already active in North Africa, such as the World Federation of Trade Unions and the International Union of Students, were considered the major conduit for any such creeping Soviet influence.[14] Prior to the Constantine massacres, neither British nor American diplomatic and military representatives in Algeria and France had a clear picture of the FLN or its forebear, the *Comité Révolutionnaire d'Unité et d'Action* (CRUA). The ideology of the FLN, its relationship with the more established nationalist parties and its role in directing the rebellion were scarcely addressed in reports filed to London and Washington in the first six months of the Algerian war.[15] French military intelligence and the SDECE failed to persuade the NATO Council that the FLN was subject to Egyptian control and ideologically committed to the communist bloc. These arguments were advanced before the rebellion even began. The relaunch of the Cairo-based Committee for North African Liberation on 4 April 1954 was, for example, held to prove a Nasserite revolutionary masterplan to seize control of the Maghreb.[16] Although advised of at least part of this intelligence material, not until the Congress of the Soummam in August 1956 did the Foreign Office devote significant reportage to the long-term ideological alignment of the FLN leadership.

Worsening Tension over Algeria and the Middle East

The contrast between the discordant Anglo-French responses to North African strategic problems and their continuing low-profile co-operation over defence facilities in sub-Saharan Africa after a preliminary conference in Dakar in March 1954 indicated that the differences between them were, at root, political.[17] In talks with Dulles and Macmillan at the Quai d'Orsay in mid-December 1955, Foreign Minister Pinay therefore shifted attention from French North Africa to the Middle East. Echoing the British, Pinay suggested that the foremost Arab threat to the western alliance lay in Egypt rather than in the disintegration of Maghreb ties to France and the western powers.[18] The impending escalation of the Arab–Israeli crisis and the descent to Suez inevitably diminished British criticism of French actions in North Africa. But this masked the fact that there had been no meeting of minds over French plans for Algeria in particular.

It bears emphasis that the ties uniting Britain and France over Suez and Nasser were always weak. France's readiness to supply Mystère jet fighters to Israel inflamed regional tension and added to the spiralling Middle East arms race which Eden had warned the Soviet government against when Czechoslovakia delivered weapons to Egypt in the autumn of 1955.[19] The Algerian link was obvious. On 11 October 1955 Ambassador Chauvel admitted that Faure's Cabinet had cancelled planned arms deliveries to Egypt and Syria 'for internal political reasons' after both countries once more opposed France over inscription of the Algerian problem onto the UN agenda.[20] Reluctantly, on 15 December Pinay conceded that French aircraft deliveries to Israel should be deferred pending discussion within the Near East Arms Co-ordinating Committee (NEACC). In return, Britain and the US were expected to intervene more rigorously against Arab states discovered supplying the Algerian and Moroccan rebels, technically a problem outside the jurisdiction of the NEACC.[21]

The British government remained anxious about the consequences across the Middle East of too cosy a relationship with the unpopular French. British representatives in Libya questioned French evidence indicating that both King Idris and his Minister of Defence had smuggled arms direct to the FLN. Grudgingly, Macmillan conceded that the Foreign Office might intervene with the Tripoli government if the French accusations were proven.[22] Here, too, issues of force deployments and arms supplies proved divisive. The Franco-Libyan treaty of friendship signed on 10 August 1955 made provision for the final withdrawal of French garrisons from Libya by 30 November 1956 by which time a final delimitation of the Libya–Algeria border was to be agreed. But the National Assembly refused to ratify the treaty whilst suspicion persisted of Libyan arms trafficking to the FLN. The discovery of oil within this frontier region added a new dimension to the problem in 1956.[23] Since its 1953 treaty with Tripoli made Britain the protecting power, French insistence on maintaining troops in the Fezzan until such time as Tunisia and Algeria were pacified caused a clash of interests. Since Britain was effectively the temporary guardian of the Fezzan, the retention of French forces in the area to block arms deliveries to the Maghreb – possibly from British client-states – was a most unwelcome diplomatic problem. In April 1955 Macmillan advised Pinay that Britain could not permit French troops to remain in the Fezzan beyond the end of that year. If Britain supported France wholeheartedly over the Fezzan and the wider problem of arms smuggling to French North Africa, its ties with friendly Arab nations would suffer, all to Nasser's benefit.[24]

For France there was no such conflict of priorities and, as Chauvel warned, strong currents of Anglophobia ran through the Quai d'Orsay's Levant section, nurtured by individuals harbouring grievances dating from the wartime disputes over Syria and Lebanon. This was particularly ironic since much of the French intelligence on Middle Eastern arms trafficking to Tunisia and Algeria derived from British sources.[25] As expected, the French made no moves to withdraw their garrison from the Fezzan as the confrontation with Nasser intensified. Libyan anger at this and the arrest of the FLN leaders in October 1956 heightened British chiefs of staff fears of an Egyptian-inspired coup in Tripoli as France's evacuation deadline approached.[26] Although this problem was quickly subsumed within the wider crisis over the Suez expedition, once again French North Africa led the Paris government to adopt a cavalier attitude towards the game of political influence in the Middle East.

Not surprisingly, in April 1955 an official French purchase request for 20 Whirlwind helicopters for use in North African operations proved just as problematic for the British government as France's earlier attempts to obtain Westland machines for use in Indo-China. Helicopters had been in service in Algeria and Morocco for several months, although not in sufficient number to meet the requirements of the ground forces locally deployed.[27] Facing trade union opposition to similar French requests for a larger order of US machines, Robert Murphy justified the American decision to provide the helicopters by arguing that the sooner France restored order in Algeria the sooner its forces could return to NATO duties in Europe. The State Department also considered linking approval for the use of US helicopters in Algeria to the rapid conclusion of a Franco-Tunisian settlement.[28] British concerns were different, although the departmental fault-lines within Whitehall were much the same as they had been during the disputes over equipment for Indo-China in 1952–53. The Ministry of Defence and the service chiefs again rejected the French proposal owing to Britain's own supply needs in Malaya. The matter was clearly important to Faure's government. Pinay raised the issue with Eden, and Jebb urged some gesture to the French.[29] Governor Soustelle was already calling for an increase to the Cabinet's recently announced 100,000 troop ceiling in Algeria. And Interior Minister Bourgès-Maunoury, an individual with considerable experience in French service ministries, insisted to US embassy staff in Paris that 20 helicopters in the Aurès mountains could accomplish more than a full infantry division. With *colon* representatives in the Constantine Chamber of Agriculture threatening to organise vigilante militias unless the French authorities intensified counter-insurgency operations in the region, a show of strength was essential.[30] In a letter to Air Minister Lord De l'Isle, Macmillan took the broad geostrategic view typical of Foreign Office assessments of France's Maghreb position:

> As you know, North Africa raises very difficult problems in our relations with the French Government. They are resentful that we have not been able to help them to maintain their forces in the Fezzan, and they accuse us of being uncooperative because we refuse to put pressure on agitators to [*sic*; 'who'] operate in French North Africa. These accusations are of course not justified, but we are under constant fire in the French Parliament and the matter threatens to embarrass our general European policy. Further I feel that we must do something to help French morale at the moment when they are at last taking the plunge and admitting the Germans into NATO.[31]

Ultimately, this helicopter supply question hinged on Britain's efforts to secure greater US arms deliveries for its forces in Malaya. By the time helicopters were made available to France in September 1955, any political benefits had disappeared.[32]

The problems thrown up by international arms deliveries soon worsened. In late 1955 the issue of Arab weapon supplies to the FLN acquired added political significance owing to the extent of French arms deals with Israel. Material support for the FLN could now be justified as part of the Arab struggle against Zionism rather than simply as a gesture of solidarity against colonialism. In January 1956 Britain's Middle East ambassadors warned that most Arab governments felt that France had betrayed its commitment to the 1950 Tripartite Declaration. Britain and the US, fellow signatories of the 1950 agreement, were accused of complicity in French plans to establish Israel as the region's major power. It would be fatal to Britain's prestige across the Middle East if Eden's government followed France's lead in supporting Israel's military build-up or, still worse, acquiesced in any Israeli scheme of preventive war against Egypt.[33]

At this stage, British strategic planning in the Middle East rested on securing Turkey's southern flank and deploying allied forces northeastwards to hold any Soviet overland advance on the line of the Zagros mountains southwest of Teheran. In order to safeguard the maximum extent of Middle Eastern territory and so preserve western oil supplies, it was vital for Britain to remain aloof from France's increasing identification with Israel. British military intelligence planners did not expect a large Soviet land campaign in the Middle East in the initial stages of a major war, instead anticipating the principal Soviet effort against allied air-bases, western Turkey and the Black Sea straits.[34] In the absence of a direct invasion, propaganda and political subversion remained key Soviet weapons in the contest for regional influence. Too close an association with France could easily damage Britain's cause. Ten days after the Algerian rebellion began, on 11 November 1954 the JIC estimated that, among the Middle Eastern states, only Turkey and Israel could withstand a sustained Soviet political threat. In most Arab countries anti-westernism and inter-state rivalries were mushrooming. To reinforce the links between western interests, colonial oppression and support for the Zionist cause would increase this animosity, a trend apparent in Syria. While Britain was anxious to break down these associations, France, through its actions in North Africa and its military support for Israel, was strengthening them.[35]

In January 1956 Eden was enraged by Quai d'Orsay leakage of French reservations about the Baghdad Pact. In subsequent weeks the *Le Monde* journalist Edouard Sablier led press criticism of Britain's Middle East policy. This merely confirmed Eden's opinion that France was irreconciled to the postwar collapse of its Middle Eastern position. Nostalgia for influence in the Levant still influenced policy-making, while anger over the universal Arab criticism of French policy in Algeria distorted French assessments of Britain's regional clients.[36] In May the Foreign Office noted that, in addition to maintaining the defensive shield of the NATO, Baghdad Pact and SEATO alliances, the western powers faced a more subtle task in preventing the growth of Soviet political and economic influence in Arab nations. Divisive French policies in North Africa and the Middle East were becoming a serious danger.[37] Quite apart from Britain's deteriorating position in Egypt, instability in Tunisia and Algeria threatened chiefs of staff plans to station forces in Libya. This left British strategic planning in the Mediterranean theatre heavily reliant upon naval and air bases in Malta and Cyprus.[38]

Unlike his Foreign Office masters, Ambassador Jebb was swiftly converted to the French military thesis that NATO might be turned from the south if pro-Soviet regimes supplanted France in North Africa. The corollary to this argument was that a French Algeria was a better long-term guarantee of western interests than any Algerian government whether democratic or not. As Paul Reynaud put it in October 1955, the French effort to build a genuine Franco-Muslim community in Algeria was a service to the free world. *Algérie française* provided a link to other Arab states and a western alternative to pan-Arabism to which other moderate Middle Eastern states might aspire.[39] Jebb was never seduced by the fiction of a functioning French Algerian society, but he assumed that the settler community had a legitimate role to play in Algeria's long-term future. Unless the country were to be partitioned – a proposition not seriously entertained before de Gaulle returned to power – the *colons* would be at the heart of Algerian politics and would remain a bulwark against anti-western government. Aside from the fact that another military humiliation so soon after Indo-China would be politically explosive in France, Jebb concluded that any French pull-out from Algeria would leave a dangerous power vacuum in North Africa. For political as well as strategic reasons, he reasoned that support for the French war effort served British and NATO interests.[40] Had the ambassador known the French army staff's forecast figures for France's troop requirements in North Africa during 1956–57, he might have been less convinced. Over the nine months from June 1956 to March 1957, force levels in newly independent Morocco and Tunisia were to remain broadly static, ranging between 91,265 to 99,765 in the former case and 42,229 to 49,986 in the latter. But in Algeria, the estimated troop requirement of 329,686 for February 1957 was exceeded by some 65,217 by 1 November 1956.[41]

The impressive nationalist lobbying machine in the US, spearheaded by the New York-based Committee for the Freedom of North Africa and the MNA's Washington representative, El-Abed Bouhafa, was quick to highlight comparisons between the intensification of the Algerian rebellion and the earlier conflict in Indo-China. In letters to Eisenhower and the Congress foreign affairs committee in January 1955, for example, Bouhafa advised the US administration to remember the lessons of Indo-China when formulating policy towards Algeria. A long colonial war would inevitably strengthen communist influence and weaken the West's moral standing. Ultimately, the US might face financial and military demands to support an exhausted colonial power.[42] Bouhafa's warnings went unanswered, but his argument resonated within the State Department. Acting on the advice of Julius Holmes, then the US diplomatic agent in Tangiers, in early October 1955 Dulles proposed an Anglo-American demarche in Paris to register concern at the dangers to NATO's southern flank inherent in the destabilisation of the Maghreb.[43] Holmes singled out Soviet arms sales to Egypt, its establishment of diplomatic relations with Libya and increasing Russian interest in the future of Tangiers as evidence of an increasing Cold War threat in North West Africa. At Jebb's prompting, Macmillan turned down Dulles' proposal.[44] But the ambassador's readiness to back French policy more openly met a chorus of Foreign Office criticism. It was dangerous to support France over Algeria when its current reform plans were so inadequate. It was unwise to jeopardise relations with Arab clients in order to win French gratitude over Algeria, and it was a nonsense to believe that the French could become constructive partners in the Middle East given their historical prejudice against Britain and their lack of physical presence or power in the region. As French opposition to the Baghdad Pact solidified, Eden and Macmillan came to share these sentiments.[45]

Istiqlal representatives, the Néo-Destour executive, the FLN's external leadership in Tunis and Cairo, and their respective envoys to Britain, the US and the UN courted international sympathy for their struggle against French rule. The UN General Assembly and a plethora of international agencies, charities and cultural partnerships were exploited to mobilise western and Muslim opinion against French colonialism and military excess in North Africa. From 1957 the Tunisian government and the FLN executive warned of enforced reliance on Egyptian, Soviet or Chinese material aid in order to win the attention of Paris, Washington and London.[46] One proof of this was John F. Kennedy's public indictment of US neglect of the Algerian war during a Senate debate on 2 July 1957. Chair of the Africa sub-committee of the Senate foreign relations committee, Kennedy warned that, just like Indo-China, Algeria was a major complication in Franco-American relations. The conflict was looming larger in the Cold War, it stripped France's NATO's contribution and undermined the liberalising reforms of the Organisation for European Economic Co-operation as France struggled to meet the cost of its military campaign.[47] Although Dulles dismissed Kennedy's intervention as an electoral ploy, it alarmed Quai d'Orsay officials, who remarked that the White House and Congress clearly saw French actions in Algeria as a liability to western policies in the Middle East.[48]

The British were also less amenable to French arguments over the military importance of the Maghreb to the NATO alliance after the humiliation of Eden's fall from grace. Egypt was clearly of far greater strategic significance than Algeria, yet Macmillan's government was coming to terms with a Middle Eastern order in which British influence in Cairo was spent. The weakness of NATO's European land force shield, occasioned in part by the reassignment of French forces to North Africa, disrupted Cabinet plans to reduce Britain's troop commitment in Germany. Macmillan shared Duncan Sandys's determination to cut Britain's continental commitment of conventional land and air forces over the next five years. The chiefs of staff squirmed at SACEUR's complaint that NATO's combat effectiveness in 1957 had diminished. Reservists were being called on to plug gaps in the line caused by French and British troop cuts.[49] Furthermore, the Foreign Office and the service departments had for several months been cool towards French efforts to secure exclusive military privileges in Morocco and Tunisia – countries which, although outside NATO's strategic perimeter, were obviously important to western supremacy in the Mediterranean, Morocco even housing US nuclear weapons.

While Britain was a past master at making base rights the cornerstone of informal influence, it was less convinced that France should follow suit. Immediately before the Suez crisis broke, Chauvel had impressed Selwyn Lloyd with the argument that French development of the Bizerta naval base, the fighter defences in Tunisia and the radar network across the country all served the interests of NATO powers in the region, including the British garrison in Libya. The African department was less convinced and preferred to explore the alternatives of a western Mediterranean security pact or a North African Colombo Plan to consolidate Maghreb ties to the western allies.[50] The latter was the more viable alternative. Several NATO states were expected to oppose NATO membership for the North African states. Even if the Americans supported Morocco's admission in an effort to safeguard their own base rights, this was bound to cause a major row among member states, particularly as the alliance was already divided over the possibility of Spanish entry.[51] By late 1957 British willingness to accommodate French base rights in North Africa had evaporated. The naval and air force facilities in Tunisia could not be integrated into the NATO command structure nor did they add much defence in depth to British bases in Malta and Cyprus.

Further Internationalisation of the Conflict

The fact that Maghreb leaders often operated outside their own countries curtailed France's ability to control them. In spite of the consolidation of the power of the ALN *wilaya* commanders within the post-Soummam

FLN executive, key rebel leaders remained beyond French reach either in their political bases in Cairo and Tunis or in military headquarters across Algeria's frontiers. This infuriated the French army leadership in Algiers. Whatever their capacity to weaken or even destroy the ALN in the field, they could not strike at its political heart. The politico-military apparatus of the FLN–ALN was like an octopus whose tentacles spread across Algeria whilst its nerve-centre stayed safe across the eastern frontier. This helps explain British scepticism towards the French war effort. Regardless of their individual successes on the ground, the French army could not pursue a key element in counter-insurgency. As Frank Furedi has observed in a more general context, 'Even in the course of a shooting war, the real target was the radical politician rather than the guerrilla.'[52] Put another way, since the FLN executive operated outside Algeria long before it reconstituted itself as a provisional government-in-exile in September 1958, from its inception the war had an international dimension which supportive Arab governments constantly emphasised. A fortnight before the crisis over Sakiet, on 25 January 1958, Tunisian deputy-premier, Bahi Ladgham, reminded French officials of the worth of his government's connections to the FLN:

> The Tunisian government considers that in maintaining contact with the FLN leadership, it encourages them to negotiate and to realise that there cannot be a purely military solution to the Algerian problem. It restrains them from seeking fresh support in the Middle East from states under Soviet influence and so pursues a forward-thinking policy useful to the West and certainly not contrary to France's long-term interests.[53]

Following the international conference of newly independent African nations at Accra in April 1958, the State Department gave fuller rein to its long-standing inclination to support constructive nationalist movements in sub-Saharan French Africa. Anxious to block Soviet opportunities to garner new allies, the State Department's increasing array of African specialists considered French colonialism a serious deficit in the wider East–West struggle. Far from prosecuting the Cold War on behalf of its western allies in Algeria, France compromised the reputation of the western powers throughout Africa.[54] The influential Martiniquan anti-colonialist Frantz Fanon – perhaps the most eloquent critic of French imperialism at the Accra conference – insisted that all nationalist struggles in Africa should be seen as part of a general revolt against western oppression. It is perhaps doubtful that FLN supporters took to heart Fanon's plea to treat the liberation of Rhodesia, Angola, indeed the whole of colonial Africa, with the same seriousness as Algeria's particular struggle. But the image of a Continent rising up with ferocious speed invoked by Fanon and other speakers at Accra made its mark on British and US political and strategic assessments of the African situation.[55] John Hargreaves puts it nicely in reference to Fanon's famous 1961 work *Les Damnés de la Terre*, 'The sense of revolutionary solidarity among colonised peoples... could no more be prevented from spreading south of the Sahara than could the radio-activity generated by French nuclear tests in southern Algeria in February 1960.'[56]

Within weeks of the Accra conference, in May 1958 the State Department's Bureau of Intelligence and Research passed its findings on the FLN leadership to the Foreign Office. Although uncertain about the distribution of power between the executive *Comité de Coordination et d'Exécution* (CCE) and the larger *Conseil National de la Révolution Algérienne* (CNRA), the State Department specialists were convinced that the FLN retained its secular, Maghrebian focus and was not prone to pan-Arabist or communist influence. While the CCE readily accepted material aid from Middle Eastern states and the Eastern bloc, this did not involve any specific political *quid pro quo*.[57] By 1958 the distinctive tenets of the FLN's programme and of an emerging grassroots Algerian nationalism were better understood in London, Washington and at NATO headquarters in Paris than in the first years of the rebellion. The FLN obviously drew on the anti-imperialism central to pan-Arab thinking, but Algerian nationalism was not integrated within any pan-Arabist movement. Similarly, although the FLN often applied a Marxist veneer to its analysis of Algeria's socio-economic problems, it had yet to draw significantly on Chinese, Soviet or Vietnamese communist models in its planning for post-independence reconstruction. In November 1958 the NATO Council debated a West German paper which stressed that the proliferation of independent African nation states heightened the risks of Soviet infiltration to the Continent. The British response was sanguine. As Sir Frank Roberts noted from Paris, since the other European colonial powers resented international scrutiny of their policies and preferred NATO to concern itself solely with alleged Soviet influence, constructive debate over possible links between African nationalism and Soviet communism was unlikely.[58]

Thanks mainly to the work of Emmanuel Sivan, the Algerian Communist Party's unsuccessful effort to co-opt the FLN and its principal nationalist rival, the MNA, into a broader pro-Soviet front is well known. So, too, the PCA's inability to make significant inroads into FLN support meant that it was already in sharp decline when finally suppressed by the French authorities in the spring of 1956.[59]

FLN leaders also shied away from proclaiming a self-styled Arab socialism akin to the Ba'athist Parties of the Middle East. During the critical Soummam Valley conference, and in subsequent editorials within the movement's newspaper *El Moudjahid*, FLN leaders criticised several Arab states for their limited backing for Algerian independence at the UN. Nasser's Egypt was accused of subordinating support for Algeria to the struggle with Israel. And whilst *El Moudjahid* acclaimed the creation of the United Arab Republic (UAR) in 1958 as a brave step towards pan-Arab unity and economic modernisation, the reality of Egyptian dominance over Syria raised concerns about Nasser's motives. FLN editorialists insisted that it was indefensible to make one Arab country the 'province' of another, an argument with obvious relevance to the prospects for Maghreb state federation.[60]

This markedly independent line tallied with British intelligence estimates of limited Egyptian and Soviet penetration of the Maghreb in the aftermath of Suez. The Algiers deuxième bureau might not have agreed. On 12 July 1957, for example, it reported that Ouamrane had just concluded the FLN's largest arms supply agreement with the Egyptian government.[61] None the less, the restoration of Franco-Egyptian commercial relations during late 1957 lent weight to British predictions. From its high-point in 1956, Radio Cairo's influence within North Africa also tailed off in the following year, superseded by the Tunisian national broadcast network and the FLN's underground 'Radio Free Algeria' which began transmissions within the country in spring 1957. UNESCO statistics indicated that radio ownership doubled in Algeria during the rebellion. But while Algerian Muslims still listened extensively to Radio Cairo transmissions, this was counter-balanced by the clearer Maghreb focus of radio propaganda from Tunisia and, later, Morocco.[62] Regardless of the decline of Egyptian radio propaganda, in January 1958 the JIC conceded that Nasser was better placed after Suez to make political inroads in all Maghreb states. This in turn facilitated Soviet efforts to lend economic, military and diplomatic support to newly independent North African regimes, a process which began earlier with the provision of economic aid to Sudan, Libya, Tunisia and Morocco in 1955–56. But the JIC stressed that the Moroccan and Tunisian regimes considered Egypt a dangerous rival in their quest for Maghreb unity rather than a partner against the West. Sensitivity to the pivotal importance of the Algerian conflict in the international politics of North Africa was vital. Anglo-American support for Moroccan and Tunisian mediation efforts made good strategic sense.[63]

Declining Imperial Power

Resentment at formal British support for the French presence in Algeria still soured relations with the Baghdad Pact nations. At the Baghdad Pact council session in Ankara in February 1958, Selwyn Lloyd suggested that full implementation of the *loi cadre* (then being watered down in the French Senate) might yet create the self-governing Algerian state favoured by Iraq and Pakistan. This was singularly unconvincing.[64] More encouraging was the convergence in British and US policy towards Algeria. But while the British and Americans shared a similar strategic outlook towards French North Africa, they had not reached a common position regarding Middle Eastern security. In practice, this brought out marked differences in the American diplomatic approach to France and Britain even though under the veneer of Anglo-American regional partnership which so antagonised de Gaulle, there was little agreement about detailed Middle East policy. As seen in the last chapter, during 1958 US pressure on Gaillard's administration was a blunt but effective instrument. By contrast, American policy in the Middle East was a more subtle, long-term affair. This was typified by Eisenhower's 5 January pledge to assist Arab nations committed to opposing communism and by congressional approval on 9 March of a Middle East resolution releasing $200 million a year for economic and military support to friendly Arab regimes. This extension of the Eisenhower Doctrine to the Middle East was informed by Washington's resolve to strengthen Saudi Arabia in opposition to Egypt, itself an alternative to US membership of the Baghdad Pact and Britain's preferred strategy of building up the Iraqi state against Nasser. Throughout 1957 Macmillan's government had pressed Washington to consider military assistance programmes for Jordan, Lebanon and, above all, Iraq.[65] Aware that Britain could not meet Iraq's requirements for modern fighter aircraft, the Treasury and the Foreign Office were ultimately disappointed by the US decision to provide a limited number of Hunter aircraft to Jordan and only a single squadron of inferior F86 jets to Iraq. As a result, in April 1958 Lloyd and Washington ambassador Sir Harold Caccia warned Macmillan that western influence in Baghdad would be irretrievably lost.[66] Their predictions were soon realised with the Iraqi coup in July 1958.

This sharp lesson in the reality of fast-diminishing British power across the Middle East only added to Britain's determination to cultivate relations with the Maghreb states. The backdrop of declining British influence within the Middle East was a key determinant of the British approach to the good offices mission established following the Sakiet bombardment. When the mission was established British strategic command in the Middle East still ran from Cyprus and Libya through to Iraq. In an echo of French operational planning in Algeria, Britain's support for the Baghdad Pact was still justified as an essential bulwark to NATO's southern flank.[67] But as the good offices teams concluded their work in the summer of 1958, the American and British military interventions in Lebanon and Jordan underlined the shift in regional power between them. The US inclination to accord both states neutral 'Austrian status' and Washington's refusal to commit financial or military aid to King Hussein's Amman regime further suggested that Eisenhower's administration was reluctant to take a more proactive role in Middle Eastern defence in order to prevent the consolidation and possible expansion of the UAR.[68] If either Jordan or Lebanon fell under UAR control, Britain's role in Middle Eastern affairs would become a sham.

De Gaulle was well aware of this. In preparation for Macmillan's first meeting with the general since his return to power, in late June the Foreign Office repeated the familiar mantra that Arab hostility to French policy in Algeria and suspicion of France's links with Israel precluded any wider French involvement in Anglo-American policy in the Middle East. Until these French ties were broken, de Gaulle's participation in any western initiative in the region was a 'positive handicap'. In May, Lloyd had been determined to keep the French 'in the dark' about Anglo-American planning over Lebanon. The regional complications of allowing French involvement when Arab hostility to events in Algeria was running so high catalysed the British inclination to exclude the French.[69] Following an acrimonious meeting in Washington between Dulles and ambassador Alphand, on 25 June de Gaulle warned London that if US or British forces entered Lebanon in support of President Camille Chamoun, the French would certainly join them. This was anathema to the British, not least because the Iraqi and Jordanian governments refused to back any western intervention involving French forces.[70] In the event, de Gaulle's posturing and the deployment of a French cruiser to the coastal waters off Beirut proved empty threats. But the outcome of the Lebanon crisis only added to de Gaulle's determination to break into the Anglo-American partnership, playing on Britain's declining Middle East position to assist him. Subsequent French interest in the extension of NATO's strategic perimeters to cover Middle Eastern, North African and even central African territory was nourished by Britain's fading regional power.[71]

On 1 August 1958 the JIC reported on Nasser's probable intentions, concluding that Egyptian efforts to achieve Arab unity might yet result in Nasserite control over Middle East oil revenues. Flushed with success in Syria and Iraq, Nasser might also countermand the Anglo-American intervention in Tunisia by supporting a Youssefist coup against Bourguiba akin to Egyptian schemes to overthrow the Libyan regime.[72] If, as expected, FLN forces in western Tunisia co-operated in such a venture, the good offices mission would be undermined.

Any such anti-western coup had wider implications for British influence in the Middle East. Britain's strategic reserve, effectively little more than a handful of professional army battalions, would be of little use to any far-flung client-power unless it was immediately reinforced by additional units drawn from the Rhine Army or the standing British forces East of Suez. Britain simply did not have the conventional forces required to play colonial, or neocolonial, fireman across large tracts of former imperial territory.[73] With only a small permanent strategic reserve in Britain, and forces committed to the Rhine and to the defence of Malaya in fulfilment of NATO and SEATO obligations, the limited garrisons in Cyprus, Hong Kong, Aden and the Persian Gulf, plus the remaining mobile forces in Kenya, hardly added up to a coherent imperial army. Not surprisingly, in October 1958 the service chiefs emphasised the urgent requirement for the local police forces and security agencies in colonial territories to play a more effective role in conserving law and order. The obvious inability of the Cyprus police force to contain EOKA guerrillas without army backing underlined the point. Preventive colonial policing and astute intelligence-gathering were vital if Britain's imperial forces were not to be over-stretched and thus undermined.[74] In client-states outside formal British control the situation was somewhat different. Ultimately, shrewd British diplomacy would have to accomplish what military power could not. In this respect, a creditable performance over Tunisia held a broader political significance for Britain's standing among Arab nations than its intrinsic importance in cementing Bourguiba's pro-western policies.

Seen from Paris, Anglo-American behaviour over Tunisia and Lebanon in 1958 was proof that the western powers were exploiting French weakness to ingratiate themselves with Arab leaders. Furthermore, the effort to promote Tunisian pro-westernism was not entirely successful. In November 1958 Bourguiba announced his policy of constructive 'non-engagement'. Tunisia would accept foreign aid only 'on condition that the doner state recognises Tunisian sovereignty and [its] independent foreign policy'. Bourguiba was clearly anxious to disarm critics who insisted that he had sold out to the West.[75] Since France's remaining naval base facilities at Bizerta were the most visible evidence of former imperial control, Franco-Tunisian clashes over the port inevitably degenerated into crisis in the months ahead.[76]

On 30 April 1959 the headquarters staff of the British forces deployed in the Arabian peninsula submitted a detailed report on the strategic outlook across the Middle East as a whole. Their conclusions reflected the speed with which Britain was forced to scale down its Middle Eastern ambitions in the aftermath of Suez, the creation of the UAR and the overthrow of the Iraqi regime in 1958:

> Our Middle East position now dwindled, apart from the garden fence of the Baghdad Pact, to a precarious position in Libya, an as yet untried settlement in Cyprus, a benevolent sponsorship of Jordan, treaty relationships with some rather doubting and doubtful Persian Gulf States and the protection of Aden and Somaliland, cannot be recovered either from Europe or from within the Middle East because we are unprepared to accept the odium of military domination and have lost the initiative of political action.[77]

Sir Frank Lee, who as Permanent Secretary at the Board of Trade had just completed a commercial tour of Middle Eastern capitals, reached much the same conclusions. He noted an 'acute and forbidding political uncertainty' caused by Egypt's regional influence, the abiding tension in Arab–Israeli relations and Britain's decline as the dominant local power.[78] Part of a wider chiefs of staff review of British strategic policy across the Middle East and Africa, both of these reports indicated that Soviet influence within several Arab nation states was facilitated by uncompromising local nationalism. Put another way, regardless of whether pan-Arabism was inherently pro-communist, its net effect was to advance Soviet interests at the West's expense. Since British and US support for 'moderate' Arab nationalism was tailored to the requirements of western strategic interests, what neither the British nor their US colleagues could admit was that their choice of conservative Arab clients was bound to leave the western powers exposed should those administrations be toppled by a more populist nationalism.[79]

Neither the service chiefs, the Foreign Office nor the Cabinet concluded from this that French insistence on the Cold War dimension to the war against the FLN made sense. Even though Soviet – and later Chinese – material support for FLN activities was proven to a greater extent than communist penetration of the UAR, the British government maintained that Algerian nationalism operated beyond the parameters of the East–West struggle. The US administration substantially agreed, although discreet approaches were made in late 1959 to known 'pro-westerners' within the FLN leadership to discourage the movement's growing links with Beijing.[80] As in previous years, France's continuing role as a key weapons provider to Israel further complicated matters, fuelling the arms race between the Israelis and the UAR. Although Algeria lay outside the Middle East strategic perimeter, it was hardly politic to antagonise friendly Arab states by making an issue of the FLN's international links. The requirements of regional stability, access to Middle East oil and the prevention of Soviet incursion added to the British determination to disengage from Arab disputes where possible. This was a sound judgment. Ultimately the FLN was beholden to no outside power; its acceptance of communist aid was militarily practical rather than politically decisive.

Dispute between London, Washington and Paris over the nature of the war in Algeria also impinged upon western efforts to prevent the spread of communism in sub-Saharan Africa.[81] Viewed from a French perspective, it was both hypocritical and illogical for Britain to put a case for closer Anglo-French military and intelligence co-operation among the emerging nations of West and East Africa whilst at the same time rejecting French arguments about FLN ideology.[82] If there was a communist threat in Ghana or French West Africa, then that threat was surely greater in Algeria. Viewed from a British perspective, closer Anglo-French military liaison over North Africa was bound to provoke arguments with established Middle East allies and potential partners in black Africa. In January 1959 known African opposition to French involvement in Algeria eased Macmillan's task in rejecting Sir Roy Welensky's unwelcome proposal for the formation of an anti-communist bloc of NATO powers and independent African states.[83] As British influence in the Middle East quickly receded after 1958, rising British interest in sub-Saharan strategic planning – typified by proposals to expand the army's strategic reserve in Kenya to a full brigade group – also suggested a concomitant reduction of commitments in North Africa where the British presence was by now confined to the small garrison in Libya devoted to internal security tasks. Where closer Anglo-French co-operation over North Africa was previously inexpedient, it was now largely irrelevant.[84]

Against this background of shifting British strategic priorities, on 16 April 1959 the three western powers began a week of tripartite discussions on Africa in Washington chaired by Robert Murphy. Britain's principal interest lay in the relocation of its main overseas strategic reserve to Kenya, but Algeria inevitably dominated French concerns. Murphy and ambassador Caccia were happy to emphasise the western interest in the stability of the Maghreb. But French State Secretary Louis Joxe went much further, reiterating the indissoluble strategic bond between North Africa and NATO's southern flank – an idea now appropriated by the Gaullist regime as it sought a more prominent role within western strategic planning. Just as France's relationship with Morocco and Tunisia was determined by their shared opposition to communism and Nasserism, so French policy in Algeria was shaped by western interests in the Middle East Cold War. Joxe demanded greater Anglo-American recognition of this, which could be registered by firmer backing for France at the UN. As so often before, while the three powers could easily agree on what they did not want to happen in the Maghreb, disagreement hinged upon French methods in Algeria and Africa more generally. French insistence that its former overseas territories should remain aligned with France set them apart, and promoted dispute with the English-speaking powers.[85]

The Cyprus settlement in 1959 also illustrated the divergence in French and British imperial strategic planning. After four years of emergency rule in an effort to contain Greek Cypriot nationalism and EOKA terrorism, the London negotiations in February 1959 over the establishment of a Cyprus Republic led to the reorganisation of the British strategic reserve on the island. The Cyprus garrison was reduced while British strategic planning in the eastern Mediterranean relied increasingly upon the presence of the US Sixth Fleet within NATO's Mediterranean command and the further development of Anglo-American security co-operation in the Middle East.[86] This trend towards cutting Britain's military cloth to fit its declining overseas imperial power contrasted markedly with the further escalation of the French military commitment in Algeria during the Challe offensive of 1959.

Unlike their French counterparts, by 1958 the British service chiefs acknowledged that imperial policing had little place within the professional army's 'true role' at the heart of western defence. Within the Ministry of Defence, opposition to France's continued diversion of military resources to Algeria steadily hardened. By 1960 the chiefs of staff were enthusiastic supporters of de Gaulle's emerging policy of negotiation and withdrawal from Algeria.[87] During a series of informal meetings held in Paris on 21–22 June 1960 the British service chiefs discussed the parameters of strategic planning for the coming decade. They predicted a future in which events in Africa would affect Britain's international status still more than had been the case in recent years. With this in view, the chiefs of staff were convinced that rapid adaptation to the requirements of postcolonial co-operation held the key to success:

> The obvious desirability of going slowly in constitutional advances in the British territories may have to be sacrificed in order to meet impatient African demands for independence if, by so doing, the vital Western and Commonwealth objective of retaining the goodwill of the newly independent countries, or at least their benevolent neutrality, stands a greater chance of being secured. Progress towards independence is likely to be very rapid.[88]

This was a lesson the French were learning. Final disengagement from Algeria was part of a wider Gaullist transformation of French strategic policy in Europe, Africa and the Middle East. This left the Algiers high command straggling behind, still convinced that pacification of Algeria had a paramount Cold War dimension. The leaders of the 'Generals' putsch' in April 1961 even expected NATO powers to endorse their coup because of de Gaulle's refusal to accept the Algerian war as the Cold War struggle it was. This was a fatal delusion. Once an Algerian settlement was in place, over the summer of 1962 the French government sought to restore contacts with Arab states that had been more or less consistently hostile since the rebellion began. By September French diplomatic relations were re-established with Syria, Jordan and Saudi Arabia. More faltering efforts were also made to thaw relations with Baghdad.[89] The final steps towards Algerian independence and their implications for Anglo-French relations form the subject of the next chapter.

7
Britain, de Gaulle and Algeria, 1958–62

For the die-hard supporters of *Algérie française*, de Gaulle's progress towards dialogue with the FLN leadership amounted to treachery. In their eyes, the general was invested as premier on 1 June 1958 with an obligation to protect Algeria's settlers and to revitalise the army's campaign against FLN terror. The revolt of General Salan's Algiers command against Pierre Pflimlin's newly installed government on 13 May, Salan's declaration of support for de Gaulle to the delight of the Algiers settlers two days later, and the obvious inability of the Paris authorities to bring Algeria back under control underlined the bonds between the final collapse of the Fourth Republic, the creation of a new Gaullist administration and prosecution of the Algerian war. The glaring divisions over Algeria within the leading parties of the old regime also suggested that an entirely new governmental structure was necessary to deal with the war. The Socialist leadership was by now implacably imposed to its erstwhile appointee as Resident, Robert Lacoste. The gulf within the MRP between Bidault's extremist support for *Algérie française* and Pflimlin's willingness to explore terms for a ceasefire could hardly have been wider. And divining a coherent Radical Party policy from politicians as individualistic as, for example, Edgar Faure, Mendès France and André Morice was near impossible. Furthermore, as Irwin Wall points out, the US government, for all its respect for Pflimlin's liberal principles and courage during the May crisis itself, conspicuously refused to pledge support for the Fourth Republic, drawing instead upon an extensive network of contacts with de Gaulle's supporters to clarify the circumstances in which the general would take power. The success of the 13 May *coup* appeared to owe as much to the disaffected officer cadres in Algeria as to the efforts of de Gaulle's political colleagues. Leading Gaullists with conflicting views of Algerian policy united to exploit the May crisis to bring about constitutional change in France.[1]

In April the general's confidant, Jacques Chaban-Delmas, while still Minister for National Defence in Félix Gaillard's embattled Cabinet, dispatched a former RPF organiser from the Nord, Léon Delbecque, to Algiers to assess local support for a Gaullist regime. The obvious dichotomy between the army commanders and the student and settler *ultras* who led the protests in Algeria and the Gaullist political community in France that profited from the resultant instability was that the former wanted to guarantee a French Algeria while the latter wanted a new Republican system in Paris. De Gaulle always presented an alternative to army rule. More gradually, he presented an alternative to continued involvement in Algeria as well. For Gaullists, the new regime was a *Union sacrée* born of national crisis, above partisan interest and yet commanding broad cross-party support. The general traded on his popular support to extend his executive authority and so circumvent due parliamentary process in order to pursue his own agenda of imperial withdrawal.[2] To Georges Bidault, a committed defender of *Algérie française,* after the last National Assembly of the Fourth Republic finally adjourned on 3 June 1958, it was de Gaulle who abused the law in pursuit of his Algerian policy. For the army officers, settlers and disaffected politicians that formed the inner core of the *Organisation de l'Armée Secrète* (OAS), the Fifth Republic had become a sham constitution in which Parliament and de Gaulle's successor as Prime Minister, the key architect of the new constitution, Michel Debré, were lap-dogs within an emerging authoritarian system controlled by de Gaulle's influential Private Office staff based at the Hotel Matignon under Georges Pompidou.[3]

It is rare to find such a fundamental misunderstanding of the aims and motives of a politico-military leader as emerged among the Algiers plotters of May 1958. Far from righting the wrongs of the previous regime by revitalising France's commitment to the war, de Gaulle broke with 130 years of French North African colonialism. The circumstances in which de Gaulle returned to power, his effective use of sweeping emergency powers, the costs of the war and the subsequent advent of OAS terrorism in France ensured continued public support for his eventual policy of negotiated withdrawal.[4] Determined to cut the crippling defence burden of the Algerian conflict to facilitate the development of France's nuclear *force de frappe,* the general was the nemesis of the insubordination within the Algiers army command. Potent symbols of this were the appointment in 1961 of the nuclear defence protagonist, General Pierre Ailleret, as commander-in-chief in Algeria and the dissolution of elite colonial parachutist and commando regiments which had spearheaded the dirty war against FLN urban terrorism and cross-frontier insurgency between 1957 and 1961.[5]

Algeria and the Consolidation of de Gaulle's Regime

From its inception, Macmillan's government speculated about the consequences for the French political system of worsening civil–military tensions in Algeria. By 1957 the Foreign Office western department considered the Algerian problem the most serious threat to the stability of the Fourth Republic. After its alarming rise in 1955–56, Poujadism waned in the following year. But the right-wing militancy it unleashed still resonated amongst the settler community in Algeria. Jebb warned in February 1957 that while most leading politicians were persuaded that autonomy or even independence for Algeria was inevitable, 'nearly all were equally convinced that it would be political suicide to say so'. Alerted by Marshal Juin to the disarray already evident among junior officers serving in Algeria, the ambassador concluded that a policy of withdrawal would provoke a *colon* revolt probably supported by key army units.[6] With hindsight, it is hard to resist the conclusion that, after the eclipse of Mendès France, only de Gaulle could meet this challenge effectively. The general learnt from Mollet's mistake in 1956 and instead remained deliberately ambiguous about his Algerian intentions.[7]

While British intelligence of Gaullist activities in the spring of 1958 does not appear to have been as detailed as the information reaching Washington, speculation about de Gaulle's plans was none the less widespread in Whitehall.[8] The Cabinet recognised that de Gaulle was man of the moment in 1958 and Macmillan's discussions with the general in Paris on 29–30 June only confirmed it. But in the Foreign Office de Gaulle's position was compared with that of Gaston Doumergue in 1934 – an elder statesman whose inability to resolve a social crisis was followed by the formation of a Popular Front. Britain's interest was to encourage US support for de Gaulle as a preferable alternative to Fourth Republic instability, and to keep quiet over Algeria pending the clarification of his policies. This proved easy. After the Sakiet affair and the fall of Gaillard, the Americans, too, wanted de Gaulle to succeed even though the storm clouds gathering over NATO, French atomic weaponry, European integration and Anglo-American policy in the Middle East were perfectly visible to Dulles' advisers.[9] The consolidation of Anglo-American relations with Morocco and Tunisia and awareness of Arab sensitivity over Algeria underscored the benefits of diplomatic silence. Perhaps most important, de Gaulle admitted his own uncertainties about Algeria. This was read in London not as indecisiveness but as refreshing flexibility. The fact that the French government needed time to fashion a policy acceptable to all sides suggested that a definitive break with past practice was on the horizon.[10] De Gaulle's great strength was that he understood public fatigue with the Algerian problem. This could only be good news. As the new regime tightened its grip in France, a viable FLN executive with which to negotiate emerged.[11]

Paradoxically, the fragmentation of the Gaullist movement gave the general greater freedom of manoeuvre over Algeria. Beginning with the defection of 27 Gaullist deputies in support of Pinay's government in March 1952 and accelerated by the Gaullists' disastrous showing in the January 1956 elections, successive splits within the Gaullist movement also marginalised leading *Algérie française* militants. De Gaulle faced bitter opposition from former Gaullists realigned in Soustelle's *Union pour le Salut et le Renouveau de l'Algérie Française* (USRAF), a movement spearheaded by five former Algiers governors – Viollette, Le Beau, Léonard, Naegelen and Soustelle himself. But he was assured of support from Michel Debré's loyalists in the revamped Gaullist movement, the *Union pour la Nouvelle République* (UNR), for whom a new constitutional system was always paramount. This insulated de Gaulle from the extremist pressure that destabilised the Gaillard and Pflimlin governments in quick succession in April–May 1958 after the USRAF leaders, Soustelle, André Morice and Roger Duchet, fulfilled their threat to provoke 'ungovernable' settler anger. Apart from Debré's UNR executive, other influential Gaullists with links to North Africa, such as the wartime Algiers resistance leader René Capitant, also accepted the need for withdrawal.[12] Few in number, these Gaullist liberals underwent a similar political conversion to that of their leader.

In the referendum on the Fifth Republic constitution between 26 and 28 September 1958 96.5 per cent of the voters in Algeria who took part supported the measure. This near-unanimous vote of confidence exceeded its equivalent in metropolitan France where some 4.5 million of the 22 million ballots cast rejected the change.[13] Bolstered by the UNR's dominance in government after the November 1958 parliamentary elections, and further reinforced by the erosion of *Algérie française* influence within the UNR executive during 1959, de Gaulle had a sure political platform from which to pursue dialogue with the FLN. The PCF's spectacular loss of support in November 1958, the continuing schisms within the Radical Party and the decline of the Socialist presence within France's major cities made a coherent left-wing challenge to

Gaullist rule unlikely. After the November elections, the UNR held 198 Assembly seats, the PCF 10, the Radicals 23 and the Socialists 44.[14]

These preconditions were essential since there was still no meeting of minds between the government and the Algiers command. Having proposed an amnesty for FLN rebels on 3 October, three weeks later de Gaulle made his first offer of a ceasefire, the so-called *paix des braves*. A day later, on 24 October, de Gaulle reminded a press conference of the army's duty to protect the Muslim population, pointing out that civilian casualties amongst the settler community were barely 15 per cent of those across the civilian population as a whole.[15] The more precisely de Gaulle defined his Algerian policy, the less the Algiers authorities liked it. General Salan's Algiers command was shocked by the *paix des braves* proposal and resented any suggestion that the army neglected the Muslim population. During May 1958 the generals refused to identify with the entrenched settler privilege personified by the *grands colons*. Salan was even jeered by the Algiers settlers until Massu appeared alongside him. The Committees of Public Safety formed across Algeria's cities by the leaders of the May coup emphasised their concern for the ordinary men and women on the street, whether settler or Muslim. And, although Salan conspicuously failed to implement government directives for the preparation of Algerian elections, the military commitment to a long-term pacification programme conducted on its own terms was beyond doubt.[16] Jebb noted the fundamental difficulty: how could de Gaulle extract the army from Algeria when its senior officers refused to leave? The reintegration within NATO of the professional cadres in Algeria was politically explosive. For troops accustomed to years of active colonial service the drudgery of life in a metropolitan base was anathema. This was captured by the soldiers' phrase 'getting back to Romorantin', a notoriously gloomy base south of Orléans.[17]

Salan's replacement on 12 December by the air force general and erstwhile Suez planner, Maurice Challe, plus the restoration of the civil post of delegate general in Algiers, confirmed the government's determination to restore executive control over policy-making in Algeria. De Gaulle's appointee as delegate general, Paul Delouvrier, a technocrat from the European Coal and Steel Community, had no colonial experience but was eminently suited to oversee a programme of economic modernisation.[18] Article 21 of the newly approved Fifth Republic constitution clarified the civil executive's ultimate responsibility for national defence and de Gaulle made the general staff directly accountable to him as head of government. This was mirrored within Algeria where the permanent secretariat of national defence came under

Delouvrier's direct authority in the implementation of military policy and the formulation of long-term defence plans. In both cases, Delouvrier's general delegation (the Algiers civil government) stressed the army's role in the government's modernisation programme for Algeria. Military pacification would enable economic and political reform to proceed uninterrupted and army personnel were to be the local agents of social change.[19]

In 1959 Delouvrier reinforced this bond between military operations and the economic transformation of Algeria by involving the prefectural authorities more closely in the enforcement of economic restrictions intended to weaken the FLN's sources of supply. The civil authorities were to supervise the movement of goods and people and the distribution of foodstuffs. In addition, on 25 November 1959 Delouvrier appointed General Parlange, the former commander in the Aurès-Nementchas, to co-ordinate the relocation of thousands of Algerians from the squalid *camps de regroupement* to purpose-built village settlements. Measures such as these helped restore the hierarchy between civil and military power which had become blurred over preceding years.[20]

The consolidation of the Gaullist regime during the autumn of 1958 was paralleled by the restructuring of the FLN executive into the Provisional Government of the Algerian Republic (Gouvernement Provisoire de la République Algérienne – GPRA), formally announced on 18 September. The GPRA was impressively organised. Presided over by the elder statesman of Algerian nationalism, Ferhat Abbas, and with key FLN and ALN leaders including Belkacem Krim as Vice-President and Armed Forces Minister, Ahmed Francis as Finance Minister and Benyoucef Ben Khedda as Social Affairs Minister, the GPRA was always credible as a government-in-waiting. Yet in response to French entreaties, the British and US governments confirmed that they would not formally recognise the GPRA. Within a fortnight of its creation, however, 13 states, including Morocco, Tunisia and most Arab governments, had done so. The Soviet Union withheld recognition, but formally wished the GPRA every success.[21]

The growing sophistication and international recognition of the FLN executive was not matched by greater ALN success against French forces. Quite the reverse. In the 18 months following May 1958 the French army achieved its most significant breakthroughs against rebel forces in the Algerian interior. The battle of the frontiers turned in the army's favour as the Morice line was expanded and reinforced with 26 additional regiments, including Bigeard's parachutists. Between July 1957 and November 1959 army engineers of the Constantine Corps command erected some 1,300 km of additional electric fencing supplied by 54 electricity generating stations. 1.2 million anti-personnel mines were laid along the Morice line alone and, by March 1959, over 80,000 troops were allocated to patrol the Tunisian and Moroccan frontier defences.[22] On 12 November Armed Forces Minister Pierre Guillaumat told a press conference that the war was being won. Rebel desertions were increasing, the frontier barriers were working and Saharan oil supplies were flowing freely. As before, War Office respect for French operational efficiency was tempered by recognition that the rebellion was far from over. The army's inability to pacify Kabylie suggested that the ALN could struggle on indefinitely. This reminded British military observers of Cyprus where a persistent EOKA threat in the mountainous interior sapped the government's will to fight on.[23] During 1958 Cyprus governor Sir Hugh Foot and the chiefs of staff convinced the Cabinet that EOKA's abiding strength demanded a more responsive system of policing and intelligence-gathering and a firm commitment to a timetable for a negotiated settlement, albeit an imposed one.[24]

By contrast, for French forces in Algeria, Challe's year of command in 1959 was akin to de Lattre's success in Indo-China eight years earlier. The major offensives of the Challe Plan – operations *Jumelles* and *Pierres Précieuses* – sought to destroy the ALN units within individual *wilayas* whilst keeping the land frontiers closed and consolidating rural pacification, in part through greater reliance upon Algerian *harki* auxiliaries. The major ALN frontier incursions attempted during the year all ended in failure.[25] The FLN met fire with fire. In January 1960 Abbas' second GPRA administration promised an intensification of the war. Three months later the French general staff reported that the FLN planned to recruit more foreign volunteers, principally from North Africa and Guinea, to join FLN 'international brigades'. At best, the military success of the Challe Plan prevented a marked increase in popular support for the FLN. As Challe's air force observers admitted, most Algerian Muslims remained shrewdly non-committal.[26]

Algeria was not the only flashpoint for France in North Africa after 1958. A key long-term consequence of the Sakiet affair was to undermine any residual Tunisian confidence in the French military across the Maghreb. Despite the best efforts of General Fernand Gambiez, commander of French forces in Tunisia, Bourguiba's administration took the events of May 1958 as further proof that the army leadership in Algeria might defy Paris in pursuit of victory, perhaps even invading Tunisia to accomplish their objective.[27] The British and US governments sympathised with Bourguiba, though for different reasons. While British intelligence assessments singled out Nasser's support for Salah Ben Youssef as the greatest threat to the Tunis regime, the State Department estimated that Bourguiba's foremost problem was to balance FLN pressure against French demands.[28] Washington was thus predisposed to reject any French requests for stronger support in Tunis.

To British discomfort, there were obvious similarities between Britain's preferential treaty arrangements in Libya and Cyprus and France's military privileges in Tunisia and Algeria. The Anglo-Libyan treaty of 1953 gave the British government a *droit de regard* over Libyan politics and the country's royal succession which exceeded French influence upon Bourguiba's administration in Tunis. In both the Libyan and the Tunisian case, the underlying British and French fear was of Egyptian-inspired political upheaval. The rationalisation of British Mediterranean command centres ordered by the Ministry of Defence in August 1958 produced a renewed commitment to maintain British garrisons within Libya.[29] Seen from the French perspective, it was disingenuous for Britain to criticise French insistence on base rights in Tunisia whilst it meanwhile imposed its requirements on the Libyan government. The fact that the Libyan royal administration was more willing than the Tunisians to join a grouping of Arab nations intent upon resisting Egyptian propaganda and subversion cut little ice in Paris.[30]

On 4 January 1960 Bourguiba formally demanded French evacuation of Bizerta on the grounds that France no longer required such base facilities. The Quai d'Orsay tried to marshal NATO support for France's right to remain before the local stalemate descended into skirmishes between the Bizerta garrison and Tunisian security forces in July 1961. Following de Gaulle's rejection of the latest in a series of Tunisian governmental requests for a total French evacuation, on 18 July Tunisian troops, encouraged by the local civilian population and the Néo-Destour militia, set up a blockade around the Bizerta base and the Saharan outpost of Garet-el-Hammel to the south. By the following day a shooting match had developed, the French authorities accusing the Tunisians of firing first. The French response was militarily effective, if woefully disproportionate. Over 1,000 Tunisians were killed after French reinforcements completed a military occupation of the city on 21 July. Civilian casualties were especially high and napalm was used. There was also severe material damage to the city and its outlying industries. Franco-Tunisian diplomatic relations were broken off before a tentative ceasefire was agreed. Although the resumption of low-level talks and an exchange of prisoners were ultimately agreed in September 1961, diplomatic contacts between Paris and Tunis were not restored until the following

July.[31] Whatever the promise after de Gaulle's rapid settlement of the Sakiet crisis, the new French regime could not dispel the Franco-Tunisian *mésentente* that had descended after independence in 1956.

Momentum for Withdrawal

Tunisia was perhaps the exception which proved the rule. The qualified success which greeted de Gaulle's acceleration of decolonisation from sub-Saharan Africa in 1958–60 reverberated through policy towards Algeria. As we have seen, government efforts during 1957–58 to push through an effective Algerian *loi cadre* enabling the enactment of reform by decree met vigorous parliamentary opposition. A much-amended *loi cadre* for Algeria was finally passed by the Senate on 19 January and approved by the Chamber on 1 February 1958. But a parallel process covering the black African colonies proved less contentious. In the months following Gaston Defferre's promulgation of his eponymous enabling law in June 1956 and the application of individual constitutional reforms across Madagascar, West and Equatorial Africa, the electoral system established under the 1946 French Union was thoroughly democratised. Elections in late March 1957 produced a number of black African governments that epitomised the 'constructive nationalism' the French craved in Algeria. In the subsequent negotiations over the terms of full self-government for the francophone colonies, the bitterest arguments took place amongst the African leaders themselves, during party conferences at Bamako and Cotonou in September 1957 and July 1958, over the retention of a federal political structure in West Africa.[32] In virtually all the black African territories, when de Gaulle took office the French were blessed with moderate negotiating partners, judged suitable as *interlocuteurs valables* because they recognised the value of close political ties to France.

The launch of the *Communauté française,* approved by the referendum of 28 September 1958, offered economic reward for those states prepared to accept preponderant French influence. As for Guinea, which rejected membership of the *Communauté,* de Gaulle insisted that it be deprived of any French assistance to prove the error of spurning French informal influence; 'Guinea must suffer', the general is reported to have ordered.[33] Although the original concept of a tightly-knit francophone Community formally linked to France became outmoded almost as soon as it was launched, de Gaulle's government maintained close ties with the majority of the newly independent black African states. In April 1960 Couve de Murville conceded during talks on Africa in Washington that the principal obstacle to a similar process for Algeria was the FLN's refusal to negotiate on de Gaulle's terms.[34]

French willingness to enact structural reform in Algeria still required nationalist representatives, backed by a clear electoral mandate, who were willing to consider a French-Algerian partnership rather than outright independence. As ever, the FLN refused to play this role. Elections in Algeria on 30 November 1958 therefore produced Muslim deputies as much tainted by their lack of contacts with the FLN as by their past associations with the Algiers administration. Morocco's influential leftist leader, Mehdi Ben Barka, assured Delouvrier that the release of Ben Bella and his fellow FLN detainees would permit meaningful talks. But the government did not respond. A further hostile UN General Assembly vote supporting Algerian self-determination in December 1959 was also ignored. Although Debré's Cabinet kept a watching brief on the UN, de Gaulle was adamant that the organisation had no place in any settlement. Despite this, UN pressure had a cumulative effect, sustaining international interest in negotiations with the FLN. In New York the Afro-Asian bloc organised a standing committee for Algeria which lobbied Alphand's UN successor, Armand Bérard, remorselessly during 1960.[35] Meanwhile, during 1958–59, the original *Communauté* project based on limited African self-government had collapsed under the weight of local pressure for complete independence. French acceptance of a new-style *Communauté* built around a voluntary contractual relationship between France and newly independent francophone African states proved more attractive to the FLN leadership.[36] Ultimately, however, this revised model of the sub-Saharan *Communauté*, enshrined in the constitutional law of 4 June 1960, was less important to talks with the FLN than de Gaulle's conviction that negotiated withdrawal was France's sole realistic option.

After de Gaulle's resounding victories in the 1958 referenda, Macmillan's administration was increasingly confident that the new regime would pursue a negotiated settlement. When Debré visited London in April 1959 the two governments agreed to continue regular bilateral talks on common problems in black Africa. Colonial secretary Alan Lennox-Boyd noted the confluence of British and French social, political and military policies across sub-Saharan Africa but lamented the persistent economic tensions between them. Technically, Algeria was beyond the scope of these exchanges, but on 4 June Macmillan reminded de Gaulle that the foremost task for Britain and France in Africa was to tackle 'multi-racial relations in complex societies'. This followed a private meeting with Soustelle that morning at Downing Street which only confirmed Macmillan's view that African problems would loom ever larger for Britain and France.[37] By the time of his 'winds of change' tour of southern Africa in early 1960 Macmillan recognised the bankruptcy of multi-racialism in British African territories, the Central African Federation above all. This had been a gradual shift. On becoming Prime Minister Macmillan had requested a 'balance sheet' measuring the benefits of empire. This inter-departmental review of the long-term prospects for British rule in Africa helped persuade several ministers, including Macmillan, Commonwealth Relations Secretary Lord Home and the new Colonial Secretary, Iain Macleod, that violence on an Algerian scale was to be avoided at all costs. An apparently benevolent term, multi-racialism actually amounted to the denial of full democratic rights to the indigenous majority for fear of the repercussions upon settler societies. The Devlin Report produced in reaction to the Nyasaland state of emergency decreed by Sir Roy Welensky's administration in Salisbury in March 1959 had proved the point. Lord Devlin's forthright criticism of the Nyasaland administration, produced amidst parliamentary and press furore over the death in custody of twelve Mau Mau detainees at the Hola 'rehabilitation' camp in Kenya, rocked Macmillan's government. The Prime Minister was hard pressed to dissuade Lennox-Boyd from resigning and had to accord far greater priority to colonial problems in the months either side of the October 1959 General Election (following which Lennox-Boyd retired).[38] Just as de Gaulle was turning away from any acceptance of settler privilege in Algeria, so Macmillan, too, was determined to change course. In 1962 he pointed to Algeria to disarm Welensky's defence of settler dominance within the Central African Federation: 'In Algeria the French have a million men under arms, and they have now suffered a humiliating defeat. It is too simple a reading of history to think that you can exercise control simply by the use of power.'[39]

That the Algerian example was but one of many factors that affected British colonial policy seems clear. A point more central to us here is to establish the basis for British governmental assessments of the final stages of the crisis. Drawing upon Foreign Office reportage, periodic military assessments and intelligence estimates, and informed by the more pervasive scepticism towards formal colonial rule, British ministers and officials discerned several factors guiding French policy towards withdrawal. These fell into three distinct categories – economic cost, Gaullist defence planning and the link between civil-military relations and French capacity to negotiate an Algerian settlement. Of these the prohibitive expense of the war and long-term reform was the first to make its mark.

De Gaulle made economic development a central plank of his Algerian strategy. Speaking in Algiers on 3 July 1958 he promised an extra 15 billion francs to the 65 billion already allocated to public works projects under the 1958 budget for Algeria. His main objectives were an ambitious house-building programme and wider educational provision over the coming decade. But the funding promised fell far short of the sums required to achieve these targets despite a further promise on 14 August of 145 billion francs over eight years to enable all Algerian children to obtain free schooling. In formulating his proposals de Gaulle borrowed from an official report compiled in 1954–55 by Councillor of State Roland Maspétiol. This set the parameters for a ten-year Algerian development plan which was further codified by an Algiers government working party in 1955.[40] Yet de Gaulle's government was never likely to commit the huge investment stipulated under the report to implement comprehensive modernisation schemes in industry, agriculture, housing, education, public health and infrastructural development. Without massive injections of private capital or increases in French taxation to fund them, de Gaulle's economic modernisation plans were unachievable. And the fact remained that approximately 6.5 million Algerians were tied to an agricultural sector in which some 22,000 *colon* farms produced much the same volume of produce as the estimated 600,000 Muslim smallholdings.[41] This imbalance could not be ignored. As Jean Morin, de Gaulle's future appointee as delegate general, recognised, Algeria's rapid population growth would perpetuate chronic land shortages.[42] Yet complete redistribution of land, FLN-style, was unacceptable.

Undeterred, de Gaulle's announcement of the so-called Constantine Plan during a visit to the city on 4 October 1958 promised the creation of 400,000 new jobs and new housing for 1 million Algerians over the next five years, plus the reallocation of 250,000 hectares of land to Muslim cultivators. Only 28 per cent of the necessary funding was to come from the metropolitan budget, the bulk being raised through commercial investment, long-term credits and the broader tax base that would be created within Algeria as general prosperity increased. In their analyses of the scheme, the African department, the Paris embassy and the Algiers consulate dismissed it as utopian. French taxpayers and investors would not meet de Gaulle's expectations of them, the plan ignored the crippling defence costs in Algeria and the oil resources of the Sahara were insufficiently developed to contribute substantially to the modernisation programme. Furthermore, there was no guarantee that Algerian nationalism would be weakened by any gradual improvement in living standards. The erstwhile followers of Ferhat Abbas that might have rallied to such reforms in 1954 were unlikely to do so now. In his fifth visit to Algeria since his return to power, in early December 1958 de Gaulle again stressed his commitment to economic development but his tantalising reference to a distinctive Algerian national personality also suggested a new focus upon constitutional reform.[43] This was to generate clashes with the military and settler *ultras* in the months ahead. Unlike the *grand colon* politicians and administrators who had blocked reform in former years, settler opposition was now dominated by younger, extremist *ultras*, typically from poor, urban backgrounds and prepared for violent confrontation with the metropolitan authorities.[44] This sent shock waves through the French military. Where they had despised the fat cat oligarchs, key professional army units identified with *ultra* frustrations.

On 10 February 1959 an executive council under premier Debré began the precise demarcation of the Constantine Plan. Armed with implementation schedules from specialist government commissions and the Algerian departmental authorities, the council submitted the final Constantine Plan for government approval on 13 June 1960. It fell to the three 'super-prefects' who administered regional government within Algeria to put the Plan into practice in liaison with their subordinate departmental prefects and the regional military commands. 1959 was thus entirely consumed by the administrative preparation of the Constantine Plan. As the emphasis shifted towards practical implementation in 1960, the fundamental obstacles to success became more apparent. The Plan reserved 50 per cent of 'category A' Algerian administrative posts to Muslim citizens in addition to between 70 and 90 per cent of positions in more junior administrative grades. In practice, the combination of years of under-education, restricted citizenship rights, FLN intimidation and committed nationalist support meant shortfalls in the recruitment of Muslim administrative staff. At the senior grade in particular, there were enough candidates to fill only one in every four posts offered.[45] As the French government edged closer to negotiations with the GPRA, so it admitted that the Constantine Plan was prohibitively expensive. On 11 April 1961 de Gaulle sounded the death knell of his economic modernisation scheme by conceding that rapid decolonisation made sound financial sense.[46]

De Gaulle, Algeria and NATO

The French crisis of confidence in NATO emerged fully during 1958 but had been brewing for years. Its fermentation quickened as a result of

Suez and Sakiet. The US finger on the nuclear trigger, the McMahon Act restrictions on sharing nuclear knowledge, distrust of the Anglo-American role in the Indo-China settlement, resentment at equivocal NATO support for French operations in North Africa and the shortcomings of integrated command revealed by the Suez expedition all sapped French belief in the structure of the western alliance.[47] Underlying these specific French complaints was a more general resentment of Britain's more privileged partnership with the US consolidated after the Macmillan–Eisenhower conference in Washington in October 1957. Henceforth, the strategic primacy of nuclear missile technology added to friction between the US, Britain and France over the deployment and usage of a US-controlled NATO missile stockpile on European soil. To no avail, the Mollet and Gaillard administrations both sought bilateral agreements with Washington modelled on Anglo-American nuclear collaboration. On 22 February 1958, Gaillard's Cabinet rejected the siting of NATO nuclear weapons in France except within a partnership deal with the US. As Maurice Vaïsse put it, what followed under Gaulle was 'a dialogue of the deaf' – neither the Americans nor the French would meet one another's nuclear demands.[48]

In June 1957 Macmillan circulated a paper on French strategic options prepared by Julian Amery, then Parliamentary Under-Secretary of State for War. Amery emphasised that France was already at the NATO 'crossroads'. Whether it committed itself further in North Africa to the exclusion of SACEUR's demands or worked more closely within a western European bloc of the Six, Britain stood to lose.[49] What Amery did not foresee was de Gaulle's determination to exploit nuclear capacity as a distinct strategic alternative. If Algeria prevented France from playing its proper role as a senior European partner inside NATO, then the *force de frappe* would restore French prestige whether inside the alliance or not. This tension between Algeria as a short-term military priority and unilateral nuclear capability as a long-term strategic goal existed throughout the rebellion. Yet, as Amery recognised when he revisited the issue in December 1958, the French commitment to nuclear capability in addition to a continued strategic presence on the African continent still posed the same dilemma for Britain. If the British government refused to help France achieve either objective, de Gaulle might turn his back on '*les Anglo-Saxons*' and encourage other Common Market states to follow suit.[50] Macmillan was acutely conscious of this throughout de Gaulle's first presidential term. After formulating his 'Grand Design' for Britain's long-term foreign policy in the months preceding Kennedy's election as US President in 1961, Macmillan tested American, NATO and Foreign

Office patience in his readiness to consider a nuclear bargain with France in exchange for admission to the EEC.[51]

As with discontent over NATO organisation, so with nuclear policy de Gaulle's return catalysed long-cherished ambitions. Mendès France had approved a nuclear research programme in December 1954. During March–April 1958 Gaillard's government had concluded a technical co-operation accord with West Germany, set a March 1960 deadline for France's first nuclear test explosion and agreed the development of French warheads for US-supplied intermediate-range ballistic missiles.[52] (France exploded its first atomic device at its Saharan test centre at Reggane on 20 February 1960.) Armed with his experience on the French atomic energy commission, de Gaulle's Armed Forces Minister, Pierre Guillaumat, injected greater urgency and a clearer ideological vision to existing strategic policy. General Paul Ely's military staff accepted that requisite nuclear spending and the costs of Algerian operations were irreconcilable. Crucially, de Gaulle's and Ely's eagerness to extend NATO's strategic compass to include the Mediterranean and North African theatres where France played a leading role was always married to the belief that nuclear deterrence at the heart of Europe was pivotal to French *grandeur*. In practice, it took the government at least 18 months to impose its nuclear priority over the Algerian commitment, and a further two years to contain the military insubordination that resulted.[53]

During 1958–59 British willingness to assist French conventional weapon design served as limited compensation for Anglo-American reluctance to share nuclear technology with France. This was consistent with Macmillan's advice to de Gaulle on 2 June 1958 to accept the inevitability of US leadership within NATO.[54] The British defence industry would obviously suffer if French manufacturers chose collaboration with German and Italian companies at British expense. Pressed by Jebb and encouraged by First Sea Lord Admiral Louis Mountbatten and Duncan Sandys' cost-conscious Ministry of Defence, Macmillan's government pursued co-operation with France in the development of short-range missiles, power-assisted bombs and helicopters. Other notable joint research and development projects included electronic guidance systems, the 'Blue Water' ground-to-ground missile, the French ENTAC anti-tank weapon and more general exchanges between the Institut Franco-Allemand at Saint Ouis and the British Armaments Research Establishment at Fort Halstead.[55]

Guillaumat's Armed Forces Ministry was also keen to develop an intermediate range ballistic missile similar to Britain's costly 'Blue Streak' system. This was more problematic. A key requirement of such a missile was a target range of at least 2,500 nautical miles enabling the French to deploy missiles against the Soviet Union from North Africa. Apart from co-operation between working groups of British and French service ministry representatives, joint research and development of missile technology and anti-tank weaponry occurred under the auspices of NATO and Western European Union agencies such as the NATO Naval Steering Group and the Moreau working party.[56] Throughout these exchanges British policy was pulled in opposite directions by Whitehall anxiety over French impatience to join the 'atomic club' and Macmillan's eagerness to conciliate de Gaulle.[57] At least the resultant British effort to guide French armaments production towards conventional weaponry for continental defence made expenditure upon the requirements of colonial warfare in Algeria seem anachronistic.

The question of French military allocation was further complicated by de Gaulle's implacable hostility to a NATO structure devised before the spread of major Cold War conflict to East Asia and Africa. This emerged within weeks of his return to power.[58] On 24 June 1958 Paul-Henri Spaak warned Sir Frank Roberts at NATO headquarters in Paris that de Gaulle opposed the preponderant Anglo-American influence within NATO, the inflexibility of the alliance regarding East–West talks, the existing framework for strategic planning and, above all, NATO's command system. Roberts remained sanguine. Until France adopted a more liberal policy in North Africa and became more co-operative over the siting of NATO ballistic missiles, its alliance partners had little cause to give ground to French demands.[59] De Gaulle's 17 September proposal for a tripartite western alliance directorate met a frosty response in Washington and London and became a running sore in Anglo-US military relations with de Gaulle's Republic. The Cabinet was anxious not to rebuff de Gaulle outright. But, contrary to Macmillan's hopes, it could not agree to Gaullist demands to share nuclear technology and admit US–British–French leadership of NATO without damaging relations with Washington. Only Jebb, whom Macmillan criticised as an 'an extreme partisan' of de Gaulle, saw merit in close tripartite co-operation on pan-African defence to block any further Soviet or Nasserite advance. In fact, French power in Africa was no asset to NATO when Algeria tied down so much French military capacity and fed anti-westernism in the Middle East, in Africa itself and at the UN. Across the Atlantic, US scepticism was stronger still. Dulles, for example, ridiculed French pretensions to become a fully-fledged nuclear power 'on the basis of one or two fire-crackers in the Sahara'.[60]

By November 1958 French representatives led by Ely were in open revolt within NATO's standing committees against plans for the further integration of European commands, arguing that vital issues such as the delineation of command boundaries, rules of engagement and priority between NATO obligations and national defence were unresolved.[61] The conflict of priority between the Algerian war and NATO defence kept these problems in sharp focus throughout 1958–62. Roberts again injected common sense to the debate a fortnight before de Gaulle won the presidential election held on 21 December. Admittedly, France could not fulfil its NATO manpower obligations in Europe, leaving SACEUR short of his 30 division requirement. But other shortfalls – in air defence and the deployment of missile defences – were more serious strategically. Above all, the diminution of French military influence within the alliance was politically dangerous. It increased NATO dependence on German forces and, paradoxically, it strengthened de Gaulle's insistence that the alliance be reordered and partly refocused on Mediterranean and African defence where French influence was stronger. Senior Foreign Office officials, including Permanent Under-Secretary Sir Frederick Hoyer-Millar, Sir Anthony Rumbold and the assistant head of the western department, A. D. F. Pemberton-Pigott, accepted Roberts' analysis. Whatever the vagaries of Anglo-French relations, a strategic interdependence between the two states remained. It was not in Britain's interest to see this weakened.[62]

Matters were little altered in 1959. The French government disputed its obligations within NATO's Mediterranean fleet, insisting that naval units could not ignore the pressing requirements of coastal policing off the Maghreb coast whatever their overarching commitments to NATO.[63] In the teeth of Cabinet and naval staff opposition, de Gaulle authorised the withdrawal of French naval forces from the Mediterranean fleet in late February 1959; according to Hervé Alphand, an action spurred by the General's fury over US abstention in a crucial General Assembly vote on Algeria in December.[64] Certainly, this gesture was politically important rather than strategically significant since the units involved were primarily devoted to convoy duties between France and North Africa. The affirmation that French ships would give priority over NATO anti-submarine defence to Algerian patrolling or the eventual protection of tankers carrying Saharan oil was further proof that de Gaulle would resist the 'denationalisation' of French forces within the fabric of the western alliance.[65] Initially at least, Gaullist intransigence over nuclear policy and the structure of NATO, plus the conflict of interest between colonial and alliance commitments, found echoes within the higher echelons of the British armed forces. There was sympathy for de Gaulle's frustration with the duality of national defence and NATO obligations within the

Mediterranean theatre and its southern margins. In late 1958 Britain's senior naval officer in the Mediterranean was also NATO's regional commander-in-chief. He headed a command organisation divided between Malta and Cyprus and faced the difficult task of reconciling Britain's national (and generally neocolonial) strategic interests with the broad requirements of NATO planning. Yet, because of his international NATO role, Britain's Mediterranean commander-in-chief could not be admitted to the chiefs of staff's Middle East advisory planning committees to discuss British strategic policy. He could not visit Cyprus without offending either Greek or Turkish NATO allies, nor could he inspect naval installations in Libya or Tunisia lest this incur Italian or French objections.[66] Naval forces formed the greater part of Britain's NATO contribution in the Mediterranean theatre whilst the lion's share of Britain's commitments under the Baghdad Pact fell to the RAF. Awareness that these forces could not be easily redeployed to meet any regional colonial emergency was profoundly discomforting to the service chiefs and their subordinate joint planning staff.[67]

Advances in missile technology and anti-submarine weaponry also increased fears among Mountbatten's naval staff that a Mediterranean NATO naval force would increasingly be attuned to anti-submarine operations. Sandys was expected to exploit this narrowing of priorities to justify cutbacks in a surface fleet hitherto adapted to a broader strategic role, including support for imperial operations.[68] As the chiefs of staff noted in early January 1959, the NATO alliance had never satisfactorily resolved the conflict of national and NATO interest that had been thrown into sharp relief by the Suez expedition. The issue had been ducked, perhaps because the requirement to place NATO above individual colonial concerns too readily equated with timid acceptance of US strategic leadership.[69] The shrinkage in British imperial commitments from 1959 onwards gradually ironed out these tensions, and the primacy of NATO obligations in Europe was anyway never in doubt. But the previous Whitehall debate was not dissimilar to that in Paris.

By August 1959 the US joint chiefs and the National Security Council were also prepared to accommodate France's short-term military obligations in Algeria in an effort to prevent a more serious breach within NATO. Eisenhower was less forgiving. He refused to support France over Algeria at the UN and he was not prepared to give in to French blackmail over control of NATO's nuclear arsenal.[70] The NSC accepted the President's view. Any US identification with the French presence in Algeria was inimical to relations with the Afro-Asian bloc and US policy in the Middle East. Although de Gaulle's 16 September proposal of a referendum on Algerian self-determination elicited strong US support, neither the US nor Britain could help the French government to overcome army and settler opposition. The underlying strategic position was unaltered. Until France extricated its 400,000 military personnel from Algeria, SACEUR's emergency defence plans were untenable.[71] Macmillan saw the logic of all this but was none the less irritated by it. Confident of the underlying solidity of the western alliance, he considered the dispute within NATO trivial next to the major problem of Britain's trade with Europe. While the Algerian crisis kept such disagreements alive, their potential to harden French opposition to British EEC membership could only increase.[72]

At the end of 1959 Algeria remained the French army's primary concern and its principal commitment. Yet, whereas the Algerian preoccupation had prevented Fourth Republic administrations from challenging NATO strategy, under de Gaulle the reverse applied.[73] In the parliamentary debate over the forthcoming year's defence budget on 19 November 1959, Debré stated that development of a French nuclear strike force took second place to operations in Algeria. According to Roberts, it was 'common knowledge' that the French land and air forces committed to NATO in West Germany treated this posting as a training ground and a reserve pool for service in Algeria. During one of the four GPRA diplomatic missions to Beijing between 1958 and 1960, Chou En-lai even thanked the Algerian delegation for having tied down NATO forces for so long. This helps explain Chancellor Adenauer's rising anxiety over communist penetration in the Maghreb and his eagerness for de Gaulle's Algerian policy to succeed.[74]

Even if the North African commitment were to end, it would take years for French conventional forces to readjust to their role within NATO's European shield force. After so many years of exceptionally high defence spending occasioned by the Algerian war and the concomitant effort to develop French nuclear defences, even de Gaulle might not withstand public pressure for substantial defence cuts immediately after final withdrawal from the Maghreb. The general was unlikely to risk public anger in order to re-establish French conventional forces within the NATO alliance whilst his objections to NATO's integrated command structure remained unresolved. Having been compelled to subordinate *la politique nucléaire* to a colonial conflict that he was determined to end, de Gaulle was sure to target defence funding towards nuclear weaponry, probably at the expense of conventional forces within NATO.[75] It was pointless for Macmillan's government to press de Gaulle to uphold France's NATO obligations. This would only reinforce Gaullist criticism of the

'Anglo-Saxon' directorate within the alliance, and would undermine Cabinet efforts to cut Britain's contribution to NATO's shield forces. Again, fear of crystallising Gaullist opposition to British admission to the EEC shaped Macmillan's response.[76]

It was hardly surprising that the French service chiefs contending with a major conflict in North Africa found it harder than their British colleagues to reconcile imperial interest with a US-led NATO alliance. It was also galling to face criticism within NATO over Algeria whilst, within the parallel councils of SEATO, US representatives edged closer to military engagement in Indo-China as the crisis in Laos escalated during 1959. American eagerness to combat the communistic Pathet Lao was surely no more justifiable than the French campaign against the FLN.[77] Why should France be expected to devote a greater share of its defence budget to NATO's European shield force whilst the West's two nuclear states, the US and Britain, alone possessed independent strategic deterrents? Why should France cut back on its operations in Algeria, over which the French government at least exerted unilateral control, in order to subsume more forces within a supposedly integrated Western European defence system where Paris would in fact play second fiddle to Washington and London? Such were the arguments put to NATO representatives in Paris in October 1959 by Debré's State Secretary, Louis Joxe. Even if de Gaulle opposed the indefinite prosecution of the Algerian war, he maintained that French forces had a clearer sense of their identity and their ultimate purpose in North Africa than within the anonymity of NATO's European command.[78]

Over the course of 1959–60 the British and US governments acknowledged that the French nuclear programme, discontent with NATO structure and resentment at Anglo-American leadership within the alliance were not purely Gaullist phenomena. De Gaulle tapped a broader vein of French nationalism which was expected to outlast his term in office. This fed Macmillan's frustration at the disruptive impact of quarrels within the western alliance on Anglo-French economic relations in Europe. On 29 June 1960 he suggested a more *attentiste* approach to France's dispute with NATO. Three months later he went further: what mattered above all was to secure Britain's export trade. This meant entry to the Common Market. The inexorable shift from Commonwealth to Continent in Britain's trade patterns underpinned his Europeanism and that of the other pro-Europeans – Christopher Soames, Duncan Sandys and Edward Heath – promoted within Macmillan's crucial Cabinet reshuffle in July 1960. Resurgent French national self-confidence, when contrasted with Britain's relatively poor economic performance next to the Six, added to

Macmillan's enthusiasm for entry to the EEC.[79] As an opponent of European federalism, de Gaulle might be amenable to British entry, especially while Algeria remained his dominant short-term concern. Sir Evelyn Shuckburgh and Sir Frank Roberts took issue with this, expressing the Atlanticism prevalent within the Foreign Office and the UK delegation to NATO. It was futile to trade concessions over NATO in a vain effort to win economic rewards for Britain in Europe from de Gaulle.[80] Out of kilter with the Foreign Office, Macmillan increasingly relied on face-to-face diplomacy with de Gaulle to circumvent Cabinet and Whitehall scepticism that the general could be won over to Britain's cause in Europe without in the process jeopardising relations with the US. The first major test of this during the meeting between the two leaders at Rambouillet on 28–29 January 1961 was encouraging if inconclusive. Although de Gaulle warmed to Macmillan's doubts about the multilateral NATO nuclear force favoured by the US, closer Anglo-French nuclear co-operation was bound to antagonise the Kennedy administration and anyway did not promise tangible rewards from the Six. This became more apparent over the coming year.[81] During 1961–62 Macmillan's efforts to win over de Gaulle to Britain's application for EEC membership were unsuccessful. Neither nuclear concessions, exploitation of French difficulties in Algeria nor broad acceptance of French prerequisites for entry sufficed to reverse de Gaulle's preferred alternative of Franco-German leadership in his Europe of States.[82]

In December 1960 the State Department Bureau of Intelligence and Research noted the friction in Anglo-French relations and concluded that de Gaulle might further consolidate his relationship with Adenauer's West Germany so diminishing the prospects for British entry to the Common Market. A month later Kennedy's Secretary of State, Dean Rusk, was told by his senior advisers that the long-term course of French foreign policy was now set. De Gaulle's administration still hankered after a tripartite directorate. Once the burden of Algeria diminished, so French leadership within the EEC would become a more effective lever either to secure de Gaulle's demands or to build a European Community as a counterweight to Anglo-Saxon power.[83] On 10 March 1961 de Gaulle's envoy, Jacques Chaban-Delmas, then president of the National Assembly, reiterated the case for a tripartite directorate to Kennedy. In these discussions Algeria was treated as a problem already in eclipse. The worsening crises in Congo and, above all, Laos were more serious focal-points of Franco-American friction. This was further confirmed when Kennedy and de Gaulle met in Paris at the end of May.[84] Kennedy concluded from his discussions with de Gaulle that the latter doubted the British commitment to the EEC over the Commonwealth and the European Free Trade Association and anyway preferred to remain the biggest fish in a small Common Market pond.[85]

During April 1961 Minister of Defence Harold Watkinson and his French opposite number, Pierre Messmer, held talks in Paris over Anglo-French defence policy and joint collaboration with NATO. Fearing that progress would be slowed by the Algerian problem, the British delegation none the less pressed Messmer regarding the development of common weapons systems and the long term co-ordination of defence programmes. The principal aim of the talks, however, was to clarify whether the French government would be prepared to guarantee NATO a role in the targeting and strategic control of French nuclear weapons. With France on the brink of a genuine independent nuclear capacity, Macmillan hoped to build bridges to de Gaulle by emphasising their shared opposition to an alliance veto on the use of national nuclear defences. But while Messmer reiterated his hostility to NATO exercising ultimate command over 'a mixed bag of strategic and tactical weapons', he also revealed a more profound French disdain for the entire fabric of multinational NATO command.[86]

As a result, the Watkinson–Messmer talks suggested that there was no basis for a British-brokered compromise between the Gaullist vision of unilateral strategic control and the multilateral requirements of NATO. It was with some relief that the Ministry of Defence concluded that the constraints imposed on French defence policy by the continuing crisis in Algeria would, for the moment at least, impose limits on French strategic independence. Moreover, much as Macmillan's government and the British chiefs of staff deplored the French obsession with an independent nuclear capability outside collective NATO control, it brought one significant consolation. De Gaulle's pursuit of the *force de frappe* during 1958–62 confirmed beyond doubt that French strategic planning would be progressively reoriented towards Europe at the direct expense of the war in Algeria. Although Britain had met limited success in pushing the French defence departments towards greater spending on conventional forces in Europe, a nuclear France at the heart of European defence was ultimately preferable to a non-nuclear ally distracted and weakened by intractable conflict in Algeria. Militarily, within General Ailleret's Paris command, Algeria was increasingly spoken of as a long-term nuclear test site rather than as France's principal theatre of overseas warfare.[87]

By 1962 the Mediterranean was less important as a focus of Anglo-French tension within NATO. Britain's strategic commitments within the region were much diminished and France was set to leave Algeria.

In preparation for the government's New Year defence white paper, in December 1961 the Foreign Office challenged the service chiefs' assumption that Britain might need to retain forces in North Africa once its existing Anglo-Libyan treaty obligations came up for review in 1963. Nor was it likely that Britain would be called on to intervene in Lebanon. The British weapons stockpile in Cyprus and its Mediterranean naval commitment could be scaled down. British Mediterranean obligations could be satisfied by reducing the status of the Malta and Gibraltar bases to forward planning centres for the navy and staging posts for the RAF. The era of major British and French military and colonial engagement in the Mediterranean was drawing to a close.[88] None the less, the principal French units repatriated from Algeria in 1962 were not reintegrated into NATO but kept as a strategic reserve under national command. Though formal French withdrawal from NATO did not occur until 1966, after the Algerian cease-fire French military priorities were never squared with the country's NATO commitments.[89]

On both sides of the Atlantic it was abundantly clear by 1962 that once an Algerian settlement was achieved, de Gaulle's administration would accelerate its nuclear programme and consolidate French leadership of the Six. In spite of US support for British admission to the EEC, Macmillan's government stood to lose ground in Washington and within Europe.[90] De Gaulle was never persuaded that Britain could fit into the EEC. But although he quickly tired of British counter-arguments, it was the resolution of the Algerian problem and the concurrent reinforcement of Franco-German relations over the course of 1962 that gave him the freedom of manoeuvre to reject British admission and oppose the Fouchet Plan for a closer political union of the Six.[91]

Civil–Military Relations, Negotiations and Withdrawal

De Gaulle's stealth over plans for Algeria was primarily dictated by the fragile relations between the French government and elements of the army in Algeria. Barricades week between 24 January and 1 February 1960 and the army *putsch* mounted by Generals Challe, Jouhaud, Salan and Zeller on 22 April 1961 were both reactions to the perceived abandonment of France's true military interest and its political obligation to the civilian population of Algeria. That British ministers remained phlegmatic about this French military disloyalty said much for their confidence in de Gaulle's popularity and resolve. Jebb's subtle reportage of the tensions within the French security forces following Massu's dismissal in January 1960 added to this sentiment. So too did his successor, Sir

Pierson Dixon's assessment of French public opinion during the Challe coup in the following year. Dixon's impression of the relative calm among the French population offset more alarming reports from the service attachés, who were profoundly shocked by signs of disloyalty within the French air force and saw few reliable units likely to resist an attempt by Challe's troops to seize control.[92]

After the Algiers street violence of barricades week de Gaulle hardened his rhetoric towards the FLN, but quickly secured renewed special powers on 25 February 1960. A number of colonels from Algiers were purged, the key *Algérie française* protagonists were removed from government, Challe was dismissed as commander-in-chief and the cinquième bureau was finally disbanded. To reassure the troops on the ground, de Gaulle conducted a tour of inspection in early March, famously borrowing a phrase coined by Massu in May 1958: there would be no Algerian Dien Bien Phu.[93] According to the rebels a year later in 1961 this promise was never kept. Justifying his actions on 22 April, Challe lambasted successive government retreats – from *Algérie française* to *Algérie algérienne* and now an independent Algeria linked to France.[94]

The trend in government policy was by now much clearer than a year before. After the unproductive opening round of negotiations with the GPRA representatives Ahmed Boumendjel and Mohammed Benyahia at Melun between 25 and 29 June 1960, French public opinion moved decisively towards support for a negotiated withdrawal. The arguments between the delegations at Melun centred on the status of the delegations, the timing of a ceasefire and the release of Ben Bella rather than the fundamental matter of whether France would leave Algeria.[95] After Dixon took over from Jebb as ambassador to Paris in the autumn of 1960, he reported to Lloyd's successor as Foreign Secretary, Lord Home, that de Gaulle regarded 'French disengagement from Algeria only as an episode in the general process of decolonisation'. In a television address on 4 November de Gaulle spoke of his expectation of an Algerian Republic.[96] On 28 November Bourguiba played on the threat of communist incursion to the Maghreb to solicit British help in pushing the French government towards wider negotiations with the FLN. Macmillan was unresponsive. He also poured cold water on Pakistan President Field Marshal Mohammed Ayab Khan's proposal to mediate with the FLN leadership days later.[97] In British eyes, de Gaulle was moving as fast as he could.

During 1961 the settler *ultras* and the army die-hards eventually united in the OAS posed a greater threat to negotiations than the instability within the second GPRA administration. Buoyed by the information provided by French radio and television, especially de Gaulle's broadcast of 23 April, the mass of soldiers and airmen serving across Algeria in 1961 refused to support the generals' coup. With the surrender of Challe and Zeller, and the formidable combination of Louis Joxe as Minister of State for Algeria, and General Jean Olié as chief of general staff, the remaining army opposition to de Gaulle's policy went underground. As independence edged closer, OAS violence expanded across Algeria and mainland France. For all the bloodshed involved, particularly in the increasingly indiscriminate murders of Algerian Muslims, the high-point of civil–military confrontation had passed. The assassination attempts against de Gaulle and bombing outrages in Paris and even at the seat of the talks in Evian failed to slow the momentum of negotiations. When Salan pleaded for British government support in a letter he sent from hiding on 3 March 1962, he was simply ignored.[98]

OAS propaganda maintained that May 1958, barricades week and the April 1961 *putsch* offered tangible proof of fraternal co-operation between the settler population, the army and those moderate Muslims who realised the imminent threat of FLN dictatorship.[99] This was an argument already rejected by the French people. In the referendum on Algerian policy on 8 January 1961 voters spurned the *Algérie française* reactionaries grouped around Bidault, Lacoste and Bourgès-Maunoury in the *Comité National pour la Défense de l'Intégrité du Territoire* and those in Soustelle's *Regroupement National pour l'Unité de la République*. Instead, by a margin of over 10 million, the electorate endorsed de Gaulle's proposal for negotiations for Algerian self-determination.[100]

Popular and press opposition to the conflict, and the increasing cohesion of both intellectual and trade union protest against the war, further strengthened the government's hand in 1960–61. While Soustelle and his co-conspirators were alienated from their former patron, the UNR establishment was broadened as the more left-wing Gaullists of the *Union Démocratique du Travail* lent their backing to the administration. The September 1961 'Manifeste des 121' leading writers, academics and artists affirming the conscripts' moral right to refuse to serve in Algeria was the most sensational of numerous anti-war petitions that gripped the public imagination. Intellectual opposition to the war stretching from François Mauriac, a darling of the Gaullist establishment, to its confirmed enemy, Jean-Paul Sartre, was impossible to ignore. At the level of popular culture, as Philip Dine has recently suggested, other high-profile anti-war gestures were perhaps still more effective. From the ten leading Algerian football players in the French League who withdrew *en masse* to form an Algerian national side in Tunis in 1958, through the consistently shocking photo-journalism of *Paris-Match*, to the leading film-makers of the French 'New Wave' who figured among the signatories of the 1961 Manifesto, hostility to the conflict was obvious.[101] Meanwhile, the January referendum confirmed that the majority thought de Gaulle's government was moving in the right direction, though few were as yet willing to end the war on any terms. This was Macmillan's impression following his talks with the General at Rambouillet immediately after the referendum result.[102]

After the collapse of the preliminary French discussions with FLN representatives at Melun in June 1960, discussion between Downing Street and the Foreign Office over the prospects for a settlement hinged on assessments of the French government's capacity to impose it, de Gaulle's ability to carry the French public with him in order to do so, and the likelihood of an Algerian partition establishing settler enclaves within the northern coastal cities.[103] The decisive element in all these problems was the future of the settler community. Amongst an Algerian population that had grown to 10,196,740 by December 1960, *colons* still comprised the majority of the 1,007,910 people that enjoyed full citizenship. Most Algerian Muslims were amongst the 8,988,906 that effectively remained second-class subjects bound by the *statut local*.[104] In his landmark address of 4 November 1960 de Gaulle famously referred to 'an Algerian Algeria' (*Algérie algérienne*). To the consternation of Debré and his Cabinet colleagues who were not consulted beforehand, de Gaulle further opined that an Algerian government 'will exist one day' (*existera un jour*).[105] Here was de Gaulle's 'winds of change'. Understandably, the rights of the Muslim majority under French rule were now of secondary interest to British observers because gradual reform was giving way to discussion of total French withdrawal. In response to de Gaulle's statements, the State Department also focused more squarely on hastening an independence settlement and building links with the GPRA.[106]

Delouvrier's successor as delegate-general, Jean Morin, the former prefect of the Haut-Garonne appointed on 23 November 1960, confronted an Algeria in which the constitutional foundations of colonial privilege remained substantially intact. But his short-term attempts to remedy this were of less concern to the Foreign or Colonial Offices in London or to the State Department in Washington than the overall thrust of his mission. As Morin knew, the fundamental question was whether de Gaulle's government could protect settler rights within an Algerian Algeria instead of insisting upon partition as an alternative. Morin has since insisted that partition was not seriously entertained as an option, the expectation being that most settlers regrouped in any designated areas along the Algerian coast would leave the country for France rather than attempt to establish a separate state.[107]

In January 1961 Macmillan initiated an inter-departmental review of the utility of talks with the French over how best to guarantee European minority populations in former colonial territory. Such discussions could easily be included within the six-monthly round of Anglo-French exchanges over policies in black Africa initiated in April 1959. Might French experience in Algeria help inform British policy in Cyprus, Kenya and the Central African Federation, or vice versa? Above all, how could negotiated guarantees to safeguard legitimate settler rights and interests be made to stick once the colonial authorities departed?[108] The answers received were revealing. The Foreign Office disliked the idea. If news of Anglo-French chats over Algeria leaked, several Commonwealth states would object. More important, recent experience from Ghana suggested that constitutional guarantees to a settler population were worthless. Only a transitional regime prior to full independence could protect a European population effectively. But gradual transfers of power were not always practicable. The Colonial and the Commonwealth Relations Offices concurred that the benefits of dialogue with France over Algeria were outweighed by the danger of international criticism. Macmillan was not so easily swayed. At the Rambouillet talks on 28 January the two leaders agreed to begin expert consultations over effective guarantees of settler minority rights.[109]

In sum, as the French government gravitated towards Algerian independence the focal point of British interest in the negotiations themselves was the fate of the *colons* within the final settlement. Preoccupation with the settler population nourished Whitehall interest in the possibility of partition. From Paris, Dixon surmised that, as Morin has since conceded, vague suggestions to partition off Algeria's more wealthy coastal hinterland or to 'regroup' settlers within a protected northern zone were largely threats to push FLN negotiators to compromise. On 14 October 1961 Louis Joxe, the chief French negotiator, confirmed that partition was neither practical nor desirable since 'it would mean a continuation of the war under conditions even worse than existing ones'.

By this point the French government accepted that the FLN represented the will of the majority in Algeria, something de Gaulle admitted openly during a tour of Corsica in mid-November.[110] A week later Foreign Office and State Department officials conferred in Washington over how best to cement western ties with the GPRA. Both sides agreed that Algeria would be second to Egypt as the 'most important country in

North Africa'. To conciliate the new regime, Deputy Under-Secretary Sir Roger Stevens confirmed that Britain would place major commercial orders for Algerian natural gas, while diplomatic contacts with GPRA leaders in Tunis were to be extended.[111]

In a convincing demonstration of their power during the last round of the Evian talks, between 6 and 14 March 1962 the ALN mounted a general offensive against the eastern barrage using an unprecedented quantity of artillery, including Soviet field guns.[112] Within a week a general ceasefire was agreed. Khrushchev immediately announced *de jure* Soviet recognition of the GPRA, prompting the withdrawal of the French ambassador from Moscow in protest.[113] On first reading, the Evian accords signed on 18 March 1962 seemed a major French diplomatic achievement. Provision was made for an orderly transfer of power based on a transitional French administration pending a referendum on independence. In addition to special legal privileges, safeguards for property rights and special statutes to protect the large *colon* communities in Algiers and Oran, the settler population had a three year period of grace in which to adopt Algerian nationality. French military forces were to be withdrawn in stages over this three-year period while Mers el-Kébir was put under French lease for 15 years. France was to keep its military facilities and test sites in the Sahara for a five-year period. Algeria would remain within the franc zone and it would receive French financial aid for three years in the first instance. The two countries were to work jointly in the exploitation of Saharan oil and mineral resources.

So far so good. But, as Home warned, the real question was whether Evian would work in practice. Once the threat of partition disappeared with the inevitable vote for independence, the Algerian government might prove less accommodating. The experience of the war made harmonious Franco-Algerian co-existence at local or inter-governmental level unlikely. Although the capture between March and April of Jouhaud and other senior OAS leaders and the army's firmer loyalty to de Gaulle suggested that the movement was past its peak, the cycle of violence and counter-terror was far from over.[114] By contrast, Macmillan was sufficiently impressed by the French concessions extracted at Evian to ask the Foreign Office to study what lessons might be learnt for forthcoming British decolonisation talks.[115]

*

By any standards, 1962 was an eventful year in French political life. As the Evian negotiations neared a settlement, OAS terrorism and massive counter-demonstrations in metropolitan France brought tanks onto the streets of Paris. Meanwhile, in mid-April, Debré's successor as Prime Minister, Georges Pompidou, a key negotiator with the FLN alongside Bruno de Leusse, became the first premier since Louis Philippe never to have previously sat in Parliament. The strong UNR and PCF performances in the 1962 elections increased the political temperature within the National Assembly. The capture and trial of Generals Salan and Jouhaud and the influx of hundreds of thousands of *colon* and Muslim refugees from Algeria over the summer kept the Algerian settlement in the public gaze long after the Evian accords received broad popular approval. The arrival over the summer of some 650,000 *pieds noirs* plus at least 130,000 Muslim *harki* families staggered the Commissariat of Planning. In subsequent years, French governmental refusal to indemnify displaced settlers for property confiscated by the Algerian authorities symbolised both the unravelling of Evian and metropolitan French discomfort at the massive *colon* influx.[116] Yet, by the end of 1962, Ambassador Dixon noted that the Algerian nightmare was fast receding from the French public mind. He ascribed this to de Gaulle's willingness to belittle his own achievement in securing a final settlement in order to focus public opinion on the greater task of cementing French leadership within Europe. Pompidou shared this European preoccupation and conspicuously avoided detailed discussion of Algeria.[117]

Furthermore, notwithstanding the problems of unanticipated immigration, the loss of French North Africa did not do serious damage to the French economy. The agricultural staples and metal ores imported from the Maghreb were still available on the open market, but French consumption of the former in particular had declined anyway in the decade before Algerian independence.[118] As for the Algerian Sahara's famous oil deposits, the infrastructure necessary for the extraction and shipment of these reserves was still in its infancy in the early 1960s. As Sir Anthony Rumbold argued from Paris in August, without the Algerian albatross to restrain it, the French government was better placed to challenge American power in Europe and to block British entry to the Common Market. Macmillan remained less pessimistic and thus was ultimately more disappointed.[119] British diplomatic observers knew that, freed from the 'Algerian obsession', de Gaulle could give vent to his hostility to British admission to the EEC during talks with Macmillan at Rambouillet in December 1962. Not surprisingly, the French veto on Britain's plans to enter the EEC between 1961 and 1963 attracted far more political interest in Britain than the end of French North Africa.[120]

Conclusion

In May 1946 Georges Bidault recalled what General de Gaulle had told him six years earlier: France would emerge victorious 'because we have the Sahara'.[1] The French determination to maintain its North African patrimony after 1945 was shaped by a wartime conviction that the empire would be fundamental to the reassertion of national power. Why then was it de Gaulle himself who finally completed the French retreat from North Africa? And what was the British response to the violence and disorder of France's most traumatic imperial retreat? This book has tried to provide some possible answers. Throughout the 1950s, management of the crises in French North Africa – Algeria foremost – was a benchmark of French strategic, colonial and diplomatic capability. During this decade the earlier imperialist consensus also gradually disintegrated, causing bitter political division. To imperial traditionalists Algeria remained central to France's status as more than a continental power. But France's increasing colonial isolation, revealed most clearly at the UN, and the adverse impact of the war on the country's ability to achieve key economic and military objectives within Europe persuaded most that *Algérie française* had become a burden. By 1960 France's leadership of the European Community and its limited nuclear capacity exemplified the triumph of this outlook which, rightly or wrongly, is near inseparable from the figure of de Gaulle.[2] Furthermore, in the early 1960s the Fifth Republic achieved impressive economic growth, the loss of empire notwithstanding.[3] What then had been the practical point of resisting decolonisation in North Africa?

A common assertion is that French imperial policies in postwar North Africa were crippled by an underlying economic determinism evident across political parties, military commands and the bureaucratic elite. Convinced that indigenous opposition to French authority derived essentially from economic causes, successive governments responded to imperial crises in the Maghreb by subordinating political reform and cultural autonomy to long-term schemes of economic modernisation. In the interim, France's security forces and intelligence services were to ensure that colonial authority was not compromised. In Morocco and Tunisia the protectorate authorities tried unsuccessfully to exploit monarchical authority as an alternative to party-based nationalism. The international connections, ideological trappings and terrorist methods of Maghreb nationalist parties were all held to prove that militant North African nationalism was an alien concept. In the Algerian case, the FLN's external bases in Cairo and Tunis, its reliance on overseas material supply and the more long-standing tradition of integral nationalism among the Algerian immigrant community in France added fuel to French arguments.

This persistent underestimation of popular political and religious grievances hardened opposition to French rule and nurtured a climate of violence. As a result, while British imperial withdrawal initially attracted greater international attention, and the smaller colonial powers – the Netherlands, Belgium and Portugal – were all poorly reconciled to their loss of overseas territory, it was France's decolonisation from Indo-China and, above all, North Africa that most clearly exemplified the trauma of imperial collapse for both the metropolitan power and the territories it vacated. Defeat in Indo-China and the impasse of Algeria broke the loyalty of the French professional army and precipitated the collapse of an entire regime in May 1958. In the Fifth Republic de Gaulle's policies and *ultra* opposition to them generated further political polarisation in France and Algeria. Two poignant examples of the French experience in the final years of the war illustrate the point. The first was the mixed public response to news of Albert Camus's sudden death in a car crash on 4 January 1960. Stung by left-wing criticism of Camus's attachment to the ideal of an egalitarian, multicultural French Algeria, his widow Francine withheld publication of the author's unfinished novel, *Le premier homme*, taken from the wreckage of his car, fearing its vilification in the media. More dramatically, the depth of police antagonism towards the North African immigrant population was starkly exposed 18 months later during the night of 17 October 1961 when Paris witnessed the most appalling outburst of security force violence since the war. At least 200 Algerians were killed following a demonstration against a selectively applied curfew imposed by the infamous prefect of police Maurice Papon. Quite apart from its inhumanity, such brutality was a contemptuous affront to French democracy, a fact underlined by Papon's blanket denial of extensive police killings and his blockage of a parliamentary investigation into the course of events.[4]

Meanwhile, British policy towards the Algerian rebellion evolved in the pragmatic, gradualistic fashion with which British officials were wont to characterise Britain's decolonisation from much of Africa. It was obviously easier to move with the times and recommend generous reform as a bystander rather than as colonial master. But it would be wrong to think that the Algerian conflict was a side-show in Anglo-French relations or in British regional policy within the Mediterranean and Middle East. British interest in an early resolution of the Algerian problem was formally defined in February 1955 by the Foreign Office Western European Section research department and African department advisers. Disorder in French North Africa tied down French forces and weakened NATO defences in Europe, complicating British efforts to cut back the Rhine Army. Rebellion fanned the flames of Arab nationalism and anti-colonialism which was bound to complicate British diplomacy in the Middle East, at the UN and within the Commonwealth. Although the evidence of communist penetration was minimal, instability in the Maghreb was a breeding ground for Soviet or Egyptian intrigue.[5] Just as important, a substantial element of the French officer corps and countless politicians genuinely believed that Algeria was France's new Cold War front-line. It is well to recall that in his initial reportage of the outbreaks in November 1954, Governor-General Roger Léonard insisted that 'the rioters had obeyed foreign orders to the letter'.[6] At his treason trial in the summer of 1962, General Salan, the disgraced leader of the OAS national council who had formerly been commander-in-chief in both Indo-China and Algeria, insisted that his postwar military career represented a long struggle against the spread of communism. In his unrepentant testimony, Salan was Cold Warrior personified. (He was sentenced to life imprisonment none the less.) It was a relief to the British government that de Gaulle's first term marked the definitive repudiation of such views as France belatedly acknowledged the fundamental differences between colonial nationalism, Arabism and the communist threat. The Algerian burden – *le boulet algérien* – was finally lifted.[7]

To these specific regional concerns, several more general – and ultimately more significant – British interests were added as Morocco and Tunisia neared independence and the Algerian war intensified. The crisis of French authority and the worsening violence across the Maghreb poisoned French politics and therefore affected aspects of Anglo-French relations with no colonial dimension. In a climate of diplomatic realpolitik this brought benefits as well as problems to the British government.

Between 1953 and 1956 intractable disputes within the French Chamber over Moroccan and Algerian policy kept the Radicals divided, helped split both the Gaullist movement and the MRP, and isolated the PCF. To a cynical British eye, there were short-term advantages in all of these. France's difficulties at the UN were another double-edged sword. From 1952 to 1962 the annual battles over inscription of Maghreb questions added to Anglo-American fears that French repression justified as a contribution to western security actually undermined respect for the West throughout North Africa.[8] UN scrutiny of Morocco, Tunisia and Algeria damaged France and French relations with the western powers whether or not the subject was debated on the General Assembly floor. None the less, it was easier for the British delegation in New York to duck the jabs as France became the favoured punch-bag for the non-aligned Afro-Asian states.

France's behaviour during the Suez crisis was less memorable for the failed attempt to oust Nasser than for the ease with which an inner-circle of ministers, generals and senior Defence Ministry officials usurped Cabinet policy-making in order to confront the Egyptian leader and thus attain the elusive strategic breakthrough in Algeria. For them, the phrase *Algérie 1956, capitale Suez* was unquestionably true.[9] This, it seems, aroused remarkably little public opposition or political recrimination after the collapse of the Suez expedition. This helps to account for the increasing divergence in French and British imperial policies in North Africa and the Middle East after 1956. Such was Britain's international humiliation over Suez that the months in late 1956 during which Eden's government became active accomplices to the French war in Algeria seemed a footnote to the more general collapse of British international power. The shock administered at Suez drove the British government closer to Eisenhower's administration, not least in the subsequent formulation of policy towards French North Africa. By contrast, for the French stopped in their tracks at Suez, an intensification of the war against the FLN inside Algeria and along its frontiers seemed the clearest strategic option. The caution in British imperial policy under Macmillan was matched by the greater assertiveness of the French military in Algeria from 1957 onwards.

Still, the fundamental dilemma remained: no government of the Fourth Republic made a clear choice between negotiation or military pacification. In making the former conditional on the success of the latter, successive administrations tied themselves to an expansion of the war.[10] The more the prospects for negotiation faded, the more emphasis was placed upon military operations. This conflict escalator played into the hands of the FLN by making the war harder for France to sustain and by rendering life even worse for millions of Muslim civilians. The FLN's capacity to meet the challenge of a widening war transformed it from an unrepresentative organisation dependent on 'compliance terrorism' to a firmly rooted national movement. British criticism of French policy in Algeria generally began from the assumption that opportunities for dialogue had been missed. From the corruption of the 1947 statute for Algeria onwards, colonial government in Algiers was poorly regarded in Whitehall. Greater British respect for French military policy stemmed, in part, from a conviction that the army was handicapped by the inadequacy of civil government and *colon* dominance of Algiers politics. With the acceleration of British decolonisation under Macmillan a shift of emphasis occurred. As the lines between settler opposition and military insubordination became blurred, British indulgence towards the military effort in Algeria diminished.

Leading British politicians and officials knew from experience that possession of empire – even an empire in trouble – helped France to punch above its weight in western alliance politics, international diplomacy and European integration. But although Whitehall observers further recognised after 1956 that the scale of French colonial breakdown in North Africa had turned an asset into a liability, few foresaw how quickly France would recover from the trauma once de Gaulle began the decisive steps towards complete withdrawal. Initially uncertain and only slowly revealed, de Gaulle's commitment to negotiate an end to the war was a practical response to its costs, its deleterious effects on foreign and defence policy and its impact on French political life. The very violence and totality of French decolonisation from North as opposed to black Africa reinforced the French commitment to the European Community, a refashioned defence policy and a clean break with past colonial policies. The rapidity of future French recovery was hard to foresee amidst the local military disorder, faltering independence talks and emerging OAS terrorism in 1960–2. Instead, Macmillan's administration overestimated its capacity to exploit French weakness in the final stages of the Algerian conflict. During de Gaulle's first term, France's Algerian commitment was a root cause of Gaullist antagonism to Anglo-American leadership of the western alliance. But its drain on French military capacity and influence within NATO made de Gaulle's tripartite directorate seem all the more ludicrous. If French ambitions for nuclear defence and leadership of the European Community, and the resultant challenge to Britain's balancing act between the US and Europe, were clear enough by 1959, the pressure of events in Algeria at least delayed the full impact of Gaullist policy in practice. Once the war ended, the dangers of misreading French intentions were soon exposed in the failure of Britain's first application to join the EEC.

For all these calculations, it would be wrong to see British policy towards French North Africa as either adversarial or coldly self-interested. The gut feeling that self-government for the protectorates was overdue and that settler power in Algeria was an unacceptable obstacle to meaningful reform were foundations of an unspoken consensus over the problems of the Maghreb. It would be easy to cry hypocrite by pointing to inconsistencies between Whitehall views of French imperial rule and British colonial practice. Still, the example of an assimilationist colonial doctrine gone disastrously wrong in Algeria was without direct parallel in spite of the persistence of white rule across southern Africa, repressive counter-insurgencies in Kenya and Cyprus and the abiding determination to maintain British imperial footholds elsewhere. Ultimately, scale was everything. Algeria was a conflict apart – more brutal, more expensive and more divisive at home and abroad than anything in Britain's postwar experience of decolonisation.

As a result, relief was always an important element in British governmental attitudes towards France's North African crisis. Such an ephemeral concept is impossible to measure. But the sentiment was there – relief that Britain's colonial wars were of lower intensity; relief that France was the choice imperial villain at the UN; relief that, after Suez, British politics were not convulsed by empire to the same extent as French; and relief that no colonial territory emptied the exchequer in the manner of Algeria. It is tempting to add the occasional glimpses of smugness among British observers of the Algerian war in particular. Here one may be more precise. Collusion between a colonial administration and settler interests had obvious parallels in recent British imperial experience, especially in southern Africa. By contrast, whether correctly or not, other aspects of the Algerian conflict were perceived as specifically French problems unlikely to occur in a British context. These included the fragmentation of political parties, the anti-colonial activities of an immigrant population, massive public protest both for and against colonial withdrawal and, above all, the break-down in civil–military relations. While British governments did not generally consider the French experience a portent, the crisis of French North Africa remained an important component in Anglo-French relations until the FLN's victory in 1962. French Cabinets split over it, the army and air force were convulsed by it and the constitutional system was reordered to cope with it. Those directly touched by the violence of North African decolonisation, especially the Algerian civilians that were its principal victim, became more and more visible to French policy-makers as the sheer horror of the war in Algeria became the most compelling reason to end it. These considerations and the wider international ramifications of the struggles for independence in North West Africa were problems too great and too tragic to ignore.

Notes

Introduction

1. Macmillan notes on Hôtel Matignon talks, 29 June 1958, PREM 11/2326, PRO. De Gaulle made similar comments to President Eisenhower during the latter's visit to Paris in September 1959: Dwight D. Eisenhower, *The White House Years. Waging Peace 1956–1961* (London: Heinemann, 1965), 429.
2. Douglas Johnson, 'Algeria: Some Problems of Modern History', *Journal of African History*, 5:2 (1964) 223; M. Semidei, 'De l'Empire à la décolonisation à travers les manuels scolaires français', *Revue Française de Science Politique*, 16:1 (1966), 56–79; Kathryn Castle, *Britannia's children. Reading colonialism through children's books and magazines* (Manchester: Manchester University Press, 1996).
3. David Carroll, 'Camus's Algeria: Birthrights, Colonial Injustice, the Fiction of a French-Algerian People', *Modern Language Notes*, 112 (1997), 529–31.
4. Philip Dine, *Images of the Algerian War. French Fiction and Film, 1954–1992* (Oxford: Clarendon Press, 1994), ch. 4; Charles-Robert Ageron, '"L'Algérie dernière chance de la puissance française". Etude d'un mythe politique (1954–1962)', *Relations Internationales*, 57 (1989), 114–15.
5. Annie Cohen-Solal, 'Camus, Sartre and the Algerian War', *Journal of European Studies*, 28:1 (1998), 44; Debré cited in Monique Gadant, *Islam et nationalisme en Algérie d'après 'El Moudjahid' organe central du FLN de 1956 à 1962* (Paris: Editions L'Harmattan, 1988), 65.
6. Service de presse et d'information (Washington) report no. 65903, 20 Oct. 1955, série Etats-Unis, vol. 342, MAE.
7. John Talbott, 'Terrorism and the Liberal Dilemma: The Case of the Battle of Algiers', *Contemporary French Civilization*, 2:2 (1978), 177–89; Dine, *Images*, 64–79.
8. State Dept. memo. for George V. Allen, 'Relationship between Algeria and France', 25 July 1955, RG 59, 751S.00, box 3375, NARA.
9. Julia A. Clancy-Smith, *Rebel and Saint. Muslim Notables, Populist Protest, Colonial Encounters (Algeria and Tunisia, 1800–1904)* (Berkeley, CA: University of California Press, 1997), 19–24, 59–60, quote at p. 20. See also R. Gallissot, 'Precolonial Algeria', *Economy and Society*, 4:4 (1975), 418–45.

10. Michael Greenhalgh, 'The New Centurions: French Reliance on the Roman Past during the Conquest of Algeria', *War and Society*, 16:1 (1998), 1–28.
11. Jean-François Guilhaume, *Les Mythes fondateurs de l'Algérie française* (Paris: Editions L'Harmattan, 1992), 188–99.
12. Patricia M. Lorcin, *Imperial Identities. Stereotyping, Prejudice and Race in Colonial Algeria* (London: I. B. Taurus, 1995), 217–25; Mustapha El Qadéry, 'Les Berbères entre le mythe colonial et la négation nationale. Le cas du Maroc', *Revue d'Histoire Moderne et Contemporaine*, 45:2 (1998), 436.
13. Daniel R. Headrick, *The Tools of Empire. Technology and European Imperialism in the Nineteenth Century* (Oxford: Oxford University Press, 1981), 66–7, 159, 200–1; Bruce Vandervort, *Wars of Imperial Conquest in Africa, 1830–1914* (London: UCL Press, 1998), 28–9.
14. P. Guiral, 'L'opinion marseillaise et les débuts de l'entreprise algérienne (1830–1841)', *Revue Historique*, 154:1 (1955), 9–34; Vandervort, *Wars*, 56–7; Anthony Clayton, *France, Soldiers and Africa* (London: Brassey's, 1988), 20–1, 52–5.
15. Charles-Robert Ageron, *Modern Algeria: A History from 1830 to the Present* (London: Hurst, 1991), 6–8; William H. Schneider, *An Empire for the Masses. The French Popular Image of Africa, 1870–1900* (Westport, Conn.: Greenwood Press, 1982), 20–1.
16. Vandervort, *Wars of Imperial Conquest*, 65–7.
17. M. Heffernan, 'The French Right and the Overseas Empire', in N. Atkin and F. Tallett (eds), *The Right in France, 1789–1997* (London: I. B. Tauris, 1997), 91–100.
18. Joëlle Redouane, 'British Trade with Algeria in the Nineteenth Century: An Ally against France?', *Maghreb Review*, 13:3–4 (1988), 175–6.
19. Headrick, *Tools of Empire*, 92–3; Clancy-Smith, *Rebel and Saint*, 156, 162–3.
20. Vandervort, *Wars of Imperial Conquest*, 58–69.
21. Clancy-Smith, *Rebel and Saint*, especially chs. 3, 4 and 6.
22. See, for example, David Prochaska, *Making Algeria French. Colonialism in Bône, 1870–1920* (Cambridge: Cambridge University Press, 1990), ch. 5, esp. 165–78.
23. Miles Kahler, *Decolonization in Britain and France. The Domestic Consequences of International Relations* (Princeton, NJ: Princeton University Press, 1984), 74–5.
24. Jacques Marseille, 'L'investissement public en Algérie après la Deuxième Guerre Mondiale', *Revue Française d'Histoire d'Outre-Mer*, LXX: 260 (1983), 180.
25. Tony Smith, 'Muslim Impoverishment in Colonial Algeria', *Revue de l'Occident Musulman et de la Méditerranée*, 156 (1974), 147–54.
26. Johnson, 'Algeria: Some Problems of Modern History', 223–9.
27. For the discussion of Charles-André Julien's *L'Afrique du Nord en marche*, see Michael Brett, 'The Colonial Period in the Maghrib and its Aftermath: the Present State of Historical Writing', *Journal of African History*, 17:2 (1976), 291–8.
28. Naegelen speech at Relizane, 21 May 1950; Thomas H. Lockett to State Dept., 25 September 1950, RG 59, 751S.00, box 3700, NARA.
29. Alan Christelow, 'Ritual, Culture and Politics of Islamic Reformism in Algeria', *Middle Eastern Studies*, 23:3 (1987), 255–69.
30. Gadant, *Islam et nationalisme en Algérie*, 64–7.

31. Martin Evans, 'Rehabilitating the traumatized War Veteran: The Case of French Conscripts from the Algerian War, 1954–1962', in Martin Evans and Ken Lunn (eds), *War and Memory in the Twentieth Century* (Oxford: Berg, 1997), 73–9.
32. John Horne, 'Immigrant Workers in France during World War I', *French Historical Studies*, 16:1 (1985), 57–88; Benjamin Stora, *La Gangrène et l'oubli. La mémoire de la guerre d'Algérie* (Paris: Editions La Découverte, 1991), 125.
33. Kahler, *Decolonization*, 73, 86–7, 94.
34. Paul Thibaud, 'Génération algérienne?', *Esprit*, 161 (1990), 46–54.
35. Regarding French operations, see John Pimlott, 'The French Army: From Indochina to Chad, 1946–1984', in Ian F. W. Beckett and John Pimlott (eds), *Armed Forces and Modern Counter-Insurgency* (London: Croom Helm, 1985), 46–67.
36. Tony Smith, *The French Stake in Algeria, 1945–1962* (Ithaca, NY: Cornell University Press, 1978), chs 6–7, and 'The French Colonial Consensus and People's War, 1946–58', *Journal of Contemporary History*, 9:4 (1974), 217–47. Smith's views are examined in C. Harrison, 'French Attitudes to Empire and the Algerian War', *African Affairs* (January 1983), 75–95.
37. Johnson, 'Algeria', 231–4. According to Johnson, by 1954 the settler community was 79.4 per cent urban.
38. Salah el Din el Zein el Tayeb, 'The Europeanized Algerians and the Emancipation of Algeria', *Middle Eastern Studies*, 22:2 (1986), 220–33.

1 Divergent Imperialism

1. General André Beaufre, *The Suez Expedition 1956*, English trans. (London: Faber and Faber, 1969), 146.
2. Frank Furedi, 'Creating a Breathing Space: The Political Management of Colonial Emergencies', *Journal of Imperial and Commonwealth History*, 21:1 (1993), 90–2.
3. Division of African affairs memo. of conversation with Bourguiba, 19 December 1946, *Foreign Relations of the United States (FRUS)*, 1946, vol. VII, 62–3. In July 1945, Algiers French military intelligence noted that the PPA 'situates its action within the framework of Anglo-Russian conflict in the Mediterranean', See: EMGDN, Section d'Afrique 2e bur. bulletin de renseignements no. 25, 11 July 1945, Affaires politiques, Carton 2116/D2, ANCOM.
4. Jacques Valette, 'Guerre Mondiale et décolonisation. Le cas du Maroc en 1945', *Revue Française d'Histoire d'Outre-Mer*, LXX: 260 (1983), 136–41.
5. As examples: Interior Ministry reports, 19 April 1946, 18 June 1946, 2 August 1946, dossier K-40–1, série Afrique-Levant, sous-série Algérie, vol. 8, MAE.
6. Sous-direction des protectorats, 'Note schematique au sujet du Destour tunisien', n.d. 1946, vol. 112, Bidault papers, AN. Abolition of protectorate status would end France's right to supervise the monarchical governments of Morocco and Tunisia.
7. Adrien Tixier to affaires étrangères/Cabinet, VI/B19, 22 June 1945, Algérie, vol. 2, MAE; Section d'Afrique 2e bur. BR no. 22, 5 June 1945, Aff. pol., C2116/D2, ANCOM; Anthony Clayton, 'The Sétif Uprising of May 1945', *Small Wars and Insurgencies*, 3:1 (1992), 7–11.

8. Roger Faligot and Pascal Krop, *La Piscine. Les services secrets français 1944–1984* (Paris: Editions du Seuil, 1985), 140.
9. Jean-Charles Jauffret, 'L'Armée et l'Algérie en 1954', *Revue Historique des Armées*, 2 (1992), 16.
10. *FRUS*, 1945, vol. VIII, 30–2.
11. J. E. M. Carvell (Algiers) to FO, 17 May 1945 and Eden minute, n.d., Z6050/900/69, FO 371/49275, PRO.
12. D. K. Fieldhouse, 'The Labour Governments and the Empire-Commonwealth, 1945–51', in Ritchie Ovendale (ed.), *The Foreign Policy of the British Labour Governments, 1945–1951* (Leicester: Leicester University Press, 1984), 88.
13. Carvell (Algiers) to FO, 9 February and 25 April 1945, Z2437/900/69, Z5441/900/69; T. V. Brenan, (Tunis) to FO, 8 April 1945, Z5336/900/69; Gilbert Mackereth (Rabat) to FO, 4 May 1945, Z5922/900/69, FO 371/49275, PRO.
14. Mast to Bidault, 8 February 1945, no. 119/CAB; Mast to Bidault, 15 March 1945, no. 219, vol. 112, Bidault papers.
15. Mackereth (Rabat) to FO, 26 June 1945, Z7869/900/69; Brenan (Tunis) to FO, 17 May 1945, Z6528/900/69; H. Farquhar (Cairo) to FO, 18 May 1945, Z6613/900/69, FO 371/49276, PRO.
16. William Roger Louis, *The British Empire in the Middle East 1945–1951. Arab Nationalism, the United States and Postwar Imperialism* (Oxford: Oxford University Press, 1984), 129–30; Jean-Charles Jauffret (ed.), *La Guerre d'Algérie par les Documents, II: Les Portes de la Guerre: des occasions manquées à l'insurrection 1946–1954* (Vincennes: SHAT, 1998), 83; FO record of conversation with Massigli, 1 August 1946, Z7290/1355/69, FO 371/60107, PRO. Original Arab League member states were Egypt, Iraq, Transjordan, Saudi Arabia, Libya, Syria and Lebanon.
17. Gabriel Puaux (Rabat) to Bidault, 22 March 1945, série Internationale, sous-série Nations Unies et Organisations Internationales (NUOI), vol. 573, MAE; Michael Thornhill, 'Britain and the Politics of the Arab League, 1943–50', in M. J. Cohen and M. Kolinsky (eds), *Demise of the British Empire in the Middle East. Britain's Responses to Nationalist Movements, 1943–55* (London: Frank Cass, 1998), 41–51; Louis, *The British Empire*, 134–6.
18. Samya el Machat, *Tunisie. Les chemins vers l'indépendance (1945–1956)* (Paris: Editions L'Harmattan, 1992), 15–20, 28.
19. R. L. Speaight minute, 3 June 1945, Z6527/900/69; Mackereth to FO, 3 August 1945, Z9370/900/69, FO 371/49276, PRO; Louis, *The British Empire*, 156–62.
20. René Girault, 'Les Décideurs français et leur perception de la puissance Française en 1948', in R. Girault and R. Frank (eds), *La Puissance française en question (1945–1949)* (Paris: Publications de la Sorbonne, 1988), 13.
21. André Nouschi, 'Modernisation au Maghreb et puissance française (1945–1948)', in Girault and Frank, *La Puissance française*, 258–9.
22. R. F. Holland, 'The Imperial Factor in British Strategies from Attlee to Macmillan, 1945–63', *Journal of Imperial and Commonwealth History*, 12:2 (1984), 166.
23. Lord Cranborne conversations, San Francisco, 15 May 1945, CO 968/162/4, PRO. Regarding Levant divisions, see A. B. Gaunson, *The Anglo-French Clash in Lebanon and Syria, 1940–1945* (London: Macmillan, 1987); Aviel Roshwald, *Estranged Bedfellows. Britain and France in the Middle East During the Second*

World War (Oxford: Oxford University Press, 1990); Louis, *The British Empire*, 147–72.

24. Post-hostilities planning sub-committee, 'Future Relations with France', 19 May 1944, PHP(44)32; COS(44)179th meeting, 1 June 1944, CAB 121/400, PRO.
25. Nicholas Owen, 'Britain and Decolonization: The Labour Governments and the Middle East, 1945–51', 4–19; John Kent, 'Britain and the Egyptian Problem, 1945–48', 142–4, both in Cohen and Kolinsky, *Demise*: *British Documents on the End of Empire Project* (*BDEEP*), series A, vol. II, part III: Ronald Hyam (ed.), *The Labour Government and the End of Empire, 1945–1951* (London: HMSO, 1992), doc. 275.
26. Bevin memo., 'Revision of the Anglo-Egyptian Treaty of 1936', 18 January 1946, CP(46)17, CAB 129/006, PRO.
27. 'The Pentagon Talks of 1947', policy documents, *FRUS*, 1947, vol. V, pp. 511–35; John Kent, *British Imperial Strategy and the Origins of the Cold War, 1944–49* (Leicester: Leicester University Press, 1993), 90–101 *passim*.
28. *BDEEP*, series A, vol. II, part I, Ronald Hyam intro., li; part II, doc. 152.
29. *BDEEP*, series A, vol. II, part II, docs. 175, 177, 178.
30. John Kent, 'Bevin's Imperialism and the Idea of Euro-Africa, 1945–49', in Michael Dockrill and John Young (eds), *British Foreign Policy, 1945–56* (London: Macmillan, 1989), 47–76; Kent, 'Britain and the Egyptian Problem, 1945–48' in Cohen and Kolinsky, *Demise of the British Empire*, 143–51.
31. Kent, *British Imperial Strategy*, 138–9; Ritchie Ovendale, *Britain, the United States and the transfer of power in the Middle East, 1945–1962* (London: Leicester University Press, 1996), 4–5.
32. Louis, *The British Empire*, 168–72.
33. Duff Cooper to FO, 21 January 1946, tel. 63, CAB 121/400; French situation reports to 1949, CO 537/4379; various reports on France, 1950, CO 537/5653, PRO.
34. Caffery to State Dept., 26 July 1946, *FRUS*, 1946, vol. VII, 56.
35. Caffery to State Dept., 26 July 1946; Consul Finley (Algiers) to Byrnes, 17 August 1946, *FRUS*, 1946, vol. VII, 54–8.
36. FO minutes on Rabat Consulate report, 13 March–8 April 1946, Z395/395/28; W. Manning, Tunis, to FO, 7 May 1946, Z4505/31/69, FO 371/60084, PRO.
37. Affaires économiques 3e bur. note, n. d. January 1946, vol. 115, Bidault papers.
38. John W. Young, *France, the Cold War and the Western Alliance, 1944–1949* (Leicester: Leicester University Press, 1990), chs. 7–8.
39. Bevin, 'Review of Soviet Policy', 5 Jan. 1948, CP(48)7, CAB 129/23, PRO.
40. Kent, *British Imperial Strategy*, 97–106; Louis, *The British Empire*, 271–8; *BDEEP*, series A, vol. II, part III, docs. 274, 275, 277, 278.
41. Record of Massigli conversation, 1 August 1946, Z7290/1355/69, FO 371/60107, PRO; Bevin memo., 'Policy in Libya', 23 September 1946, CP(46)354, CAB 129/13; *BDEEP*, *op. cit.*, docs. 297, 298.
42. *BDEEP*, *op. cit.*, docs. 296, 297.
43. *BDEEP*, *op. cit.*, docs. 301, 302; memo. by assistant chief of the division of African affairs, 13 May 1948, *FRUS*, 1948, vol. III, 692–4.
44. Bevin memo., 'Former Italian Colonies', 13 September 1948, CP(48)222, CAB 129/29; FO and WO memo., 'Cyrenaica', 9 November 1948, CP(48)261, CAB

129/30, PRO. The principal French garrisons in the Fezzan were at Ghat, Ghadames and Sebha.

45. Sir Frederick Hoyer-Millar note, 'North West Africa', 9 January 1947, Z300/52/69, FO 371/67710, PRO.
46. Afrique du Nord Arab Libre communiqué, n.d. 1944, F^{60}/835, AN.
47. Cabinet diplomatique (Rabat) memo., 'La question marocaine à l'ONU', 27 August 1947, NUOI vol. 573, MAE; Samya el Machat, *Tunisie*, 27; Jauffret (ed.), *La Guerre d'Algérie par les Documents, II*, 89.
48. Edmond Mouret and Jean-Pierre Azéma (eds), *Vincent Auriol. Journal du Septennat, 1947–1954, tome II, 1948* (Paris: Armand Colin, 1974), entry for 13 February 1948, 92.
49. Mast to Bidault, 12 February 1945, no. 122, vol. 112, Bidault papers.
50. Residency report, 'Situation politique en Tunisie', 1 February 1946, *ibid.*
51. Residency report, 'Situation politique en Tunisie', 17 June 1946, vol. 112, Bidault papers. This report pleaded for funding to support DGER/SDECE activities in Tunisia.
52. Direction Afrique-Levant note pour le ministre, 8 May 1946, Tunisie 1944–49, vol. 93, MAE.
53. Benjamin Stora and Zakya Daoud, *Ferhat Abbas une utopie algérienne* (Paris: Editions Denoël, 1995), 171.
54. Duff Cooper to Bevin, 12 Sept. 1946, Z8121/2830/17, FO 371/60048, PRO.
55. Bidault to Mast, 2 September 1946, no. 1222; Massigli to Bidault, 9 September 1946, no. 2697, Tunisie 1944–1949, vol. 93, MAE.
56. Residency tel. to direction Afrique-Levant, 3 October 1946, no. 740, Tunisie 1944–1949, vol. 93, MAE.
57. Jauffret, *La Guerre d'Algérie par les Documents, II*, 51–3.
58. Bureau d'études note, 24 January 1947, vol. 112, Bidault papers. For background to Blum's visit, see Young, *France, the Cold War*, 131–3.
59. Ashley Clarke to Hoyer-Millar, 14 January 1947, Z835/52/69, FO 371/67710, PRO.
60. Consular heads, 3rd meeting, 23 January 1947, Z1574/52/69, FO 371/67710, PRO.
61. W. I. Mallet to Sir William Strang, 18 July 1949 – record of Bevin's 1947 pronouncement, J6058/1055/69, FO 371/73728, PRO.
62. Director of office of Near Eastern and African affairs memo., 14 April 1947, *FRUS*, 1947, vol. V, 678–9.
63. 'Maroc – Questions politiques', 22 January 1946, vol. 115, Bidault papers; Will D. Swearingen, *Moroccan Mirages. Agrarian Dreams and Deceptions* (Princeton, NJ: Princeton University Press, 1987), 122–5.
64. Nouschi, 'Modernisation au Maghreb', 261–3.
65. Schuman note, 'La crise marocaine', 8 January 1945, vol. 115, Bidault papers.
66. Pasquet to Secretary of State, 7 August 1946, *FRUS*, 1946, vol. VII, 57.
67. El Mustafa Azzou, 'Le nationalisme marocain et les Etats-Unis 1945–1956', *Guerres Mondiales et Conflits Contemporains*, 177 (1994), 131–8.
68. Stéphane Bernard, *The Franco-Moroccan Conflict 1943–1956* (New Haven: Yale University Press, 1968), 42.
69. Raphaële Ulrich, 'Vincent Auriol et la Tunisie', *Revue d'Histoire Diplomatique*, 110 (1996), 225–7; Aline Fonveille-Vojtovic, *Paul Ramadier (1881–1961) Elu local et homme d'état* (Paris: Publications de la Sorbonne, 1993), 360.

70. James I. Lewis, 'The MRP and the Genesis of the French Union, 1944–1948', *French History*, 12:3 (1998), 306–12; Entry, 12 February 1948, *Journal du Septennat, tome II, 1948*, 88.
71. Caffery to Secretary of State, 17 May 1947, *FRUS*, 1947, vol. V, 684; Bernard, *Franco-Moroccan Conflict*, 43–59.
72. Jauffret (ed.), *La Guerre d'Algérie par les Documents, II*, 137–41.
73. Section d'Afrique 2e bur., 'Note sur le statut d'Algérie', n. d. May 1947, Aff. pol., C2116/D2, ANCOM; James I. Lewis, 'French Politics and the Algerian Statute of 1947', *Maghreb Review*, 17 (1992), 146–72.
74. 'Compte rendu analytique des séances d'études tenues au comité de l'AFN en Octobre 1946', 4Q119/D8, SHAT.
75. Duff Cooper to Bevin, 26 August 1946, Z7714/2830/17, FO 371/60048, PRO.
76. Salah el Din el Zein el Tayeb, 'The Europeanized Algerians', 206–35; Stora and Daoud, *Ferhat Abbas*, 178–80.
77. Creech Jones circular to colonial governments, 4 February 1949, CO 537/4379, PRO; Young, *France, the Cold War*, 166.
78. Robert Bourgi, *Le Général de Gaulle et l'Afrique noire 1940–1969* (Paris: LGDJ, 1980), 142–3, 156.
79. Tait (Algiers) to State Dept., 3 March 1950, RG 59, 751S.00, box 3700, NARA.
80. Pierre Letamendia, *Le Mouvement Républicain Populaire. Histoire d'un grand parti français* (Paris: Beauchesne Editeur, 1995), 355.
81. Algiers consul to Bevin, 31 December 1947, Z131/131/69, FO 371/73024, PRO.
82. Thomas Lockett memo., 24 July 1951, RG 59, 751S.00, box 3700, NARA.
83. Sir Oliver Harvey to FO, 9 April 1948, Z3038/131/69, FO 371/73024, PRO.
84. Entry for 7 April 1948, Auriol, *Journal du Septennat, tome II, 1948*, 166.
85. Algiers consul to FO, 15 April 1948, Z3349/131/69, FO 371/73024, PRO.
86. Smith, 'Muslim Impoverishment', 139–40; Algiers consul to State Dept., 9 November 1950, RG 59, 751S.00, box 3700, NARA. *Beni-oui-oui*: literally, 'sons of yes-yes'.
87. T. V. Brenan memo., 'The nationalist movement in Morocco', 6 January 1947, Z383/52/69; Tangiers consulate memo., 'Moroccan nationalism', 4 January 1947, Z760/52/69, FO 371/67710, PRO.
88. Clayton, *Wars of French Decolonization*, 94.
89. Maréchal Juin, *Mémoires*, vol. II (Paris: Fayard, 1960), 135–7.
90. Lewis, 'The MRP', 310–11; Fonveille-Vojtovic, *Paul Ramadier*, 360–5; Anthony Clayton, 'Emergency in Morocco, 1950–56', *Journal of Imperial and Commonwealth History*, 21:3 (1993), 134.
91. Juin to Bidault, 15 September 1947, no. 3, vol. 115, Bidault papers.
92. Harvey to Attlee, 15 January 1948, Z426/73/69; C. F. Cane (Rabat) to FO, 9 September 1948, Z7561/73/69, FO 371/73022, PRO.
93. C. F. Cane reports on Moroccan riots, 8–9 June 1948, Z4732/73/69, Z4733/73/69, Z4758/73/69, FO 371/73022, PRO; Furedi, 'Creating a Breathing Space', 94–5.
94. Owen, 'Britain and decolonization', 12–13.
95. Sous-direction des protectorats note, 9 September 1946; bureau politique du Parti Libéral Constitutionaliste to HMG, 24 August 1946, vol. 112, Bidault papers.

96. Antoine Daveau, 'Le Poids de la guerre d'Indochine', *Revue d'Histoire Diplomatique*, 107:4 (1993), 337–8.
97. EMGDN, comité de l'Afrique du Nord, études 1946, 4Q119, SHAT; direction d'Afrique-Levant, note for Bidault, 31 January 1947, vol. 112, Bidault papers.
98. Jean Chauvel to Bidault, 15 April 1947, vol. 112, Bidault papers.
99. Hurst (Tunis) to Western dept., 24 December 1947, Z91/91/69, FO 371/73023; Harvey report on tour of North Africa, 31 March 1949, J2771/1019/69, FO 371/73721, PRO.
100. *BDEEP*, series A, vol. II, part II, doc. 184.
101. Allen reports on visits to Algeria and Morocco, 1949; comments on Algeria report by Sybil Crowe, October 1950; CO minutes, 5 Jan. 1951, CO 537/5654, PRO. The fallout from Allen's visit did prompt changes to arrangements for future tours of French colonies to ensure contact with the local population.

2 Towards Independence for Morocco and Tunisia

1. Letamendia, *Le Mouvement Républicain Populaire*, 352–3.
2. Juin to affaires étrangères, 27 June 1950, tel. 445, NUOI, vol. 573, MAE.
3. Tunis residency, 'Notes schematiques sur la situation politique en Tunisie', n.d. 1950, vol. 113, Bidault papers; note by Roger Allen, African Dept., 19 December 1950, JF1076/1, FO 371/90236, PRO; Jauffret (ed.), *La Guerre d'Algérie par les Documents, II*, 100–1.
4. Bourguiba *Jeunesse destourienne* speech, 19 March 1950, Tunisie, vol. 300, MAE.
5. Sous-direction de l'Algérie note, 24 April 1950, Tunisie, vol. 300, MAE.
6. A. S. Calvert (Tunis) to R. Allen, 20 September 1950, CO 537/5654, PRO. French scrutiny of Tunisian ministerial documents was established by beylical decree in 1947.
7. Letamendia, *Mouvement Républicain Populaire*, 352–3; Harvey to FO, 1 June 1950, JF1018/13, FO 371/80619; Calvert to R. Allen, 25 October 1950, CO 537/5654, PRO.
8. Schuman to Sidi Mohammed Lamine Bey, 26 November 1952, Tunisie, vol. 335, MAE.
9. Direction d'Afrique-Levant, 'L'évolution politique de la Tunisie', 2 April 1952, Tunisie, vol. 335, MAE.
10. Sir Cyril Caine to African Dept., 5 January 1951, JF1013/2, FO 371/90234, PRO.
11. Bevin memos., CP(50)114, CP(50)115, CAB 129/40, PRO.
12. William I. Hitchcock, *France Restored. Cold War Diplomacy and the Quest for Leadership in Europe, 1944–1954* (Chapel Hill, NC: University of North Carolina Press, 1998), 160.
13. Kahler, *Decolonization*, 82–3.
14. Direction d'Afrique-Levant, 'L'évolution politique de la Tunisie', 2 April 1952, Tunisie, vol. 335, MAE.
15. Letamendia, *Mouvement Républicain Populaire*, 353–4; Direction d'Afrique-Levant note, 2 January 1952, Tunisie, vol. 340, MAE.

16. Section Afrique-Levant, profile of Habib Bourguiba, 22 January 1951, Tunisie, vol. 300; Service d'information et de presse note, 16 April 1951, NUOI vol. 573, MAE.
17. Section Afrique du Nord note, 30 August 1951, Tunisie, vol. 300, MAE.
18. Perkins, 'North African Propaganda', 68–70.
19. Frank Giles, *The Locust Years, The Story of the Fourth French Republic, 1946–1958* (New York: Carroll and Graf, 1991), 132, 136–7.
20. Périllier to Schuman, 1 March 1951, no. 317, Tunisie, vol. 495, MAE.
21. Jauffret (ed.), *La Guerre d'Algérie par les Documents, II*, 72–3.
22. Henri Queuille instruction, 'Organisation et fonctionnement des secrétariats permanents de la défense nationale en AFN', 3 July 1951, no. 730/DN, 1H1104/D1, SHAT; Daveau, 'Le Poids de la guerre', 342–5, 348–9.
23. PPS memo., 'Problem of the French Budget in Calendar Year 1951', 27 September 1950, RG 59, PPS files 250/D/12/01, box 15, NARA; Hitchcock, *France Restored*, 148–9.
24. 'Notes sur les entretiens avec le Général Eisenhower', 4 September 1951; 'Entretiens – Département d'état', séance, 17 September 1951, 10H173, SHAT.
25. Michel, 'De Lattre et les débuts de l'américanisation', 328–31; Meetings with General de Lattre, 7 September 1951, RG 59, PPS files, 250/D/12/01, NARA.
26. 'Valeur des forces rebelles à la date du 24 décembre 1951', 10H173, SHAT.
27. State Dept. briefing paper, 14 June 1952; bureau of Far Eastern affairs note on JCS evaluation of the Letourneau plan, 4 May 1953, RG 59, PPS files, 250/D/12/01, box 18, NARA; COS(53)56th meeting, 30 April 1953, DEFE 11/62, PRO.
28. Supply of helicopters to France, 1952 fiches, COS(52)49th meeting, 7 April 1952, AIR 8/1660, PRO.
29. Makins to Eden, 28 March 1953, WF10345/5, FO 371/107443, PRO.
30. Selwyn Lloyd record of conversation with Massigli, 19 May 1953, WF1071/22, FO 371/107446, PRO.
31. COS(53)56th meeting, 30 April 1953, DEFE 11/62, PRO.
32. Churchill minute to Strang, 1 May 1953, FF10317/43, FO 371/106751, PRO.
33. Regarding France and EDC, see: Hitchcock, *France Restored*, ch. 5.
34. G. R. Gauntlett (Algiers) to Eden, 12 November 1952, JF1193/2, FO 371/97117, PRO.
35. Martin S. Alexander and Philip C. F. Bankwitz, 'From Politiques en Képi to Military Technocrats. De Gaulle and the Recovery of the French Army after Indochina and Algeria', in G. J. Andreopoulos and H. E. Selesky (eds), *The Aftermath of Defeat. Societies, Armed Forces and the Challenge of Recovery* (New Haven, Conn.: Yale University Press, 1994), 81–4.
36. JIC report, 'The Future of the War in Indo-China', 26 March 1954, JIC(54)26, CAB 158/17, PRO; Jean-Marc Marill, 'L'Héritage indochinois: adaptation de l'Armée française en Algérie (1954–1956)', *Revue Historique des Armées*, 2 (1992), 27–8.
37. Eden note, 'Indo-China', 18 March 1954, CP(54)108, CAB 129/67, PRO.
38. Richard H. Immerman, 'Between the Unattainable and the Unacceptable: Eisenhower and Dien Bien Phu', in Richard A. Melanson and David Mayers (eds), *Reevaluating Eisenhower. American Foreign Policy in the Fifties* (Urbana, Ill.: University of Chicago Press, 1987), 124–45.

39. Charles G. Cogan, 'De la politique du mensonge à la farce de Suez: appréhensions et réactions américaines', in Maurice Vaïsse (ed.), *La France et l'opération de Suez de 1956* (Paris: ADDIM, 1997), 126.
40. Entries for 9 and 20 July 1954, fos. 78–9, 102, 1st series Diaries, d. 17, Macmillan papers.
41. Lacroix-Riz, *Les Protectorats d'Afrique du Nord*, 56–7, 68–9.
42. Algiers consul to State Dept., 11 August 1950; Consulate memo., 'Political Attitudes of Algerian Nationalist Parties', 4 June 1951, RG 59, 751S.00, box 3700, NARA.
43. R. H. McBride (Rabat) to State Dept., 15 September 1950, RG 59, 771.00, box 3989, NARA.
44. J. C. Vincent (Tangiers), 'Developments in Moroccan Nationalist Movement, 1949–1952', 21 May 1952, RG 59, 771.00, box 3991, NARA.
45. McBride (Rabat) to State Dept., 21 February 1951, RG 59, 771.00, box 3990, NARA; Irving, *Christian Democracy*, 210; Bidwell, *Morocco under Colonial Rule*, 151.
46. McBride to State Dept., 24 March 1950, RG 59, 771.00, box 3989, NARA.
47. Algiers Consulate memo., 28 February 1952, RG 59, 751S.00, box 3700, NARA.
48. Acheson memo. for Truman, 16 March 1951, RG 59, 771.00, box 3990; State Dept. brief, 15 May 1952, 751S.00, box 3700, NARA.
49. Harvey, 'France – Annual Review for 1952', 21 January 1953, WF1101/1, FO 371/107433, PRO.
50. Garbay to EMA, 9 January 1952, no. 58/ORG, Tunisie, vol. 495, MAE.
51. De Hauteclocque to Schuman, 23 January 1952, no. 115/AM, Tunisie, vol. 340, MAE.
52. 'Note d'ensemble sur la situation tunisienne de 1950 à 1952', n.d., vol. 113, Bidault papers; De Hauteclocque to DN, 17 January 1952, no. 106, Tunisie, vol. 340, MAE.
53. Direction d'Afrique-Levant note, 10 January 1952, Tunisie, vol. 340, MAE; Harvey to FO, 16 January 1952, JF1041/2, FO 371/97090, PRO.
54. Harvey to FO, 19 January 1952, JF1041/6, FO 371/97090, PRO.
55. Harvey to FO, 21 January 1952, JF1041/11, FO 371/97090, PRO. Schumann, René Pleven, Robert Schuman, Georges Bidault and Edgar Faure sat on the committee.
56. Harvey to FO, 23 January 1952, JF1041/13, FO 371/97090, PRO.
57. Bonnet to Schuman, no. 1197, 7 March 1952, Etats-Unis, vol. 346, MAE.
58. Sangmuah, 'Interest Groups and Decolonization', 168–72.
59. Bonnet to Schuman, 11 April 1952, no. 1810; Bonnet to Schuman, 18 April 1952, no. 1924, Etats-Unis, vol. 346, MAE; Bonnet note, 'Problèmes politiques de l'Afrique française sur la scene intérnationale', 25 April 1952, vol. 113, Bidault papers.
60. Quoted in Wall, *United States*, 232.
61. D. W. Warehouse memo., 'The Moroccan Question in the 7th and 8th UN General Assembly', 11 December 1954, RG 59, 771.00, box 3997, NARA.
62. Le Roy to Schuman, 9 April 1952, no. 503, Grande-Bretagne, vol. 79, MAE.
63. Ingrid Geay, 'Les débats sur les recours de la Tunisie à l'ONU de 1952 à 1954', *Revue d'Histoire Diplomatique*, 110 (1996), 241–54.

64. Dillon memo., 'Lessons from the Present Government Crisis', 23 June 1953, RG 59, PPS files, 250/D/12/01, box 18, NARA.
65. Bonnet to Schuman, 2 January 1953, no. 28, Etats-Unis, vol. 341, MAE.
66. Raymond Poidevin, 'René Mayer et la politique extérieure de la France (1943–1953)', *Revue d'Histoire de la Deuxième Guerre Mondiale*, 134 (1984), 88.
67. Harvey, 'France – Annual Review, 1952', 21 January 1953, WF1101/1, FO 371/107433, PRO; Roger Vaurs to Bidault, 18 December 1952, vol. 113, Bidault papers.
68. Maurice Schumann to Bidault, 4 March 1953; Section d'Afrique-Levant, 'Note – situation en Tunisie', 7 March 1953, vol. 113, Bidault papers.
69. Harvey, 'France – Annual Review, 1952', 21 January 1953, WF1101/1, FO 371/107433, PRO.
70. Calvert to Roger Allen, 9 January 1953, JF1015/2, FO 371/102937, PRO.
71. J. Dorman (Rabat) to State Dept., 25 October 1951, RG 59, 771.00, box 3991, NARA.
72. Rabat quarterly political report, 26 January 1953, JM1013/2, FO 371/102973, PRO.
73. Rabat quarterly political report, 13 April 1953, JM1013/8, FO 371/102973, PRO.
74. 'French Proposals for Moroccan Reforms', 3 September 1953, RG 59, 771.00, box 3995, NARA.
75. Bidwell, *Morocco under Colonial Rule*, 124.
76. Rabat quarterly report, 5 October 1953, JM1013/14, FO 371/102973, PRO; Rabat consulate record of Oujda trial, 28 December 1954, RG 59, 771.00, box 3998, NARA.
77. J. Dorman to State Dept., 17 August 1953, RG 59, 771.00, box 3995, NARA.
78. Rabat quarterly report, 5 October 1953, JM1013/14, FO 371/102973, PRO.
79. Georges Bidault, *Resistance, the Political Autobiography of Georges Bidault* (London: Weidenfeld and Nicolson, 1967), 182–6.
80. Henri Descamps, *La Démocratie Chrétienne et le MRP: de 1946 à 1959* (Paris: LGDJ, 1981), 152–3.
81. Lewis, 'The MRP', 302.
82. Mohamed Fathi Al Dib, *Abdel Nasser et la Révolution Algérienne* (Paris: Editions L'Harmattan, 1985), 11–14.
83. W. K. Scott, State Dept. executive secretariat, to General Smith, 18 August 1953, RG 59, 771.00, box 3995, NARA.
84. Annual Report on France, 1953, 30 January 1954, WF1011/1, FO 371/112774, PRO.
85. W. D. McIntyre, *Background to the ANZUS Pact. Policy-Making, Strategy and Diplomacy, 1945–55* (New York: St. Martin's Press 1995); Richard J. Aldrich and John Zametica, 'The Rise and Decline of a Strategic Concept: the Middle East, 1945–51', in R. J. Aldrich (ed.), *British Intelligence, Strategy and the Cold War* (London: Routledge, 1992), 253, 256 and 263.
86. Peter L. Hahn, 'Containment and Egyptian Nationalism: The Unsuccessful Effort to Establish the Middle East Command, 1950–53', *Diplomatic History*, 11 (1987), 35–7; Michael J. Cohen, *Fighting World War Three from the Middle East. Allied Contingency Plans, 1945–1954* (London: Frank Cass, 1997), 91–3, 243–5.
87. Middle East redeployment working party, note on Army Plan D, 16 May 1952, COS(52)60, DEFE 10/324, PRO.

88. David Goldsworthy, 'Keeping Change within Bounds: Aspects of Colonial Policy during the Churchill and Eden Governments, 1951–57', *Journal of Imperial and Commonwealth History*, 18:1 (1990), 84–103 *passim*.
89. Massigli to Schuman, 23 January 1951, no. 170/AS, Grande-Bretagne, vol. 95, MAE.
90. PPS memo., 'French Objection to their Exclusion from Malta Talks', 19 March 1951, RG 59, PPS files, 250/D/12/01, box 15, NARA; direction d'Europe note, 17 March 1951, Grande-Bretagne, vol. 79, MAE.
91. Sous-direction du Levant, 'Entretiens franco-britanniques', 10–11 May 1951, Grande-Bretagne, vol. 79, MAE.
92. Eden memo., 'Middle East Policy', 7 January 1954, CP(54)6, CAB 129/65, PRO.
93. Entries for 29 December 1953, 1 January 1954, fos. 7–8, 13, 1st series Diaries, d. 16, Macmillan papers.
94. Affaires étrangères memo., 'La Ligue Arabe', n. d. 1955, Tunisie, vol. 390, MAE.
95. Sous-direction du Levant, 'Entretiens franco-britanniques', 10–11 May 1951, Grande-Bretagne, vol. 79, MAE.
96. Poidevin, 'René Mayer et la politique extérieure de la France (1943–1953)', 90–2.
97. Rioux, *The Fourth Republic*, 202–3.
98. PPS memo., 'French Requests for Assurances at Bermuda', 3 March 1954, RG 59, PPS files, 250/D/13/04, box 87, NARA; Dalloz, *Georges Bidault*, 328–9.
99. *Memoirs of Lord Gladwyn*, 271.
100. Tunis consulate report, 3 July 1953, JF1015/17, FO 371/102937, PRO; Irving, *Christian Democracy*, 210.
101. J. Price memo., 8 December 1953, JF1015/33, FO 371/102937, PRO.
102. Harvey to Eden, 25 February 1954, F1892/1, FO 371/108610, PRO.
103. On the impact of Mendès France, see François Bédarida and Jean-Pierre Rioux, *Pierre Mendès France et le mendésisme. L'expérience gouvernementale et sa postérité (1954–1955)* (Paris: Fayard, 1985); J. Chêne, E. Aberdam and H. Morsel (eds), *Pierre Mendès France la morale en politique* (Grenoble: Presses Universitaires de Grenoble, 1990); René Girault *et al.* (eds), *Pierre Mendès-France et le rôle de la France dans le monde* (Grenoble: Presses Universitaires de Grenoble, 1991).
104. Pierre Mendès France, *Oeuvres complètes. III: Gouverner c'est choisir 1954–1955* (Paris: Gallimard, 1986), 211–20.
105. *Memoirs of Lord Gladwyn*, 271–6.
106. Anne Deighton, 'The Last Piece of the Jigsaw: Britain and the Creation of the Western European Union, 1954', *Contemporary European History*, 7:2 (1998), 186–9; Mendès France, *Gouverner*, 331.
107. Jebb to FO, 27 August 1954, FO 371/108954, PRO; Mendès France, *Gouverner*, 181–6, 252–5.
108. Pierre Guillen, 'Le gouvernement Pierre Mendès France face aux problèmes marocain et tunisien' in Bédarida and Rioux (eds), *Pierre Mendès France et le mendésisme*, 317–29; Pierre Guillen, 'Pierre Mendès France et la décolonisation' in Chêne *et al.*, *Pierre Mendès France*, 194–8.
109. Mendès France, *Gouverner*, 421; Alexander and Bankwitz, 'From Politiques en Képi', 85–6.

110. Guillen, 'Pierre Mendès France et la décolonisation', 199–200.
111. *FRUS*, 1952–54, vol. XVI, Part 1, 181–4.
112. Dulles tel. to Cabot Lodge, 10 December 1954, RG 59, 771.00, box 3997, NARA; El Machat, *Les Etats-Unis et le Maroc*, 117–18.
113. El Machat, *Les Etats-Unis et le Maroc*, 91–3.
114. Paris embassy meetings on French North Africa, 1st meeting, 1 August 1955, RG 59, 751S.00, box 3376, NARA; El Machat, *Les Etats-Unis et la Tunisie*, 72–3.
115. Rabat consulate to Dulles, 31 December 1954, RG 59, 771.00, box 3998, NARA.
116. FO notes, 'French North Africa', n. d. December 1954, FO 371/108594, PRO.
117. Jean-François Sirinelli, 'Les intellectuels dans la mêlée', in Jean-Pierre Rioux (ed.), *La Guerre d'Algérie et les Français* (Paris: Fayard, 1990), 116–30.
118. Williams, *Crisis and Compromise*, 46–7; *DDF*, 1955, I, no. 26, Francis Lacoste to Christian Fouchet, 12 January 1955; no. 71, Note de la direction générale au ministère des affaires marocaines et tunisiennes, 11 February 1955.
119. Clayton, 'Emergency in Morocco', 131–2, 144.
120. Clark to State Dept., 25 January 1955, RG 59, 751S.00, box 3375, NARA; C. O. Wakefield-Harrey (Algiers) to FO, 14 April 1955, FO 371/113788, PRO.
121. *DDF*, 1955, I, no. 232, Pinay circular tel., 28 April 1955.
122. *DDF*, 1955, I, no. 280, Lacoste (Rabat) to Pierre July, 14 May 1955, no. 343, Lacoste to July, 16 July 1955. Lacoste learnt of his dismissal in the media.
123. *DDF*, 1955, II, nos. 25, 26, 27, 75, 76.
124. *FRUS*, 1955–1957, vol. XVIII Africa, no. 26, French Embassy to State Dept., 5 June 1955, 95–7; Livingston Merchant to Dulles, 2 July 1955; Dillon to Dulles, 15 June 1955, RG 59, 751S.00, box 3375, NARA.
125. Rioux, *Fourth Republic*, 228, 238; *DDF*, 1955, II, no. 131, Grandval to Pierre July, 23 August 1955, n. 1.
126. *DDF*, 1955, II, no. 145, Entretiens franco-marocains d'Aix-les-Bains, procès-verbaux, 22–28 August 1955.
127. *Journal de Septennat, VII: 1953–1954*, 372–77; Christine Bougeard, *René Pleven. Un Français libre en politique* (Rennes: Presses Universitaires de Rennes, 1994), 250.
128. Bernard, *Franco-Moroccan Conflict*, 300–7, 323–4; Henri Lerner, *Catroux* (Paris: Albin Michel, 1990), 325–6. Regarding Catroux's mission, see: *DDF*, 1955, II, nos. 157, 172, 199. Si Ould Embarek Bekkaï had been Pacha of Sefrou.
129. *DDF*, 1955, II, no. 343, Pinay to overseas ambassadors, 2 November 1955.
130. Kahler, *Decolonization*, 113–14.
131. A. M. Williams (Tunis) to African dept., 3 February 1955; P. C. Bell (Tunis) to African dept., 8 August 1955, FO 371/113788; PRO.
132. Direction d'Afrique-Levant memo., 'Un grand événement: l'autonomie interne', n. d., 1955, Tunisie, vol. 390/DA1, MAE.
133. *DDF*, 1956, I, no. 44, Roger Seydoux to Quai, 26 January 1956; regarding Bourguiba's rivalry with Salah Ben Youssef, see *DDF*, 1955, II, no. 295, Seydoux to Pierre July, 13 October 1955; General Bruno Chaix, 'La France et la réconstitution de l'armée Tunisienne en 1956', *Revue d'Histoire Diplomatique*, 110 (1996), 286–7.

134. *DDF*, 1956, I, no. 77, Alain Savary to André-Louis Dubois (Rabat), 6 February 1956; no. 108, note de la direction des affaires économiques et financières, 17 February 1956.
135. Maryvonne Prévot, 'Convergences maghrébines autour d'Alain Savary, secrétaire d'Etat aux affaires marocaines et tunisiennes en 1956', *Revue Historique*, CCI: 3 (1999), 509–17; *DDF*, 1956, I, no. 126, note de la direction générale des affaires marocaines et tunisiennes, 25 February 1956; no. 167, Compte rendus des négociations franco-tunisiennes, 29 February–12 March 1956.
136. *DDF*, 1956, I, nos. 159, 202, direction générale notes, 10 and 26 March 1956.
137. Jebb to FO, 3 March 1956, PREM 11/1350, PRO; *DDF*, 1956, I, no. 226, Compte rendus des négociations franco-tunisiennes, 4–7 April 1956; no. 307, note de la direction des affaires marocaines et tunisiennes, 10 May 1956; no. 376, note du secrétariat d'état aux affaires marocaines et tunisiennes, 8 June 1956.
138. *DDF*, 1956, II, nos. 3 and 11, André-Louis Dubois to secrétariat d'état aux affaires marocaines et tunisiennes, 2 and 5 July 1956, no. 19, Savary to Dubois, 6 July 1956; Chaix, 'La France et la réconstitution', 296–7.
139. African dept. draft recognition doc., 29 March 1956, JF1052/4; Jebb to FO, 12 May 1956, JF1052/17, FO 371/119377, PRO.
140. El Machat, *Les Etats-Unis et le Maroc*, 131–2; W. M. Rountree memo., 19 November 1955, RG 59, lot files, office of North African affairs, file 19, box 4, NARA.
141. *DDF*, 1956, I, no. 376, Secrétariat d'état aux affaires marocaines et tunisiennes note, 8 June 1956; no. 385, Bourgès-Maunoury to Pineau, 11 June 1956; *DDF*, 1956, II, no. 78, Service des pactes note, 25 July 1956. French base rights in Morocco were to expire in 1960.
142. 'Political review of events in Tunisia', 5 August 1956, JN1013/1, FO 371/119552, PRO; *DDF*, 1956, I, no. 373, Alain Savary to overseas embassies, 7 June 1956.
143. 'Political review', *op. cit.*; Fathi Al Dib, *Abdel Nasser et la Révolution*, 89–91.
144. Malcolm to Lloyd, 30 July 1956, JN10137/6, FO 371/119558; Malcolm to Lloyd, 20 February 1957, JN10317/5, FO 371/125841, PRO; Chaix, 'La France et la réconstitution', 289.
145. Jean Mathieu, direction des travaux publics, memo., 11 August 1954, Tunisie, vol. 390, MAE; *DDF*, 1956, II, no. 24, Dubois to Savary, 7 July 1956.
146. 'Tunisia: Annual Review for 1956', 28 January 1957, JN1011/1, FO 371/125828, PRO; Chauvel to Pineau, 18 July 1956, no. 2887, Grande-Bretagne, vol. 142, MAE.
147. Pyman (Rabat), 'Moroccan foreign policy', 18 September 1956, JM1026/3, FO 371/119481, PRO; Donald R. Norland to John A. Bovey, 23 August 1956, RG 59, State Dept. lot files, box 4, file 15, NARA; El Machat, *Les Etats-Unis et le Maroc*, 195–6.
148. Rabat Chancery to FO, 5 July 1956, JM10317/5, FO 371/119483, PRO.
149. H. Freese-Pennefather to FO, 29 June 1956, JM1026/1, FO 371/119481; FO minutes, 1 August 1956, JM10317/10, FO 371/119483, PRO.

3 The Algerian War as a Colonial Problem

1. Colonel Badille, chef du secrétariat permanent de la défense nationale, 'Plan quadriennal de modernisation et d'équipment', 16 November 1953, 1H1104/D2, SHAT.
2. Marseille, 'L'investissement public en Algérie', 180–9; Tableaux de l'économie algérienne, 1960, 1H1106/D1, SHAT.
3. Marseille, 'L'investissement public en Algérie', 180.
4. Ageron, '"L'Algérie dernière chance de la puissance française"', 114; Nathalie Ruz, 'La force du "Cartiérisme"', in Rioux (ed.), *La Guerre d'Algérie*, 328–33.
5. Smith, 'Muslim Impoverishment in Colonial Algeria', 142–6; *DDF*, vol. I, 1960, no. 206, de Gaulle–Nehru conversation, 8 May 1960.
6. Mill-Irving to African dept., 28 January 1956. JF1015/8, FO 371/119350, PRO.
7. Holland, 'The Imperial Factor in British Strategies', 170–1.
8. Marseille, 'L'investissement public en Algérie', 190; Algiers consulate tri-monthly review, 8 July 1955. FO 371/113788, PRO.
9. Kahler, *Decolonization*, 85.
10. Goldsworthy, 'Keeping Change within Bounds', 83–7.
11. E. M. Wilson to State Dept., 23 June 1955, RG 59, 751S.00, box 3375, NARA.
12. Algiers consulate tri-monthly review, 8 July 1955, FO 371/113788, PRO.
13. C. O. I. Ramsden minute, 23 May 1955, JF1051/10, FO 371/113803, PRO.
14. Jebb to Macmillan, 7 July 1955, JF1019/17, FO 371/113795, PRO; R. P. Joyce (Paris) memo., 'British thinking on Tunisia and Algeria', 28 July 1955, RG 59, 751S.00, box 3376, NARA.
15. Mill-Irving to African dept., 14 January 1956, JF1019/19, FO 371/119356, PRO; Ageron, '"L'Algérie dernière chance de la puissance française"', 117.
16. Jebb to FO, 4 February 1956, JF1019/43, FO 371/119357, PRO.
17. Mill-Irving to African dept., 14 January 1956, JF1019/19, FO 371/119356, PRO.
18. Paris chancery to African dept., 13 January 1956, JF1019/20; Algiers consulate to African dept., 18 January 1956, JF1019/24, FO 371/119356, PRO.
19. African affairs position paper on Algeria, 30 August 1956, RG 59, 751S.00, box 3377, NARA. Bône was granted departmental status a year earlier in August 1955.
20. Jebb to FO, 7 February 1956, JF1019/44, FO 371/119357; R. F. G. Sarell, monthly report for Algeria, December 1956, 9 January 1957, JR1013/1, FO 371/125915, PRO.
21. Acting consul Dugdale to African dept., 8 July 1955, FO 371/113788; Mill-Irving to Lloyd, 26 January 1956, JF1019/33, FO 371/119357; Mill-Irving to African dept., 16 February 1956, JF1019/64, FO 371/119358, PRO. The FLN executive even ordered a temporary relaxation of the boycotts on 23 June 1955.
22. Colonel Acworth interview with Lt.-Col. Esteuille, deuxième bureau deputy chief, Algiers, 27 February 1956, JF1015/15, FO 371/119350, PRO.
23. Colonel Paynaud, SPDN, 'Note sur le problème de l'intégration du point de vue de la défense nationale', 4 June 1958, no. 1360/DN, 1H1104/D5, SHAT.
24. M. Calcat, 'Comment résoudre en Algérie l'équation démographie-ressources', 22 July 1946, Cours professés au Centre de Hautes Etudes d'Administration Musulmane, Aff. pol. C2299/D3, ANCOM.

25. Roger Quillot, *La S.F.I.O. et l'exercise du pouvoir 1944–1958* (Paris: Fayard, 1972), 268.
26. *DDF*, 1955, I, no. 15, Mendès France to Mitterrand, 7 January 1955.
27. Clark to State Dept., 14 January 1955, 25 January 1955, RG 59, 751S.00, box 3375, NARA; Mendès France, *Gouverner*, 718; Rioux, *The Fourth Republic*, 233–4.
28. Clark to State Dept., 25 January 1955; tel. 3143, Dillon to Dulles, 26 January 1955; Clark to State Dept., 31 January 1955, RG 59, 751S.00, box 3375, NARA; Bernard Ullmann, *Jacques Soustelle. Le mal aimé* (Paris: Plon, 1995), 186–90.
29. Clark to John Wesley Jones, 22 April 1955, RG 59, 751S.00, box 3375, NARA.
30. Couve de Murville to Quai, 7 February 1956, no. 748, Etats-Unis, vol. 342, MAE; Denis Lefebvre, *Guy Mollet. Le mal aimé* (Paris: Plon, 1992), 183–9.
31. Jebb to FO, 18 February 1956, JF1019/63, FO 371/119358; 'French North Africa', 20 February 1956, intell. 27, PREM 11/1350, PRO.
32. Clark to Dulles, 14 February 1956; M. N. Coates (Algiers) to WEA, 29 February 1956, RG 59, 751S.00, box 3376, NARA; Philippe Bourdrel, *La Dernière chance de l'Algérie française. Du gouvernement socialiste au retour de De Gaulle, 1956–1958* (Paris: Albin Michel, 1996), 21–8; Alistair Horne, *A Savage War of Peace: Algeria 1954–1962* (London: Macmillan, 1987), 148–55.
33. Leon G. Dorros memo., 5 August 1955, RG 59, 751S.00, box 3376, NARA.
34. Theodore Achilles (Paris) to Dulles, 13 January 1956, RG 59, 751S.00, box 3376, NARA; Dugdale to African dept., 8 July 1955, FO 371/113788; Sarell, annual review for Algeria, 1956, 14 January 1957, FO 371/125913, PRO; Ullmann, *Jacques Soustelle*, ch.2; Geoffrey Adams, *The Call of Conscience. French Protestant Responses to the Algerian War, 1954–1962* (Waterloo: Wilfrid Laurier University Press, 1998), 27–8.
35. Annual report for France, 1956, 21 January 1957, WF1011/1, FO 371/130625, PRO.
36. J. G. S. Beith (Paris) to Wakefield-Harrey, 24 January 1955, JF1019/2; Wakefield-Harrey to Patrick Reilly (Paris), 5 February 1955, JF1019/5, FO 371/113795, PRO.
37. Hugh Roberts, 'Algeria's ruinous impasse and the honourable way out', *International Affairs*, 71:2 (1995), 249–50.
38. Naegelen, *Mission en Algérie*, 200–10.
39. Algiers consulate, quarterly political review, 7 November 1951, JF1013/16, FO 371/90234, PRO; regarding the *Organisation Spéciale*, see Jauffret (ed.), *La Guerre d'Algérie, II*, 181–2.
40. Wakefield-Harrey, quarterly political reviews for Algeria, 15 January 1954, 8 April 1954, FO 371/108586, PRO.
41. Wakefield-Harrey, quarterly political review, 14 Oct. 1954, FO 371/108586; Record of Mollet-Pineau-Gaitskell meeting, 10 May 1956, PREM 11/1351, PRO; Martin Evans, *The Memory of Resistance. French Opposition to the Algerian War (1954–1962)* (Oxford: Berg, 1997), 173–5; Charles-Robert Ageron, 'Les Français devant la guerre civile algérienne', in Rioux (ed.), *La Guerre d'Algérie*, 55–6.
42. Wakefield-Harrey to Beith, 17 February 1955, JF1019/4, FO 371/113795, PRO.
43. *DDF*, 1955, II, no. 77, Boyer de Latour to Pierre July, 2 August 1955.
44. Algiers consulate to African dept., 26 April 1955, JF1019/6, FO 371/113795, PRO. Recorded participation among the Muslim electorate was 53 per cent.

45. Clark to Dulles, 6 June 1956, RG 59, 751S.00, box 3377, NARA.
46. J. W. Jones, WEA, to C. Burke Elbrick, 19 September 1956, RG 59, 751S.00, box 3377, NARA; G. P. Young to J. H. A. Watson, 16 January 1957, JR10317/14, FO 371/125928, PRO.
47. Sarell to Beith, 21 February 1957, JR1013/2, FO 371/125915, PRO.
48. Christelow, 'Ritual, Culture and Politics of Islamic Reformism', 264–8.
49. Direction d'Afrique-Levant report on Ulama activity, 3 Oct. 1947, Algérie, vol. 2, MAE.
50. Clark to State Dept., 24 July 1951, RG 59, 751S.00, box 3700, NARA.
51. Couve de Murville to Schuman, 21 March 1952, no. 451, Algérie, vol. 4, MAE; Fathi Al Dib, *Abdel Nasser et la Révolution*, 50–1; Clark to Dulles, 17 January 1956, RG 59, 751S.00, box 3376, NARA; Mohammed Harbi, *Les Archives de la révolution algérienne* (Paris: Editions J.A., 1981), doc. 18.
52. State Dept. bureau of intelligence and research report, 22 May 1958, JR1016/26, FO 371/131663, PRO; Horne, *A Savage War*, 402–3; Algiers to State Dept., 11 August 1950, RG 59, 751S.00, box 3700, NARA.
53. Wakefield-Harrey to Beith, 17 February 1955, JF1019/4, FO 371/113795, PRO.
54. *DDF*, 1955, I, no. 26, Francis Lacoste (Rabat) to Christian Fouchet, 12 January 1955.
55. Brigadier J. A. H. Mitchell, 'Report on visit to 10e military region', 16–31 October 1958, JR1193/19, FO 371/131685, PRO.
56. Neil MacMaster and Toni Lewis, 'Orientalism: from unveiling to hyperveiling', *Journal of European Studies*, 28:1 (1998), 257–7; Benjamin Stora, 'Mémoires comparées: femmes françaises, femmes algériennes. Les écrits de femmes, la guerre d'Algérie et l'exil', in Charles-Robert Ageron and Marc Michel (eds), *L'ère des décolonisations* (Paris: Karthala, 1995), 172–83.
57. Furedi, 'Creating a Breathing Space', 96–100.
58. Stephen Howe, *Anticolonialism in British Politics. The Left and the End of Empire 1918–1964* (Oxford: Clarendon Press, 1993), 235–6.
59. Dine, *Images*, 72.
60. Clark to State Dept., desp. 176, RG 59, 751S.00, box 3379, Service de presse et d'information, French Affairs no. 47, 3 June 1957, Etats-Unis, vol. 343, MAE; Martha Crenshaw Hutchinson, *Revolutionary Terrorism. The FLN in Algeria, 1954–1962* (Stanford CA: Hoover Institution Press, 1978), 44–9. Between 315 and 374 men were killed.
61. C. d'Abzac-Epezy and F. Pernot, 'Les opérations en Algérie, décembre 1958–avril 1960. Le général Challe parle', *Revue Historique des Armées*, 3 (1995), 64–8; Philip Dine, 'French culture and the Algerian war: mobilizing icons', *Journal of European Studies*, 28:1 (1998), 53 and note 1.
62. The six *wilaya* commands were: W1: Aurès-Nementchas; W2: Northern Constantine; W3: Kabylie; W4: the Algérois; W5: Oranie; W6: the Saharan territory. Each *wilaya* was subdivided into sectors (*mintaka*) and smaller *quartiers* (*nahla*).
63. Jauffret, 'L'Armée et l'Algérie en 1954', 19–20; Jauffret (ed.), *La Guerre d'Algérie par les Documents, II*, 359–61.
64. Fathi Al Dib, *Abdel Nasser et la Révolution*, 45, 174. Ben Boulaïd was assassinated in 1956 after refusing to recognise the ALN leadership which emerged from the Soummam Valley Congress in August.
65. Clark to State Dept., 13 April 1955, RG 59, 751S.00, box 3375, NARA.

66. EMA-3, 'Algérie – organisation territoriale', 5 February 1955, 1H1374/D2, SHAT.
67. Memo. from C. Burke Elbrick and J. D. Jernigan for Robert Murphy, 15 September 1955, RG 59, 751S.00, box 3376, NARA.
68. For example: Lacoste Directive générale, 19 May 1956, Carton Z23344, SHAA.
69. Between 1949–51 and 1956–58, Papon completed two tours of service in the prefectural and departmental administration of Constantine and in 1954 worked as secretary-general in the protectorate administration in Rabat. With dreadful consequences for Algerian immigrants, Papon was appointed prefect of Paris police by Félix Gaillard's government in March 1958. See Richard J. Golsan, 'Memory's *bombes à retardement*: Maurice Papon, crimes against humanity and 17 October 1961', *Journal of European Studies*, 28:1 (1998), 159–61. Clark to Dulles, 15 March 1956, RG 59, 751S.00, box 3377, NARA.
70. Clark to Dulles, 15 March 1956, RG 59, 751S.00, box 3377, NARA; Frédéric Guelton and Geneviève Errera, 'Transmissions et guerre subversive en Algérie', *Revue Historique des Armées*, 1 (1990), 77–9.
71. Algiers consulate memo., 'Impact of nationalist terrorism on the Algerian economy', 9 April 1956, RG 59, 751S.00, box 3377, NARA.
72. Dillon to Dulles, 12 April 1956, RG 59, 751S.00, box 3377, NARA.
73. Lacoste general directives 4 and 5, April and September 1957, Fonds de la préfecture d'Alger, Carton S5/D33, ANCOM.
74. Clark desp. 134, 'Trends within the French Army in Algeria', RG 59, 751S.00, box 3379, NARA.
75. General Jean Delmas, 'A la recherche des signes de la puissance: l'armée entre Algérie et bombe A 1956–1962', *Relations Internationales*, 57 (1989), 80–1.
76. Peter Paret, *French Revolutionary Warfare from Indochina to Algeria. The Analysis of a Political and Military Doctrine* (Princeton, NJ: Princeton University Press, 1964); George Armstrong Kelly, *Lost Soldiers. The French Army and Empire in Crisis, 1947–1962* (Cambridge, Mass.: MIT Press, 1965); Capitaine Jean-Marc Marill, 'L'Héritage indochinois: adaptation de l'Armée française en Algérie (1954–1956)', *Revue Historique des Armées*, 2 (1992), 26–32; François Pernot, 'La Guerre psychologique en Algérie vue à travers les archives de l'armée de l'air', *Revue Historique des Armées*, 1 (1993), 90–9; Grégor Mathias, *Les sections administratives spécialisées en Algérie. Entre idéal et réalité (1955–1962)* (Paris: Editions L'Harmattan, 1998).
77. Rapport du Colonel Alazard, chef du bureau psychologique EMFA, 26 November 1956, no. 2192, Z23344, SHAA.
78. COS comm., 'Psychological warfare requirements in limited war and local actions', 7 May 1958, COS(58)132, DEFE 5/83, PRO.
79. General C. R. Baillif, 'Forces armées et psychologie', *Revue de Défense Nationale*, 16 (1960), 820–1.
80. WO report on operations in Algeria, 19–31 July 1958, JR1193/8, FO 371/131685, PRO; Salan, *Mémoires*, III, 44, 69; Salan letter to Admiral Radford, 4 Jan. 1957, box 4/folder 091, Records of Joint Chiefs of Staff, RG 218, NARA.
81. Henry Descombin, *Guerre d'Algérie 1959–60. Le Cinquième Bureau ou 'Le théorème du poisson'* (Paris: Editions L'Harmattan, 1994), 28.

82. Séance d'Etat-Major mixte – regroupement des populations, 7 November 1957, 1H1104/D8; Commandement supérieur interarmées, 'Réunion barrage et frontière Est', 26 February 1958, 1H2036/D1, SHAT.
83. Michel Cornaton, *Les Camps de regroupement de la guerre d'Algérie* (Paris: Editions L'Harmattan, 1998), 54–6, 74–5.
84. Peynaud note, 'Regroupement des populations', 22 March 1958, 1H1104/D8, SHAT.
85. Sarell to Paris embassy, 15 December 1958, JR1193/19, FO 371/131685; Paris chancery to African dept., 3 February 1958, JR1551/1, FO 371/131690, PRO.
86. Pernot, 'La guerre psychologique', 91–3; I. C. Alexander (Algiers) to H. F. T. Smith, 9 August 1958, JR1193/6, FO 371/131685, PRO.
87. 'Document du SHAT: Directive générale sur la guerre subversive du général de division Massu', *Revue Historique des Armées*, 3 (1995), 45–61.
88. Jauffret, 'L'Armée et l'Algérie', 16–17; Pernot, 'La guerre psychologique', 97–9; Descombin, *La Guerre d'Algérie*, 52–8.
89. Lt-Col. A. J. Wilson report on visit to operations in Algeria, 10–18 July 1958, JR1193/7, FO 371/131685, PRO.
90. FLN directive, 'Lutte contre la SAS', n. d. 1957, Carton S5/D33, ANCOM.
91. Wilson report on visit to Algeria, 8–16 January 1957, JR1201/3, FO 371/125945; Sarell to Watson, 3 December 1958, JR1193/21, FO 371/131685, PRO.
92. Wilson report, 'Visit to Grand Kabylie', 13 March 1957, JR1201/6, FO 371/125945, PRO; Lorcin, *Imperial Identities*, 234–5.
93. Lord Birdwood report on official MOD visit to Algeria, 28 January 1957, JR1201/1, FO 371/125945, PRO.
94. Sarell, 'Annual review – Algeria, 1957', 18 January 1958, FO 371/131654, PRO.
95. EMA-3, Instruction des disponibles', 11 April 1956, 1H1379/D1, SHAT.
96. Wilson report, JR1201/3; Sarell to Beith, 20 March 1957, JR1201/7; Sarell to Watson, 22 March 1957, JR1201/8, FO 371/125945, PRO.
97. Sarell to Lloyd, 9 August 1957, JR1201/13, FO 371/125945, PRO.
98. Sarell to Brigadier Jackson, 6 August 1957, JR1201/15, FO 371/125945, PRO.
99. As examples: Lord Birdwood report, 28 January 1957; Wilson report, 8–16 January 1957; Brigadier Jackson report, 'The present military situation in Algeria', 1 March 1958, FO 371/131663, PRO.
100. Acworth report, sent to African dept, 12 August 1957, JR1201/16, FO 371/125945, PRO.
101. I. C. Alexander to H. F. T. Smith, 3 May 1958, JR1016/9, FO 371/131663; WO situation report, Algeria, 1–18 July 1958, JR1193/4, FO 371/131685, PRO; Harbi, *Le F.L.N.*, 127, 150–1, 157, 237.
102. Alexander to Lt-Col. P. H. Flower, 25 July 1958, JR1193/5, FO 371/131685, PRO. *Groupes mobiles de sécurité* were an offshoot of the *groupes mobiles de police rurale* founded in January 1955 under the auspices of the *sûreté nationale*.
103. Archives Corps d'Armée, zone nord Algerois: caractéristiques du Barrage Est 1956–1961, 1H2968/D1; zone de l'ouest Oranais: le Barrage de la frontière du Maroc, rapport no. 226/200/2/S, 25 January 1959, 1H2039/D1, SHAT.
104. SPDN, 'Instruction provisoire sur l'organisation des services de surveillance et de fermeture des frontières' 15 October 1957, 1H1104/D4, SHAT.

105. Brigadier Jackson, final report, 12 May 1958, JR1016/24, FO 371/131663; Brigadier J. A. H. Mitchell, 'Report on visit to 10e military region', 16–31 October 1958, JR1193/19, FO 371/131685, PRO.

4 1956: the Algerian War Extended and the Suez Intervention

1. Bourdrel, *La Dernière chance de l'Algérie française*, 17–18.
2. Mill-Irving to African dept., 31 December 1955, JF1019/6, FO 371/119356, PRO.
3. Paris chancery to African dept., 2 January 1956, JF1019/11, FO 371/119356, PRO. The gendarme was only given a disciplinary reprimand.
4. Jebb to FO, 30 December 1955, JF1019/1; Mill-Irving to African dept., 31 December 1955, JF1019/5, FO 371/119356, PRO.
5. General Paul Ely, *Mémoires, II: Suez... Le 13 Mai* (Paris: Plon, 1969), 15–16.
6. Situation des effectifs stationées en AFN, 1 January 1956, 1H1374/D2, SHAT.
7. Algiers Consulate to African dept., 27 September 1955, JF1019/60, FO 371/113797; Consulate to African dept., 10 January 1956, JF1019/14, FO 371/119356; Mill-Irving to African dept., 19 January 1956, JF1019/26, FO 371/119357, PRO.
8. Bernard, *The Franco-Moroccan Conflict*, ch. 8; Rioux, *The Fourth Republic*, 244–53.
9. Williams, *Crisis and Compromise*, 47–8, 163–9; Jebb to FO, 7 February 1956, JF1019/44, PRO, FO 371/119357; Jebb reports on the Poujadist movement, 14 February 1956, PREM 11/1848, PRO.
10. Paris chancery to African dept., 14 January 1956, JF1019/16, FO 371/119356, PRO.
11. Jebb to Macmillan, 7 July 1955, JF1019/17, FO 371/113795; Blackham minute, 19 January 1956, JF1019/16, FO 371/119356, PRO; Achilles (Paris) to Dulles, 13 January 1956, Clark (Algiers) to Dulles, 13 Jan. 1956, RG 59, 751S.00, box 3376, NARA.
12. Clark to Dulles, 14 and 17 January 1956, RG 59, 751S.00, box 3376, NARA; Ullmann, *Jacques Soustelle*, 216.
13. Williams, *Crisis and Compromise*, 48–9, app. V; Lefebvre, *Guy Mollet*, 177–8.
14. Robert Frank, 'The French Alternative: Economic Power through the Empire or through Europe?', in Ennio di Nolfo (ed.), *Power in Europe? II: Great Britain, France, Germany and Italy and the Origins of the EEC, 1952–1957* (Berlin: 1992), 167.
15. Harrison, 'French Attitudes', 78–92; Bourdrel, *La Dernière chance*, 27–8.
16. Adam Watson, 'The Aftermath of Suez: Consequences for French Decolonization', in William Roger Louis and Roger Owen (eds), *Suez 1956: The Crisis and its Consequences* (Oxford: Oxford University Press, 1993), 341–2.
17. Weekly French political summary no. 12, 26 March 1947, Z3091/58/17, FO 371/67680, PRO.
18. Daniel Le Couriard, 'Les Socialistes et les Débuts de la Guerre d'Indochine', 339–48; Gérard Bossuat, 'Guy Mollet: La puissance française autrement', *Relations Internationales*, 57 (1989), 26–7; Lefebvre, *Guy Mollet*, 195–6.

19. Stora, *La gangrène et l'oubli*, 75–9; Larkin, *France since the Popular Front*, 258; regarding working-class racism towards Algerians, see MacMaster, *Colonial Migrants*, ch. 7.
20. Evans, *The Memory of Resistance*, 170–3; MacMaster, *Colonial Migrants*, 195–6; Danièle Joly, *The French Communist Party and the Algerian War* (London: Macmillan, 1991), 93–9.
21. Alain Ruscio, 'French Public Opinion and the War in Indochina', 121; Alexander and Bankwitz, 'From Politiques en Képi', 88–9. SHAT, 1H1374/D3, fiche, 'Situation des effectifs des trois Armées en Algérie, 1956'.
22. Capitaine Jean-Marc Marill, 'L'Héritage indochinois: adaptation de l'armée française en Algérie (1954–1956)', *Revue Historique des Armées*, 2 (1992), 31–2.
23. Sarell (Algiers), 'Algeria, annual review for 1956'. 14 January 1957, FO 371/125913, PRO.
24. Clark to State Dept., 11 February 1955, RG 59, 751S.00, box 3375, NARA; I. C. Alexander minute, 5 May 1956, J1023/16, FO 371/118676, PRO.
25. Danièle Joly, 'France's Military Involvement in Algeria: the PCF and the *Oppositionnels*', in M. Scriven and P. Wagstaff (eds), *War and Society in Twentieth Century France* (Oxford: Berg, 1992), 130–4.
26. Joly, 'France's Military Involvement in Algeria', 137–9.
27. Regarding the initial call-up, see: EMA-1, 'Plan d'urgence – 1e partie', 18 March 1956, no. 17605, 1H1379/D1, SHAT; Ely, *Mémoires*, II, 26–7.
28. Joly, 'France's Military Involvement', 141–5; Evans, *The Memory*, 138–9.
29. John Kent, *The Internationalization of Colonialism: Britain, France and Black Africa, 1939–1956* (Oxford: Clarendon Press, 1992), 279–87.
30. FO memo. to Jebb, 'Communism and Africa', 21 April 1956, J1023/6G, FO 371/118676, PRO; *BDEEP*, series A, vol. III, part I: David Goldsworthy (ed.), *The Conservative Government and the End of Empire 1951–1957* (London: HMSO, 1994), doc. 99.
31. I. C. Alexander minute, 5 May 1956, J1023/16, FO 371/118676, PRO.
32. Direction d'Afrique-Levant, bureau de liaison pour les affaires nord-africaines to overseas missions, n. d. November 1955, Etats-Unis, vol. 342, MAE.
33. Anthony Adamthwaite, 'Suez Revisited', *International Affairs*, 64:3 (1988), 452.
34. Entry for 28 June 1956, fo. 87; entry for 5 July, fo. 96, 1st series Diaries, d. 26, Macmillan diaries.
35. Harold Dooley, 'Great Britain's "Last Battle" in the Middle East: Notes on Cabinet Planning during the Suez Crisis of 1956', *International History Review*, 11:3 (1989), 487–90; Kyle, *Suez*, 56–9, 91–6; W. Scott Lucas, *Divided We Stand. Britain, the US and the Suez Crisis* (London: Hodder and Stoughton, 1991), 93–7.
36. William Roger Louis, 'Dulles, Suez and the British', in Richard H. Immerman (ed.), *John Foster Dulles and the Diplomacy of the Cold War* (Princeton, NJ: Princeton University Press, 1990), 136–42; Nigel John Ashton, *Eisenhower, Macmillan and the Problem of Nasser. Anglo-American Relations and Arab Nationalism, 1955–59* (London: Macmillan, 1996), ch. 3; Ara Sanjian, 'The Formulation of the Baghdad Pact', *Middle Eastern Studies*, 33:2 (1997), 226–66.
37. For Indian views of the Baghdad Pact, see First Sea Lord Mountbatten letter to Monckton, 13 February 1956, box 6, 1956 correspondence, Walter Monckton papers, Bodleian Library.

38. Auchinleck draft memo., 'Note on Pakistan', n.d. March 1956, box 6, 1956 correspondence, Monckton papers.
39. Patrick Seale, *The Struggle for Syria. A Study of Post-War Arab Politics, 1945–1958*, 2nd edn. (London: I. B. Taurus, 1986), chs. 16 and 17.
40. *DDF*, 1955, I, no. 138, Pinay to Middle East ambassadors, 22 March 1955.
41. Eden tel. for Jebb, n. d. March 1956, T269/56; Patrick Reilly (Paris) to FO, 26 March 1956, PREM 11/1344, PRO.
42. *DDF*, 1956, I, no. 37, Note de la direction d'Afrique-Levant, 23 January 1956; no. 57, Chauvel (London) to Pinay, 30 January 1956; no. 147, compte rendus (SEATO meeting, Karachi), 7 March 1956; Sir Ivone Kirkpatrick note, 4 January 1956, V1072/1, FO 371/121244; Jebb to Lloyd, 18 April 1956, V1072/47, FO 371/121245, PRO.
43. William Stivers, 'Eisenhower and the Middle East', in Melanson and Mayers (eds), *Reevaluating Eisenhower*, 196; entry for 30 July 1956, fo. 13, 1st series Diaries, d. 27, Macmillan papers.
44. SDECE intercept, 'Les nationalistes marocaines et les "frères musulmans" contre les pachas et caïds', 19 June 1953, no. 3734/232, NUOI, vol. 111, MAE; Faligot and Krop, *La Piscine*, 139–44; Douglas Porch, *The French Secret Services. From the Dreyfus Affair to the Gulf War* (London: Macmillan, 1996), 366.
45. Lucas, *Divided*, 158–60; Faligot and Krop, *La Piscine*, 148; Porch, *French Secret Services*, 366–72.
46. Entry for 3 August 1956, fos. 25–6, d. 27, Macmillan papers; Nigel Ashton, 'Macmillan and the Middle East', in Richard Aldous and Sabine Lee (eds), *Harold Macmillan and Britain's World Role* (London: Macmillan, 1996), 43–4.
47. *Memoirs of Lord Gladwyn*, 282; 'France and the Middle East', 7 August 1956 EG(56)9, CAB 134/1217, PRO.
48. Dooley, 'Great Britain's "Last Battle"', 495–6; entry for 3 August 1956, fo. 25, d. 27, Macmillan papers; Kyle, *Suez*, 174–5.
49. Kyle, *Suez*, 175–8.
50. Vice-Amiral Barjot projet pour Général Keightley, n. d. Nov. 1956, 9U4/D53, SHAT; Beaufre, *The Suez Expedition*, 36–7.
51. Entry for 20 August 1956, recording lunch with Jebb, fo. 48, d. 27, Macmillan papers; Lefebvre, *Guy Mollet*, 255–6.
52. Chauvel to Pineau, 3 September 1956, no. 1598/DP, Grande-Bretagne, vol. 139, MAE.
53. Rapport du Général Brohon, 27 November 1956, no. 281/GH1, 9U4/D51, SHAT. Mobilised reservists were shipped from Marseilles to Algeria from May 1956, see: EMA-1, 'Fiche relative au rappel des disponibles', no date, 1956, 1H1379/D1, SHAT.
54. Entry for 23 August 1956, fo. 55, d. 27, Macmillan papers; Lucas, *Divided*, 175–8.
55. Couve de Murville (Washington) to Foreign Ministry, 21 March 1956, no. 1899, Etats-Unis, vol. 342, MAE. American negotiators refused to provide weaponry for the aircraft, suggesting that the French try to purchase this in Britain.
56. WEA memo., 29 March 1956, RG 59, 751S.00, box 3377, NARA; *DDF*, 1956, I, no. 147, Karachi compte rendus, 7 March 1956.

57. Stivers, 'Eisenhower and the Middle East', 213; for the American perception of Algeria and Suez, see Irwin M. Wall, *France, the United States and the Algerian War, 1954–1962* (Berkeley CA: University of California Press, 2000), ch. 2.
58. Clark to Dulles, 6 June 1956, RG 59, 751S.00, box 3377, NARA.
59. Alphand (Washington) to Pineau, 10 September 1956, no. 2755, Etats-Unis, vol. 342, MAE; Sarell, 'Algeria, annual review for 1956', 14 January 1957, FO 371/125913, PRO.
60. As an example: Clark to Dulles, record of conversation with *chef de cabinet* Maison Neuve, Prefect Collaveri, Mayor Chevallier and General Quenard, 6 August 1956, RG 59, 751S.00, box 3377, NARA.
61. Redha Malek, *L'Algérie à Evian. Histoire des négociations secrètes 1956–1962* (Paris: Editions du Seuil, 1995), 24–6; Harbi, *Le F.L.N.*, 197; Kyle, *Suez*, 116, 144.
62. Paris Embassy to Dulles, 4 September 1956, RG 59, 751S.00, box 3377, NARA.
63. Georgette Elgey, 'Le gouvernement Guy Mollet et l'intervention', Charles-Robert Ageron, 'L'opération de Suez et la guerre d'Algérie', both in Vaïsse (ed.), *La France et l'opération de Suez*, 27–8, 43–9; *DDF*, 1956, II, no. 109, André-Louis Dubois (Rabat) to Savary, 2 August 1956; no. 112, Pineau to Rabat/Tunis ambassadors, 3 August 1956.
64. As examples, see: *DDF*, 1956, I, nos. 187, 236, 253; regarding Morocco and Tunisia, see A. C. E. Malcolm (Tunis) to Lloyd, 23 October 1956, JN10317/13, Malcolm to African dept., 24 October 1956, JN10317/15, FO 371/119558; Malcolm to J. H. A. Watson, 7 February 1957, and minutes, JN10317/3, FO 371/125841, PRO.
65. Beaufre, *The Suez Expedition*, 23, 147.
66. EMA-3, 'Instruction des unités du plan d'urgence 2e partie et du Plan Valmy', 18 May 1956, no. 9772, 1H1379/D1; EMA-1, 'Plan Bugeaud I', 27 June 1956, no. 3522, 1H1374/D3, SHAT. Regarding the air force call-up, see EMAA-1, instruction no. 6021, 27 April 1956, Z23344/D1, SHAA.
67. Dillon to Dulles, 23 October 1956, RG 59, 751S.00, box 3378, NARA; Jean-Pierre Dubois, 'L'Aéronautique Navale et les Opérations d'Algérie, 1954–1962', *Revue Historique des Armées*, 187 (1992), 113; Horne, *A Savage War*, 158–9. The five arrested were Ahmed Ben Bella, Mohammed Boudiaf, Hocine Aït Ahmed, Mohammed Khider and Mustafa Lacheraf (FLN information officer). Only the latter was not a member of the original CRUA. The *Athos*, first registered as the *Saint-Brivels*, had been British-owned before Ben Bella organised the vessel's purchase in Beirut in July, see Fathi Al Dib, *Abdel Nasser et la Révolution*, 175–6.
68. Clark to State Dept., 27 October 1956, RG 59, 751S.00, box 3378, NARA.
69. *DDF*, 1956, II, no. 301, Department note, 'Sur les ingérences égyptiennes en Afrique du Nord', 20 October 1956.
70. Dillon interview with Alain Savary's *chef de cabinet*, Chazelle, 24 October 1956, RG 59, 751S.00, box 3378, NARA; Lefebvre, *Guy Mollet*, 228–32.
71. Harbi, *Le F.L.N.*, 184–92; State dept bureau of intelligence and research memo., 'The leadership of the Algerian National Liberation Front', 22 May 1958, JR1016/26, FO 371/131663, PRO.
72. *FRUS*, 1955–1957, vol. XVIII Africa, no. 74, M'hammed Yazid to Eisenhower, 23 October 1956, n.2; *DDF*, 1956, II, no. 306, Roger Lalouette (Rabat) to Savary, 23 October 1956.

73. *DDF*, 1956, II, no. 240, Savary to Dubois (Rabat), 3 October 1956; 'Prospects for Franco-Moroccan co-operation, 14 November 1956, JM10317/37, FO 371/119483, PRO.
74. Dillon to Dulles, 24 October 1956, RG 59, 751S.00, box 3378, NARA; Irwin M. Wall, 'The United States, Algeria, and the Fall of the French Fourth Republic', *Diplomatic History*, 18:4 (1994), 493–4; Anthony Nutting, *No End of a Lesson. The Story of Suez* (London: Constable, 1967), 100–1; *DDF*, 1956, II, Pierre de Leusse (Tunis) to secrétariat d'état aux affaires marocaines et tunisiennes, 23 October 1956. Twenty people also died in clashes in Tunisia during the arrests crisis.
75. Fathi Al Dib, *Abdel Nasser et la Révolution*, 41–3, 175–6; Malek, *L'Algérie à Evian*, 22–9.
76. Kyle, *Suez*, 112. By late 1956 a network of Egyptian military attachés in Paris, Madrid, Rabat and Tripoli all assisted in covert arms trafficking, see: Fathi Al Dib, *Abdel Nasser et la Révolution*, 204. This was well known to the SDECE.
77. Mohamed H. Heikal, *Cutting the Lion's Tail: Suez through Egyptian Eyes* (London: André Deutsch, 1986), 74, 98–9, 112–13; Malek, *L'Algérie à Evian*, 23–9; Lefebvre, *Guy Mollet*, 200–3; *DDF*, 1956, II, no. 59, note 2.
78. Mahmoud Fawzi, *Suez 1956. An Egyptian Perspective* (London: Shorouk International, 1987).
79. Robert J. Bookmiller, 'The Algerian war of words: broadcasting and revolution, 1954–1962', *The Maghreb Review*, 14:3–4 (1989), 198–201; *DDF*, 1956, II, no. 301, Department note, 20 October 1956.
80. JIC, 'Egyptian arms imports', 19 June 1954, JIC(54)57, CAB 158/17, PRO.
81. JIC secretary's note, 'Egyptian anti-British propaganda in the Middle East'. 31 December 1954, JIC(54)53, CAB 158/17; JIC report, 'The activities of Cairo Radio and their impact on the territories towards which they are directed', 23 July 1956, JIC(56)78, CAB 158/25, PRO; Kyle, *Suez*, 54, 59–60.
82. Sir Ralph Stevenson (Cairo) to FO, 31 July 1954, FO 371/108598, PRO.
83. Makins (Washington) to FO, 20 November 1954, FO 371/108597, PRO.
84. Wall, *The United States and the Making of Postwar France*, 282–95.
85. Mill-Irving to African dept., 21 Dec. 1955, JF1019/2, FO 371/119356, PRO. M. A. B. refers to the arms maker – *Manufacture d'Armes Basque*.
86. Fathi Al Dib, *Abdel Nasser et la Révolution*, 82–8.
87. Reilly (Paris) to African dept, 5 October 1955; Cairo Embassy report to African dept., 7 October 1955, FO 371/113802, PRO.
88. Ovendale, *Britain, the United States and the Transfer of Power*, 96.
89. *DDF*, 1955, II, no. 6, Antoine Pinay to Chauvel, 4 July 1955, note 1, no. 81, 'Arrangement militaire franco-britannique', 3 August 1955.
90. CIGS note, 'The situation in Libya', 1 November 1956, COS(56)393, DEFE 5/72, PRO; *DDF*, 1955, I, department note, 21 April 1955.
91. Lloyd (Karachi) to FO, 8 March 1956; record of Eden-Mollet discussions (Chequers), 11 March 1956; Jebb to FO, 20 March 1956; Eden to Jebb – for Mollet; Jebb to FO, 21 March 1956, PREM 11/1344, PRO; Kyle, *Suez*, 112–16, 144.
92. PM's minute, 17 March 1956, JF1023/3, FO 371/119368, PRO.
93. W. D. Graham to Lloyd, 15 August 1956, JF1051/17, FO 371/119376, PRO.
94. Baghdad and Damascus tels. to FO, 26 March, 30 March, 1 April and 13 April 1956, JF1023/6; JF1023/7; JF1023/8; JF1023/15, FO 371/119368, PRO.

95. *DDF*, 1956, I, no. 334, Dumarçay (Tripoli) to Pineau, 23 May 1956; Fathi Al Dib, *Abdel Nasser et la Révolution*, 41. Fathi Al Dib states that, in exchange for Egyptian political support, the Libyan premier selected a sub-prefect, Abdel Hamid Darna, to organise the concealment of Egyptian weapons for the FLN in Libya.
96. T. G. Beagley (NATO delegation, Paris) to FO, 7 July 1956, JF1025/3; Graham (Tripoli) to FO, 24 October 1956, JF1025/9; Sir Humphrey Trevelyan (Cairo) to FO, 27 October 1956, JF1024/16, FO 371/119372, PRO.
97. Beaufre, *The Suez Expedition*, 142; The Foreign Office was also concerned that the Quai d'Orsay failed to explain Britain's North Africa policy to Mollet's government: Beith (Paris) to J. H. A. Watson, 21 September 1956, JF1195/26, FO 371/119392, PRO.
98. Maurice Vaïsse, 'France and the Suez Crisis', in Louis and Owen (eds), *Suez 1956*, 131–3.
99. Mill-Irving to African dept., 31 December 1955, JF1019/7, FO 371/119356, PRO.
100. Kyle, *Suez*, 116–17; Vaïsse, 'France and the Suez Crisis', 134; Abel Thomas, *Comment Israel fut sauvé. Les Secrets de l'expédition de Suez* (Paris: Albin Michel, 1978), 83–90.
101. Regarding the Chantilly exchanges, see: Kyle, *Suez*, 117–18.
102. Paris chancery to African dept: *Journal Officiel* decrees, 17 February 1956, JF1019/66, FO 371/119358, PRO.
103. Regarding the Sèvres talks, see: Avi Shlaim, 'The Protocol of Sèvres, 1956: anatomy of a war plot', *International Affairs*, 73:3 (1997), 509–29.
104. Shlaim, 'The Protocol of Sèvres, 1956', 511–12.
105. *Memoirs of Lord Gladwyn*, 282.
106. Shlaim, 'The Protocol of Sèvres, 1956', 514–15.
107. Cogan, 'De la politique du mensonge', in Vaïsse (ed.), *La France et l'opération de Suez*, 130–1; William Roger Louis, 'American anti-colonialism and the dissolution of the British Empire', *International Affairs*, 61:3 (1985), 414; Lucas, *Divided*, 330.
108. Louis, 'Dulles, Suez and the British', 152–3.
109. Isaacson (Paris) to FO, 10 November 1956, Selwyn Lloyd papers, FO 800/727, PRO.
110. Eden to Eisenhower, 5 August 1956, tel. 3568, Lloyd papers, FO 800/726, PRO.
111. *DDF*, 1956, I, no. 161, Mollet tel. to Eden, 11 March 1956.
112. *Memoirs of Lord Gladwyn*, 283–4.
113. Draft notes on Suez Committee proceedings, n.d. September 1956, box 7, 1956 Correspondence, Monckton papers; entries for 1 August 1956, fos. 15–16, 17 August 1956, fos. 44–6, 11 September 1956, fo. 90, d. 27, Macmillan papers.
114. Eden to Eisenhower, 6 September 1956, tel. 4061; Eden to Eisenhower, 5 November 1956, tel. 5181; reply to Eden, 3 November 1956, tel. 4060, FO 800/726, Lloyd papers, PRO.
115. *DDF*, 1956, III, no. 74, Alphand to Pineau; no. 77, Pineau circular to overseas ambassadors, both 31 October 1956.
116. *DDF*, 1956, III, nos. 107, 139, Chauvel to Pineau, 4 and 7 November 1956, no. 126, Dejean to Pineau, 6 November 1956. A day earlier the Soviet

government threatened Mollet with military intervention under UN auspices to end the fighting in Egypt.

117. Brief for MOD and COS chairman, 7 November 1956, FS/56/24; strategic exports comm. note, 'Export of Arms to the Middle East', 13 November 1956, DEFE 13/214, PRO.
118. Smith, 'Muslim Impoverishment in Colonial Algeria', 145, n. 16.
119. Text of Cairo press conference, 25 April 1956, JF1581/2, FO 371/119415, PRO.
120. Vaïsse, 'France and the Suez Crisis', 134–7.
121. Eden–Mollet discussions, Chequers, 11 March 1956, PREM 11/1344, PRO.
122. Jebb to western dept., annual report for France, 1956, 21 January 1957, WF1011/1, FO 371/130625, PRO; Dooley, 'Great Britain's "Last Battle"', 509–10.
123. Piers Dixon, *Double Diploma: the life of Sir Pierson Dixon, don and diplomat* (London: Hutchinson, 1968), 278: cited in Adamthwaite, 'Suez Revisited', 449–50.
124. Shlaim, 'The Protocol of Sèvres', 514; on Templer and Mountbatten, see: Kyle, *Suez*, 201–3, 419–20, 438–9; Adamthwaite, 'Suez Revisited', 454–8.
125. Jebb to western dept., annual report for France, 1956, 21 January 1957, WF1011/1, FO 371/130625, PRO; Maurice Vaïsse, 'Aux origines du mémorandum de septembre 1958', *Relations Internationales*, 58 (1989), 254.
126. Isaacson (Paris) to FO, 26 October 1956, JF1025/12, FO 371/119372, PRO; Clark memo. on CRUA, 20 June 1955, RG 59, 751S.00, box 3375, NARA.
127. Clark to Dulles, 9 October 1956, RG 59, 751S.00, box 3378, NARA.
128. David G. Nes (Tripoli) to State Dept., 20 December 1955; Peter R. Chase (Cairo) to State Dept., 21 December 1955, RG 59, 751S.00, box 3376, NARA.
129. *Memoirs of Lord Gladwyn*, 285.
130. Murray, political adviser to UK C-in-C., to Sir Ivone Kirkpatrick, 1 November 1956, Lloyd papers, FO 800/727, PRO.
131. Eden to Mollet, 1 November 1956, tel. 2363; Jebb to Eden, 2 November 1956, tel. 397; Murray to Kirkpatrick, 3 November 1956, Lloyd papers, FO 800/727, PRO. For succinct descriptions of the French military operations, see: Kyle, *Suez*, ch. 22; Philippe Masson, 'Origines et bilan d'une défaite', *Revue Historique des Armées*, 4 (1986), 51–8; Vaïsse (ed.), *La France et l'opération de Suez*, deuxième partie.
132. Peter Hennessy and Mark Laity, 'Suez – what the papers say', *Contemporary Record*, I (April 1987), 8; also cited in Adamthwaite, 'Suez Revisited', 453, and Keith Kyle in Louis and Owen (eds), *Suez 1956*, 130.
133. General Keightley dispatch, 'Operations in Egypt, November to December 1956', 10 June 1957, DEFE 7/1127, PRO.
134. Situation militaire au Moyen-Orient, 27 September 1956, no. 17/EM/OPS, 9U4/D15; Rapport du Général Brohon, 27 November 1956, no. 281/GH1, 9U4/D51, SHAT.
135. Clark to State Dept., 9 October 1956, RG 59, 751S.00, box 3378, NARA.
136. Rapport du Général Brohon, 27 November 1956, no. 281/GH1, 9U4/D51, SHAT.
137. Beaufre, *The Suez Expedition*, 108–21.
138. Auchinleck letter to Monckton, 22 November 1956, box 8, General Correspondence, November–December 1956, Monckton papers.

139. Christopher Brady, 'The Cabinet System and Management of the Suez Crisis', *Contemporary British History*, 11:2 (1997), 77–84; Chauvel to Pineau, tel. 1983/EU, Grande-Bretagne, vol. 139, MAE.
140. Barjot projet pour Général Keightley, n. d. November 1956, 9U4/D53, SHAT.
141. Barjot report, 'Conclusions à tirer de l'opération EGYPTE', 31 December 1956, no. 1008/CCFFO, 9U4/D52, SHAT.
142. Ely, *Mémoires*, II, 205–6; Delmas, 'A la recherche des signes', 78; Vaïsse, 'Aux origines du mémorandum', 254–60; Watson, 'The Aftermath of Suez', 342.
143. Dillon to Dulles, 13 November 1956, RG 59, 751S.00, box 3378, NARA.
144. Harbi, *Le F.L.N.*, 180–92; Fathi Al Dib, *Abdel Nasser et la Révolution*, 171–4.
145. Situation des effectifs stationées en AFN, 1 December 1956, 1H1374/D2, SHAT.
146. *DDF*, 1956, III, no. 158, Note de la direction générale politique, 10 November 1956; Fathi Al Dib, *Abdel Nasser et la Révolution*, 203–4.
147. Memo. of conversation with Pineau, 16 November 1956, RG 59, 751S.00, box 3378, NARA; *DDF*, 1956, III, no. 281, Compte rendu, 10 December 1956. Pineau, Joxe, Daridan and Alphand led the French delegation.
148. Vaïsse, 'Aux origines du mémorandum', 255; *Memoirs of Lord Gladwyn*, 285. For Mollet's TV address: Jebb to FO, 9 January 1957, JR10317/2, FO 371/125928, PRO.

5 France Undermined?

1. S. H. Perowne minute, 14 November 1951, CO 537/7136, PRO.
2. Jacques Marseille, 'The Phases of French Colonial Imperialism: Towards a New Periodization', *Journal of Imperial and Commonwealth History*, 13:3 (1985), 132–40.
3. *Memoirs of Lord Gladwyn*, 268.
4. *Ibid.*, 269.
5. *BDEEP* series A, vol. III, part I, docs. 118, 122.
6. Jebb to Macmillan, 7 July 1955, JF1019/17, FO 371/113795, PRO.
7. G. W. Harrison minute, 22 May 1956, JF1581/1; Sir Ivone Kirkpatrick minute, 30 June 1956, JF1581/5, FO 371/119415, PRO.
8. E. M. Wilson (London) to State Dept., 23 June 1955, RG 59, 751S.00, box 3375, NARA; *DDF*, 1955, I, no. 253, direction générale des affaires marocaines et tunisiennes note, 5 May 1955.
9. Jebb to Eden, 11 February 1955, JF1015/3, FO 371/113789, PRO.
10. Sous-direction de Tunisie note, 16 February 1956; Moroccan and Tunisian affairs officers meeting, 18 April 1956, dossier Tunisie 1955–56, série NUOI, vol. III, MAE.
11. Reilly (Paris), to Wakefield-Harrey, 25 November 1954; Wakefield-Harrey to African dept., 3 December 1954, FO 371/108611; George Bowker (Bône) report, 13 May 1955, JF1019/17, FO 371/113795, PRO.
12. See, for example, War Office and Royal Marine requests vetoed by Selwyn Lloyd in 1956. These are detailed in FO 371/119399, PRO.
13. R. Allen (Bonn) to FO, 23 August 1955, FO 371/118302; Mill-Irving to FO, 23 August 1955, JF1019/28, FO 371/113796; app. 1, JF1019/57, FO 371/113797, PRO.

14. Sir M. Wright (Baghdad), Sir H. Trevelyan (Cairo), Sir R. Scott (Washington), tels. to FO, 25, 27 and 30 August 1955, FO 371/118302, PRO.
15. Jackson (Paris) report on alleged French atrocities, 17 November 1955, FO 443/174; Mill-Irving to Macmillan, 27 August 1955, JF1019/33, FO 371/113796, PRO.
16. Jackson report (note 15 above).
17. Central Office memo., 'Questions of policy – Kenya: detentions without trial', no date, 1955, CCO4/6/33, Conservative Party archive.
18. Wakefield-Harrey survey of political events in Algeria, last quarter, 1954, 21 January 1955, FO 371/113788, PRO.
19. Mill-Irving to African dept., 10 September 1955, minutes by J. Phillips and C. O. Ramsden, 12 September 1955, JF1019/44; Mill-Irving to African dept., 7 February 1956, FO 371/113796; Adam Watson minute, 28 February 1956, JF1019/69, FO 371/119358, PRO.
20. Couve de Murville to Pinay, 26 May 1955, no. 2836, Etats-Unis, vol. 342, MAE; *DDF*, 1955, I, no. 354, Pinay to Louis de Guiringaud (San Francisco), 22 June 1955.
21. *DDF*, I, 1955, no. 300, Pinay to Couve de Murville, 26 May 1955.
22. *DDF*, I, 1955, no. 293, Comité de défense nationale, 24 May 1955.
23. For details of the troop movements, see. PRO, FO 371/113812; *DDF*, I, 1955, no. 315, Note de la direction politique, 3 June 1955.
24. *DDF*, 1955, II, no. 14, Alexandre Parodi (NATO Council) to Pinay, 6 July 1955, no. 74, Fiche de l'état-major des forces armées, 1 August 1955.
25. Embassy meetings on North Africa, 1–3 August 1955, RG 59, 751S.00, box 3376, NARA.
26. John W. Jones, WEA director, to Livingston Merchant, 6 February 1956, RG 59, 751S.00, box 3376, NARA.
27. Secrétaire d'état aux forces armées memo., 'Renforts supplémentaires pour l'Afrique du Nord', 26 April 1956, 1H1379/D1, SHAT.
28. Défense Nationale Cabinet to EMAA, 18 April 1956, Z23344/D1, SHAA.
29. Algiers consulate to African dept., 8 March 1956, JF1051/2, FO 371/119376, PRO; *FRUS*, 1955–1957, vol. XVIII Africa, no. 67, Paris embassy tel. to State Dept., 7 March 1956; no. 68, Hoover tel. to Paris embassy, 8 March 1956; no. 70, Dillon to State Dept., 20 March 1956, 234–41 *passim*.
30. FO instructions to Mill-Irving, 28 March 1956, JF1051/3; African dept. note, 20 March 1956, JF1051/4, FO 371/119376, PRO.
31. Dillon to Dulles, 31 May 1956, RG 59, 751S.00, box 3377, NARA.
32. Geay, 'Les débats sur les recours de la Tunisie à l'ONU', 241–54.
33. Robert Holland, *Britain and the Revolt in Cyprus 1954–1959* (Oxford: Clarendon Press, 1998), 41–4.
34. *DDF*, 1955, II, no. 93, note du secrétariat des conférences, 6 August 1955; no. 99, Couve de Murville to Pinay, 9 August 1955.
35. *BDEEP*, series A, vol. III, part I, doc. 108.
36. *DDF*, 1955, II, no. 135, Charles Lucet (UN) to Pinay, 24 August 1955.
37. Pinay speech, 30 September 1955, no. 6903, Etats-Unis, vol. 342, MAE.
38. Couve de Murville to Foreign Ministry, 11 May 1956, Etats-Unis, vol. 342, MAE.
39. UK del., UN, to FO, 30 September 1955, tel. 890, PREM 11/902, PRO; *DDF*, 1955, II, nos. 175, 260, n. 1.

40. Hervé Alphand, *L'étonnement d'être. Journal (1939–1973)* (Paris: Fayard, 1977), 275.
41. UK del., UN, to FO, both 1 October 1955, tels. 898/2353, PREM 11/902, PRO; René Girault, 'La France en accusation à l'ONU, ou les pouvoirs d'une organisation internationale', *Relations Internationales*, 76 (1993), 413–14.
42. *DDF*, 1955, II, no. 260, note 1; no. 261, note du secrétariat des conférences, 1 October 1955; no. 266, Couve de Murville to Pinay, 3 October 1955; no. 277, Pinay reply, 6 October 1955, no. 283, Louis de Guiringaud (UN) to Foreign Minister, 8 October 1955; Maurice Vaïsse, 'La Guerre perdue à l'ONU?', in Rioux (ed.), *La Guerre d'Algérie*, 452–3.
43. *DDF*, 1955, II, no. 347, note du département, 'Assemblée générale des Nations Unies, Question algérienne', 4 November 1955.
44. *DDF*, 1956, I, no. 231, n. 2.
45. *DDF*, 1956, I, Alphand (Washington) to Pineau, 28 June 1956; Vaïsse, 'La Guerre perdue à l'ONU?', 453.
46. *DDF*, 1956, II, no. 23, Dejean (Moscow) to Pineau, 7 July 1956; Sir William Hayter (Moscow) to FO, 7 July 1956, JF1025/1A, FO 371/119372, PRO.
47. *DDF*, 1956, II, Dejean (Moscow) to Pineau, 20 July 1956, n. 1.
48. African dept. brief for Eden visit to France, 28 September 1956, JF1051/19, FO 371/119376, PRO; African affairs position paper on Algeria, 30 August 1956, RG 59, 751S.00, NARA; Holland, *Britain and the Revolt in Cyprus*, 43–4.
49. *DDF*, 1956, II, no. 312, note du secrétariat des conférences, 23 October 1956.
50. Girault, 'La France en accusation à l'ONU', 416.
51. Parker (Jedda) to FO, 31 October 1956, JF1025/17, FO 371/119372, PRO; *FRUS*, 1955–1957, vol. XVIII Africa, no. 74, Yazid to Eisenhower, 23 October 1956, 246.
52. Charles Lucet (Washington) to Pineau, 11 December 1956, Etats-Unis, vol. 342, MAE.
53. A. A. Duff (Paris) to H. F. T. Smith, 12 January 1957, JR10345/2, FO 371/125933; Algeria, annual review for 1956, 14 January 1957, FO 371/125913, PRO.
54. Sir H. Caccia to FO, 14 January 1957, JR10317/8, FO 371/125928, PRO.
55. Clark to Dulles, 4 January 1957, RG 59, 751S.00, box 3379, NARA.
56. Isaacson (Paris) to FO, 26 October 1956, JF1025/12, FO 371/119372, PRO; Dillon to Dulles, 13 November 1956, no. 2372, RG 59, Box 3378, 751S.00, NARA. The Tunisians helped arrange the first official negotiations with the FLN at Melun in June 1960, see: *DDF*, vol. I, 1960, no. 291, Raoul-Duval (Tunis) to Foreign Ministry, 24 June 1960.
57. Pineau-Dulles talks, 19 November 1957, RG 59, 751S.00, box 3381, NARA.
58. D. M. Bane memo., 'Algeria', 11 June 1957; memo. of conversation with J. E. Coulson, 3 July 1957; W. R. Tyler to J. W. Jones, 12 July 1957, RG 59, 751S.00, box 3380; Cabot Lodge to Dulles, 27 November 1957, 751S.00, box 3381, NARA.
59. Clark memos., 'Trends within the French Army in Algeria' I and II, 10 January 1957, 27 June 1957, desps. 134 and 251; Clark to State Dept., desp. 11, RG 59, 751S.00, boxes 3379 and 3380, EUR memo., 'British working paper' 30 January 1958, 751S.00, box 3382, NARA.
60. Matthew Connelly, 'The French–American Conflict over North Africa and the Fall of the Fourth Republic', *Revue Française d'Histoire d'Outre-Mer*, 84:315

(1997), 13–19; Irwin M. Wall, 'The United States, Algeria and the Fall of the French Fourth Republic', *Diplomatic History*, 18:4 (1994), 502; Caccia to FO, 13 June 1957, JR10345/3, FO 371/125933, PRO.

61. Sarell to Beith (Paris), 21 February 1957, JR1013/2, FO 371/125915, PRO; Vaïsse, 'La Guerre perdue à l'ONU?', 454–5.
62. *DDF*, I, 1957, no. 312, Pineau circular tel., 13 April 1957; Lacoste to Pineau, 20 May 1957, Etats-Unis, vol. 343, MAE.
63. Alphand to Pineau, 25 May 1957, tel. 1414, Etats-Unis, vol. 343, MAE.
64. Rousso, *The Vichy Syndrome*, 75–6.
65. Paris chancery to African dept., 30 July 1957, JR1551/1; J. H. A. Watson minute, 3 September 1957, JR1551/3, FO 371/125949, PRO.
66. Jebb to Lloyd, 27 December 1957, JR10317/1, FO 371/131674, PRO. The worst cases of maltreatment related in the Beteille report concerned Algerian detainees confined overnight in wine cellars. Eighty-eight died, overcome by fumes.
67. Jebb to FO, 29 January 1958, JR10317/3, FO 371/131674, PRO.
68. Sarell to Lloyd, 10 September 1957, JR1551/7; Sarell to African dept., 18 September 1957, JR1551/10, FO 371/125949, PRO.
69. Rioux, *The Fourth Republic*, 291–3. The citation of Massu during a 1970 libel trial against *L'Express*, in addition to Yacef Saadi's 1962 memoir and Gillo Pontecorvo's famous film about the battle of Algiers, prompted the General to write his self-justificatory *La Vraie bataille d'Alger*, published by Plon in 1971.
70. Cyprus government white paper, 'Allegations of brutality in Cyprus', no date, 1957, CCO4/7/167, Conservative Party archive; C. T. Collingford to FO, 5 March 1958, JR1661/1, FO 371/131696; JR1661/2, FO to Ethele Powell, 13 March 1958; COS comm., 'Present military situation in Cyprus', 22 April 1958, COS(58)119, DEFE 5/83, PRO; Horne, *A Savage War*, 199–201.
71. Jebb, 'France – annual review for 1957', 17 January 1958, and Juliet Collings minute, 7 March 1958, WF1011/1, FO 371/137237, PRO; Michael Dockrill, 'Restoring the "Special Relationship": the Bermuda and Washington Conferences, 1957', in Dick Richardson and Glyn Stone (eds), *Decisions and Diplomacy: Essays in Twentieth Century International History* (London: Routledge, 1995), 205–23.
72. Entry for 19 May 1957, fo. 41, 2nd series Diaries, d. 29, Macmillan papers.
73. Georges Bidault, 'La France défend son destin en Algérie', *Carrefour*, 4 October 1957, 3–4.
74. Bénard to Gorse, 23 November 1957, no. 7422, NUOI, vol. 111, MAE; Claude Paillat, *Dossier secret de l'Algérie 1954–1958*, II (Paris: Presses de la Cité, 1962), 490.
75. Clark memo., 'Responsibility for the Sakiet incident', 14 February 1958, RG 59, 751S.00, box 3382, NARA; *FRUS*, 1958–1960, vol. VII, Pt. 2, Western Europe, no. 4, Dulles to Bonn Embassy, 2 April 1958 Wall, *France, the United States and the Algerian War*, ch. 4.
76. Irwin M. Wall, 'Les Etats-Unis, la Grande-Bretagne et l'affaire de Sakiet-Sidi-Youssef', *Revue d'Histoire Diplomatique*, 110 (1996), 307–27; *France, the United States and the Algerian War*, ch. 4.
77. J. C. Holmes, 'US initiative on North Africa', 20 February 1958, box 3382; SHAPE liaison officer memo., 'Algerian problem', 26 March 1958, 751S.00, box 3383, NARA.

78. Connelly, 'The French-American Conflict', 18–19.
79. Michael M. Harrison, 'French Anti-Americanism', in D. Lacorne *et al.* (eds), *The Rise and Fall of Anti-Americanism* (London: Macmillan, 1990), 169, 173–5.
80. Gorse (Tunis) to Foreign Ministry, 8 February 1957, NUOI, vol. 111, MAE.
81. Jauffret, 'L'Armée et l'Algérie en 1954', 20.
82. Alain Ruscio, 'Dien Bien Phu: Du coup de génie à l'aberration', *Revue Française d'Histoire d'Outre-Mer,* LXXII: 268 (1985), 340–4.
83. Zone nord-Algérois, Commandement du Génie, 'Les Travaux de la frontière Franco-Tunisienne', 30 July 1958, 1H2968/D1; EMI-3, 'La Barrage avant de la frontière Tunisienne', n.d. March 1960, 1H2035/D1, SHAT.
84. General Dulac to General Olié, 23 February 1959, 1H2036/D1, SHAT.
85. Basdevant circular tel., 4 June 1957, no. 2237, NUOI, vol. 111, MAE.
86. *DDF,* 1956, I, no. 24, Soustelle (Algiers) to Bourgès-Maunoury, 14 January 1956.
87. *DDF,* 1957, I, no. 400, Maurice Faure to Robert Lacoste, 16 May 1957; no. 449, Chargé d'affaires Lalouette (Rabat) to Maurice Faure, 7 June 1957.
88. Bénard (Tunis) interview with Bahi Ladgham and Dr Mokkadem, 25 January 1958, no. 687, NUOI, vol. 111, MAE.
89. Chaix, 'La France et la réconstitution', 298–304.
90. Philippe Vial, 'Algérie ou A. F. N.? Le destin partagé de la Ve région aérienne (1946–1962)', *Revue Historique des Armées,* 1 (1993), 86–9.
91. Regarding 1956 incidents, see: *DDF,* 1956, II, nos. 55 and 165.
92. 'Incidents à la frontière algéro-tunisienne', no date, September 1957, 1H1759/D1, SHAT; Bénard (Tunis) to Foreign Ministry, 2 September 1957, no. 5122; Gorse (Tunis) to Foreign Ministry, 12 September 1957, no. 5357; Colonel Ruyssen to *chef de cabinet,* 8 November 1957, no. 3051; General Scutari (Algiers) to secretary for Moroccan and Tunisian affairs, 18 November 1957, no. 3132, NUOI, vol. 111, MAE; EMI-2, General Salan, synthèse mensuelle, November 1957, 18 December 1957, 1H1425/D1, SHAT.
93. Direction générale des affaires marocaines et tunisiennes memo., 25 May 1958, no. 45, NUOI, vol. 112, MAE.
94. El Machat, *Les Etats-Unis et la Tunisie,* 121–56; Vaïsse, 'Aux origines', 257–8.
95. El Machat, *ibid.,* 114–15; Martin Thomas, 'Policing Algeria's Borders, 1956–1960: Arms Supplies, Frontier Defences and the Sakiet Affair', *War and Society,* 13:1 (1995), 91.
96. Malcolm to Watson, 18 April 1957, JR1201/11, FO 371/125945, PRO.
97. Lloyd to Rabat, 31 May 1957, JN10317/21, FO 371/125841, PRO; El Machat, *Les Etats-Unis et la Tunisie,* 81–90.
98. Pierre Mélandri, 'La France et le "jeu double" des Etats-Unis', in Rioux (ed.), *La Guerre d'Algérie,* 429–31.
99. Elly Hermon, 'A propos du plan Félix Gaillard de Pacte Méditerranéen', *Revue d'Histoire Diplomatique,* 109 (1995), 10; Joint communiqué, 26 November 1957, PREM 11/1830A, PRO.
100. Alistair Horne, *Macmillan II: 1957–1986* (London: Macmillan, 1989), 35.
101. HMG communication to Dulles, 25 November 1957, PREM 11/1849, PRO.
102. Secrétariat des conférences memo., 17 February 1958, NUOI, vol. 112, MAE.
103. Wall, 'Les Etats-Unis', 312–25; Connelly, 'The French-American Conflict', 18–24; CC(58)26th conclusions, 27 March 1958, CAB 128/31, PRO.

104. Acworth report, 12 August 1957, JR1201/16, FO 371/125946, PRO.
105. UK reply to NATO review, 30 May 1958, COS(58)145, DEFE 5/84, PRO.
106. UK reply to NATO review, 17 June 1958, COS(58)158, DEFE 5/84, PRO.
107. Roberts to A. D. M. Ross, 1 October 1957, JR10317/59, FO 371/125944, PRO.
108. John Beith to P. F. Hancock, 27 January 1958, WUN11913/2; N. Cheetham (NATO, Paris) to Hancock, 1 February 1958, WUN11913/9, FO 371/137865, PRO.
109. Watson to C. E. F. Gough (MOD) and reply, 23 December 1957 and 14 February 1958; Pemberton-Pigott minute, 28 February 1958, FO 371/125944, PRO.
110. Hermon, 'A propos du plan Félix Gaillard', 7–9, 15–17.
111. *Ibid.*, 7–21.
112. Bénard (Tunis) to Gorse, 23 November 1957, no. 7422, NUOI, vol. 111, MAE.
113. Secrétariat d'état, pièces addressées à l'ONU, 12 February 1958, no. 490, NUOI, vol. 111, MAE; Harbi, *Le F.L.N.*, 213–14.
114. Wall, 'Les Etats-Unis', 316–23; Maurice Couve de Murville, *Une politique étrangère 1958–1969* (Paris: Plon, 1971), 22.
115. Wall, 'Les Etats-Unis', 321–7, *France, the United States and the Algerian War*, ch. 4; Jebb meeting with Joxe, 3 March 1958, JN10317/208, FO 371/131585; C. Hourani to Beeley, 29 May 1958, JN10317/359, FO 371/131591, PRO.

6 The Algerian Conflict – a Cold War Front Line?

1. Sir Frank Roberts to A. Ross, 1 October 1957, JR10317/59, FO 371/125944, PRO.
2. Memo. for Paris meeting, 'General North African Situation', 26 November 1954, NATO briefing papers, R 12, NARA.
3. Makins to FO, 23 November 1954, FO 371/108597; A. A. Duff (Paris) to Tom Bromley (African dept.), 16 November 1954, FO 371/108596, PRO.
4. Wall, 'The United States, Algeria', 490.
5. JIC report, 'Political developments in the Middle East and their impact upon western interests', 11 November 1954, JIC(54)72, CAB 158/18; COS comm., 'Directive to Commanders-in-chief, Middle East', 28 March 1958, COS(58)87, DEFE 5/83, PRO.
6. Rabat Cabinet diplomatique memo., 'Istiqlal et communisme', 25 August 1951; Juin memo., 'Nationalisme marocaine et procédés de guerre froide', 8 September, 1951, NUOI, vol. 573, MAE.
7. Ageron, '"L'Algérie dernière chance de la puissance française"', 122.
8. General L.-M. Chassin, 'Vers un encerclement de l'Occident?', *Revue de Défense Nationale*, (1956), 531–53.
9. General Paul Ely, 'Notre politique militaire', *Revue de Défense Nationale*, (1957), 1037–9.
10. Stivers, 'Eisenhower and the Middle East', 193–203.
11. *Memoirs of Lord Gladwyn*, 280; see Jebb dispatches in FO 371/113803, PRO.
12. 'Review of current NEA problems with British representative', 28 January 1955, RG 59, 751S.00, Box 3375, NARA.
13. Director of plans brief for CAS, 28 July 1954, AIR 8/1877, PRO.

14. JIC, 'Survey of world communism in 1954', 24 March 1955, JIC(55)10, CAB 158/19, PRO.
15. The first substantial report on the FLN/CRUA from the US Consulate in Algiers was dispatched in June 1955, see: Lewis Clark report on CRUA, 20 June 1955, RG 59, 751S.00, Box 3375, NARA; William B. Quandt, *Revolution and Political Leadership: Algeria, 1954–1968* (Cambridge, Mass.: MIT Press, 1969), 91–3.
16. Ageron, 'L'opération de Suez', in Vaïsse (ed.), *La France et l'opération*, 44–6.
17. Dakar conference working party on West African defence facilities, Quai d'Orsay meeting, 10 January 1956, DEFE 7/957, PRO.
18. Quai d'Orsay talks, 15 December 1955, V1024/17G, *ibid.*
19. Eden tel. to Bulganin, 20 October, 1955, EG/40, FO 800/669, Macmillan papers, PRO.
20. Macmillan to Jebb, 11 October 1955, V1022/23, FO 800/678, PRO.
21. Quai d'Orsay talks, 15 December 1955, V1024/17G, *op. cit.*
22. Jebb to Macmillan, 10 June 1955, FO 800/663, Macmillan papers, PRO.
23. L. G. Dorros to John A. Bovey, 14 November 1956, RG 59, State Dept. lot files, office of North African affairs, box 4, file R12, NARA.
24. Record of meeting with Pinay, 21 April 1955, JT10317/76, FO 800/672, Macmillan papers, PRO.
25. Macmillan to Jebb, 13 April 1955, JT10317/67; WF1051/33, Macmillan to Jebb, 7 June 1955, WF1051/33, *ibid.*
26. CIGS note, 'Situation in Libya', 1 November 1956, COS(56)393, DEFE 5/72, PRO.
27. EMA-3, 'Récapitulation – principaux éléments des forces terrestres stationnées en AFN', 15 May 1955, 1H1374/D2, SHAT.
28. Murphy to Walter P. Reuther, President of CIO, 7 September 1955, Etats-Unis, vol. 342, MAE; *DDF*, I, 1955, no. 307, Note du secrétaire général, 'Envoi d'effectifs OTAN en Algérie', 31 May 1955.
29. COS(55)29th meeting, 28 April 1955, and comment by J. Alexander, 29 April 1955, AIR 8/1660, PRO; *Memoirs of Lord Gladwyn*, 282.
30. Dillon to Dulles, 3 June 1955; Clark to State Dept., 9 June 1955, RG 59, 751S.00, box 3375, NARA.
31. Macmillan to Lord De l'Isle, 29 April 1955, AIR 8/1660, PRO.
32. DC(55)23rd meeting of defence committee, 2 May 1955; Air Ministry to Minister of Supply, Reginald Maudling, 28 September 1955, AIR 8/1660, PRO.
33. Lloyd to Eden, 25 January 1956, FO 800/731, Selwyn Lloyd papers, PRO.
34. JPS memo., app. A, 'Strategic background', 2 June 1955, JP(55)46, DEFE 7/957; JIC report, 'Soviet threat to the Middle East in a general war up to the end of 1959', 14 January 1955, JIC(54)64, CAB 158/18; JIC report on Soviet navy and air force employment in general war, 15 August 1955, JIC(55)6, CAB 158/19, PRO.
35. JIC report, 'Political developments in the Middle East and their impact upon western interests', 11 November 1954, JIC(54)72, CAB 158/18, PRO.
36. Record of Eden–Chauvel conversation, 23 January 1956, V1072/15; FO brief for Lloyd – Mollet meeting, 11 March 1956, V1072/28G, FO 371/121244; Paris chancery to African dept., 29 March 1956, V1072/38, FO 371/121245, PRO.
37. FO memo., 'The future of NATO', 2 May 1956, CP(56)112, CAB 129/81, PRO.

38. Macmillan to Reilly, 21 April 1955, JT10317/76, FO 800/672, Macmillan papers; Walter Monckton memo., 'The strategic importance of Malta', COS annex, 5 September 1956, CP(56)205, CAB 129/83, PRO.
39. SPI report, 20 October 1955, no. 65903, Etats-Unis, vol. 342, MAE.
40. *Memoirs of Lord Gladwyn*, 281–2.
41. EMA-3, 'Situation prévisionnelle des effectifs en Afrique du Nord', no date, 1956; EMA-3, 'Situation des effectifs en Afrique Français du Nord', 1 November 1956, 1H1374/D2, SHAT. These figures included colonial troops.
42. Juniac (Washington) to Foreign Ministry, 24 January 1955, no. 566, Etats-Unis, vol. 342, MAE.
43. *FRUS*, 1955–1957, vol. XVIII, Holmes memo. to Dulles, 29 September 1955, 105–12; Macmillan to Makins, 6 October 1955, FO 800/672, Macmillan papers, PRO.
44. Near Eastern and African affairs memo. of conversation on French North Africa, 3 October 1955, RG 59, 751S.00, Box 3376, NARA; Jebb letter to Macmillan, 11 October 1955, JF1072/23, FO 371/113806, PRO.
45. Jebb to Eden, 23 March 1955, JF1051/3; African dept memo., 29 March 1955, JF1051/4, FO 371/113803; Baghdad pact correspondence, PREM 11/1344, PRO.
46. Connelly, 'The French-American Conflict', 14–15; Harbi, *Archives de la Guerre*, doc. 28.
47. Paul J. Zingg, 'The Cold War in North Africa: American Foreign Policy and Postwar Muslim Nationalism 1945–1962', *The Historian*, 39:1 (1976), 58–9; Congressional Record, 2 July 1957, JR10345/4, FO 371/125933, PRO.
48. Washington embassy dispatches to Pineau, 1 July, 18 July and 2 August 1957, nos. 4580, 1853, 1974, Etats-Unis, vol. 343, MAE.
49. COS comm., 'SACEUR's combat effectiveness report, 1957', 15 April 1958, COS(58)106, DEFE 5/83, PRO; Simon J. Ball, 'Macmillan and British Defence Policy', in Aldous and Lee (eds), *Harold Macmillan and Britain's World Role*, 75–81.
50. Lloyd to Jebb, 17 July 1956, JN1037/4, FO 371/119558; African dept. brief for Eden visit to France, 28 September 1956, JF1019/19, FO 371/119376, PRO.
51. Roberts to A. Ross, 29 March 1957, JM1022/6, FO 371/125765, PRO.
52. Furedi, 'Creating a Breathing Space', 97.
53. Bénard interview with Bahi Ladgham and Dr Mokkadem, 25 January 1958, no. 687, NUOI, vol. 111, MAE.
54. Noraogo Kinda, 'Les Etats-Unis et le nationalisme en Afrique noire à l'épreuve de la décolonisation (Deuxième Guerre Mondiale-1960)', *Revue Française d'Histoire d'Outre-Mer*, LXXIX: 297 (1992), 547–53.
55. Regarding Fanon at Accra, see Gadant, *Islam et nationalisme en Algérie*, 68.
56. Hargreaves, *Decolonization in Africa*, 173.
57. Bureau of Intelligence and Research memo., 'The leadership of the Algerian National Liberation Front', 22 May 1958, JR1016/26, FO 371/131663, PRO. In August 1957 the CCE and the CNRA were expanded, the former from 5 to 9 members and the latter from 34 to 54.
58. UK delegation, NATO, to African dept., 19 November 1958, J1079/1; Sir Frank Roberts to FO, 25 November 1958, J1079/2, FO 371/131198, PRO.
59. Emmanuel Sivan, *Communisme et nationalisme en Algérie 1920–1962* (Paris: FNSP, 1976), ch. VI.

60. Gadant, *Islam et nationalisme en Algérie*, 58–62.
61. EM-2, synthèse mensuelle, June 1957, 12 July 1957, 1H1425/D1, SHAT.
62. Treasury Overseas Finance Division: Franco-Egyptian commercial negotiations, 1957, T 236/4787; JIC memo., 'The Activities of Radio Cairo', 15 August 1957, JIC(57)36, CAB 158/28, PRO; Bookmiller, 'The Algerian war of words', 197–205.
63. JIC memo., 'Soviet and Egyptian penetration of the newly independent Arab countries in Africa', 1 January 1958, JIC(57)112, CAB 158/30, PRO.
64. Baghdad Pact council brief, January–February 1958, JR1051/2, FO 371/131678, PRO.
65. Stivers, 'Eisenhower and the Middle East', 192; Ashton, *Eisenhower*, 107–13; Cabinet defence committee memo., 'Supply of Hunter Aircraft to Iraq', 22 January 1957, DEFE 13/214, PRO.
66. Lloyd to Macmillan, 26 April 1958, PM/58/34; Sir Harold Caccia to FO, 29 April 1958, DEFE 13/214, PRO.
67. COS comm. directive, 28 March 1958, COS(58)87, DEFE 5/83, PRO.
68. Ritchie Ovendale, 'Great Britain and the Anglo-American Invasion of Jordan and Lebanon in 1958', *International History Review*, 16:2 (1994), 290–303; Ashton, *Eisenhower*, 182–6.
69. Lloyd to Jebb, 24 June 1956, tel. 1373; Jebb to Lloyd, 25 June 1958, tel. 331; FO briefs for PM's visit to Paris, 29–30 June 1958, PREM 11/2326, PRO; Ashton, *Eisenhower*, 155–6.
70. FO minutes, VL1015/322, FO 371/134123; Jebb to Lloyd, 25 June 1958, tel. 331, PREM 11/2326; Sir William Hayter minute, 25 June 1958, VL1015/376, FO 371/134125, PRO.
71. Pemberton-Pigott minute, 8 July 1958, WUN10719/6, FO 371/137819, PRO.
72. JIC memo., 'Nasser's probable policy and aims over the next six months', 1 August 1958, JIC(58)77, CAB 158/33, PRO.
73. COS memo., 'Implications of maintaining present readiness in the Middle East', 7 August 1958, COS(58)190, DEFE 5/84, PRO.
74. COS memo., 'Release of military manpower from police duties in colonial territories', 30 October 1958, COS(58)243, DEFE 5/85; Defence co-ordination committee report, 'Cyprus', 1 December 1958, COS(58)272, DEFE 5/87, PRO.
75. 'Situation politique en Tunisie, Novembre 1958', NUOI, vol. 112, MAE.
76. Maurice Vaïsse and Chantal Morelle, 'Les relations Franco-Tunisiennes (Juin 1958–Mars 1962)', *Revue d'Histoire Diplomatique*, 110 (1996), 341–80.
77. British Forces Arabia Peninsula memo., 30 April 1959, COS(59)122, DEFE 5/91, PRO.
78. Sir Frank Lee memo., 'Commercial Prospects in the Middle East', 20 April 1959, UEE10439/21, DEFE 7/1295, PRO.
79. Stivers, 'Eisenhower and the Middle East', 203–4, 214–5.
80. J. C. Satterthwaite to Dulles, 16 November 1959, RG 59, 751S.00, box 3388, NARA.
81. British Forces Arabia Peninsula memo., 30 April 1959, COS(59)122, DEFE 5/91; COS memo., 'Defence in the Middle East – general policy', 8 December 1959, and Air Ministry note, 30 August 1960, COS(60)240, DEFE 7/2200, PRO.
82. JPS, 'Review of defence machinery concerned with Africa', 14 February 1958, JP(57)143, CO 968/697, PRO.

83. C. Ramsden minute, 8 October 1956, JF1196/2, FO 371/119394; CO tels. to East African governors, 6 June 1958 and 7 January 1959, CO 968/697, PRO.
84. COS comm. memo., 'Long-term deployment of the Army', 24 June 1959, COS(59)146, DEFE 5/92, PRO.
85. Record of tripartite talks on Africa, 16–22 April 1959, CO 968/497, PRO.
86. Brief for ministers' meeting, 8 December 1959; JPS report, 'Current requirements in the eastern Mediterranean', 6 July 1960, JP(60)80, DEFE 7/2200, PRO.
87. COS memo., 'Release of military manpower from police duties in colonial territories', 30 October 1958, COS(58)243, DEFE 5/85; COS comments, 6 July 1959, COS(59)162, DEFE 5/92; COS memo., 'Military strategy for circumstances short of global war', 21 June 1960, COS(PAR)(60), DEFE 4/132, PRO.
88. COS 1st meeting, 21 June 1960, COS(PAR)(60), DEFE 4/132, PRO.
89. Maurice Vaïsse, *La Grandeur. Politique étrangère du général de Gaulle 1958–1969* (Paris: Fayard, 1998), 66; G. F. Hiller minute, 7 September 1962, CF1022/14, FO 371/163494, PRO.

7 Britain, de Gaulle and Algeria, 1958–62

1. Anthony Hartley, *Gaullism. The Rise and Fall of a Political Movement* (London: Routledge, 1972), 148–51; Jean Charlot, *Le Gaullisme d'opposition 1946–1958. Histoire politique du Gaullisme* (Paris: Fayard, 1983), 347–60; Odile Rudelle, *Mai 1958, de Gaulle et la République* (Paris: Plon, 1988), 103–10 and deuxième partie; Wall, *France, the United States and the Algerian War*, ch. 5.
2. Alexander and Bankwitz, 'From Politiques en Képi', 80, 89–91; Claude d'Abzac-Epezy, 'La Société militaire, de l'ingérence à l'ignorance', in Rioux (ed.), *La Guerre d'Algérie*, 245–9; Hartley, *Gaullism*, 152–7.
3. Bidault, 'Ma Position. Discours et écrits sur l'Algérie depuis le 16 Septembre 1959', *Les Documents d'Actualité*, 2 (1959); Serge Berstein, *The Republic of de Gaulle 1958–1969* (Cambridge: Cambridge University Press, 1989), 5.
4. Hartley, *Gaullism*, 157–60.
5. Delmas, 'A la recherche des signes de la puissance', 85; Alexander and Bankwitz, 'From Politiques en Képi', 91–102, esp. 94–5.
6. Western dept. comments on Jebb's annual review for France, 21 January 1957, WF1011/1, FO 371/130625, PRO.
7. Bossuat, 'Guy Mollet', 29.
8. Regarding US intelligence contacts, see Algiers consulate report, 'Rumors of insurrection', 28 March 1958, RG 59, 751S.00, box 3383, NARA. Regrettably, in 1988 certain Cabinet documents relating to May 1958 were destroyed on the authority of the Prime Minister's Office, see PREM 11/2339, PRO.
9. FO memo., 'General de Gaulle', 6 June 1958, PREM 11/2339, PRO; *FRUS*, 1958–1960, vol. VII, Pt. 2, nos. 12 and 27, Assistant Secretary of State for European affairs memos., 27 May and 26 June 1958; Wall, 'The United States, Algeria', 505–11.
10. CC(58)46, 4 June 1958, CAB 128/32; FO brief, 29–30 June 1958; FO to Dulles, 2 July 1958, tel. 4176, PREM 11/2326, PRO.
11. Vaïsse, *La grandeur*, 60–1; C. M. Anderson minute, 20 September 1958, WUN10317/12, FO 371/137819, PRO.

12. Kahler, *Decolonization*, 91–7; Sarell, annual report for Algeria, 1958, 23 January 1959, FO 371/138569, PRO.
13. Charles de Gaulle, *Memoirs of Hope* (London: Weidenfeld and Nicolson, 1971), 34.
14. Kahler, *Decolonization*, 105–7; Hartley, *Gaullism*, 163–4.
15. Michèle Cointet, *De Gaulle et l'Algérie française 1958–1962* (Paris: Perrin, 1995), 24; Malek, *L'Algérie à Evian*, 38; *DDF*, vol. II, 1958, no. 285, n. 1; Jebb to FO, 24 October 1958, JR1193/16, FO 371/131685, PRO.
16. Sarell, annual report for Algeria, 1958, 23 January 1959, FO 371/138569, PRO.
17. Jebb to Lloyd, 27 November 1958, JR1193/19, FO 371/131685, PRO.
18. De Gaulle, *Memoirs of Hope*, 60–2; Cointet, *De Gaulle et l'Algérie française*, 38–9.
19. SPDN note, 26 November 1958, no. 2705/DN, 1H1104/D1, SHAT.
20. Délégation générale decision, 27 May 1959, no. 4520; Delouvrier to corps commanders and prefects, 28 October 1959, no. 2564/DN, 1H1104/D6, SHAT; Cornaton, *Les Camps de regroupement*, 68–71.
21. JR1024/8, JR1024/9, JR1024/20, JR1024/27, FO 371/131672, PRO.
22. General Allard to General Challe, 8 March 1959, no. 443; Challe, 'Note de Service', 13 April 1960, no. 3879, 1H2036/D1; EMI-3, 'Le Barrage avant de la frontière Tunisienne', n. d., March 1960, 1H2035/D1, SHAT.
23. Paris chancery to African dept., 18 November 1958, JR1193/18; WO situation report, 17 October–17 November 1958, JR1193/20, FO 371/131685, PRO.
24. COS comm., 'Present military situation in Cyprus', 22 April 1958, COS(58)119, DEFE 5/83; Defence co-ordination committee, Middle East, report, 'Cyprus', 1 December 1958, DEFE 5/87, PRO; Holland, *Britain and the Revolt in Cyprus*, 243–7.
25. General Martial Valin, 'Notes sur certains aspects de la situation militaire en Algérie', January 1959, Z23344/Mission AFN, SHAA; EMI-3, 'Programme d'équipement de la frontière est, 1959', 11 December 1958; Olié to Challe, 3 January 1960, 1H2036/D1, SHAT; d'Abzac-Epezy and Pernot, 'Les opérations en Algérie', 64–70.
26. *DDF*, vol. I, 1960, nos. 19 and 27, Tréca (Tripoli) to Couve de Murville, 15 and 21 Jan. 1960, no. 107, EMGDN note, 11 March 1960; General Valin, compte rendu, 'Mission d'information' 14–18 September 1959, Z23344/Dossier: Mission AFN, SHAA.
27. Dulles meeting with M. Slim, 27 May 1958, RG 59, 751S.00, box 3383, NARA.
28. R. D. Baum to John Bovey, 27 February 1959, RG 59, Lot files: office of North African affairs position papers, box 4, file R8, NARA.
29. C.-in-C. Med. to GOC Middle East land forces, 'US and UK planning in Libya', 7 Aug. 1958, DEFE 7/1013; COS memo., 14 July 1958, RWM/324; MOD Defence Committee, brief D(58)24, 'Libya Garrison', n.d., DEFE 7/1013, PRO.
30. Dixon (UN) to FO, 23 August 1958, tel. 953, DEFE 7/1013, PRO.
31. *DDF*, 1960, vol. I, nos. 24, 88; 1961, vol. II, nos. 5, 7, 17, 32, 42, 45; Nicole Grimaud, 'La Crise de Bizerte', *Revue d'Histoire Diplomatique*, 110 (1996), 337–8; Brian Urquhart, *Hammarskjold* (London: Bodley Head, 1972), ch. 20; de Gaulle, *Memoirs of Hope*, 117.
32. Bourgi, *Le Général de Gaulle et l'Afrique noire*, 326–41.
33. Watson, 'The Aftermath of Suez' in Louis and Owen (eds), *Suez 1956*, 343.
34. Vaïsse, *La grandeur*, 92–103; *FRUS*, 1958–1960, vol. XIV Africa, no. 29, State dept. exchange of views on Africa, 15 April 1960.

35. Vaïsse, *La grandeur*, 63, 71–2; Malek, *L'Algérie à Evian*, 52–4; *DDF*, vol. I, 1960, no. 83, Bérard (New York) to Couve de Murville, 22 February 1960.
36. Bourgi, *Le Général de Gaulle et l'Afrique noire*, 363–9.
37. Downing Street meeting with Debré, 14 April 1959, J1074/20; tel. T294/59, 4 June 1959, PREM 11/2694, PRO; Entry for 4 June 1959, fo. 119, 2nd series Diaries, d. 35, Macmillan papers.
38. John Darwin 'The Central African Emergency, 1959', *Journal of Imperial and Commonwealth History*, 21:1 (1993), 220–9; Entries for 22 June, 13 July 1959, fos. 26–7, 64–7, 2nd series Diaries, d. 36, Macmillan papers.
39. Ritchie Ovendale, 'Macmillan and the Wind of Change in Africa, 1957–1960', *Historical Journal*, 38:2 (1995), 455–77; Horne, *Macmillan* II, 193–200; Quote from Philip E. Hemming, 'Macmillan and the End of the British Empire in Africa', in Aldous and Lee (eds), *Harold Macmillan and Britain's World Role*, 111.
40. De Gaulle, *Memoirs of Hope*, 61; Daniel Lefeuvre, 'L'Echec du plan de Constantine', in Rioux (ed.), *La Guerre d'Algérie*, 321.
41. Paris chancery to Lloyd, 14 August 1958, JR1102/4, FO 371/131682, PRO; 'Rapport sur le programme arrêté par les députés d'Algérie et du Sahara', 8 December 1958, Marius Moutet papers, PA 28, C28/D170, ANCOM.
42. Jean Morin, *De Gaulle et l'Algérie. Mon témoignage 1960–1962* (Paris: Albin Michel, 1999), 52.
43. Watson minute, 30 August 1958, JR1102/4; Sarell memo., 22 October 1958, JR1102/5; Sarell to Lloyd, 12 December 1958, JR1102/7, FO 371/131682, PRO; Cointet, *De Gaulle et l'Algérie française*, 25–8.
44. R. G. Johnson to State Dept., 29 January 1959, RG 59, 751S.00, box 3385, NARA.
45. Statistique générale de l'Algérie, 'Plan de Constantine', 1960, 1H1106/D3, SHAT.
46. Lefeuvre, 'L'Echec du plan de Constantine', 320.
47. Lothar Ruehl, *La politique militaire de la cinquième république* (Paris: Presses de la fondation nationale des sciences politiques, 1976), ch. III; Couve de Murville, *Une politique étrangère*, 60–75 *passim*.
48. Jan Melisson, 'Nuclearizing NATO, 1957–1959: the "Anglo-Saxons", Nuclear Sharing and the Fourth Country Problem', *Review of International Studies*, 20 (1994), 256–62; Maurice Vaïsse, 'Un dialogue de sourds: les relations nucléaires franco-américaines de 1957 à 1960', *Relations internationales*, 60 (1991), 407–23.
49. Amery to Macmillan, 12 June 1957, PREM 11/2333, PRO.
50. Amery memo., 3 December 1958, PREM 11/2696, PRO.
51. Macmillan's motives are examined in Constantine A. Pagedas, 'The Limits of Personal Influence: Harold Macmillan and Anglo-French Relations, 1960–1963', in T. G. Otte and Constantine A. Pagedas (eds), *Personalities, War and Diplomacy. Essays in International History* (London: Frank Cass, 1997), 254–82.
52. Vaïsse, 'Aux origines du mémorandum', 253–68; Delmas, 'A la recherche', 78–81.
53. Jebb memo., 2 June 1958, PREM 11/2339, PRO; Delmas, 'A la recherche', 82–6; Vaïsse, 'Aux origines du mémorandum', 258–67; Jean Doise and Maurice Vaïsse, *Diplomatie et outil militaire 1871–1991* (Paris: Imprimerie Nationale, 1987), 587–94, 601–4; Ely, *Mémoires* II, ch. 3, 409–15. Ely had resigned in the

May crisis over the transfer of three other generals. De Gaulle quickly reinstated him.

54. Macmillan to de Gaulle, 2 June 1958, PREM 11/2339, PRO.
55. First Sea Lord's weekly meeting, 19 December 1957, ADM 205/204; MOD committee on interdependence in research and production meeting, 30 June 1958, PCIRP(58)29; tel. 97, Gladwyn Jebb to FO/UK del., NATO, 14 March 1958, DEFE 7/264, PRO.
56. MOD note, 23 December 1959, WUN1191/1, FO 371/154573; MOD Under-Secretary, G. Wheeler, letter to General Lavaud, n.d., DEFE 7/265, PRO.
57. Roberts to FO, 23 October 1959, DEFE 7/265, PRO; Pagedas, 'The Limits', 256–7.
58. Macmillan–Chauvel conversation, 20 June 1958, PREM 11/2326, PRO; Eisenhower, *Waging Peace*, 427.
59. Roberts report, 24 June 1958, WUN10719/2; Roberts tel., 'General de Gaulle's attitude to NATO', 3 July 1958, WUN10719/6, FO 371/137819, PRO.
60. Tels. 477, 483 and 3047, PREM 11/3002, PRO; Vaïsse, *La grandeur*, 117–20, 129–32; Geoffrey Warner, 'De Gaulle and the Anglo-American 'Special Relationship' 1958–1966: Perceptions and Realities', in Maurice Vaïsse *et al.* (eds), *La France et l'OTAN* (Paris: Editions Complexe, 1996), 250–5.
61. 21st meeting of NATO military committee, Paris, 25–26 November 1958, COS(58)271, DEFE 5/87, PRO.
62. Roberts memo., 9 December 1958, WUN11913/22, FO 371/137865, PRO; Pemberton-Pigott memo. and minutes, 23 Jan. 1959, WUN11922/2, FO 371/146393, PRO.
63. COS comm. memo., 2 January 1959, COS(59)4, DEFE 5/88, PRO.
64. Assistant Secretary memo., 3 March 1959, RG 59, 751S.00, box 3385, NARA.
65. Roberts to Lloyd, 2 and 6 March 1959, WUN11922/7, WUN11922/19; Admiralty directorate of plans memo., 4 March 1959, WUN11922/27, FO 371/146394, PRO. The naval units involved were the US-supplied aircraft carrier *Bois Bellau*, one cruiser, two submarines, 20 escort vessels and 26 minesweepers.
66. COS comm. memo., 2 January 1959, COS(59)4, DEFE 5/88, PRO.
67. COS(58)81st meeting, minute 5, 23 September 1958; JPS report, 'Future Command Organisation in the Middle East', 27 October 1958, JP(58)145, CO 968/547, PRO.
68. First Sea Lord's weekly meeting, 23 October 1957, ADM 205/204, PRO.
69. COS comm. memo., 2 January 1959, COS(59)4, DEFE 5/88, PRO.
70. *FRUS*, 1958–1960, vol. VII, Pt. 2, no. 128, NSC 417th meeting, 18 August 1959; Alphand, *L'étonnement d'être*, 313–16.
71. *FRUS*, 1958–1960, vol. VII, Pt. 2, no. 145, NSC 5910/1, 4 November 1959.
72. PM minute to Lloyd, 22 December 1959, PREM 11/3002, PRO.
73. Roberts memo., 24 February 1959, WUN1011/1, FO 371/146300, PRO.
74. *DDF*, 1960, II, no. 170, note 1; In Bonn, Eisenhower found Adenauer 'almost obsessed with the Algerian problem' in August 1959: Eisenhower, *Waging Peace*, 417.
75. Roberts memo., 5 December 1959, WUN11922/189, PREM 11/3002, PRO.
76. Horne, *Macmillan*, II, 108–11; Pagedas, 'The Limits', 258–60.
77. COS comm., 'Report on 10th SEATO military advisers' conference, Wellington, NZ', 2–4 April 1959, COS(59)92, DEFE 5/91, PRO.

78. Roberts to FO, 23 October 1959, tel. 109/013, DEFE 7/265, PRO.
79. Sabine Lee, 'Staying in the Game? Coming into the Game? Macmillan and European Integration', in Aldous and Lee (eds), *Harold Macmillan and Britain's World Role*, 128–32, 139; P. M. H. Bell, *France and Britain 1940–1994. The Long Separation* (London: Longman, 1997), 183–5.
80. PM minute, 29 June 1960; PM to Tim Bligh, 16 September 1960; Shuckburgh minute, 16 September 1960, PRO, PREM 11/3334, PRO; Horne, *Macmillan* II, 256–7.
81. Pagedas, 'The Limits', 260–3; Ian Clark, *Nuclear Diplomacy and the Special Relationship. Britain's Deterrent and America, 1957–1962* (Oxford: Clarendon Press, 1994), 306–15 *passim*.
82. Maurice Vaïsse, 'De Gaulle and the British "Application" to Join the Common Market', in George Wilkes (ed.), *Britain's Failure to Enter the European Community 1961–63* (London: Frank Cass, 1997), 51–67.
83. *FRUS*, 1958–1960, vol. VII, Pt. 2, no. 201, Bureau of Intelligence and Research report, 6 December 1960; *FRUS*, 1961–1963, vol. XIII West Europe and Canada, no. 223, Assistant Secretary of State for European affairs memo., 24 January 1961.
84. *FRUS*, 1961–1963, vol. XIII West Europe and Canada, no. 225, memo. of conversation, 10 March 1961; no. 228, President's visit, talking points, 27 May 1961; no. 230, memo. of conversation, 2 June 1961.
85. *FRUS*, 1961–1963, vol. XIII West Europe and Canada, no. 231, memo. of Kennedy conversation with congressional leaders, 6 June 1961.
86. Conversations ministerielles franco-britanniques, 13 April 1961; record of 4th meeting with Messmer, 13 April 1961, DEFE 13/178, PRO.
87. Alexander and Bankwitz, 'From Politiques en Képi', 98.
88. JPS report, 'British strategy in the Sixties', 19 December 1961, JPS(61)149; draft MOD brief for PM, 19 December 1961, DEFE 7/2234, PRO.
89. Ruehl, *La politique militaire*, 101–2; Couve de Murville, *Une politique*, 73–4.
90. *FRUS*, 1961–1963, vol. XIII West Europe and Canada, nos. 236 and 239, James M. Gavin (Paris) to State Dept., 6 November 1961 and 21 February 1962; Vaïsse, 'De Gaulle and the British "Application"', 55.
91. Vaïsse, *La grandeur*, 208–10, 148–54; Bell, *France and Britain 1940–1994*, 189–97; Pierre Gerbet, 'The Fouchet Negotiations for Political Union and the British Application', in Wilkes (ed.), *Britain's Failure*, 138–42.
92. Jebb reports to FO, 23 January to 3 February 1960, PRO, PREM 11/3200; Dixon to FO, 23 April 1961, tel. 204; Dixon to FO, 24 April 1961, tel. 215; CC(61)23, 25 April 1961, CAB 128/35, PRO.
93. Hartley, *Gaullism*, 172–4; *DDF*, vol. I, 1960, no. 125, Couve de Murville circular tel., 23 March 1960. De Gaulle dismissed Algerian independence as 'à la fois une catastrophe, une sottise, une monstrosité'.
94. Malek, *L'Algérie à Evian*, 114.
95. *DDF*, 1960, II, no. 7, Roger Moris, 'Conclusions sur les entretiens de Melun', 5 July 1960; Malek, *L'Algérie à Evian*, 62–6.
96. 'France, annual review, 1960', 2 February 1961, WF1011/1, FO 371/161091, PRO.
97. Conversations with Abubakar Tafawa Balewa, 28 Nov. 1960, PREM 11/3200; PM tel. to Ayab Khan, T740/60, 25 December 1960, PREM 11/3201, PRO.

98. Jacques Chaban-Delmas, *Mémoires pour demain* (Paris: Flammarion, 1997), 312–38; Salan to Macmillan, 3 March 1962, PREM 11/361, PRO. The best treatment of the OAS is Alexander Harrison, *Challenging De Gaulle. The O.A.S. and the counterrevolution in Algeria, 1954–1962* (New York: Praeger, 1989), esp. chs. 1–3.
99. Ageron, '"L'Algérie dernière chance de la puissance française"', 128–9.
100. Hartley, *Gaullism*, 176–7.
101. Hartley, *Gaullism*, 186–7; Jean-François Sirinelli, 'Guerre d'Algérie, guerre des pétitions? Quelques jalons', *Revue Historique*, 291:1 (1988), 73–100; Dine, 'French culture', 56–66.
102. CC(61)3, 31 January 1961, CAB 128/35, PRO.
103. FO conversations at French Embassy, 25 November 1960, PREM 11/3200, PRO. Regarding the initial Evian talks, see: Malek, *L'Algérie à Evian*, ch. 8.
104. General Peynaud, chef du SPDN, 'Dénombrement de la population, 1960', 15 Dec. 1961, 1H1104/D8, SHAT.
105. Morin, *De Gaulle et l'Algérie*, 8–9.
106. J. C. Satterthwaite memo., 30 January 1961, RG 59, Lot files: Africa, office of North African affairs position papers, box 1, file A20, NARA.
107. Morin, *De Gaulle et l'Algérie*, ch. IX.
108. Philip de Zulueta to Macmillan, 5 and 13 January 1961, PREM 11/3336, PRO.
109. PM/61/3 and PM/61/6, 10 January 1961; Commonwealth Relations secretary letter, 11 Jan. 1961; extract from Rambouillet talks, 28 January 1961, PREM 11/3336, PRO.
110. Dixon tels to FO, 29 June 1961, 14 October 1961, 10 November 1961, nos. 307, 326 and 346, PREM 11/4094, PRO.
111. 'US/UK talks on post-independence Algeria', 21 November 1961, RG 59, Lot files: Africa, office of North African affairs – UK discussions, box 1, file A8, NARA.
112. Artillery report, 30 March 1962, no. 89/ART, 1H2036/D1, SHAT.
113. Couve de Murville, *Une politique étrangère*, 188.
114. Evans (Algiers) to FO, 15 March 1962, tel. 14, PREM 11/4094; Home memo., 'The Evian agreements', 3 April 1962, C(62)58, CAB 129/109, PRO. For the original text of the Evian accords, see: Malek, *L'Algérie à Evian*, annex IV.
115. Note for the record, Algeria pt. 3, 19 March 1962, PREM 11/4094, PRO.
116. William B. Cohen, 'Legacy of Empire: the Algerian Connection', *Journal of Contemporary History*, 15:1 (1980), 99–110.
117. Dixon, 'France, annual review, 1962', 3 January 1963, CF1011/1, FO 371/169107; Dixon to FO, 6 February 1962, CF1022/2, FO 371/163494, PRO.
118. Marseille, 'Phases of French Colonial Imperialism', 135–9.
119. Rumbold (Paris) to Home, 23 August 1962, CF1022/3; Macmillan minute, 20 September 1962, FO 371/163494, PRO; Horne, *Macmillan* II, 445–51.
120. George Wilkes, 'Eye-witness Views of the Brussels Breakdown', in Wilkes (ed.), *Britain's Failure*, 229, 234. The most nuanced account of Britain's application, the Brussels entry talks in particular, is now N. Piers Ludlow, *Dealing with Britain. The Six and the First UK Application to the EEC* (Cambridge: Cambridge University Press, 1997).

Conclusion

1. Bevin conversation with Bidault, 17 May 1946, CP(46)197, CAB 121/400, PRO.
2. René Girault, 'De la puissance et de la France d'aujourd'hui', *Relations Internationales*, 58 (1989), 163–4.
3. Marseille, 'Phases of French Colonial Imperialism', 135–9.
4. Carroll, 'Camus's Algeria', 538–9, n.10. *Le premier homme* was finally published in 1994. On the 1961 killings, see: Jean-Luc Einaudi, *La bataille de Paris: 17 octobre 1961* (Paris: Editions du Seuil, 1994); Mike Mason, 'Batailles pour la Mémoire', *Journal of African History*, 35 (1994), 304; Golsan, 'Memory's *bombes à retardement', 162–7.*
5. Western European Section report, 10 February 1955, JF1054/4, FO 371/113789, PRO.
6. Ageron, 'L'opération de Suez', in Vaïsse (ed.), *La France et l'opération de Suez*, 43.
7. Alexander and Bankwitz, 'From Politiques en Képi', 95; David L. Schalk, 'Reflections *d'outre-mer* on French colonialism', *Journal of European Studies*, 28:1 (1998), 9.
8. Geay, 'Les débats sur les recours de la Tunisie à l'ONU', 254; William Rountree memo. for Dulles, 28 August 1957, RG 59, 751S.00, box 3380, NARA.
9. Ageron, 'L'opération de Suez', 43.
10. Clark memo., 'Pacification or negotiation', 1 March 1957, RG 59, 751S.00, box 3379, NARA.

Bibliography

Primary Sources – Great Britain

Public Record Office, London

Cabinet files
CAB 121 – Special Secret Information Centre files
CAB 127 – Private Collections, ministers and officials
CAB 128 – Cabinet minutes
CAB 129 – Cabinet memoranda
CAB 130 – Ad hoc Cabinet Committees
CAB 131 – Cabinet Defence Committee
CAB 134 – Cabinet Committees, general series from 1945
CAB 158 – Chiefs of Staff Joint Intelligence Committee memoranda
CAB 159 – Chiefs of Staff Joint Intelligence Committee minutes

Admiralty files

ADM 205 – First Sea Lord Papers

Air Ministry files

AIR 8 – Chief of Air Staff papers

Colonial Office files

CO 537 – Colonial Office confidential original correspondence
CO 968 – Colonial Office defence original correspondence

Ministry of Defence files

DEFE 2 – Combined Operations HQ reports
DEFE 4 – Chiefs of Staff Committee minutes
DEFE 5 – Chiefs of Staff Committee memoranda
DEFE 7 – Registered files, general series
DEFE 11 – Chiefs of Staff Committee registered files
DEFE 13 – Ministry of Defence Private Office files

Foreign Office

FO 371 – Foreign Office general correspondence
FO 413 – Confidential print: Morocco/North West Africa
FO 443 – Foreign Office files, Morocco
FO 800 – Private Papers: Ernest Bevin; Anthony Eden; Selwyn Lloyd; Harold Macmillan

Premier's Office

PREM 11 – Prime Minister's office files

Treasury

T 236 – Overseas Finance Division files

War Office

WO 216 – Chief of Imperial General Staff papers

Bodleian Library, Oxford

Conservative Party Archives – Subject file series: Colonial Affairs 1946–1966; Imperial Policy; Relations with Right-Wing Parties
Harold Macmillan papers: Diaries, first series 1950–1956; second series 1957–1963
Sir Anthony Rumbold papers
1st Viscount (Walter) Monckton papers

Churchill College, Cambridge

Alfred Duff Cooper papers
Duncan Sandys papers
J. Selwyn Lloyd papers

Primary Sources – France

Archives Nationales, Paris (AN)

Georges Bidault papers (457AP); René Pleven papers (560AP)
Série F^{60} – Premier's Office files (1944–45)

Archives Nationales Centre des Archives d'Outre-Mer, Aix-en-Provence (ANCOM)

Marius Moutet papers (PA28)
Ministère de la France d'Outre-Mer direction des affaires politiques files
Département d'Alger: Série 1K – Cabinet files

Ministère des Affaires Etrangères, Paris (MAE)

Série files: Afrique-Levant, 1944–59; Amérique, 1952–63; Asie-Océanie, 1944–55; Europe, 1944–60; Internationale, 1944–49
Sous-Série files: Algérie; Etats-Unis; Grande-Bretagne; Maroc; Nations Unies et Organisations Internationales; Tunisie

Service Historique de l'Armée de l'Air, Vincennes (SHAA)

Série I Algeria files: Cartons Z23344 Opérations en AFN; Z23345 Fonds de Général Valin; Z23363 Indochine/Algérie documents divers

Service Historique de l'Armée de Terre, Vincennes (SHAT)

Série 1H – Algérie: Archives du Cabinet Militaire de la Délégation Générale du Gouvernement en Algérie; Etat-Major Interarmées (EMI) premier bureau, deuxième bureau, troisième bureau; Secrétariat Permanent de la Défense Nationale (SPDN)
Série 2H – Tunisie; Série 3H – Maroc; Série 10H – Indochine
Sous-Série 4Q – Etat-Major de la Défense Nationale; 9U – Opérations de Suez 1956–57

Primary Sources – USA

National Archives and Records Administration, College Park, MD. (NARA)

RG 59 – General Records of the Department of State
Decimal files – 751 (Algeria); 771 (Morocco)
Lot files – Office of Western European Affairs (French Desk); Office of African Affairs
Policy Planning Staff files 1947–63
RG 218 – Records of the Joint Chiefs of Staff

Published Document Collections

British Documents on the End of Empire Project (BDEEP), series A, vol. II, parts I-III: Ronald Hyam (ed.), *The Labour Government and the End of Empire, 1945–1951* London: HMSO, 1992; series A, vol. III, part I: David Goldsworthy (ed.), *The Conservative Government and the End of Empire 1951–1957* London: HMSO, 1994.

Documents on British Policy Overseas series I, vol. VII: H. J. Yasamee and K. A. Hamilton (eds); series II, vol. II: Roger Bullen and others (eds), London: HMSO, 1987 *et seq*.

Documents Diplomatiques Français, 1944, vol. II/ 1945, vol. I Ministère des Affaires Etrangères, Paris: Imprimerie Nationale, 1996 *et seq*.

Documents Diplomatiques Français, 1954–1961 19 vols, Ministère des Affaires Etrangères, Paris: Imprimerie Nationale, 1987 *et seq*.

Foreign Relations of the United States Washington: US Government Printing Office, 1969 *et seq*. Volumes consulted: 1945, vol. VIII; 1946, vol. VII; 1947, vol. V; 1948, vol. III; 1949, vol. VI; 1950, vol. V; 1952–1954, vol. VI pt. 2, vol. XI; 1955–1957, vol. XVIII; 1958–1960, vol. VII pt. 2, vol. XIV; 1961–1963, vol. XIII.

La Guerre d'Algérie par les Documents, I: L'Avertissement, 1943–1946, Jean-Charles Jauffret (ed.), Vincennes: SHAT, 1990; *II: Les Portes de la Guerre: des occasions manquées à l'insurrection 1946–1954* Vincennes: SHAT, 1998

Memoirs and Diaries

Alphand, Hervé, *L'Étonnement d'être. Journal (1939–1973)*, Paris: Fayard, 1977.

Auriol, Vincent, *Journal du Septennat, 1947–1954*, 7 vols., Paris: Armand Colin, 1971 *et seq*.

Beaufre, André, *The Suez Expedition 1956*, trans., London: Faber and Faber, 1969.
Bidault, Georges, *Resistance, the Political Autobiography of Georges Bidault*, London: Weidenfeld and Nicolson, 1967.
Chaban-Delmas, Jacques, *Mémoires pour demain*, Paris: Flammarion, 1997.
Couve de Murville, Maurice, *Une politique étrangère 1958–1969*, Paris: Plon, 1971.
Debré, Michel, *Trois républiques pour une France. Mémoires*, Paris: Albin Michel, 1984, *et seq*.
Dixon, Piers, *Double Diploma: the Life of Sir Pierson Dixon, Don and Diplomat* London: Hutchinson, 1968.
Ely, General Paul, *Mémoires*, 2 vols., Paris: Plon, 1969.
Eisenhower, Dwight D., *The White House Years. Waging Peace 1956–1961*, London: Heinemann, 1965.
Fawzi, Mahmoud, *Suez 1956. An Egyptian Perspective*, London: Shorouk International, 1987.
de Gaulle, Charles, *Discours et messages*, III and IV, Paris: Plon, 1970.
——*Memoirs of Hope*, London: Weidenfeld and Nicolson, 1971.
Lord Gladwyn, *The Memoirs of Lord Gladwyn*, London: Weidenfeld and Nicolson, 1972.
Jouhaud, Edmond, *Ce que je n'ai pas dit*, Paris: Fayard, 1977.
Juin, Maréchal Alphonse, *Mémoires*, vol. II, Paris: Fayard, 1960.
Macmillan, Harold, *Riding the Storm*, London: Macmillan, 1971.
——*Pointing the Way*, London: Macmillan, 1972.
——*At the End of the Day*, London: Macmillan, 1973.
Malek, Redha, *L'Algérie à Evian. Histoire des négociations secrètes 1956–1962*, Paris: Editions du Seuil, 1995.
Massigli, René, *Une Comédie des Erreurs*, Paris: Plon, 1978.
Massu, Jacques, *La vraie bataille d'Alger*, Paris: Plon, 1971.
Mendès France, Pierre, *Oeuvres complètes III: Gouverner, c'est choisir 1954–1955*, Paris: Gallimard, 1986.
Morin, Jean, *De Gaulle et l'Algérie. Mon témoignage 1960–1962*, Paris: Albin Michel, 1999.
Naegelen, Marcel-Edmond, *Mission en Algérie*, Paris: Flammarion, 1962.
Nutting, Anthony, *No End of a Lesson. The Story of Suez*, London: Constable, 1967.
Paillat, Claude, *Dossier secret de l'Algérie, 1954–1958*, Paris: Presses de la Cité, 1962.
Pineau, Christian, *Suez 1956*, Paris: Editions Robert Laffont, 1976.
Rusk, Dean, *As I Saw It. A Secretary of State's Memoirs*, London: I. B. Taurus, 1991.
Salan, Raoul, *Mémoires. III: Fin d'un Empire*, Paris: Presses de la Cité, 1972.
Teitgen, Pierre-Henri, *Faites entrer le témoin suivant – 1940–1958: De la Résistance à la Vième République*, Ouest-France, 1988.

Books

Adams, Geoffrey, *The Call of Conscience. French Protestant Responses to the Algerian War, 1954–1962*, Waterloo: Wilfrid Laurier University Press, 1998.
Ageron, Charles-Robert, *France coloniale ou parti colonial?*, Paris: Presses Universitaires de France, 1978.
——*Histoire de l'Algérie contemporaine, II: De l'insurrection de 1871 au déclenchement de la guerre de libération (1954)*, Paris: Presses Universitaires de France, 1979.

——(ed.), *Les Chemins de la décolonisation de l'empire colonial français, 1936–1956*, Actes du Colloque, October 1974, Paris: Editions CNRS, 1986.
——*Modern Algeria: A History from 1830 to the Present*, London: Hurst, 1991.
and Marc Michel, *L'Afrique noire française: l'heure des Indépendances*, Paris: Editions CNRS, 1992.
——*L'ère des décolonisations. Actes du Colloque d'Aix-en-Provence*, Paris: Karthala, 1995.
——*La guerre d'Algérie et les Algériens 1954–1962*, Paris: Armand Colin, 1997.
Aimaq, Jasmine, *For Europe or Empire? French Colonial Ambitions and the European Army Plan*, Lund: Lund University Press, 1996.
Al Dib, Mohamed Fathi, *Abdel Nasser et la Révolution Algérienne*, Paris: Editions L'Harmattan, 1985.
Aldous, Richard, and Sabine Lee (eds), *Harold Macmillan and Britain's World Role*, London: Macmillan, 1996.
Aldrich, Richard J., *British Intelligence, Strategy and the Cold War, 1945–51*, London: Routledge, 1992.
Aldrich, Robert, *Greater France. A History of French Overseas Expansion*, London: Macmillan, 1996.
Alleg, Henri, (ed.), *La Guerre d'Algérie*, 3 vols, Paris: Temps Actuels, 1981.
Ambler, John, *The French Army in Politics, 1945–1962*, Columbus OH: Ohio State University Press, 1965.
Andrews, William G., and Stanley Hoffman (eds), *The Impact of the Fifth Republic on France*, Albany, NY: State University of New York Press, 1981.
Ashton, Nigel John, *Eisenhower, Macmillan and the Problem of Nasser. Anglo-American Relations and Arab Nationalism, 1955–59*, London: Macmillan, 1996.
Atkin, Nicholas, and Frank Tallett (eds), *The Right in France, 1789–1997*, London: I. B. Taurus, 1997.
Beckett, Ian F. W., and John Pimlott, *Armed Forces and Modern Counter-Insurgency*, London: Croom Helm, 1985.
Bédarida, François, and Jean-Pierre Rioux, *Pierre Mendès France et le mendésisme. L'expérience gouvernementale et sa postérité (1954–1955)*, Paris: Fayard, 1985.
Bell, P. M. H., *France and Britain 1940–1994. The Long Separation*, London: Longman, 1997.
Bergot, Erwan, *La Guerre des appelés en Algérie, 1956–1962*, Paris: Presses de la Cité, 1980.
Bernard, Stéphane, *The Franco-Moroccan Conflict, 1943–1956*, New Haven: Yale University Press, 1968.
Berstein, Serge, *The Republic of de Gaulle, 1958–1969*, Cambridge: Cambridge University Press, 1993.
Berstein, Serge, Jean-Marie Mayeur and Pierre Milza (eds), *Le MRP et la Construction Européenne*, Paris: Editions Complexe, 1993.
Betts, Raymond, *France and Decolonisation, 1900–1960*, London: Macmillan, 1991.
Biondi, Jean-Pierre, *Les anticolonialistes (1881–1962)*, Paris: Editions Robert Laffont, 1992.
Bougeard, Christian, *René Pleven. Un Français libre en politique*, Rennes: Presses Universitaires de Rennes, 1994.
Bourdrel, Philippe, *La Dernière chance de l'Algérie Française. Du gouvernement socialiste au retour de De Gaulle, 1956–1958*, Paris: Albin Michel, 1996.
Bourgi, Robert, *Le Général de Gaulle et l'Afrique noire 1940–1969*, Paris: LGDJ, 1980.

Cable, James, *The Geneva Conference of 1954 on Indochina*, London: Macmillan, 1986.
Centre d'études d'histoire de la Défense, *La France et l'opération de Suez de 1956*, Paris: ADDIM, 1997.
——*La IVe République face aux problèmes d'armement*, Paris: ADDIM, 1998.
Charlot, Jean, *Le Gaullisme d'opposition, 1946–1958. Histoire politique du Gaullisme*, Paris: Fayard, 1983.
Chêne, Janine, Edith Aberdam and Henri Morsel (eds), *Pierre Mendès France la morale en politique*, Grenoble: Presses Universitaires de Grenoble, 1990.
Clancy-Smith, Julia A., *Rebel and Saint. Muslim Notables, Populist Protest, Colonial Encounters (Algeria and Tunisia, 1800–1904)*, Berkeley, CA: University of California Press, 1997.
Clark, Ian, *Nuclear Diplomacy and the Special Relationship: Britain's Deterrent and America, 1957–1962*, Oxford: Clarendon Press, 1994.
Clayton, Anthony, *France, Soldiers and Africa*, London: Brassey's, 1988.
——*The Wars of French Decolonization*, London: Longman, 1994.
Cohen, Michael J., *Fighting World War Three from the Middle East. Allied Contingency Plans, 1945–1954*, London: Frank Cass, 1997.
Cohen, Michael J., and Martin Kolinsky (eds), *Demise of the British Empire in the Middle East. Britain's Responses to Nationalist Movements, 1943–55*, London: Frank Cass, 1998.
Cointet, Michèle, *De Gaulle et l'Algérie Française, 1958–1962*, Paris: Perrin, 1995.
Collot, Claude, *Les Institutions de l'Algérie durant la période coloniale (1830–1962)*, Paris: Editions du CNRS, 1987.
Colombani, Olivier, *Mémoires Coloniales: la fin de l'Empire français d'Afrique vue par les administrateurs coloniaux*, Paris: Editions de la Découverte, 1991.
Cornaton, Michel, *Les Camps de regroupement de la guerre d'Algérie*, Paris: Editions L'Harmattan, 1998.
Dalloz, Jacques, *The War in Indo-China, 1945–1954*, Gill and Macmillan: Dublin, 1990.
——*Georges Bidault. Biographie Politique*, Paris: Editions L'Harmattan, 1992.
Deighton, Anne (ed.), *Building Postwar Europe: National Decision-Makers and European Institutions, 1948–63*, London: Macmillan 1995.
Demory, Jean-Claude, *Georges Bidault 1899–1983*, Paris: Editions Julliard, 1995.
Descamps, Henri, *La Démocratie Chrétienne et le MRP: de 1946 à 1959*, Paris: LGDJ, 1981.
Descombin, Henry, *Guerre d'Algérie 1959–60. Le Cinquième Bureau ou 'Le théorème du poisson'*, Paris: Editions L'Harmattan, 1994.
Devereux, David R., *The Formulation of British Defence Policy towards the Middle East, 1948–56*, London: Macmillan, 1990.
Dine, Philip, *Images of the Algerian War. French Fiction and Film, 1954–1992*, Oxford: Clarendon Press, 1994.
Di Nolfo, Ennio (ed.), *Power in Europe? II: Great Britain, France, Germany and Italy and the Origins of the EEC, 1952–1957*, Berlin: Walter de Gruyter, 1992.
Dockrill, Michael, *British Defence since 1945*, Oxford: Basil Blackwell, 1988.
——and J. W. Young (eds), *British Foreign Policy, 1945–56*, London: Macmillan, 1989.
Droz, Bernard, and Evelyne Lever, *Histoire de la Guerre d'Algérie 1954–1962*, Paris: Editions du Seuil, 1982.

Einaudi, Jean-Luc, *La Bataille de Paris: 17 octobre 1961*, Paris: Editions du Seuil, 1994.
Elgey, Georgette, *La République des illusions, 1945–1951, ou la vie secrète de la IVe République*, Paris: Fayard, 1965.
El Machat, Samya, *La Tunisie, les chemins vers l'indépendance, 1945–1956*, Paris: Editions L'Harmattan, 1992.
——*Les Etats-Unis et la Tunisie. De l'ambiguité à l'entente 1945–1959*, Paris: Editions L'Harmattan, 1996.
——*Les Etats-Unis et le Maroc. Le choix stratégique 1945–1959*, Paris: Editions L'Harmattan, 1996.
——*Les Etats-Unis et l'Algérie. De la méconnaissance à la reconnaissance 1945–1962*, Paris: Editions L'Harmattan, 1996.
Evans, Martin, *The Memory of Resistance. French Opposition to the Algerian War (1954–1962)*, Oxford: Berg, 1997.
——and Ken Lunn (eds), *War and Memory in the Twentieth Century*, Oxford: Berg, 1997.
Faligot, Roger and Pascal Krop, *La Piscine. Les services secrets français 1944–1984*, Paris: Editions du Seuil, 1985.
Fonveille-Vojtovic, Aline, *Paul Ramadier (1881–1961) Elu local et homme d'état*, Paris: Publications de la Sorbonne, 1993.
Gadant, Monique, *Islam et Nationalisme en Algérie d'après 'EL Moudjahid' organe central du FLN de 1956 à 1962*, Paris: Editions L'Harmattan, 1988.
Giles, Frank, *The Locust Years. The Story of the French Fourth Republic, 1946–1958*, New York: Carroll and Graf, 1991.
Girault, René, and Robert Frank (eds), *La Puissance Française en Question (1945–1949)*, Paris: Publications de la Sorbonne, 1988.
Girault, René *et al.* (eds), *Pierre Mendès France et le rôle de la France dans le monde*, Grenoble: Presses Universitaires de Grenoble, 1991.
Goldsworthy, David, *Colonial Issues in British Politics, 1945–1961*, Oxford: Clarendon Press, 1971.
Graham, B. D., *Choice and Democratic Order. The French Socialist Party, 1937–1950*, Cambridge: Cambridge University Press, 1994.
Guilhaume, Jean-François, *Les mythes fondateurs de l'Algérie française*, Paris: Editions L'Harmattan, 1992.
Guillaume, Sylvie, *Antoine Pinay ou la confiance en politique*, Paris: FNSP, 1984.
Hadhri, Mohieddine, *L'URSS et le Maghreb: De la révolution d'octobre à l'indépendance de l'Algérie, 1917–1962*, Paris: Editions L'Harmattan, 1985.
Hahn, Peter L., *The United States, Great Britain and Egypt, 1945–1956*, Chapel Hill, NC: University of North Carolina Press, 1991.
Harbi, Mohammed, *Les Archives de la révolution algérienne*, Paris: Editions J.A., 1981.
——*Le F.L.N. Mirage et Réalité: des origines à la prise du pouvoir (1945–1962)* 2nd edn, Paris: Editions J.A., 1985.
——*1954: La Guerre commence en Algérie*, Brussels: Editions Complexe, 1989.
Harrison, Alexander, *Challenging De Gaulle. The O.A.S. and the counterrevolution in Algeria, 1954–1962*, New York: Praeger, 1989.
Hartley, Anthony, *Gaullism. The Rise and Fall of a Political Movement*, London: Routledge, 1972.

Headrick, Daniel R., *The Tools of Empire. Technology and European Imperialism in the Nineteenth Century*, Oxford: Oxford University Press, 1981.
Hélie, Jérôme, *Les Accords d'Evian. Histoire de la paix ratée en Algérie*, Paris: Olivier Orban, 1992.
Hitchcock, W. I., *France Restored. Cold War Diplomacy and the Quest for Leadership in Europe, 1944–1954*, Chapel Hill, NC: University of North Carolina Press, 1998.
Holland, Robert, *Britain and the Revolt in Cyprus 1954–1959*, Oxford: Clarendon Press, 1998.
Horne, Alistair, *The French Army and Politics, 1870–1970*, London: Macmillan, 1984.
——*A Savage War of Peace: Algeria 1954–1962*, London: Macmillan, 1987.
——*Macmillan*, 2 vols., London: Macmillan, 1988 and 1989.
Howe, Stephen, *Anticolonialism in British Politics. The Left and the End of Empire 1918–1964*, Oxford: Clarendon Press, 1993.
Hutchinson, Martha Crenshaw, *Revolutionary Terrorism. The FLN in Algeria, 1954–1962*, Stanford, CA: Hoover Institution Press, 1978.
Immerman, Richard H., *John Foster Dulles and the Diplomacy of the Cold War*, Princeton, NJ: Princeton University Press, 1990.
Irving, R. E. M., *Christian Democracy in France*, London: Allen and Unwin, 1973.
Jackson, Henry F., *The FLN in Algeria. Party Development in a Revolutionary Society*, London: Greenwood Press, 1977.
Joly, Danièle, *The French Communist Party and the Algerian War*, London: Macmillan, 1991.
Kahler, Miles, *Decolonization in Britain and France. The Domestic Consequences of International Relations*, Princeton, NJ: Princeton University Press, 1984.
Kaiser, Wolfram, *Using Europe, Abusing the Europeans. Britain and European Integration, 1945–63*, London: Macmillan, 1996.
Kaplan, Lawrence, Denise Artaud and Mark R. Rubin (eds), *Dien Bien Phu and the Crisis of Franco-American Relations, 1954–1955*, Wilmington, Del: SR books, 1990.
Kelly, George Armstrong, *Lost Soldiers. The French Army and Empire in Crisis, 1947–1962*, Cambridge, Mass: MIT Press, 1965.
Kent, John, *The Internationalization of Colonialism: Britain, France and Black Africa, 1939–1956*, Oxford: Clarendon Press, 1992.
——*British Imperial Strategy and the Origins of the Cold War, 1944–49*, Leicester: Leicester University Press, 1993.
Kettle, Michael, *De Gaulle and Algeria, 1940–1960*, London: Quartet, 1993.
Kyle, Keith, *Suez*, London: Weidenfeld and Nicolson, 1992.
Lacorne, Denis, *et al.* (eds), *The Rise and Fall of Anti-Americanism. A Century of French Perception*, London: Macmillan, 1990.
Lacouture, Jean, *Pierre Mendès-France*, London, Holmes and Meier, 1984.
——*De Gaulle II: The Ruler, 1945–1970*, London, Collins, 1991.
Lacroix-Riz, Annie, *Les Protectorats d'Afrique du Nord entre la France et Washington du débarquement à l'indépendance. Maroc et Tunisie, 1942–1956*, Paris: Editions L'Harmattan, 1988.
Lefebvre, Denis, *Guy Mollet. Le mal aimé*, Paris: Plon, 1992.
Le Goyet, Pierre, *La Guerre d'Algérie*, Paris: Perrin, 1989.
Letamendia, Pierre, *Le Mouvement Républicain Populaire. Histoire d'un grand parti français*, Paris: Beauchesne Editeur, 1995.

Lorcin, Patricia M., *Imperial Identities. Stereotyping, Prejudice and Race in Colonial Algeria*, London: I. B. Taurus, 1995.
Louis, William Roger, *The British Empire in the Middle East 1945–51. Arab Nationalism, the United States and Postwar Imperialism*, Oxford: Oxford University Press, 1984
——and Roger Owen (eds), *Suez 1956: The Crisis and its Consequences*, Oxford: Oxford University Press, 1993.
Lucas, W. Scott, *Divided we Stand. Britain, the US and the Suez Crisis*, London: Hodder and Stoughton, 1991.
Ludlow, N. Piers, *Dealing with Britain. The Six and the First UK Application to the EEC*, Cambridge: Cambridge University Press, 1997.
MacMaster, Neil, *Colonial Migrants and Racism. Algerians in France, 1900–62*, London: Macmillan, 1997.
MacRae Jr, Duncan, *Parliament, Parties and Society in France 1948–1958*, London: Macmillan, 1967.
Maquin, Etienne, *Le Parti Socialiste et la Guerre d'Algérie 1954–1958*, Paris: Editions L'Harmattan, 1990.
Mathias, Grégor, *Les Sections administratives spécialisées en Algérie. Entre idéal et réalité (1955–1962)*, Paris: Editions L'Harmattan, 1998.
McLellan, David S., *Dean Acheson The State Department Years*, New York: Dodd, Mead and Co., 1976.
Melanson, Richard A., and David Mayers (eds), *Reevaluating Eisenhower. American Foreign Policy in the Fifties*, Urbana, Ill.: University of Chicago Press, 1987.
Merle, Marcel (ed.), *Les Eglises chrétiennes et la décolonisation*, Paris: Presses de la Fondation Nationale des Sciences Politiques, 1967.
Morgan, Ted, *A Covert Life. Jay Lovestone: Communist, Anti-Communist and Spymaster*, New York: Random House, 1999.
Nouschi, André. *L'Algérie Amère 1914–1994*, Paris: Editions de la Maison des Sciences de l'Homme, 1995.
Otte, T. G., and Constantine A. Pagedas (eds), *Personalities, War and Diplomacy. Essays in International History*, London: Frank Cass, 1997.
Ovendale, Ritchie (ed.), *The Foreign Policy of the British Labour Governments, 1945–1951*, Leicester: Leicester University Press, 1984.
——*Britain, the United States and the Transfer of Power in the Middle East, 1945–1962*, London: Leicester University Press, 1996.
Paret, Peter, *French Revolutionary Warfare from Indochina to Algeria. The Analysis of a Political and Military Doctrine*, London: Pall Mall Press, 1964.
Pervillé, Guy, *De l'Empire français à la décolonisation*, Paris: Hachette, 1991.
Poidevin, Raymond, *Robert Schuman homme d'Etat 1886–1963*, Paris: Imprimerie Nationale, 1986.
Porter, A. N., and A. J. Stockwell, *British Imperial Policy and Decolonization, 1938–1964. vol. II: 1951–64*, New York: St. Martin's Press, 1989.
Prochaska, David, *Making Algeria French. Colonialism in Bône, 1870–1920*, Cambridge: Cambridge University Press, 1990.
Quandt, William B., *Revolution and Political Leadership: Algeria, 1954–1968*, Cambridge, Mass.: MIT Press, 1969.
Quillot, Roger, *La S.F.I.O. et l'exercise du pouvoir, 1944–1958*, Paris: Fayard, 1972.
Richardson, Dick, and Glyn Stone (eds), *Decisions and Diplomacy: Essays in Twentieth-Century International History*, London: Routledge, 1995.

Rice-Maximin, Edward, *Accommodation and Resistance. The French Left, Indochina and the Cold War, 1944–1954*, Westport, Conn.: Greenwood Press, 1986.
Rioux, Jean-Pierre, *The Fourth Republic, 1944–1958*, Cambridge: Cambridge University Press, 1987.
—— (ed.), *La Guerre d'Algérie et les Français*, Paris: Fayard, 1990.
Rudelle, Odile, *Mai 1958. De Gaulle et la République*, Paris: Plon, 1988.
Ruehl, Lothar, *La Politique militaire de la cinquième république*, Paris: Presses de la Fondation Nationale des Sciences Politiques, 1976.
Sarfady, Simon, *France, de Gaulle and Europe. The Policy of the Fourth and Fifth Republics towards the Continent*, Baltimore: Johns Hopkins University Press, 1968.
Schalk, David L., *War and the Ivory Tower. Algeria and Vietnam*, New York: Oxford University Press, 1991.
Schneider, William H., *An Empire for the Masses. The French Popular Image of Africa, 1870–1900*, Westport, Conn.: Greenwood Press, 1982.
Scriven, Michael, and Peter Wagstaff (eds), *War and Society in Twentieth Century France*, Oxford: Berg, 1992.
Seale, Patrick, *The Struggle for Syria. A Study of Post-War Arab Politics, 1945–1958* 2nd edn, London: I. B. Taurus, 1986.
Shennan, Andrew, *Rethinking France. Plans for Renewal, 1940–1946*, Oxford: Oxford University Press, 1989.
Sivan, Emmanuel, *Communisme et nationalisme en Algérie, 1920–1962*, Paris: FNSP, 1976.
Smith, Tony, *The French Stake in Algeria, 1945–1962*, Ithaca, NY: Cornell University Press, 1978.
Smouts, Marie-Claude, *La France à l'ONU. Premiers Rôles et Second Rang*, Paris: Presses de la Fondation Nationale des Sciences Politiques, 1979.
Spillmann, Georges, *Du protectorat à l'indépendance*, Paris: Plon, 1967.
Stora, Benjamin, *La Gangrène et l'oubli. La mémoire de la guerre d'Algérie*, Paris: Editions La Découverte, 1991.
—— and Zakya Daoud, *Ferhat Abbas une utopie algérienne*, Paris: Editions Dénoël, 1995.
Swearingen, Will D., *Moroccan Mirages. Agrarian Dreams and Deceptions*, Princeton, NJ: Princeton University Press, 1987.
Talbott, John, *The War without a Name. France in Algeria, 1954–1962*, London: Faber and Faber, 1981.
Thomas, Abel, *Comment Israel fut sauvé. Les Secrets de l'expédition de Suez*, Paris: Albin Michel, 1978.
Ullman, Bernard, *Jacques Soustelle. Le mal aimé*, Paris: Plon, 1995.
Urquhart, Brian, *Hammarskjold*, London: Bodley Head, 1972.
Vaïsse, Maurice (ed.), *La France et l'opération de Suez de 1956*, Paris: ADDIM, 1997.
——*La grandeur. Politique étrangère du général de Gaulle 1958–1969*, Paris: Fayard, 1998.
—— and Pierre Melandri, Frédéric Bozo (eds), *La France et l'OTAN, 1949–1996*, Paris: Editions Complexe, 1997.
Vandervort, Bruce, *Wars of Imperial Conquest in Africa, 1830–1914*, London: UCL Press, 1998.
Vinen, Richard, *Bourgeois Politics in France, 1945–1951*, Cambridge: Cambridge University Press, 1995.

Wall, Irwin M., *The United States and the Making of Postwar France, 1945–1954*, Cambridge: Cambridge University Press, 1991.
——*France, the United States and the Algerian War, 1954–1962*, Berkeley CA: University of California Press, 2000.
Wilkes, George (ed.), *Britain's Failure to Enter the European Community 1961–63*, London: Frank Cass, 1997.
Williams, Philip M., and Martin Harrison, *Politics and Society in De Gaulle's Republic*, London: Longman, 1971.
Young, John W. (ed.), *The Foreign Policy of Churchill's Peacetime Administration, 1951–1955*, Leicester: Leicester University Press, 1988.
——*France, the Cold War and the Western Alliance, 1944–1949: French Foreign Policy and Post-war Europe*, Leicester: Leicester University Press, 1990.
——*Winston Churchill's Last Campaign. Britain and the Cold War, 1951–5*, Oxford: Clarendon Press, 1996.

Articles

Abzac-Epezy, Claude and François Pernot, 'Les opérations en Algérie, décembre 1958–avril 1960. Le général Challe parle', *Revue Historique des Armées*, 3 (1995) 62–73.
Adamthwaite, Anthony, 'Overstretched and overstrung: Eden, the Foreign Office and the making of policy, 1951–5', *International Affairs*, 64:2 (1988) 241–59.
——'Suez Revisited', *International Affairs*, 64:3 (1988) 449–64.
Ageron, Charles-Robert, 'L'Opinion française devant la guerre d'Algérie', *Revue de la France d'Outre-Mer*, 231 (1976) 256–85.
——'La survivance d'un mythe: la puissance par l'Empire colonial, 1944–1947', *Revue Française d'Histoire d'Outre-Mer*, LXXII: 269 (1985) 387–405.
——'"L'Algérie dernière chance de la puissance française". Etude d'un mythe politique (1954–1962)', *Relations Internationales*, 57 (1989) 113–39.
——'Vers un syndicalisme national en Algérie (1946–1956)', *Revue d'Histoire Moderne et Contemporaine*, 36 (1989) 450–63.
Alexander, Martin S. and Philip C. F. Bankwitz, 'From Politiques en Képi to Military Technocrats. De Gaulle and the Recovery of the French Army after Indochina and Algeria', in G. J. Andreopoulos and H. E. Selesky (eds), *The Aftermath of Defeat. Societies, Armed Forces and the Challenge of Recovery*, New Haven, Conn.: Yale University Press, 1994, 79–102.
Andrew, Christopher and A. S. Kanya-Forstner, 'Centre and Periphery in the Making of the Second French Colonial Empire, 1815–1920', *Journal of Imperial and Commonwealth History*, 16:3 (1988) 9–34.
Ashton, Nigel John, 'The Hijacking of a Pact: the Formation of the Baghdad Pact and Anglo-American Tensions in the Middle East, 1955–1958', *Review of International Studies*, 19 (1993) 123–37.
Baillif, General, 'Forces armées et psychologie', *Revue de Défense Nationale*, 16 (1960) 819–29.
Barral, Pierre, 'La Méditerranée dans la guerre froide', *Relations Internationales*, 87 (1996) 293–308.
Battesti, Michèle, 'Les ambiguités de Suez', *Revue Historique des Armées*, 4 (1986) 3–14.

Beaussant, Amiral, 'La politique navale française de 1945 à 1965', *Revue Historique des Armées*, 3 (1991) 48–57.

Bessis, Juliette, 'Sur Moncef Bey et le moncéfisme: la Tunisie de 1942 à 1948', *Revue Française d'Histoire d'Outre-Mer*, LXX: 260 (1983) 97–131.

Binoche-Guedra, Jacques, 'Le rôle des élus de l'Algérie et des colonies au Parlement sous la Troisième République (1871–1940)', *Revue Française d'Histoire d'Outre-Mer*, LXXV: 280 (1988) 309–46.

Bookmiller, Robert J., 'The Algerian war of words: broadcasting and revolution, 1954–1962', *The Maghreb Review*, 14:3–4 (1989) 196–213.

Bossuat, Gérard, 'Guy Mollet: La puissance française autrement', *Relations Internationales*, 57 (1989) 25–48.

Brady, Christopher, 'The Cabinet System and Management of the Suez Crisis', *Contemporary British History*, 11:2 (1997) 65–93.

Brett, Michael, 'The Colonial Period in the Maghreb and its Aftermath: the Present State of Historical Writing', *Journal of African History*, 17:2 (1976) 291–305.

——'Anglo-Saxon Attitudes: the Algerian War of Independence in Retrospect', *Journal of African History*, 35 (1994) 217–35.

Brocard, Rémi, 'L'organisation politico-administrative et militaire du F.L.N. vue à travers les archives du 5e bureau de l'E.M.I.', *Revue Historique des Armées*, 2 (1992) 44–53.

Burke, Edmund, 'Pan-Islam and Moroccan Resistance to French Colonial Penetration, 1900–1912', *Journal of African History*, 13 (1972) 97–118.

Carroll, David, 'Camus's Algeria: Birthrights, Colonial Injustice, the Fiction of a French-Algerian People', *Modern Language Notes*, 112 (1997) 517–49.

Chaix, General Bruno, 'La France et la réconstitution de l'armée Tunisienne en 1956', *Revue d'Histoire Diplomatique*, 110 (1996) 279–306.

Chassin, General L.-M., 'Vers un encerclement de l'Occident?', *Revue de Défense Nationale*, 12 (1956) 531–53.

Christelow, Allan, 'Ritual, Culture and Politics of Islamic Reformism in Algeria', *Middle Eastern Studies*, 23:3 (1987) 255–73.

Clayton, Anthony, 'The Sétif Uprising of May 1945', *Small Wars and Insurgencies*, 3:1 (1992) 1–21.

——'Emergency in Morocco, 1950–56', *Journal of Imperial and Commonwealth History*, 21:3 (1993) 129–47.

Cochet, François, 'Les attitudes de la France en Tunisie (1945–1962): les rapports des sources orales', *Revue d'Histoire Diplomatique*, 110 (1996) 203–20.

Cohen, William B., 'Legacy of Empire: The Algerian Connection', *Journal of Contemporary History*, 15:1 (1980) 97–123.

Cohen-Solal, Annie, 'Camus, Sartre and the Algerian war', *Journal of European Studies*, 28:1 (1998) 43–50.

Connelly, Matthew, 'The French-American Conflict over North Africa and the Fall of the Fourth Republic', *Revue Française d'Histoire d'Outre-Mer*, 84:315 (1997) 9–27.

Costigliola, Frank, 'The Failed Design: Kennedy, de Gaulle and the Struggle for Europe', *Diplomatic History*, 8:3 (1984) 227–51.

Dalloz, Jacques, 'L'opposition M.R.P. à la guerre d'Indochine', *Revue d'Histoire Moderne et Contemporaine*, 43:1 (1996) 106–18.

Darwin, John, 'British Decolonization since 1945: A Pattern or a Puzzle?', *Journal of Imperial and Commonwealth History*, 12:2 (1984) 187–209.

——'The Central African Emergency, 1959', *Journal of Imperial and Commonwealth History*, 21:3 (1993) 217–34.

Daveau, Antoine, 'Le poids de la guerre d'Indochine', *Revue d'Histoire Diplomatique*, 107:4 (1993) 333–57.

Davis, Richard, ''Why did the General do it?' De Gaulle, Polaris and the French Veto of Britain's Application to join the Common Market', *European History Quarterly*, 28:3 (1998) 373–97.

De Cock, Laurence, 'La France et Bourguiba: 1945–1956', *Revue d'Histoire Diplomatique*, 110 (1996) 255–64.

Deighton, Anne, 'The Last Piece of the Jigsaw: Britain and the Creation of the Western European Union, 1954', *Contemporary European History*, 7:2 (1998) 181–96.

Delmas, General Jean, 'A la recherche des signes de la puissance: l'armée entre Algérie et bombe A 1956–1962', *Relations Internationales*, 57 (1989) 77–87.

Dine, Philip, 'French culture and the Algerian war: mobilizing icons', *Journal of European Studies*, 28:1 (1998) 51–68.

Dockrill, Michael, 'British Attitudes Towards France as a Military Ally', *Diplomacy and Statecraft*, 1 (1990) 49–70.

Dooley, Howard J., 'Great Britain's ''Last Battle'' in the Middle East: Notes on Cabinet Planning during the Suez Crisis of 1956', *International History Review*, 11:3 (1989) 486–517.

Duhamel, Eric, 'Pleven et Mitterrand', *Vingtième Siècle*, 45 (1995) 67–75.

Duval, Marcel and Pierre Melandri, 'Les Etats-Unis et la prolifération nucléaire: le cas français', *Revue d'Histoire Diplomatique*, 109 (1995) 193–220.

El Mustafa, Azzou, 'Le Nationalisme Marocain et les Etats-Unis 1945–1956', *Guerres Mondiales et Conflits Contemporains*, 177 (1994) 131–8.

——'Les Hommes d'affaires américains au Maroc avant 1956', *Guerres Mondiales et Conflits Contemporains*, 180 (1995) 129–43.

El Qadéry, Mustapha, 'Les Berbères entre le mythe colonial et la négation nationale. Le cas du Maroc', *Revue d'Histoire Moderne et Contemporaine*, 45:2 (1998) 425–50.

El Tayeb, Salah el Din el Zein, 'The Europeanized Algerians and the Emancipation of Algeria', *Middle Eastern Studies*, 22:2 (1986) 206–35.

Ely, General Paul, 'Notre politique militaire', *Revue de Défense Nationale*, July (1957) 1033–51.

Facon, Patrick, 'L'Algérie et la politique générale de l'armée de l'air (1954–1958)', *Revue Historique des Armées*, 2 (1992) 76–85.

Faivre, Maurice, 'Les Français musulmans dans la guerre d'Algérie I: De l'engagement à la mobilisation', *Guerres Mondiales et Conflits Contemporains*, 177 (1994) 139–65.

——'Les Français musulmans dans la guerre d'Algérie II: Les représailles et l'oubli de la France', *Guerres Mondiales et Conflits Contemporains*, 180 (1995) 145–70.

Fraser, Cary, 'Understanding American Policy Towards the Decolonization of European Empires, 1945–64', *Diplomacy and Statecraft*, 3:1 (1992) 105–25.

Frémeaux, Jacques, 'Vision perspective sur la guerre d'Algérie', *Histoire et Défense*, 25:1 (1992) 49–67.

Furedi, Frank, 'Creating a Breathing Space: The Political Management of Colonial Emergencies', *Journal of Imperial and Commonwealth History*, 21:3 (1993) 89–106.

Gallissot, R., 'Precolonial Algeria', *Economy and Society*, 4:4 (1975) 418–45.

Geay, Ingrid, 'Les débats sur les recours de la Tunisie à l'ONU de 1952 à 1954', *Revue d'Histoire Diplomatique*, 110 (1996) 241–54.

Gibbs, David N., 'Political Parties and International Relations: The United States and the Decolonization of Sub-Saharan Africa', *International History Review*, 17:2 (1995) 306–27.

Girault, René, 'De la puissance et de la France d'aujourd'hui', *Relations Internationales*, 58 (1989) 159–67.

——'La France en accusation à l'ONU, ou les pouvoirs d'une organisation internationale', *Relations Internationales*, 76 (1993) 411–22.

Goldsworthy, David, 'Keeping Change within Bounds: Aspects of Colonial Policy during the Churchill and Eden Governments, 1951–57', *Journal of Imperial and Commonwealth History*, 18:1 (1990) 81–108.

Golsan, Richard J., 'Memory's *bombes à retardement*: Maurice Papon, crimes against humanity and 17 October 1961', *Journal of European Studies*, 28:1 (1998) 153–72.

Greene, Daniel P. O'C., 'John Foster Dulles and the End of the Franco-American Entente in Indochina', *Diplomatic History*, 16:4 (1992) 551–71.

Greenhalgh, Michael, 'The New Centurions: French Reliance on the Roman Past during the Conquest of Algeria', *War and Society*, 16:1 (1998) 1–28.

Grimaud, Nicole, 'La crise de Bizerte', *Revue d'Histoire Diplomatique*, 110 (1996) 328–40.

Guelton, Frédéric, and Geneviève Errera, 'Transmissions et guerre subversive en Algérie', *Revue Historique des Armées*, 1 (1990) 74–83.

Guiral, P., 'L'opinion marseillaise et les débuts de l'entreprise algérienne (1830–1841)', *Revue Historique*, 154:1 (1955) 9–34.

Hahn, Peter L., 'Containment and Egyptian Nationalism: the Unsuccessful Effort to Establish the Middle East Command, 1950–53', *Diplomatic History*, 11 (1987) 23–40.

Hamon, Olivier, 'Chronique du conflit Algérien, 1954–1962', *Revue Historique des Armées*, 2 (1992) 33–43.

Hamoumou, Mohand, 'Les harkis, un trou de mémoire franco-algérien', *Esprit*, 161 (1990) 25–45.

Hanley, David, 'From Co-operation to Conflict: the French Political System and the Onset of the Cold War', *French Cultural Studies*, 8 (1997) 3–15.

Harrison, Christopher, 'French Attitudes to Empire and the Algerian War', *African Affairs*, (1983) 75–95.

Hermon, Elly, 'A propos du plan Félix Gaillard de Pacte Méditerranéen', *Revue d'Histoire Diplomatique*, 109 (1995) 2–28.

Hoisington, William, 'Commerce and Conflict: French Businessmen in Morocco, 1952–55', *Journal of Contemporary History*, 9 (1974) 49–67.

Holland, Robert F., 'The Imperial Factor in British Strategies from Attlee to Macmillan, 1945–63', *Journal of Imperial and Commonwealth History*, 12:2 (1984) 165–86.

Jasse, Richard L. 'The Baghdad Pact: Cold War or Colonialism?', *Middle Eastern Studies*, 27:1 (1991) 140–56.

Jauffret, Jean-Charles, 'Du 8 mai 1945 au 1er novembre 1954. Une nouvelle lecture des débuts de la guerre d'Algérie', *Histoire et Défense*, 25:1 (1992) 23–47.

——'L'armée et l'Algérie en 1954', *Revue Historique des Armées*, 2 (1992) 15–25.

——'The Origins of the Algerian War: The Reaction of France and its Army to the two Emergencies of 8 May 1945 and 1 November 1954', *Journal of Imperial and Commonwealth History*, 21:3 (1993) 17–29.

Johnson, Douglas, 'Algeria: Some Problems of Modern History', *Journal of African History*, 5:2 (1964) 221–42.

Kaiser, Wolfram, 'The Bomb and Europe: Britain, France and the EEC Entry Negotiations (1961–63)', *Journal of European Integration History*, 1:1 (1995) 65–85.

——'La question française dans la politique européenne et nucléaire britannique (1957–1963)', *Revue d'Histoire Diplomatique*, 2 (1998) 173–204.

Khane, Mohammed, 'Perceptions of Algerian identity in the 1950s: *Le Monde*'s treatment of intellectuals' views', *Bulletin of Francophone Africa*, 2 (1993) 47–75.

Kinda, Noraogo, 'Les Etats-Unis et le nationalisme en Afrique noire à l'épreuve de la décolonisation (Deuxième Guerre Mondiale–1960)', *Revue Française d'Histoire d'Outre-Mer*, LXXIX: 297 (1992) 533–55.

Kyle, Keith, 'The Politics of the Independence of Kenya', *Contemporary British History*, 11:4 (1997) 42–65.

Le Couriard, Daniel, 'Les Socialistes et les débuts de la guerre d'Indochine (1946–1947)', *Revue d'Histoire Moderne et Contemporaine*, 31 (1984) 334–53.

Lefebvre, Jeffery A., 'Kennedy's Algerian Dilemma: Containment, Alliance Politics and the "Rebel Dialogue"', *Middle Eastern Studies*, 35:2 (1999) 61–82.

Lévizze-Touzé, Christine, 'La situation intérieure de l'Algérie pendant la Seconde Guerre Mondiale', *Histoire et Défense*, 25:1 (1992) 5–21.

Lewis, James I., 'French Politics and the Algerian Statute of 1947', *Maghreb Review*, 17: 3–4 (1992) 146–72.

——'The MRP and the Genesis of the French Union, 1944–1948', *French History*, 12:3 (1998) 276–314.

Louis, William Roger, 'American Anti-colonialism and the Dissolution of the British Empire', *International Affairs*, 61:3 (1985) 395–420.

——and Ronald Robinson, 'The Imperialism of Decolonization', *Journal of Imperial and Commonwealth History*, 22:3 (1994) 462–511.

Lucas, W. S. 'Redefining the Suez "Collusion": A Regional Approach', *Middle Eastern Studies*, 26:1 (1990).

——and Ray Takeyh, 'Alliance and Balance: The Anglo-American Relationship and Egyptian Nationalism, 1950–57', *Diplomacy and Statecraft*, 7:3 (1996) 631–51.

MacMaster, Neil, and Toni Lewis, 'Orientalism: from unveiling to hyperveiling', *Journal of European Studies*, 28:1 (1998) 121–36.

Marill, Capitaine Jean-Marc, 'L'Héritage indochinois: adaptation de l'Armée française en Algérie (1954–1956)', *Revue Historique des Armées*, 2 (1992) 26–32.

Marseille, Jacques, 'L'investissement public en Algérie après la Deuxième Guerre Mondiale', *Revue Française d'Histoire d'Outre-Mer*, LXX: 260 (1983) 179–97.

——'The Phases of French Colonial Imperialism: Towards a New Periodization', *Journal of Imperial and Commonwealth History*, 13:3 (1985) 127–41.

Masson, Philippe, 'Origines et bilan d'une défaite', *Revue Historique des Armées*, 4 (1986) 51–8.

Melissen, Jan, 'Nuclearizing NATO, 1957–1959: the "Anglo-Saxons", nuclear sharing and the fourth country problem', *Review of International Studies*, 20 (1994) 253–75.

Metz, Steven, 'American Attitudes toward Decolonization in Africa', *Political Science Quarterly*, 99:3 (1984) 515–34.
Michel, Marc, 'De Lattre et les débuts de l'américanisation de la guerre d'Indochine', *Revue Française d'Histoire d'Outre-Mer*, LXXI: 268 (1985) 321–34.
——'De Lattre, la conférence de Singapour et ses suites', *Revue Française d'Histoire d'Outre-Mer*, LXXIX: 295 (1992) 199–211.
Nachmani, Amikan, '"It's a Matter of Getting the Mixture Right": Britain's Post-War Relations with America in the Middle East', *Journal of Contemporary History*, 18:1 (1983) 117–40.
Ovendale, Ritchie, 'Great Britain and the Anglo-American Invasion of Jordan and Lebanon in 1958', *International History Review*, 16:2 (1994) 284–303.
——'Macmillan and the Wind of Change in Africa, 1957–1960', *Historical Journal*, 38:2 (1995) 455–77.
Paillard, Jacques, 'La S. A. S. d'Arris, mars 1960–mars 1962', *Revue Historique des Armées*, 2 (1992) 54–8.
Payre, Gabriel, 'Les origines et le rôle du Contrôle Civil dans la Régence de Tunis (1881–1956)', *Revue d'Histoire Diplomatique*, 98 (1984) 267–88.
Perkins, Kenneth J., 'North African Propaganda and the United States, 1946–1956', *African Studies Review*, 14:3 (1976) 65–77.
Pernot, François, 'La guerre psychologique en Algérie vue à travers les archives de l'armée de l'air', *Revue Historique des Armées*, 1 (1993) 90–9.
Pervillé, Guy, 'Les principes de 1789 et le Mouvement national algérien', *Revue Française d'Histoire d'Outre-Mer*, 76:282 (1989) 231–7.
Pignol, Armand, 'L'image de de Gaulle dans les pays arabes du Proche-Orient: la genèse socio-politique d'un stéréotype', *Revue Historique*, 272:2 (1984) 403–20.
Poidevin, Raymond, 'René Mayer et la politique extérieure de la France (1943–1953)', *Revue d'Histoire de la Deuxième Guerre Mondiale*, 134 (1984) 73–97.
Prévot, Maryvonne, 'Convergences maghrébines autour d'Alain Savary, secrétaire d'Etat aux affaires marocaines et tunisiennes en 1956', *Revue Historique*, CCI:3 (1999) 507–36.
Redouane, Joëlle, 'British Trade with Algeria in the Nineteenth Century: An Ally against France?', *The Maghreb Review*, 13:3–4 (1988) 175–82.
Rice-Maximin, Edward, 'The United States and the French Left, 1945–1949: The View from the State Department', *Journal of Contemporary History*, 19:4 (1984) 729–47.
Rivlin, Benjamin, 'The United States and Moroccan International Status, 1943–1956: a Contributory Factor in Morocco's reassertion of Independence from France', *International Journal of African Historical Studies*, 15:1 (1982) 64–82.
Roberts, Hugh, 'The Algerian State and the Challenge of Democracy', *Government and Opposition*, 27:4 (1992) 433–54.
——'Algeria's Ruinous Impasse and the Honourable Way Out', *International Affairs*, 71:2 (1995) 247–67.
Rolland, Denis, 'Jacques Soustelle, de l'ethnologie à la politique', *Revue d'Histoire Moderne et Contemporaine*, 43:1 (1996) 137–50.
Ruane, Kevin, 'Anthony Eden, British Diplomacy and the Origins of the Geneva Conference of 1954', *Historical Journal*, 37:1 (1994) 153–72.
——'Refusing to Pay the Price: British Foreign Policy and the Pursuit of Victory in Vietnam, 1952–4', *English Historical Review*, 110 (1995) 70–92.

Ruscio, Alain, 'Le Mendésisme et l'Indochine', *Revue d'Histoire Moderne et Contemporaine*, 29 (1982) 324–42.
——'Dien Bien Phu: Du coup de génie à l'abérration ou comment les contemporains ont vécu l'ultime bataille de la guerre française de l'Indochine', *Revue Française d'Histoire d'Outre-Mer*, LXXII: 268 (1985) 335–47.
Sangmuah, Egya N., 'Interest Groups and Decolonization: American Businessmen and Organized Labour in French North Africa, 1948–56', *Maghreb Review*, 13:3 (1988) 161–74.
Sanjian, Ara, 'The Formulation of the Baghdad Pact', *Middle Eastern Studies*, 33:2 (1997) 226–66.
Schalk, David L., 'Reflections *d'outre-mer* on French colonialism', *Journal of European Studies*, 28:1 (1998) 5–24.
Schenk, Catherine R., 'Decolonization and European Economic Integration: the Free Trade Area Negotiations, 1956–58', *Journal of Imperial and Commonwealth History*, 24:3 (1996) 444–63.
Schillinger, Philippe, 'Le "testament" du Général Salan ou pourquoi Dien Bien Phu?', *Revue Historique des Armées*, 4 (1989) 58–64.
Semidei, M., 'De l'Empire à la décolonisation à travers les manuels scolaires français', *Revue Française de Science Politique*, 16:1 (1966) 56–79.
Shlaim, Avi, 'The Protocol of Sèvres, 1956: anatomy of a war plot', *International Affairs*, 73:3 (1997) 509–29.
Sirinelli, Jean-François, 'Guerre d'Algérie, guerre des pétitions? Quelques jalons', *Revue Historique*, 279:1 (1988) 73–100.
Sivan, Emmanuel, 'Colonialism and Popular Culture in Algeria', *Journal of Contemporary History*, 14:1 (1979) 21–53.
Smith, T. Alexander, 'Algeria and the French *Modérés*: the Politics of Immoderation?', *Western Political Quarterly*, 18:86 (1965) 116–34.
Smith, Tony, 'The French Colonial Consensus and People's War, 1946–58', *Journal of Contemporary History*, 9 (1974) 217–47.
——'Muslim Impoverishment in Colonial Algeria', *Revue de l'Occident Musulman et de la Méditerranée*, 156 (1974) 139–72.
——'The French Economic Stake in Colonial Algeria', *French Historical Studies*, 9:1 (1975) 184–9.
Soutou, Georges-Henri, 'La politique nucléaire de Pierre Mendès France', *Relations Internationales*, 59 (1989) 317–30.
——'Georges Bidault et la construction européenne', *Revue d'Histoire Diplomatique*, 105 (1991) 267–306.
Stora, Benjamin, 'Algeria: the War without a Name', *Journal of Imperial and Commonwealth History*, 21:3 (1993) 208–16.
Talbott, John E., 'The Myth and Reality of the Paratrooper in the Algerian War', *Armed Forces and Society*, 3:1 (1976) 69–86.
——'Terrorism and the Liberal Dilemma: The Case of the Battle of Algiers', *Contemporary French Civilization*, 2:2 (1978) 177–89.
Thomas, Martin, 'The Dilemmas of an Ally of France: Britain's Policy towards the Algerian Rebellion, 1954–62', *Journal of Imperial and Commonwealth History*, 23:1 (1995) 129–54.
——'Policing Algeria's Borders, 1956–1960: Arms Supplies, Frontier Defences and the Sakiet Affair', *War and Society*, 13:1 (1995) 81–99.

Turpin, Frédéric, 'Le Mouvement Républicain Populaire et la Guerre d'Indochine (1944–1954)', *Revue d'Histoire Diplomatique*, 110 (1996) 157–90.

Ulrich, Raphaële, 'Vincent Auriol et la Tunisie', *Revue d'Histoire Diplomatique*, 110 (1996) 221–40.

Vaïsse, Maurice, 'Aux origines du mémorandum de septembre 1958', *Relations Internationales*, 58 (1989) 253–68.

——'Un dialogue de sourds: les relations nucléaires franco-américaines de 1957 à 1960', *Relations Internationales*, 60 (1991) 407–23.

——'Le Choix atomique de la France (1945–1958)', *Vingtième Siècle*, 36 (1992) 21–30.

——'De Gaulle et la première "candidature" britannique au Marché Commun', *Revue d'Histoire Diplomatique*, 108 (1994) 129–50.

——and Chantal Morelle, 'Les relations Franco-Tunisiennes (Juin 1958–Mars 1962)', *Revue d'Histoire Diplomatique*, 110 (1996) 341–80.

Valette, Jacques, 'Guerre mondiale et décolonisation. Le cas du Maroc en 1945', *Revue Française d'Histoire d'Outre-Mer*, LXX:260 (1983) 133–50.

——'France et Viet Minh à la conférence de Genève en 1954', *Guerres Mondiales et Conflits Contemporains*, 176 (1994) 119–37.

Vial, Philippe, 'Algérie ou A. F. N.? Le destin partagé de la Ve région aérienne (1946–1962)', *Revue Historique des Armées*, 1 (1993) 80–9.

Vidal-Naquet, Pierre, 'Une Fidélité Têtue. La résistance française à la guerre d'Algérie', *Vingtième Siècle*, 10 (1986) 3–18.

Vinen, Richard C., 'The End of an Ideology? Right-wing anti-Semitism in France, 1944–1970', *Historical Journal*, 37:2 (1994) 365–88.

Wall, Irwin M., 'The United States, Algeria, and the Fall of the French Fourth Republic', *Diplomatic History*, 18:4 (1994) 489–511.

——'Les Etats-Unis, la Grande-Bretagne et l'affaire de Sakiet-Sidi-Youssef', *Revue d'Histoire Diplomatique*, 110 (1996) 307–27.

Warner, Geoffrey, 'Eisenhower, Dulles and the Unity of Western Europe, 1955–1957', *International Affairs*, 69:2 (1993) 319–29.

——'The United States and the Western Alliance, 1958–63', *International Affairs*, 71:4 (1995) 801–18.

Zingg, Paul J., 'The Cold War in North Africa: American Foreign Policy and Postwar Muslim Nationalism 1945–1962', *The Historian*, 39:1 (1976) 40–61.

Zoubir, Yahia H., 'The United States, the Soviet Union and Decolonization of the Maghreb, 1945–62', *Middle Eastern Studies*, 31:1 (1995) 58–84.

——'U.S. and Soviet Policies towards France's Struggle with Anticolonial Nationalism in North Africa', *Canadian Journal of History*, 30 (1995) 439–66.

Index